First World War
and Army of Occupation
War Diary
France, Belgium and Germany

16 DIVISION
49 Infantry Brigade
Royal Inniskilling Fusiliers
8th Battalion
3 February 1916 - 23 August 1917

WO95/1977/3

The Naval & Military Press Ltd
www.nmarchive.com
Published in association with The National Archives

Published by

The Naval & Military Press Ltd

Unit 10 Ridgewood Industrial Park,

Uckfield, East Sussex,

TN22 5QE England

Tel: +44 (0) 1825 749494

www.naval-military-press.com

www.nmarchive.com

This diary has been reprinted in facsimile from the original. Any imperfections are inevitably reproduced and the quality may fall short of modern type and cartographic standards.

© **Crown Copyright**
Images reproduced by permission of The National Archives, London, England, 2015.

Contents

Document type	Place/Title	Date From	Date To
Heading	1977/3 8 Battalion Royal Iniskilling Fusiliers Feb 1916-Aug 1917		
Heading	16th Division 49th Infy Bde 8th Bn Roy Innis Fus Feb 1916-1917 Aug		
Miscellaneous	From O.C 8th Royal Billing Fusiliers To D.A.G 3rd Echelon	31/03/1916	31/03/1916
War Diary	Bordon	03/02/1916	17/02/1916
War Diary	Southampton	17/02/1916	19/02/1916
War Diary	Havre	20/02/1916	21/02/1916
War Diary	Lillers	22/02/1916	22/02/1916
War Diary	Ligny-Lez Aire	25/02/1916	25/02/1916
War Diary	Lieres	26/02/1916	26/02/1916
War Diary	Bellerive	02/03/1916	02/03/1916
War Diary	Philosophe	03/03/1916	11/03/1916
War Diary	Noeux-Les-Mines	11/03/1916	20/03/1916
War Diary	Raimbert	21/03/1916	27/03/1916
War Diary	Philosophe E	27/03/1916	28/03/1916
War Diary	Mazingarbe	28/03/1916	28/03/1916
War Diary	Philosophe	31/03/1916	31/03/1916
War Diary	Noeux Les Mines	03/04/1916	29/04/1916
War Diary	In The Line	24/05/1916	25/05/1916
War Diary	Philosophe East	26/05/1916	26/05/1916
War Diary	Drouvin	26/05/1916	28/05/1916
War Diary	Hesdingeuil	29/05/1916	29/05/1916
War Diary	Condette	29/05/1916	31/05/1916
War Diary	Condette	01/06/1916	14/06/1916
War Diary	Philosophe	14/06/1916	15/06/1916
War Diary	10th Ave	16/06/1916	19/06/1916
War Diary	In The Line	23/06/1916	23/06/1916
War Diary	Mazingarbe	28/06/1916	28/06/1916
War Diary	Condette	13/06/1916	19/06/1916
War Diary	In The Line	20/06/1916	27/06/1916
Heading	War Diary 8th (S) Battalion Royal Fus 1st. July To 31st. July 1916. Volume No. 6		
War Diary	Mazingarbe	01/07/1916	07/07/1916
War Diary	Left Sub-Section Loos	05/07/1916	07/07/1916
War Diary	Philosophe E.	07/07/1916	12/07/1916
War Diary	Left Sub Section Loos	13/07/1916	19/07/1916
War Diary	Noeux-Les-Mines	20/07/1916	21/07/1916
War Diary	Left Sub-Section Hulluch	22/07/1916	24/07/1916
War Diary	Noeux-Les-Mines	24/07/1916	31/07/1916
Heading	War Diary 8th Royal Inniskilling Fusiliers Month Of August 1916. Volume 7		
War Diary	Left Sub. Sect. 14 Bis.	09/08/1916	12/08/1916
War Diary	Philosophe W	05/08/1916	08/08/1916
War Diary	Rl Sub. Sect 14 Bis.	09/08/1916	12/08/1916
War Diary	10th Ave	12/08/1916	16/08/1916
War Diary	Rl Sub. Sect 14 Bis	16/08/1916	20/08/1916
War Diary	Mazingarbe	20/08/1916	23/08/1916
War Diary	Houchin	24/08/1916	25/08/1916

War Diary	Labeuvriere	26/08/1916	29/08/1916
War Diary	Longueau	29/08/1916	29/08/1916
War Diary	Sailly-Le-Sec	30/08/1916	31/08/1916
Heading	War Diary 8th Royal InnisKilling Fusiliers For Month of September 1916 Volume 8		
War Diary	Happy Valley	01/09/1916	02/09/1916
War Diary	Citadel	03/09/1916	03/09/1916
War Diary	Billon Farm	04/09/1916	04/09/1916
War Diary	Guillemont	05/09/1916	07/09/1916
War Diary	Bernafay Wood	08/09/1916	08/09/1916
War Diary	Guillemont	09/09/1916	09/09/1916
War Diary	Ginchy Guillemont	10/09/1916	10/09/1916
War Diary	Billon Farm	11/09/1916	11/09/1916
War Diary	Sailly-Le Sec.	11/09/1916	18/09/1916
War Diary	Sorel	18/09/1916	21/09/1916
War Diary	Bailleul	22/09/1916	22/09/1916
War Diary	Locre	22/09/1916	23/09/1916
War Diary	Front Line	23/09/1916	27/09/1916
War Diary	Locre	28/09/1916	30/09/1916
Heading	War Diary Month Of October, 1916. 8th Royal Inniskilling Fusiliers. Vol 9		
War Diary	Locre	01/10/1916	03/10/1916
War Diary	Front Line	03/10/1916	09/10/1916
War Diary	Locre	09/10/1916	14/10/1916
War Diary	Front Line	14/10/1916	17/10/1916
War Diary	Locre	17/10/1916	21/10/1916
War Diary	Front Line	21/10/1916	26/10/1916
War Diary	Locre	26/10/1916	31/10/1916
Heading	War Diary For Month Of November, 1916. Volume 10 8th R. Inniskilling Fusiliers Vol 10		
War Diary	Locre	01/11/1916	01/11/1916
War Diary	Front Line	01/11/1916	06/11/1916
War Diary	Locre	06/11/1916	12/11/1916
War Diary	Front Line	12/11/1916	18/11/1916
War Diary	Locre	18/11/1916	24/11/1916
War Diary	Front Line	24/11/1916	30/11/1916
War Diary	Locre	30/11/1916	30/11/1916
Heading	War Diary For Month Of December, 1916. Volume 11 8th R Inniskilling Fusiliers		
War Diary	Locre	01/10/1916	06/10/1916
War Diary	Front Line	06/12/1916	12/12/1916
War Diary	Locre	12/12/1916	18/12/1916
War Diary	Front Line	18/12/1916	21/12/1916
War Diary	Kemmel Shelters	24/12/1916	30/12/1916
War Diary	Front Line	30/12/1916	31/12/1916
Miscellaneous	Report of Patrol	25/05/1916	25/05/1916
Miscellaneous	A Form. Messages And Signals.		
Miscellaneous	Report On Gap H19 C.9.9		
Miscellaneous			
Miscellaneous	Report On Wire At H.19.C.99	25/06/1916	25/06/1916
Miscellaneous	H25 G.55	25/06/1916	25/06/1916
Miscellaneous	Report Of Officer Patrol	24/06/1916	24/06/1916
Miscellaneous	Patrol Report Attached From Perch	26/06/1915	26/06/1915
Miscellaneous	H.Q 49th Inf Bde		
Miscellaneous	A Form. Messages And Signals.		
Miscellaneous	Perch		

Miscellaneous	D.A.G., Base.	21/06/1916	21/06/1916
Miscellaneous	Prisoners		
Miscellaneous	7th. R. Innis. Fus.	21/06/1916	21/06/1916
Miscellaneous	Report On Operation Between 11 Pm To 3.30 am 15/18-7-8	16/07/1916	16/07/1916
Miscellaneous	Report On Mine Explosion Seaforth Crate And Raid	17/07/1916	17/07/1916
Miscellaneous	S to B Canal 11-1145		
Miscellaneous			
Miscellaneous	H.Q Div Infantry Brigade Raid Scheme Left Sub Section Left Section		
Miscellaneous	Report On Operation Carried Out On 9th Sept., 1916 Appendix II	10/09/1916	10/09/1916
Miscellaneous	16th. Div. No. 6520/1 (G).-31/8/16	31/08/1916	31/08/1916
Miscellaneous	O.C. 8th R. Innis Fus B.M.C VIII/ 2261		
Operation(al) Order(s)	49th Infantry Brigade Order No. 52, 2/9/16	02/09/1916	02/09/1916
Operation(al) Order(s)	8th R. Innis. Fus. Operation Order No. 44	02/09/1916	02/09/1916
Operation(al) Order(s)	8th R. Innis. Fus. Operation Order No. 46	14/09/1916	14/09/1916
Miscellaneous	7th. R. Innis. Fus.	03/09/1916	03/09/1916
Operation(al) Order(s)	8th R. Innis Fus Op Order No. 46	00/09/1916	00/09/1916
Miscellaneous		07/09/1916	07/09/1916
Operation(al) Order(s)	49th. Infantry Brigade Order No. 52	02/09/1916	02/09/1916
Miscellaneous	B/X/468	08/10/1916	08/10/1916
Heading	War Diary For Month Of January, 1917. Volume 12 8th R Inniskilling Fusiliers Vol 12		
War Diary	Locre	17/01/1917	23/01/1917
War Diary	Front Line	23/01/1917	29/01/1917
War Diary	Wakefield Huts	29/01/1917	31/01/1917
Heading	War Diary For Month Of February, 1917. Volume 13 8th Royal Inniskilling Fus.		
War Diary	Wakefield Huts	01/02/1917	06/02/1917
War Diary	Derry Huts & Kemmel Chateau	06/02/1917	10/02/1917
War Diary	Front Line	10/02/1917	14/02/1917
War Diary	Kemmel Shelters	14/02/1917	22/02/1917
War Diary	Derry Huts Kemmel Chateau	22/02/1917	26/02/1917
War Diary	Front Line	26/02/1917	28/02/1917
Heading	War Diary For Month Of March, 1917. Volume 14 8th Btn Ro Inniskilling Fus		
War Diary	Front Line	01/03/1917	02/03/1917
War Diary	Doncaster Huts	02/03/1917	19/03/1917
War Diary	Front Line	19/03/1917	23/03/1917
War Diary	Butterfly Farm	23/03/1917	29/03/1917
War Diary	Front Line	29/03/1917	31/03/1917
Heading	War Diary for Month of April, 1917. Volume 15 8th R. Inniskilling Fus.		
War Diary	Front Line	01/04/1917	01/04/1917
War Diary	Locre	01/04/1917	03/04/1917
War Diary	Clare Camp	07/04/1917	13/04/1917
War Diary	Hazebrouck	13/04/1917	14/04/1917
War Diary	Arques	14/04/1917	15/04/1917
War Diary	Mentque	15/04/1917	28/04/1917
War Diary	Arques	28/04/1917	29/04/1917
War Diary	Hazebrouck	13/04/1917	30/04/1917
War Diary	Locre	30/04/1917	30/04/1917
Heading	War Diary Volume:-16 for Month of May, 1917. 8th R. Inniskilling Fusrs		
War Diary	Weston Camp Scherpenburg	01/05/1917	01/05/1917

Type	Description	From	To
War Diary	Front Line	01/05/1917	05/05/1917
War Diary	Ridge Wood	07/05/1917	07/05/1917
War Diary	Curragh Camp. Scherpenburg	09/05/1917	10/05/1917
War Diary	Front Line	10/05/1917	10/05/1917
War Diary	Butterfly Farm	14/04/1917	18/04/1917
War Diary	Renmore Camp Brulooze	18/05/1917	02/06/1917
War Diary	Bde Support	03/06/1917	04/06/1917
War Diary	Vierstraat Switch	04/06/1917	04/06/1917
War Diary	Front Line	04/06/1917	06/06/1917
War Diary	Doncaster Huts. Locre	06/06/1917	06/06/1917
War Diary	Front Line	07/06/1917	09/06/1917
War Diary	Doncaster Huts. Locre	09/06/1917	12/06/1917
War Diary	Locre	13/06/1917	13/06/1917
War Diary	Merris	16/06/1917	16/06/1917
War Diary	Clare Camp	17/06/1917	17/06/1917
War Diary	Merris	18/06/1917	18/06/1917
War Diary	Eecke	20/06/1917	20/06/1917
War Diary	Broxeele	22/06/1917	29/06/1917
War Diary	Etrehem & Leulinghem	30/06/1917	08/07/1917
War Diary	Rubrouck Area	08/07/1917	08/07/1917
War Diary	Winnizeele Area	09/07/1917	26/07/1917
War Diary	Watou No 2 Area	26/07/1917	30/07/1917
War Diary	Red Rose Camp	30/07/1917	31/07/1917
Heading	War Diary Of 8th Pm R. Innis Fus. For August 1917		
Heading	War Diary. for Month of August, 1917. Volume 19 8th R. Inniskilling Fuslrs		
War Diary	Vlamertinghe No. 3 Area H 16 a & d.	01/08/1917	01/08/1917
War Diary	Red Rose Camp	01/08/1917	03/08/1917
War Diary	Forward Area	04/08/1917	05/08/1917
War Diary	Front Line	06/08/1917	07/08/1917
War Diary	H 17 a.o.9	08/07/1917	14/07/1917
War Diary	Front Line	15/08/1917	17/08/1917
War Diary	Support	17/08/1917	17/08/1917
War Diary	H 17 a.o.9	18/08/1917	18/08/1917
War Diary	Watou No. 3 Area	18/08/1917	20/08/1917
War Diary	Godwaersvelde	20/08/1917	22/08/1917
War Diary	Achiet-Le-Petit	22/08/1917	23/08/1917
Operation(al) Order(s)	B R. Inniskilling Fusiliers Operation Order No. 91/1	25/04/1917	25/04/1917
Miscellaneous	Issued For Instructional Purposes Only	25/04/1917	25/04/1917
Miscellaneous	Copy No. 1 to O.C. Coy.		
Miscellaneous	Second Army Q/1173/22	20/04/1917	20/04/1917
Miscellaneous	49th. I.B. No. S.C.C X1/108	03/06/1917	03/06/1917
Miscellaneous	49th I.B. S.O.C. XI/100	28/05/1917	28/05/1917
Miscellaneous	8th Royal Inniskilling Fusiliers	23/05/1917	23/05/1917
Map			
Map	Traffic Routes		
Map	Traffic Routes IX Corps.		
Miscellaneous	Preliminary Instruction No. 1 By Major T.F. O'Donnell H.O. Commanding 7/8th	23/05/1917	23/05/1917
Map	49th Inf Bde.		
Miscellaneous	49th Infantry Brigade Instructions For The Offensive.	25/05/1917	25/05/1917
Miscellaneous		02/06/1917	02/06/1917
Miscellaneous	49th Inf. Bde. No. S.O. 60-25-5-17	25/05/1917	25/05/1917
Miscellaneous	49th. I.B. No. S.C.C. IX/188/7	28/05/1917	28/05/1917
Miscellaneous	49th Infantry Brigade Administrative Instructions For The Offensive.	25/05/1917	25/05/1917

Miscellaneous	49th Infantry Brigade. Administrative Instruction For The Offensive.		
Miscellaneous	1. Rations.		
Miscellaneous	2. Medical		
Miscellaneous	3. Veterinary.		
Miscellaneous	8.a. Orders For Guards Over Prisoners Of War.		
Miscellaneous	8.b. Orders For Officers Or N.C.O'S. In Command Of Escorts To Prisoners Of War.		
War Diary	9. Reinforcements.		
Miscellaneous	11. Storage Of Spare Kit		
Miscellaneous	49th Inf. Bde. No. S.O. 60-27-5-17	27/05/1917	27/05/1917
Miscellaneous	49th Infantry Brigade Instructions For The Offensive. Appendix D		
Miscellaneous	A Carrying Party. Load For First Journey.		
Miscellaneous	B and "C" Carrying Parties. Loads For First Journey.		
Miscellaneous	B And "C" Carrying Parties. Load For Second Journey.		
Miscellaneous	A Carrying Party. Load For First Journey.		
Miscellaneous	B And "C" Carrying Parties. Load For Second Journey.		
Miscellaneous	B And "C" Carrying Parties. Load For First Journey.		
Miscellaneous	49th Inf. Bde. No. S.O. 60-28-5-17	28/05/1917	28/05/1917
Miscellaneous	49th Infantry Brigade Instructions For The Offensive.	28/05/1917	28/05/1917
Miscellaneous	49th Inf. Bde. No. S.O. 60-27-5-17	27/05/1917	27/05/1917
Miscellaneous Diagram etc	Signal Instructions For The Offensive. Appendix C		
Miscellaneous	49th Inf. Bde. No. S.O. 60-30-5-17	30/05/1917	30/05/1917
Miscellaneous	49th Infantry Brigade Instructions For The Offensive.		
Miscellaneous	49th Inf. Bde. No. S.O. 60	31/05/1917	31/05/1917
Miscellaneous	49th Infantry Brigade Instructions For The Offensive.		
Miscellaneous	49th I.B. No. S.C.C XI/102	31/05/1917	31/05/1917
Miscellaneous	Appendix "A" Company Order By Captain W.L.C. Moore Brabazon, Commanding "A" Coy. 2nd. Battalion, The Royal Irish Regiment.		
War Diary	Appendix "B" Company Orders By Captain R.A. Belemore, Commanding, "B" Coy. 2nd. Battalion, The Royal Irish Regiment.		
Miscellaneous	Appendix "C" Company Orders By Captain P.J.G. Gordon Ralph, Commanding, "C" Company. 2nd. Battalion, The Royal Irish Regiment.		
Miscellaneous	Appendix "D" Company Orders By Captain J.I. Cotter, Commanding, "D" Coy 2nd. Battalion, The Royal Irish Regiment.		
Miscellaneous	Appendix "E"		
Miscellaneous	Appendix "F" Carrying Party		
Map	A Carrying Party Load for 21st Journey.		
Operation(al) Order(s)	Operation Order No. 30 By Lieut Colonel H.G. Gregorie D.S.O. Commanding 2nd Battn. The Royal Irish Regt.	02/06/1917	02/06/1917
Operation(al) Order(s)	Operation Orders No. 30 By Lieut. Colonel H.G. Gregorie, D.S.O., Commanding, 2nd. Battalion, The Royal Irish Regiment.	29/05/1917	29/05/1917
Miscellaneous		02/06/1917	02/06/1917
Miscellaneous	Reg. No. S.O. /160/VI.	04/06/1917	04/06/1917
Miscellaneous	Orders For Raid	01/06/1917	01/06/1917
Operation(al) Order(s)	Left Group Operation Order No. 56	04/06/1917	04/06/1917
Operation(al) Order(s)	8th R. Inniskilling Fusiliers. Operation Order No. 103 By Lieut. Colonel. T.H. Boardman D.S.O.	04/06/1917	04/06/1917

Miscellaneous	B And "C" Carrying Parties. Load For First Journey.		
Miscellaneous	Report Of Raid Carried Out By 8th Bn. R. Inniskilling Fus On The Right Of 5th June 17	05/05/1917	05/05/1917
Miscellaneous	Attack on Wytschaete Ridge - 7th June. 1917	07/06/1917	07/06/1917
Miscellaneous	Report Of Raid Carried Out By 8th R. Inniskilling Fusiliers, 49th Inf. Bde. On The Night 15th/16th July	15/07/1917	15/07/1917
Diagram etc			
Miscellaneous	Orders For Raid.		
Miscellaneous	Detail of Carrying Parties. Appendix "C"		
Miscellaneous	Scheme For 3" Stokes Bombardment To Assist Raid On Night 5th/6th.	04/06/1917	04/06/1917
Operation(al) Order(s)	Right Group Operation Order No. 10. Lieut. Colonel. L.E.S. Ward D.S.O. R.F.A. Commdg.	05/06/1917	05/06/1917
Operation(al) Order(s)	Left Group Operation Order No. 56	04/06/1917	04/06/1917
Miscellaneous	Orders For Raid.	03/06/1917	03/06/1917
Miscellaneous	Action Of Machine Guns.	03/06/1917	03/06/1917
Miscellaneous	B & "C" Carrying Parties. Load For Second Journey.		
Miscellaneous	A Carrying Party. Load For First Journey.		
Operation(al) Order(s)	Operation Order No. 103 Appendix		
Miscellaneous	B Coy. 8th R. Innis. Fus. Mopping Up For 7th R. Innis. Fus. Appendix "B"		
Miscellaneous	D Coy. 8th R. Innis. Fus. Mopping Up For 7/8th R. Irish Fus. Appendix "A"		
Operation(al) Order(s)	8th. R. Inniskilling Fusiliers. Operation Order No. 103 By Lieut. Colonel. T.H. Boardman D.S.O.	04/06/1917	04/06/1917
Miscellaneous	Appendix "Z" Attack On Wytschaete 7th June 1917 Operation Order No. 103 Report On Operation Maps (2)		
Operation(al) Order(s)	8th. R. Inniskilling Fusiliers. Operation Order No. 103 By Lieut. Colonel. T.H. Boardman D.S.O.	04/06/1917	04/06/1917
Miscellaneous	Odd Spare Shuts Of O.O. 103 (Offensive)		
Miscellaneous	A Carrying Party. Load For First Journey.		
Miscellaneous	S.O./1 /5	04/06/1917	04/06/1917
Miscellaneous	Instructions For The Offensive	04/06/1917	04/06/1917
Miscellaneous	Appendix C to S.O/1	04/06/1917	04/06/1917
Miscellaneous	Accommodations And Arrangements In S.P. 13	04/06/1917	04/06/1917
Diagram etc			
Map	Meter Gauge Railway Shewn Thus		
Heading	War Diary. For Month Of June, 1917. Volume.-17 Unit 8th Battn R. Inniskilling Fusiliers		
Miscellaneous	A Form Messages And Signals	05/06/1917	05/06/1917
Miscellaneous	List of Machine Gun Emplacements, Strong Points etc in enemy's line opposite Vierstraat Sector suggested for treatment by Heavy Artillery.		
Miscellaneous	Machine Gun Emplacements.		
Miscellaneous	Headquarters		
Miscellaneous	Blue Clay		
Miscellaneous	49th I.B. No. Q/28 8/R. Innis. Fus.	04/06/1917	04/06/1917
Miscellaneous			
Miscellaneous	49th I.B. Q. 42	05/06/1917	05/06/1917
Miscellaneous	49th I.B. No. S.C.C. XI/110	05/06/1917	05/06/1917
Miscellaneous	O.C. 8th R. Innis Fus.	05/06/1917	05/06/1917
Miscellaneous	Special Order.	05/06/1917	05/06/1917
Miscellaneous	49th I.B. No. Q. 47	06/06/1917	06/06/1917
Miscellaneous	49th I.B. No. Q. 48	06/06/1917	06/06/1917
Miscellaneous	49th. Inf. Bde. No. S.M. 121	06/06/1917	06/06/1917

Type	Description	Date From	Date To
Miscellaneous	Instructions For The Demolition of Hostile Guns With 3" Stokes Trench Mortar Bombs and Special Slow Fuze.		
Miscellaneous	49th Inf. Bde. No. B.O. 130/1	06/06/1917	06/06/1917
Miscellaneous	2/R. Irish Regt. and T.O.	06/06/1917	06/06/1917
Miscellaneous	49th Inf. Bde. No. S.O. 60	06/06/1917	06/06/1917
Miscellaneous	49th Infantry Brigade Instructions For The Offensive.		
Miscellaneous	Between 33rd Inf. Bde. and Xth Corps.		
Miscellaneous	49th I.B. No. Q55	07/06/1917	07/06/1917
Operation(al) Order(s)	8th. R. Inniskilling Fusiliers Operation Order No. 109	29/06/1917	29/06/1917
Map	Second Army Barrage Map. June 1917		
Miscellaneous	8th Royal Inniskilling Fus. Reference Operation Order No. 30	04/06/1917	04/06/1917
Miscellaneous	Instructions For The Offensive	01/06/1917	01/06/1917
Miscellaneous	Appendix. C. to S.O/I. d/30.5.17	30/05/1917	30/05/1917
Miscellaneous	49th. I.B. No. S.C.C. IX/188/11	01/06/1917	01/06/1917
Miscellaneous	Officer Commanding 8th Royal Inniskilling Fusiliers.	02/06/1917	02/06/1917
Operation(al) Order(s)	Operation Orders. No. 1	02/06/1917	02/06/1917
Miscellaneous	Appendix "A" 49th Infantry Brigade Administrative Instructions For The Offensive	02/06/1917	02/06/1917
Miscellaneous	A Carrying Party. Load For First Journey.		
Miscellaneous	B And "C" Carrying Parties. Load For First Journey.		
Miscellaneous	B And "C" Carrying Parties. Load For Second Journey		
Miscellaneous	Appendix A. 49th Infantry Brigade Instructions For The Offensive.		
Miscellaneous	Table Showing Scale Of S.A.A. Grenades, & C, To Be Kept At Brigade And Battalion Dumps.		
Miscellaneous	Table Showing Scale Of S.A.A., Grenades, &c, To Be Kept At Brigade And Battalion Dumps In Addition To The Amounts Already Held By The Brigade In The Line.		
Miscellaneous	Amendments To Appendix "A" Of 49th Infantry Brigade Administrative Instructions For The Offensive.	04/06/1917	04/06/1917
Miscellaneous	Appendix B. Action Of Divisional Machine Guns		
Miscellaneous	49th Infantry Brigade Instructions For The Offensive.	02/06/1917	02/06/1917
Miscellaneous	49th Inf. Bde. No. S.O. 60	03/06/1917	03/06/1917
Miscellaneous	49th Infantry Brigade Instructions For The Offensive		
Miscellaneous	Continuation Of Operation Orders No. 1. Issued On Sheet 8	04/06/1917	04/06/1917
Miscellaneous	The Officer Commanding 8th R. Innis Fus.	05/06/1917	05/06/1917
Operation(al) Order(s)	Operation Order No. 37 By, Lieut Col. H.N. Young, D.S.O.	06/06/1917	06/06/1917
Miscellaneous	Dear Boardman	10/06/1917	10/06/1917
Miscellaneous	Dear Boardman		
Miscellaneous	A Form Messages And Signals.		
Miscellaneous	Big Officers	01/06/1917	01/06/1917
Miscellaneous	Instructions For The Offensive	30/05/1917	30/05/1917
Miscellaneous	A Form Messages And Signals.		
Map	Part Of Sheet 5A (Belgium) Second Army Area		
Miscellaneous	49th Inf. Bde. No. S.O. 83	03/06/1917	03/06/1917
Miscellaneous	Tanks.		
Miscellaneous	Appendix F. Contact Patrols		
Miscellaneous	Code Letters For Liaison Between Infantry And Aircraft.		
Miscellaneous		16/07/1916	16/07/1916
Miscellaneous	B Form Messages And Signals.		

Miscellaneous	A Form Messages And Signals.		
Miscellaneous	B Form Messages And Signals.		
Miscellaneous	Instructions For The Offensive		
Miscellaneous	S 138	15/07/1916	15/07/1916
Miscellaneous			
Miscellaneous	B Form Messages And Signals.		
Miscellaneous	2. Craters		
Map	Secret Copy No. 5 Map A		
Miscellaneous	A Form Messages And Signals.	12/07/1916	12/07/1916
Miscellaneous	8th Inniskilling	14/07/1916	14/07/1916
Miscellaneous	Appendix. 49th Infantry Brigade Raid Scheme.	14/07/1916	14/07/1916
Miscellaneous	49th Inf. Bde. Raid Scheme.		
Miscellaneous	R.E. Scheme In Conjunction With 49th Brigade Infantry Scheme.		
Miscellaneous	Appendix III	16/08/1917	16/08/1917
Miscellaneous	O.C. 8. R Innis Fusrs.	14/08/1917	14/08/1917
Operation(al) Order(s)	Operation Orders No. 118	10/08/1917	10/08/1917
Operation(al) Order(s)	Operation Order No. 119 B R Innis Fus.	14/08/1917	14/08/1917
Miscellaneous			
Operation(al) Order(s)	8th R. Innis Fus. Operation Orders No. 115	03/08/1917	03/08/1917
Miscellaneous	Provisional Orders For The Attack 8th R. Innis. Fusiliers. Appendix I		
Map	Communication Chart		
Operation(al) Order(s)	Operation Order No. 121 8 R. Innis. Fus. Appendix II	15/08/1917	15/08/1917
Operation(al) Order(s)	Operation Orders No. 4. By. Lieut. Colonel. K.C. Weldon D.S.O. Comdg Royal Irish Fusiliers.	14/08/1917	14/08/1917
Operation(al) Order(s)	Operation Order No. 120 8 R. Innis Fus	15/08/1917	15/08/1917
Operation(al) Order(s)	O.C. 8. R Innis Fusrs	14/08/1917	14/08/1917
Miscellaneous	Scheme For Raid by 2nd. Battalion, The Royal Irish Regiment.		
Operation(al) Order(s)	O.O. No. 42. Page 2 after line 13 Insert		
Operation(al) Order(s)	Operation Order No. 42 by Major J.D. Scott, Commanding. 2nd. Battalion, The Royal Irish Regiment.	15/08/1917	15/08/1917
Miscellaneous	49th I.B. No. S.C.C. 9/306	06/09/1917	06/09/1917
Miscellaneous	49th Infantry Brigade. Special Administrative Instruction No. 15 Issue Of Ammunition	03/08/1917	03/08/1917
Miscellaneous	49th Infantry Brigade.	05/08/1917	05/08/1917
Operation(al) Order(s)	8th Royal Inniskilling Fusiliers Operation Order No. 122	20/03/1917	20/03/1917
Operation(al) Order(s)	8th R. Inniskilling Operation Orders No. 117		
Operation(al) Order(s)	8th RI Innis Fus OO/116	05/08/1917	05/08/1917
Operation(al) Order(s)	8th R. Innis Fus. Operation Order No. 116	06/11/1917	06/11/1917
Map	1:10,000. Second Army Front Map D.		
Map	1:10,000. Second Army Front. Map E		
Map	1:10,000. Second Army Front. Map F		

3/feb?

8 Battalion Regal Inniskilling Fusiliers

Feb 14/16 - Aug 1917

16TH DIVISION
49TH INFY BDE

8TH BN ROY. INNIS FUS

FEB 1916 - ~~MAY 1918~~ 1917 AUG

became 7/8 BN Aug 1917

From O.C. 8th Royal Inniskilling Fusiliers

To. D.A.G. 3rd Echelon

Herewith War Diary of "8" (S) Bn Royal Inniskilling Fusiliers to date.

H. Montgomery
Major
Commanding
(S) Battalion R. Innis. Fusiliers.

31.3.16

Army Form C., 2118.

WAR DIARY
or
INTELLIGENCE SUMMARY.
(Erase heading not required.)

Instructions regarding War Diaries and Intelligence Summaries are contained in F. S. Regs., Part II. and the Staff Manual respectively. Title pages will be prepared in manuscript.

Place	Date	Hour	Summary of Events and Information	Remarks and references to Appendices
BORDON	3.2.16		Orders received to mobilize as from 1st February 1916	Wilson
BORDON	17.2.16		Battalion left BORDON and proceeded to SOUTHAMPTON in 3 trainloads. 1st Trainload under Lieut Col A.J. Downing, D.S.O. 2nd Trainload under Capt. C. Knipe. 3rd Trainload under Major W.J. & Jeffreys	Wilson
SOUTHAMPTON	17.2.16		Arrived. 6 Officers, 231 O.R. entrained Transport Embarked for HAVRE in S.S. "HUNTSCRAFT". Two officers and 126 O.R. under command of Capt. T.A. Clarke (Remainder of the Battn, 26 Officers and 726 O.R. proceeded to Rest Camp)	Wilson
SOUTHAMPTON	18.2.16		Remainder of Battn embarked for HAVRE in S.S. "MARGUERITE". Ship sailed from SOUTHAMPTON Docks about 11pm. Weather too rough	Wilson
SOUTHAMPTON	19.2.16		Ship sails again and from anchorage HAVRE shortly after midnight.	Wilson
HAVRE	20.2.16		Disembarked and proceeded to No.1. Rest Camp. SNWO took over the rest of the Battn was met.	Wilson

Army Form C. 2118.

WAR DIARY
or
INTELLIGENCE SUMMARY.
(Erase heading not required.)

Instructions regarding War Diaries and Intelligence Summaries are contained in F. S. Regs., Part II. and the Staff Manual respectively. Title pages will be prepared in manuscript.

Place	Date	Hour	Summary of Events and Information	Remarks and references to Appendices
HAVRE	21.2.16		Battalion moved from Rest Camp HAVRE in two parties	
			1st Party 3 officers & 125 O.R. under Major NP Salzul Walton	
			2nd Party Remainder of Battalion under Lieut. Col. A.T. Downing D.S.O	
			1st Party Entrained from Pond 6, 2nd Party from Pond 3	
		3.9h	Left HAVRE	
LILLERS	22.2.16		Arrived at LILLERS and detrained proceeding by march route to nearby billets at	Western
LIGNY-LEZ-AIRE				
LIGNY-LEZ-AIRE	25.2.16		Orders received from 49th INF. BDE. to move to LIERES, when Battalion was billeted for one night	Western
LIERES	26.2.16		Battalion proceed from LIERES and marches to BELLERIVE, as part of Division in reserve 1st Army Corps	Western
BELLERIVE	2.3.16		Battalion moved from BELLERIVE on attachment for training to 15th DIVISION and occupies billets in PHILOSOPHE	Western
PHILOSOPHE	3.3.16		2 Companies proceed to the trenches for training, being attached as under:—	Western
			C Coy 1 Platoon to each of the Companies of 6th Cameron Hrs. known as 56th INF. BDE., occupying centre subsection, HULLUCH SECTON	

2353 Wt.W2541/1454 700,000 5/15 D.D.&L. A.D.S.S./Form/C. 2118.

Army Form C. 2118.

WAR DIARY
or
INTELLIGENCE SUMMARY.
(Erase heading not required.)

Instructions regarding War Diaries and Intelligence Summaries are contained in F. S. Regs., Part II. and the Staff Manual respectively. Title pages will be prepared in manuscript.

Place	Date	Hour	Summary of Events and Information	Remarks and references to Appendices
PHILOSOPHE	5.3.16		D Coy 1 platoon attached to each of the Coys of 11th A & S Highrs in left sub section of HULLUCH SECTION.	w.o.f. S
			C & D Coys came down from trenches and A & B Coys went up on attachment in similar manner. 1 platoon to each Coy of 13th Royal Scots in Right Sub section of HULLUCH SECTOR. B Coy attached — 1 platoon to each Coy of Seaforth Highrs in centre sub section HULLUCH SECTOR	
	7.3.16		A & B Coys came down from trenches to huts in PHILOSOPHE w. coy. D Coy went to trenches attached.	w.o.f. S.
	11.3.16		C & D Coys came down from trenches to billets PHILOSOPHE A & B Coy went up to Right sub section HULLUCH SECTOR. A Coy 2 platoons forming Bn 2 platoons forming support B Coy 2 platoons forming line 2 platoons support. C & D Coys proceeded to TENTH AVENUE where A & B Coy joined them as Battn. took over from 8th SEAFORTH S.	w.o.f. S
NOEUX-LES-MINES.	17.3.16		Battn. returned by 8th SEAFORTH S and proceeded to relieve 9th BLACK WATCH in PONT STREET RIGHT SUB SECTOR HULLUCH SECTOR. Distribution as follows C Coy in firing line D Coy in support on L. B Coy in support A Coy in reserve. Weather fine. Officer & 1 shell shock	
			1 O.R. killed 3 O.R. wounded. Heavy shelling in afternoon from rifle	w.o.f. S
	20/3/16		Relieved about 6 p.m by 10th Scottish Rifles. Marched to NOEUX-LES-MINES and spent night in huts.	w.o.f. S

Army Form C. 2118.

WAR DIARY
or
INTELLIGENCE SUMMARY.
(Erase heading not required.)

Instructions regarding War Diaries and Intelligence Summaries are contained in F. S. Regs., Part II. and the Staff Manual respectively. Title pages will be prepared in manuscript.

Place	Date	Hour	Summary of Events and Information	Remarks and references to Appendices
RAMBERT	23.3.16 to 27.3.16		Marched to RAMBERT where battalion was in Billets. Weather cold and snowy.	W.H.S
PHILOSOPHE W	27.3.16 to 28.3.16		Battn moved to PHILOSOPHE W by march and train as Bde reserve to 47 Inf Bde.	W.H.S
MAZINGARBE	28.3.16		To MAZINGARBE. Brigade in Divisional Reserve. Weather fine and warmer.	W.H.S
PHILOSOPHE E	31.3.16		To PHILOSOPHE — Bde reserve to 49 Inf Bde	W.H.S

2353 Wt. W2344/1454 700,000 5/15 D.D.&L. A.D.S.S./Forms/C. 2118.

WAR DIARY
or
INTELLIGENCE SUMMARY

8 Innis Killings
Vol 3

XVI

Place	Date April 1916	Hour	Summary of Events and Information	Remarks and references to Appendices
PHILOSOPHE	31 - 3		In billets in Bde Reserve. Weather fine.	
NOEUX-LES-MINES	3 - 6		Marched to TENTH AVENUE where we took over from Battn. in support 7th R Irish Fus. Weather fine.	
	6 - 12		Took over left sub section Puits 14 sub section from 7th R Irish killing two on nights 6/7 April. Previous to taking over front line was heavily bombarded by enemy. During period 6 to 12 enemy shelled this sub section intermittently. Battn. Headquarters in GUN TRENCH. A B & C Coys each Coy 2 platoons in firing line in front and firing line support D Coy in Reserve in RESERVE TRENCH. two platoons support. Weather fine. Casualties Killed O.R. 1. C Died of wounds O.R. 1. C. Wounded O.R. 3 B & C. Accidental self inflicted O.R. 2. Wounded at Duty O.R.1 missing whilst prisoner of war O.R. 1.	
	13		Battn. was relieved by 9th R Dublin Fus on night 12/13 April. Proceeded to NOEUX-LES-MINES as Bde. in Divisional Reserve.	
NOEUX-LES-MINES	13 - 20		In billets in Divisional Reserve	

Army Form C. 2118.

WAR DIARY
or
INTELLIGENCE SUMMARY.
(Erase heading not required.)

Instructions regarding War Diaries and Intelligence Summaries are contained in F. S. Regs., Part II. and the Staff Manual respectively. Title pages will be prepared in manuscript.

Place	Date	Hour	Summary of Events and Information	Remarks and references to Appendices
NOEUX-LES-MINES.	April 20	9am	Moves up to relieve 6th Bn CONNAUGHT RANGERS in Rt Subsection HULLUCH SECTOR.	
	20-24		Rt Subsection occupied with 3 Coys. (D.A.B.) Rt Subsection occupied with 3 Coys. each with 2 platoons in firing line & 2 in Support. C Coy in Reserve. During this period Enemy were very active with Rifle Grenades and Trench Mortar fire. Casualties: Killed O.R. 1. Wounded O.R. 9.	Weather fine
	24.		Battalion was relieved by 7th Bn. Royal Inniskilling Fusrs and moved into BRIGADE RESERVE - Billets PHILOSOPHE WEST.	Weather fine
	24-27		In billets PHILOSOPHE WEST - weather fine	Weather fine
	27th		On morning 27th a very heavy bombardment was commenced by Enemy about 5.10am. The Battalion stood to ready to move up into the line. About 6am A Coy moves into L VILLAGE LINE. A Coy with right on NORTHERN DR. C Coy with left on LE RUTOIRE ALLEY. About 5am—6am Enemy shells PHILOSOPHE WEST heavily with lacrymatory shells, and a cloud of poison gas also encountered. About 7am the bombs of B. & D Coys were moved into LE MENDE and placed as	between 9am 10am

1577 Wt.W10791/1773 500,000 1/15 D. D. & L. A.D.S.S./Forms/C. 2118.

Army Form C. 2118.

WAR DIARY
or
INTELLIGENCE SUMMARY.
(Erase heading not required.)

Instructions regarding War Diaries and Intelligence Summaries are contained in F. S. Regs., Part II. and the Staff Manual respectively. Title pages will be prepared in manuscript.

Place	Date April	Hour	Summary of Events and Information	Remarks and references to Appendices
	28th		Arrival of O.C. 7th R. IRISH FUS. in BRIGADE SUPPORT. The bombardment ceased shortly afterwards. "A" & "B" Coys remained in the line until night returning to billets in PHILOSOPHE about 11.30 p.m. The bombers of B & D Coys remained in the line.	Wire
			Battalion moved up to relieve 7th Bn. Royal INNISKIL'G FUS'RS. in Sub Sector HULLUCH SECTOR. Disposition as follows: Batt. Headquarters FORT 37. D.A.& B. Coys each with 2 platoons in firing line & 2 platoons in support.	Wire
	29th	3.45 am	Enemy liberated gas and moved safely started heavy shelling on Support lines. Shelling was not very effective, and casualties from shell fire were few. M.G. and rifle fire was opened through the gas cloud which was very dense. The Enemy liberated gas from two tubes which were half way across No mans land. Gas came over in two clouds. The first of a greenish colour. The second of a yellowish orange colour from HULLUCH SOUTH. Gas was driven back over Enemy line. It must have suffered heavy casualties as ambulances were seen coming up BENIFONTAINE - VENDIN-LE-VIEIL Road. Enemy made no attempt to attack on our front. Gas lasted about 5 am. and Enemy was absolutely quiet throughout rest of day. Our casualties from gas	

1577 Wt. W16791/1773 500,000 1/15 D.D.&L. A.D.S.S./Forms/C. 2118.

Army Form C. 2118.

WAR DIARY
or
INTELLIGENCE SUMMARY.
(Erase heading not required.)

Instructions regarding War Diaries and Intelligence Summaries are contained in F. S. Regs., Part II. and the Staff Manual respectively. Title pages will be prepared in manuscript.

Place	Date	Hour	Summary of Events and Information	Remarks and references to Appendices
Rubouf	21st May		Much work was done on trenches during this period. There was considerable shelling activity on both sides. Casualties; Died of wounds LIEUT. DE NEWALL 25.5.16 wounded 2/LIEUT M? RATER 22.5.16. 2/LIEUT R.J. MCWHIRTER 21.5.16. OR Killed 24 wounded 7.	
Rubouf	23rd May		Battalion relieved by 1st Royal Innis. Fus. in left No. B. Section LOOS SECTOR and moved back to Brigade Support ANGRES, HULLS PHILOSOPHE EST. 1 platoon in LENS REDOUBT	
PHILOSOPHE EAST	24th		Battalion relieved in B.D.E. Reserve by 1st Royal BERKS REGT. on relief A/See marched to BRUAY. BULLETS at BRUAY.	
BRUAY	26th 27th		In Billets — weather fine.	
BRUAY	28th		Battalion marched to BETHUNE and entrained to M. DINGEN.	
M. DINGEN	29th		Battalion detrained and marched to CONDETTE and billeted to be attached on our of instruction	
CONDETTE	30th/31st		Under canvas — weather fine.	

End of Month —

J. Musadware Major
Commanding 9th Batt. Innis. Fus.

Army Form C. 2118.

WAR DIARY
or
INTELLIGENCE SUMMARY
(Erase heading not required.)

Vol S. 8 Innishkilling
June
H 9/16
XVI

Instructions regarding War Diaries and Intelligence Summaries are contained in F.S. Regs., Part II. and the Staff Manual respectively. Title pages will be prepared in manuscript.

Place	Date	Hour	Summary of Events and Information	Remarks and references to Appendices
CONDETTE	1st to 1st		Under Canvas at CONDETTE – weather fine	Weather
CONDETTE	2		Draft of 3 nuns [arrived] from 10th Bn. & [Gibralty]	Weather
"	7		Draft of 52 men [arrived] from 10th [Bn.] [Base] at [10].	Weather
"	11		Battn. marched to the Joining [Neuve] and bivouacked moving off at 11 am. Advanced at [proper]	Weather
			LES NIEPPES and marched to billets at [Mussilville West]	
	13		Seven M.Gs moved up and relieved 5th M.G.R. [there] two in [Eifeld] [section]. [Rest] in	Weather
MAILLY=MAILLET	14		B1 SECTOR	
"	15		Battn moved up to relieve 1st R. Irish Fus in Redoubts No 3 & 4 B.1. SECTOR	
			but one Coy to [reinforce] King's [own] at [Euston] Dump. Relief complete on [Sur 10.15]	
			a.m. 15/6 VENUE.	
MAILLY	16		March in and relieves Kings Own Bn. on the [4th] [inst]. [Relief] [2] hs. A.3 SECTOR	Weather
			Battn. HQ [Euston] ST.	
	18/19		2nd Lieut Weir was [wounded] by [shell] [in] [Ruin Knol]	

Army Form C. 2118.

WAR DIARY
or
INTELLIGENCE SUMMARY.
(Erase heading not required.)

Place	Date June	Hour	Summary of Events and Information	Remarks and references to Appendices
In line	23rd		Draft of 40 men joined from Base Depot.	
"	23rd		Draft of 23 OR from 7th R/Innis two joined the Battalion	
MAZIN PROBE	23rd		Draft of 11 OR joined from Base Depot.	
			The following officers joined during the month	
CONDETTE			Lt J.J. KENNEDY } from 19th Reserve Battalion	
"			2/Lt R.J. WOODS }	
"	1st		7/Lt R.E. PALMGREN on appointment from 11th Hussars	
"	15th		2/Lt W.F. GREEN on attachment from 4th D.G.	
"	19th		2/Lt F.R. STRONG on attachment from 7th M.M.G. Coy.	
			End of Month.	

Lieut. Colonel, Commanding
11th (S) Battalion R. Innis. Fusiliers.

Army Form C. 2118.

WAR DIARY
or
INTELLIGENCE SUMMARY

(Erase heading not required.)

Instructions regarding War Diaries and Intelligence Summaries are contained in F. S. Regs., Part II. and the Staff Manual respectively. Title pages will be prepared in manuscript.

Place	Date	Hour	Summary of Events and Information	Remarks and references to Appendices
Kuhn	20/21		Battalion relieved by 7th R Innis Fus in left Sub Section, & Bis Section in right Sub Section of relief Batln moves into Bde Support in 10th AVENUE. During afternoon Enemy was extremely quiet 20 rounds Trench Mortar and rifle grenade and trench mortars fire which came rather infrequently	Appdx
"	21/22		In Brigade Support in 10th AVE. – Situation very quiet	Appdx
"	23/24		Batln moved in and relieved 7th R Innis Fus in left Sub Section. Bn H.Q. 14 Bns Batt=H.Q. - CURZON ST. B Coys in Front line – C, A, B from right to left. D Coy in Reserve	
"	24/26		There was no particular activity during two days beyond shelling our front & Support trenches	4 pm
"	26/27		Battalion were relieved by 9th Royal Dublin Fusiliers and moved into billets in Sukhm	Appdx
			Divisional Reserve at NIEPPE ON RBE	27/4/16
			Casualties during trench tours of twelve days expressed – 1 officer W.J. Thomas 3rd O.E. died of wounds 2nd of wounded, O.R. 31. Killed O.R. 3 wounded, O.R. 36 O.R. Total – 36 O.R.	Appx

WAR DIARY

8th (S) Battalion
Royal Inniskilling Fus

1st. July to 31st. July 1916.

VOLUME No. 6

Army Form C. 2118.

WAR DIARY
or
INTELLIGENCE SUMMARY.
(Erase heading not required.)

8TH (S) BATTALION
C 298
2 AUG 1916
R. INNIS. FUSILIERS.

Instructions regarding War Diaries and Intelligence Summaries are contained in F.S. Regs., Part II. and the Staff Manual respectively. Title pages will be prepared in manuscript.

Place	Date	Hour	Summary of Events and Information	Remarks and references to Appendices
MAZINGARBE	July 1/3		In billets in Div. Reserve MAZ IN GARBE	Within
"	2d.		Battalion moved up to relief of 8th Bn. Connaught Rangers in Gt Tuberbrun LOOS SECTOR as Batt. N.2. G3b a. 3/-5. 3 Coys in front line, and 1 Coy in Reserve. Relieve Cmo in front line	Within
		7th.		Within
LEFT SUB SECTION 5/6th. LOOS		11.30	Gas was discharged on Batt. front from ENGLISH ALLEY to SCOTS ALLEY. No infantry attack was carried out by this Batt. Enemy artillery fired in retaliation but damage very little, damage being done by their fire	Within
"	3/7th.		With exception of above observation the situation was normal during this tour of front line. CASUALTIES during this tour. DIED OF WOUNDS 1. O.R. wounded 8. O.R.	Within
"	7th.		Battalion relieved by 7th R. Innis Fus. and moved into Bde Reserve in PHILOSOPHE E. with 1 Coy. in VILLAGE LINE, this Coy. forming garrison of LEWIS No.8 REDOUBT	Within
PHILOSOPHE E.	7/8th.		Battn. in Bde. Reserve. Weather fine	Within

Army Form C. 2118.

WAR DIARY
or
INTELLIGENCE SUMMARY.

(Erase heading not required.)

Instructions regarding War Diaries and Intelligence Summaries are contained in F.S. Regs., Part II. and the Staff Manual respectively. Title pages will be prepared in manuscript.

Place	Date	Hour	Summary of Events and Information	Remarks and references to Appendices
PHILOSOPHE E	12th	1 pm	Battalion moved up to relieve 7th R. Irish Rus. in Left sub-sector, LOOS SECTOR. Batln. H.Q. 9.36 a 3/2-5. 3 Coys in front line, 1 Coy in Reserve - 8 Lewis Guns in front and support lines.	6/15/tm
LEFT P.R. SECTION LOOS	13th		Battalion distributed as above. Situation normal. CAPT. C. SEMER wounded.	alex
"	15/16th		At 11.30 pm two mines were exploded as SEAFORTH CRATER on right of battalion front. A raiding party under of 3 N.C.O.s & 18 men under 2/Lt. CAPT. WRAY entered enemy trench, bombed dug-outs for a distance of 200 yards. Party returns after being in enemy trench for about 35 minutes. 1 Prisoner was taken, and many casualties inflicted on enemy. The CRATERS were consolidated by two parties each of 2 - 25 men under 2Lt. W.G. FLEMING R.9.E. and 2Lt. H.A. GREEN. R.E parties were also employed. CASUALTIES KILLED - 2/Lt. CAPT. WRAY, 1 no. O.R. WOUNDED - 2/Lt. W.G. FLEMING R.9.E. and 28 O.R. 10 O.R. killed 27 OR wounded. TOTAL CASUALTIES during this tour - 1 Officer killed, 3 Others wounded, by 7th R. Inniskilling Fus. Battalion relieved in Left Sub Section LOOS SECTOR by 7th R. Inniskilling Fus. and moved into Btn. Subsect. Ph. N.2 - PHILOSOPHE E. 2 Coys in ENCLOSURE under OC R. Sub Section 1 Coy in DUKE ST. and 1 Coy in REST tent OC Left Sub Section.	alex

Army Form C. 2118.

WAR DIARY
or
INTELLIGENCE SUMMARY.
(Erase heading not required.)

Instructions regarding War Diaries and Intelligence Summaries are contained in F.S. Regs., Part II. and the Staff Manual respectively. Title pages will be prepared in manuscript.

Place	Date	Hour	Summary of Events and Information	Remarks and references to Appendices
	16/19th		Battn in Batt Support. H.Q. Anicole Pitt.	Weather
	19th		Battn relieved in Batt Support by 7th R.I. Rifles, and moves back to hute in NOEUX LES MINES - Divisional Reserve	Weather
NOEUX-LES-MINES	20th		In Divisional Reserve - Huts - Weather fine	Weather
"	21st		Battn moves up and relieves 6th Cameron Highrs in Lyhtol section. HULLUCH SECTOR. 3 Coy's in front line one 1 Coy in Reserve - B.L.M Co n Battn. H.Q. DEVON LANE front and support lines.	Weather
LEFT SUB SECTION	22 & 23		Lyhtol section. HULLUCH. Battn find considerably shelled with Enemy T.M.S. Stand on during this time otherwise normal	Weather
HULLUCH				
"	24th		Battn relieved by 8th Royal Dublin Fusiliers, and moves into Divisional Reserve Huts. NOEUX- LES- MINES - CASUALTIES during the tour 50R. killed, 1 died of wounds, 15 wounded	Weather
NOEUX-LES-MINES.	24/30th		In Divisional Reserve - Huts NOEUX LES MINES - weather fine	Weather
"	31st		Battalion moved with 4 Trenches, and relieved 8th Royal Munsters two in Lys sub section Puits 14 BIS SECTOR. Battn. H.Q. CURZON ST 3 Coys in front line 1 Coy in support line sighted Group	Weather

2353 Wt. W2511/1434 700,000 5/15 D. D. & L. A.D.S.S./Form/C. 2118.

Vol 7

R4

WAR DIARY.

8th Royal Iniskilling Fusiliers

MONTH OF AUGUST, 1916.

VOLUME:- 7

Army Form C. 2118.

WAR DIARY
of
INTELLIGENCE SUMMARY
(Erase heading not required.)

Instructions regarding War Diaries and Intelligence Summaries are contained in F. S. Regs., Part II. and the Staff Manual respectively. Title pages will be prepared in manuscript.

8TH (S) BATTALION
-2 SEP. 1916
R. INNIS. FUS. "S"

Place	Date August	Hour	Summary of Events and Information	Remarks and references to Appendices
Left Sub Sectⁿ in Pts 5.	3rd	10th	Holding Left Subsection Pts TS 14 B15 SECTOR. A B & D Coys in front line from Right to Left. C Coy in Reserve – Battⁿ H.Q. PONT ST. Shooting during the 24th quiet except for enemy T.M.s at Boyan. Casualties :- 20 O.R. killed. 12 O.R. wounded. Battⁿ relieved by 9th R. Inniskilling Fus and moved into Boyan Reserve. PHILOSOPHE W.	Copy within
"	4th			Copy within
PHILOSOPHE W.	5th / 6th		Battalion in Boyan Reserve. Batt H.Q. PHILOSOPHE W. Weather fine.	Copy within
"	8th		Battalion moves up, and relieves 7th R.I. Fus, in readjustment of 1st Corps front. A & B Coys in front line from Boyan 47 to H 25.a.5.b. 2 Coys in Reserve. Battⁿ H.Q. 98th. TOSH ALLEY - 936.a.7.b.8.	
R^t Sub Sectⁿ 14 B15.	9th	9th	C Coy from Reserve moved up to relieve 1 Coy. 13th E. Surrey Regt from Boyan 47 to Boyan 47, completion of the relocation of the new R^t Sub Section Puits 14 B15.	
"	9/10th		Holding R^t Sub Section PUITS 14 B15 – Enemy very quiet during this period. Casualties :- 2 nd/Lt. R.G. CARSON, wounded 12.2.16. 1 O.R. killed. 6 O.R. wounded.	Copy within
"	11th		Battalion relieved by 9th K.R. Inniskilling Fus and on completion of relief moves into Bde Support Distribution :- C & A & B Coys. 10th A.V.E. holding 65 Puits Point to NORTHERN Ave. RESERVATS. D Coy in Gun TRENCH. Battⁿ H.Q. - 10th AVE.	Copy within
10th AVE	12/16th		Battalion in Bde Support in 10th AVE.	Copy within

Army Form C. 2118.

WAR DIARY
or
INTELLIGENCE SUMMARY
(Erase heading not required.)

Instructions regarding War Diaries and Intelligence Summaries are contained in F.S. Regs., Part II. and the Staff Manual respectively. Title pages will be prepared in manuscript.

Place	Date August	Hour	Summary of Events and Information	Remarks and references to Appendices
10th AVE.	18th		Batt. moved up, and relieved 7th K.R. from holding fire trenches in M/Sd. Section Puits 14 Bis. Distribution: D.C. "A" Coy in front line from Right to left. Batt. H.Q. Posh Alley 9.36 a 7½.8	15thm
N.Sub. Sec. P.15	19th		Battalion holding M.Sub. section. Puits 14 Bis. Enemy much more active than usual with Trench Mortars. This fire which was especially directed against my right front was very successful and very little damage was done. Casualties :- 1 O.R. killed, 6 O.R. wounded.	15thm
"	20th		Battalion relieved by 7th R.I have Battn. 8vo., and marched into Bde. Reserve - MAZINGARBE NORTH HUTS	15thm
MAZINGARBE	20/21st		L. Bde. Reserve - MAZIN GARBE. Weather fine	15thm
"	"	23.0 1pm	Battalion marched to camp at HOUCHIN.	15thm
HOUCHIN	24/25st		In camp at HOUCHIN. Orders received on 25th inst. to march on 26th inst. to LABEUVRIERE.	15thm
LABEUVRIERE	26th /27th		In Billets - weather variable. Orders received to move by train on morning 29th inst. from FOUQUEREUIL.	15thm
"	29th	2.30am	Battalion moved by march route to FOUQUEREUIL and entrained for LONGUEAU. Entraining Strength 32 Officers 845 O.R.	15thm
LONGUEAU	29th	11.10am	Battalion detrained at LONGUEAU and marched to billets at SAULLY-LE-SEC	15thm
SAULLY-LE-SEC	30th		In billets - weather very wet - attached VII Corps 4st Army	15thm

2353 Wt. W23/4/1454 750,000 5/15 D/D.& L. A.D.S.S./Forms/C. 2118.

Army Form C. 2118.

WAR DIARY
or
INTELLIGENCE SUMMARY.
(Erase heading not required.)

Place	Date	Hour	Summary of Events and Information	Remarks and references to Appendices
SAILLY-LE-SEC	August 31st	1.45am	Orders received to march to HAPPY VALLEY.	With
"		7.10am	Battalion reaches HAPPY VALLEY, and Encamps there. Strength 31 officers 615 O.R.	
			Officers joined during the month.	
			2/Lieut A.F. PORTER - 5. 8. 16.	With
			" W. TURNER - 21. 8. 16.	
			" S. McCONNELL - 23. 8. 16. (from 5th. R. Innis Fus on attachment)	
			Drafts received during the month.	
			48 O.R. from 16th A.B.D. 4. 8. 16	With
			11 O.R. " " 7. 8. 16	
			5 O.R. " " 15. 8. 16	
			12 O.R. " " 25. 8. 16	
			96 O.R. Connaught Rangers (from No.6 Entrenching Battn.) 26. 8. 16	

[signature]
Lieut.-Colonel, Commanding
8th (S) Battalion R. Innis. Fusiliers.

WAR DIARY

8th Royal Inniskilling Fusiliers

FOR MONTH OF SEPTEMBER, 1916.

VOLUME 8

Army Form C. 2118.

WAR DIARY
INTELLIGENCE SUMMARY.
(Erase heading not required.)

Place	Date	Hour	Summary of Events and Information	Remarks and references to Appendices
HAPPY VALLEY	1.9.16		Battalion in camp at HAPPY VALLEY as part of DIVN. in Corps Reserve	Weather
"	2.9.16		Battalion in camp at HAPPY VALLEY. Orders received to move on 3rd inst. at 10am to CITADEL (F.21.b)	Weather
CITADEL	3.9.16		Battalion moved into camp at CITADEL (F.21.b)	
		7.10pm	Orders received to move to BILLON FARM at (F.29) at 8.20 pm	Weather
		7.20pm	Battalion with transport complete moved to BILLON FARM	
BILLON FARM	4.9.16	2 am	Battalion arrives at BILLON FARM and bivouacs	Weather
"		5 pm	Orders received to move up to trenches to relieve a unit of 59th Inf. Bde. (20th Div) in support on E. side of GUILLEMONT	Ref. sheet 57c. S.W. 3
GUILLEMONT	5.9.16	6.50am	Battalion relieved 8th Bn. SOMERSET L.I. (59th Bde. 20th Div) in occupation of GUILLEMONT. Battalion dispositions as follows:— Batln. HQ. T.25.b.3.5½. A & B Coys holding old GERMAN LINE from T.25.b.3.8½ to T.25.b.3.3. C Coy holding line of strong posts T.25.b.1½.5 - T.25.b.1½.9. D Coy holding posts at T.19.c.1.3. T.25.a.3.6. Battalion holding positions as on 5th inst.	Weather
GUILLEMONT	6.9.16	12 noon	A coy sent forward to reinforce 7th R. Innis. Fus. on GINCHY-WEDGE WOOD ROAD line with left flank on cross roads T.20.c.2.4. The situation on Bn. front then being:— 7th R. Innis. Fus. holding line N. corner of LEUZE WOOD to about T.20.d.0.5 with 1 coy. Line from S.W. corner of LEUZE WOOD to about T.20.d.1.4. 2 Coys. on GINCHY-WEDGE WOOD ROAD line.	Weather
		5.15pm	Orders received from 49th I.B. that units from N. corner of LEUZE WOOD to T.20.d.2.5. thence to T.20.c.9.8 and from S.W. corner of LEUZE WOOD to T.20.d.0.5. thence to T.20.c.5.5 were to be Aug. night bn/7th This Battalion to dig and hold Front line from T.20.d.5.6 to T.20.c.9.8	Weather

5/15 D.D. & L. A.D.S.S. (Form) C. 2118.

Army Form C. 2118.

WAR DIARY
or
INTELLIGENCE SUMMARY.
(Erase heading not required.)

Instructions regarding War Diaries and Intelligence
Summaries are contained in F. S. Regs., Part II.
and the Staff Manual respectively. Title pages
will be prepared in manuscript.

Place	Date	Hour	Summary of Events and Information	Remarks and references to Appendices
GUILLEMONT	6.9.16		Support line from T.20 d.3.2 to T.20 c.5.5. About dusk GERMANS attacked to raid our positions in LEUZE WOOD and consolidation above orders did not take place until 5am.	658th
do	7.9.16	5am	The situation on our own left also has not been clear. Battalion moves forward in 3 Coys (A.B & C) advancing to line T.20 d.5.6. T.20 c.9.8. D Coy remaining in reserve in GINCHY-WEDGE WOOD ROAD LINE immediately South of Cross Roads T.20 d.2.4 Consolidation was commenced about 5am and front and support lines consolidated by about 7am. The position was held by Batt throughout the day. Enemy inflicted a number of casualties by sniping from high ground T.20 a. and from N.E of GINCHY. Position previously held in GUILLEMONT was taken over by 2/R.I.R. 56th Div. 9/R.B.Fus.	658th
do.	7.9.16	10.35pm	Battalion was relieved in above position by 12th LONDON REGT. (Welsh Inf Bde. 56th Div.) & 2/R.Fus. IRISH REGT. (47th I.B. 16th Div.) occupied line from cross roads T.20 C.2.4. to T.20 d.2.3. On completion of this relief Battalion moved into Divnl. RESERVE in BERNAFAY WOOD	658th 658th
BERNAFAY WOOD	8.9.16		In Divisional Reserve. BERNAFAY WOOD	658th
"	"	4pm 11.30pm	Orders received for attack by XIV Corps. on 9th inst. Battalion moves off and proceeds to occupy line N.E of GINCHY from T.9 d.8.6.2 to T.9 a.3.6	658th
GUILLEMONT	9.9.16	7am 7.10am	Battalion in position as leading Battalion of Brigade in Divnl. Reserve. Our heavies commence bombardment - Shells fell very short causing many casualties in our hole by Battalion. About 2.15 am it was found necessary to evacuate the hole this was carried out by 3 Coys. which occupied temporarily line along N.W. corner of GUILLEMONT	658th
		7am	LIEUT. COL. H.P. DALZELL-WALTON KILLED in action.	658th

Army Form C. 2118.

WAR DIARY
or
INTELLIGENCE SUMMARY.
(Erase heading not required.)

Instructions regarding War Diaries and Intelligence Summaries are contained in F. S. Regs., Part II and the Staff Manual respectively. Title pages will be prepared in manuscript.

Place	Date	Hour	Summary of Events and Information	Remarks and references to Appendices
POLLEMONT	9.9.16	9 am	Major A.J. WALKER took on command of Battn.	Weather
		9.45am	Original line re-occupied	Appendix II
			Report on action and attack on FINCH & attaches	Weather
		about 1 pm	Battalion relieved by 1 Coy 1st Grenadier Guards – and on completion of relief moved to BILLON FARM.	
Vicinity POLLEMONT	10.9.16		Casualties during operations 4th/10th September 1916:–	
			KILLED:– LIEUT. COL. H.P. DALZELL-WALTON . 9. 9. 16.	
			LIEUT. T.J. KENNEDY 9. 9. 16.	
			2/LIEUT. D.C. O'CONNELL 9. 9. 16.	
			(4th Conn. Rang.)	
			DIED of WOUNDS:– 2/LIEUT. R.S. PURDY (5th Bn.) 11. 9. 16 (wounded 10.9.16.)	
			WOUNDED:– 2/LIEUT. R.F. CASEY 5. 9. 16	
			2/LIEUT. E.H. SHAW (6th Bn.) 6. 9. 16	
			MAJOR J.M. WARDROPE 6. 9. 16	
			2/LIEUT. J.J. BRUEN 7. 9. 16	
			(4th Conn. Rang.)	
			CAPT. C. SEAVER. 9. 9. 16	
			CAPT. C.H. GODSLAND 9. 9. 16	
			(1st Bn.)	
			2/LIEUT. H.V.L.A. SMITH 9. 9. 16.	
			2/LIEUT. W.A. CAMPBELL 9. 9. 16.	
			(5th R. Irish Fus)		Weather

Army Form C. 2118.

WAR DIARY
or
INTELLIGENCE SUMMARY.
(Erase heading not required.)

Instructions regarding War Diaries and Intelligence Summaries are contained in F.S. Regs., Part II. and the Staff Manual respectively. Title pages will be prepared in manuscript.

Place	Date	Hour	Summary of Events and Information	Remarks and references to Appendices
			Casualties 4th/10th Continued:-	
			WOUNDED :- 2/LIEUT. L. W. L. LEADER. 9.9.'16. (4th Lon. Ramg.)	
			2/LIEUT. E. W. McKEGNEY. (5th Bn.) 9.9.'16.	
			2/LIEUT. MAJOR A. J. WALKER 9.9.'16.	
			WOUNDED (at duty) :- 2/LIEUT (To CAPT.) H. A. GREEN. 9.9.'16.	
			2/LIEUT. S. McCONNELL 9.9.-16. (5thBn)	
			MISSING :- 2/LIEUT. S. B. COGHILL (Bn.) 9.9.'16.	
			O.R. Killed, Wounded & Missing :- 219.	
			Strength 10.9.16:- 22 Officers 422 O.R.	
BILLON FARM	11.9.'16.		Batt. in bivouacs.	Watson
			MAJOR T. H. BOARDMAN, 8th R. IRISH FuS. took over temporary Command of the Battalion	
		12 noon	Orders received to move with 49th I.B. Group to SAILLY-LE-SEC	
		3.50pm ~3.30pm~	Battalion complete with transport moved to SAILLY-LE-SEC with 49th I.B. Group.	Watson
		5.30pm	Arrived SAILLY-LE-SEC, and billeted here.	Watson
SAILLY-LE-SEC.	12.9.16.		In billets SAILLY-LE-SEC.	Watson

WAR DIARY
or
INTELLIGENCE SUMMARY.
(Erase heading not required.)

Army Form C. 2118.

Instructions regarding War Diaries and Intelligence Summaries are contained in F.S. Regs., Part II. and the Staff Manual respectively. Title pages will be prepared in manuscript.

Place	Date	Hour	Summary of Events and Information	Remarks and references to Appendices
SAILLY-LE-SEC	17.9.16		Orders received to transport to LA CHAUSSÉE area, and continue march following day to MALLEN COURT area, where 10th Division was to concentrate preliminary to being transferred to 2nd. ARMY.	WMM
		1.30pm	Transport moves as ordered above	WMM
SAILLY-LE-SEC	18.9.16	10.15am	In accordance with orders received on 17th inst. Battalion (less transport) moved to LA NEUVILLE, moving thence by bus to SOREL, where it billeted	WMM
SOREL	18/		In billets at SOREL	WMM
	21.9.16	1.30pm	Battalion moved to PONT REMY and entrained there —	WMM
	21.9.16	4.8pm	Train departed from PONT REMY	WMM
BAILLEUL	22.9.16	1.30am	Arrived BAILLEUL STATION, and advanced, marching to camp at LOCRE.	WMM
LOCRE	22.9.16		Battalion In Camp DONCASTER HUTS. Orders received to relieve Bn of 12th CANADIAN INF. Bde in Trenches on 23rd. inst.	WMM
LOCRE	23.9.16	9 a.m	Battn. moves up to front line, and relieved 78th CAN. INF. BN in Sectors J2. E inclusive. 4 Coys in front line A.B.C.D from Right to Left. 1 Coy. BN. R.IRISH FUS in Support in J.D. 10.12. Battn. HQ LA POLKA (N. 21 d.7.5.)	WMM
Trenches	23/24th		Relieving took over as above. Situation during this period Extremely quiet Coy walking-2.O.R. wounded	WMM

Place	Date	Hour	Summary of Events and Information	Remarks and references to Appendices
	29.9.16		Battn relieved in front line by 3 companies 9th R Dublin Fusiliers, and 1 coy 7th R.Irish Fusiliers on completion of relief Battn moved into Divisional Reserve, DONCASTER HUTS. LOCRE	Wthr m
LOCRE	30.9.16		In Divisional Reserve, DONCASTER HUTS. LOCRE	Wthr m
			Officers joined during month:-	
			LIEUT. H BRADLEY, 2nd Bn 2.9.16	
			2/LIEUT. J.E. FAGAN, 6th Bn 15.9.16	
			2/LIEUT. R.V. POLLE J, 5th R.IRISH FUS 15.9.16	
			2/LIEUT. J.J. BRUEN, 4th CONNAUGHT RANGERS - returned from Hospital (wounded) 16.9.16	
			2/LIEUT. H.W. L A SMITH, " 19.9.16	Wthr m
			Drafts joined during the month from Base Depot.	
			5 OR 5.9.16	
			3 12.9.16	
			6 16.9.16	
			8 22.9.16	
			10 21.9.16	
			7 25.9.16	
			3 29.9.16	
			40	
			— End of month —	

T M Bowman
Major
"Lieut-Colonel", Commanding
8th (S) Battalion R. Innis. Fusiliers.

Miss West

WAR DIARY

MONTH OF OCTOBER, 1916.

VOLUME 9

8th Royal Inniskilling Fusiliers

Army Form C. 2118.

WAR DIARY
INTELLIGENCE SUMMARY.
(Erase heading not required.)

Instructions regarding War Diaries and Intelligence Summaries are contained in F. S. Regs., Part II. and the Staff Manual respectively. Title pages will be prepared in manuscript.

Place	Date	Hour	Summary of Events and Information	Remarks and references to Appendices
LOCRE	1/3.10.16	—	In Divisional Reserve – DONCASTER HUTS. LOCRE.	20/4m
"	2.10.16		Battalion moves up and relieves 7th. R. IRISH Fus in left sub-section of 49th. I.B. front. Dispositions: Batt. H-Q KEMMEL CHATEAU. C & B Coys front line D & A Coys reserve	1. B.T.m
Front Line	3/9.10.16		Holding front line as above.	18 B.Tm
"	9.10.16		Battalion relieved in left sub-section by 7th. R. IRISH Fus, and on completion of relief moves into Divisional Reserve at LOCRE. About from occasional trench mortar activity the line was very quiet. Casualties: 2/Lieut. J.E. FAGAN, died of wounds. 5.10.16 3 O.R. killed. 7 O.R. wounded.	23/4m
LOCRE	9/11.10.16		In Divisional Reserve – DONCASTER HUTS. LOCRE.	20/4m
"	14.10.16		Battalion moves up and relieves 7th. R. IRISH Fus in L.H. sub-section. Dispositions: Batt. H.Q. KEMMEL CHATEAU D & A Coys frontline, C & B Coys Reserve	19/4m
Frontline	14/17.10.16		Holding front line as above	18 B.Tm
"	17.10.16		Battalion relieved by 1st.R.Bn. THE ROYAL IRISH REGIMENT and moved into Divisional Reserve. LOCRE. The tour was very quiet, there being practically no activity on either side. Casualties: 2/Lt. J.P. DIGNAN, 4th Connaught Rangers att. killed in action 15.10.16 5 O.R. wounded	18/4m

Army Form C. 2118.

WAR DIARY
INTELLIGENCE SUMMARY.
(Erase heading not required.)

Place	Date	Hour	Summary of Events and Information	Remarks and references to Appendices
LOCRE	19/20.10.16		In Divisional Reserve. DONCASTER HUTS. LOCRE	
"	21.10.16		Battalion moved into and relieved 7th R. INNIS. Fus in right sub-section. Sub-sectors Battn. HQ. FORT VICTORIA. N.28.C.3/2.5 Bn. O Coys front line N.O Coys Reserve	Ref. French trench Map Sheet 28 Sw. 1/20,000
"	22-25.10.16		Holding right sub. section as above	
Doulieu	26.10.16		Battalion relieved by 7th R. INNIS. Fus and in completion of relief moved into Divisional Reserve. LOCRE. This tour was also very quiet. Casualties :- 2 O.R wounded	
LOCRE	27-30.10.16		In Divisional Reserve. DONCASTER HUTS. LOCRE.	
	31.10.16		The following officers joined during the month :- MAJOR W.E. ROTHWELL. 2nd Bn. R.Inn. Innis Fus 19.10.16 LIEUT. O.J. WHITE } from 9th Bn. 25.10.16 2/LIEUT. C.J. COGGINS 2/LIEUT. A.M. RATTRAY from ditto 30.10.16 Royal Innis Fus LIEUT. C.A. LE PETON } from 7th ROYAL IRISH Fus. 31.10.16 2/LIEUT. T.E. PRIZELLE	

Army Form C. 2118.

WAR DIARY
or
INTELLIGENCE SUMMARY
(Erase heading not required.)

29.

Instructions regarding War Diaries and Intelligence
Summaries are contained in F.S. Regs., Part II.
and the Staff Manual respectively. Title pages
will be prepared in manuscript.

Place	Date	Hour	Summary of Events and Information	Remarks and references to Appendices
LoCRE			The following drafts joined the Battalion during the month	125th
			From 16 R. Inf. Base Depot 3 O.R. 2. 10. 16.	
			12 " 11. 10. 16.	
			14 " 15. 10. 16.	
			11 " 21. 10. 16.	
			3 " 26. 10. 16.	
			— End of Month —	

W. Beauchamp
"Lieut.-Colonel, Commanding"
7th (S) Battalion R. Innis. Fusiliers.

WAR DIARY.

FOR

MONTH OF NOVEMBER, 1916.

VOLUME 10

8th R. Iniskilling Fusiliers

Army Form C. 2118.

WAR DIARY
or
INTELLIGENCE SUMMARY.
(Erase heading not required.)

Instructions regarding War Diaries and Intelligence Summaries are contained in F. S. Regs., Part II. and Staff Manual respectively. Title pages will be prepared in manuscript.

Place	Date	Hour	Summary of Events and Information	Remarks and references to Appendices
LOCRE	Month/y		Battalion moved up to front line and relieved 7th R. INNIS. FUS. in Rt Sub Section Shepherds Do A Coys trenches. CUR Coys SubSect. Reserve. Battn HQ. FORT VICTORIA	
Trenches	3/6/16		Holding Rt Sub-section as above	
	4th		Battalion relieved by 9th R. INNIS FUS and in completion of relief moved into Divisional Reserve. DONCASTER Hut C. LOCRE. Weishaken Lingerd Huts Kemmel. Shooting Butts westerly on Behier hutts. Casualties 2 OR wounded	
LOCRE	5/6 12h		In Divisional Reserve. DONCASTER Huts. LOCRE	
	12h		Battalion moved to front line and relieves 7th R. INNIS FUS in Rt Sub Section Shepherds Bn Coys front line. MFP Coys Shepherds Reserve. Battn HQ. FORT VICTORIA.	
Front line	12/13/th		Holding front line as above	
	13th		Battalion relieved by 7th R. INNIS. FUS and on completion of relief moved into Divisional Reserve. DONCASTER HUTS. LOCRE. During the two previous days head quarters Sunk shafts were sent forward. Casualties — OR killed, OR wounded	
LUCRE	14th		In Divisional Reserve. DONCASTER HUT. LOCRE	
	24th		Battalion moves to front line and relieves 7th R. INNIS FUS in Rt Sub actor Subsection D. A Coys front line. B.C. Coys Subsect and Reserve. Battn HQ. FORT VICTORIA	

Army Form C. 2118.

WAR DIARY
or
INTELLIGENCE SUMMARY.
(Erase heading not required.)

Instructions regarding War Diaries and Intelligence Summaries are contained in F. S. Regs., Part II. and Staff Manual respectively. Title pages will be prepared in manuscript.

Place	Date	Hour	Summary of Events and Information	Remarks and references to Appendices
Trenches	29th/30th		Nothing of interest to report	
	30th		Battalion relieved by 7th R. INNIS. F¤B, and on completion of relief marched viâ Brigade Reserve DONCASTER HUTS to R.E. Dump and arriving at T.M. Bombardment at 11pm. March to billets throughout this town was broken up. Casualties — 1 R. wounded	
LoCRE	30th		In Divisional Reserve DONCASTER HUTS to R.E. PIPER W.E. RIDDELL R. INNIS F¤B, Lt Kdln R. INNIS F¤B & 1 R. INNIS F¤B & 2 other ministers The following officers joined during the month: — 2/Lt R. H. BORCHARDS } 5½c. Ro " F. B. KEOGH } " J. C. BROWN } Casualty officers from 10th R. INNIS. F¤B. " R. T. BROWN } Drafts of O.R. joined the Battalion during the month as under from 16th I.B.D. 4 OR — 11.11.16 3a " — 14.11.16 29 " — 13.11.16 5 " — 20.11.16 7 " — 24.11.16 4 " — 29.11.16	

M. ....
"Lieut.-Colonel, Commanding"
8th (S) Battalion, R. Innis. Fusiliers.

WAR DIARY FOR MONTH OF DECEMBER, 1916.

VOLUME 11

8th R. Inniskilling Fusiliers

WAR DIARY or INTELLIGENCE SUMMARY

Army Form C. 2118.

(Erase heading not required.)

Place	Date December	Hour	Summary of Events and Information	Remarks and references to Appendices
LOCRE	1st.		In Divisional Reserve LOCRE	With M
"	1/6th		In Divisional Reserve LOCRE	With M
"	6th.		Battalion moved up and relieved 7th R. INNIS. Fus in right Sub-section. Baybachere Batt. HQ FORT VICTORIA. B & C Coys front line. D & A Coys support and reserve.	With M
Front line	6/12th		Holding Rt Subsection as above	With M
"	12th		Battalion relieved by 7th R. INNIS. Fus. and moved into Divisional Reserve LOCRE. The Enemy shewed considerable T.M activity throughout this tour doing considerable damage to our trenches. Casualties 1 O.R. wounded (attd R.E.)	With M
LOCRE	12/13th		In Divisional Reserve DONCASTER HUTS LOCRE	With M
"	18th.		Battalion moved up and relieved 7th R. INNIS. Fus in Rt Subsection Baybachere. A & D Coys on front line. C & B Coys support and reserve. Batt. HQ FORT VICTORIA	With M
Front line	18th 24th		Holding Rt Subsection as above.	With M

Army Form C. 2118.

WAR DIARY
or
INTELLIGENCE SUMMARY.
(Erase heading not required.)

8TH (S) BATTALION
1 JAN. 1917

Instructions regarding War Diaries and Intelligence Summaries are contained in F. S. Regs., Part II. and the Staff Manual respectively. Title pages will be prepared in manuscript.

Place	Date Dec.	Hour	Summary of Events and Information	Remarks and references to Appendices
Front line	26th		Battalion relieved in Right subsection by 7th R. Innis Fus. and on completion of relief moved into Brigade Reserve KEMMEL SHELTERS. Apart from the usual artillery activity this period was very quiet. Casualties 1 O.R. wounded	Other
KEMMEL SHELTERS	27th	12 mn	In Brigade Reserve KEMMEL SHELTERS - nothing to report	Other
"	27		In Brigade Reserve KEMMEL SHELTERS. Enemy shelled camp with 10-12 rounds H.E. (5.9 cm?). Casualties 2 O.R. killed 5 O.R wounded	Other
"	28		In Brigade Reserve KEMMEL SHELTERS - Also took on board about 5.15 pm completely destroying 2 buildings and a quantity of equipment and materiel. No casualties occurred	Other
"	28/30		In Brigade Reserve - KEMMEL SHELTERS	Other
"	30		Batt'n moved to front line relieved 7 R.P. INNIS FUS. in right subsection. Disposition B+C Coys Front line; A+D Support + Reserve; Batt. H.Q. Fort Victoria	✗
Front line	30/31		Holding front line as above	✗

WAR DIARY
or
INTELLIGENCE SUMMARY.
(Erase heading not required.)

Army Form C. 2118.

Place	Date	Hour	Summary of Events and Information	Remarks and references to Appendices
	Dec 1		2/Lieut W. H. Allen 7/8 R. Irish Fus. reported as 7/8 R. Irish Fus. auth 16th Inst letter A/2/91 11/12/16	11/12/16 JC
			2/Lieut J.J. Bruton ⎫ " J.C. Brown ⎬ 4th The Connaught Rangers attd. joined "A" Battn M.G. Corps (Heavy Branch) " F.B. Keogh ⎪ " R.T. Crouin ⎭ 23/12/16 — auth AG's A/18532/133 — 18/12/16	JC
			2/Lieut U.G. Groombridge rejoined Battn 13/12/16 (wounded 15.7.16) Posted to A Coy.	JC
			2/Lieut M.P. Hanlon 6th R. Inniskilling Fus. joined Battn 14/12/16 Posted to B Coy	JC

			Drafts joined the Battalion during the month as under :—
			From 16 M.I.B.D.
			    4 O.R. — 3.12.16
			    4 " — 16.12.16
			    9 " — 22.12.16
			    5 " — 30.12.16
				JC

A.J. Walker Major
Comm'g 8th R. Innis. Fus.
1/1/17.

Report of Patrol 25/5/1916.
H.31.b.25

The patrol consisting of Sgt Tuohy & myself left a point 4 bays right of bogey 49. We advanced in the direction of the enemy gap. A little over half way across we came across about 15ˣ in front of our wire which [was] damaged by HE we found the track of an enemy patrol obviously made lately.

We proceeded and at a little over half way across on the lead of the undulation we heard a patrol in front not more than 10ˣ away.

We listened for 5 minutes and ascertained that they were others to our left. They were stationary for a time.

They made a noise like
the striking of a match
softly on a door
three times — repeated.

I sent Sgt Daly back
to report and [word crossed out]
and explained 5 agons
then lay circling bay
right.

I was in sight of
the enemy wire &
could not see anyone
making thoff a
noise of wire was
heard.

The time was then
7 minutes within returning
time so I hastened
by my same route

Owing to shortage of
time I am unable

to report definitely on the exact state of the enemy wire

The patrol returned at 11:20 p.m.

J. W. Ledgerwood

At the same time that patrol was out, my wiring party made several gaps in my wire opposite same point as patrol went out from. not a single shot was fired by the enemy during this period. As soon as

The Patrol was in
Machine guns were
turned on enemy were
is still firing.
Please say if things
will remain as per
your orders, on account
of patrol not being
able to withdraw if
gap in enemy wire
still exists

11.45 Am   Edw Haskns
2.5   Lieut
───
6-16 Comd A Coy
              PIRE

N.B. a.p.S.
Received message
Ref S.O. 449.

"A" Form.
MESSAGES AND SIGNALS.

Army Form C. 2121.

Concentrate on in your old front line and CHINESE WALL north of MAYO Street HQ BYRON FARM aaa The new Zero hour for the further advance of new troops is 3.10 PM aaa acknowledge

From: 49 IB
Place:
Time: 12.5 PM

"A" Form.
MESSAGES AND SIGNALS.

Army Form C. 2121.

No. of Message............

Prefix....... Code......m.	Words	Charge	This message is on a/c of:	Recd. at........m.
Office of Origin and Service Instructions.				
	Sent		.............Service.	Date............
Secret	At........m.			From............
	To........			
	By........		(Signature of "Franking Officer.")	By............

TO { All units

| Sender's Number | Day of Month | In reply to Number | AAA |
| *BMC 140 | 7 | | |

The 4⁸ᵗʰ Inf Bde will send 2 Bns to occupy and consolidate the MAUVE LINE from Railway Junction O.21.C.5.1 to junction of railway and OIL TRENCH relieving the remnants of 7/8 R Innis Fus and the platoon of 2ⁿᵈ R Innis at SONEY FM which will rejoin their Bns any Bns will hold their present fronts ~~strength in depth continuing~~ ~~the consolidation~~ as follows:—
2ⁿᵈ R Innis BLACK and GREEN LINES ans 7/8 R Innis Fus and 7ᵗʰ R Innis fills BLUE and RED LINE NAIL SWITCH and NANCY Subkept locality of bns 8ᵗʰ R Inns Fus will

From ....
Place ....
Time ....

The above may be forwarded as now corrected.   (Z)

Censor.   Signature of Addressor or person authorised to telegraph in his name.

* This line should be erased if not required.
(A1) ... Ltd., London— W.14042/M.44. 150,000 Pads. 12/15. Form C.2121.

Report on Gap H 19 C 9.9

Two small breaches have been made in the wire about 15 yards apart, each being from three to six feet broad. The wire is fairly cut & lies about loosely. The right gap is not so complete as the left.

Two or three shells have made a very slight opening about five yards to the right, but admits of no passage.

L.W. Pocock. 2/Lieut.

R. King   L.Cpl.

W Shields Pte.

Patrol Report
B. Coy

F Tron O.C. B Coy

PERCH

To Adjt PERCH

To night between 11 pm and 11.45 pm with Serjt COLSTON and Cpls HEGARTY and GREEN I patrolled the german wire opposite section of our trench bounded by BOYAUS 60 & 61 and found a gap of about 15 yds through which men could pass with little difficulty. To the right there are two very weak spots in the wire of about 5 yds length and 7 yds apart.

On return for some distance we were followed by a man clothed in white. At post this object appeared to be a newly made shell hole.

Signed Norman Wray 2nd Lt
C Coy 6th R Innis Fus

26th June
12.15 am.

W Colston Sjt
W Green Cpl
L Cpl Hegarty J

Bn Orderly

REPORT ON WIRE AT H.19.C.99.

"There is a gap in the wire
30 yds wide.
The wire on either side of
the gap is broken in many
places.
Large shell holes are in &
around the gap.

E. A Strain 2/Lieut
J Slater C.S.M.
W Cunningham Cpl.

25/6/16.

To Capt PERCH.

H 25 6 55

Patrolling the enemy wire opposite BOYAU 61 tonight between 9 pm and 11.45 pm with Sergts CAROLAN and COLSTON I found that the gap which was there last night is, except for about 8 yds, closed with loose wire and "gooseberries."

About 6 yds to the right a gap of about 20 yds has been made. Like the former gap last night there are some loose strands lying in the gap but not sufficient to hinder men stalking though.

25th June   Thomas Strafford Lt
11.59 pm   M Carolan Sgt
By Orderly   W. Colston

24/6/16.

Report of Officers Patrol

I left with Sgt Tedy at 11.0 and got through our wire at exit H.31.8.

The trip wire on the far side gave some difficulty and it was 11.15 pm. before we got through.

Our progress was then easy. We saw what seemed a small patrol about 100x in front of the enemy's wire, to our left which we ignored

We immediately moved about 50x parallel to our front and then made straight for the gap in the Hun wire.

Our progress was once more retarded by a shower of enemy verey lights which fell about 50x in front of their wire.

We got to within 30 yds of the gap and owing to the numerous verey lights sent up by the enemy from the end

2.

of the small sap to the right of the gap it was clearly seen that a clear space has been made which I consider easily passable by Infantry. I estimate the length of the gap to be not less than 15 feet.

The enemy were working ~~them~~ repairing them wire at the point. Numbers of very ~~entrenched~~ at light. They dropped whip their own lights went up. Owing to the short space of time at our disposal it was impossible to collect much information of a general nature but it was noticed that:—

The enemy was very quiet and except for slight shovelling at various points on his front line no sounds were heard.

A green rocket was sent up by the enemy at a point on their front line opposite X roads at 11.30pm. No result was noticed.

3.

The patrol started to return at 11.40 p.m. We missed the gap in our own wire and were forced to make our way through with the aid of wire cutters, at a point opposite boyau 47. Our wire was very good at this point and it took us fully 5 mins. to cut through.

On returning our Machine Guns opened fire on the gap in the enemy wire.

W. Ledgerwood Lieut
7th Royal Irish Fus.

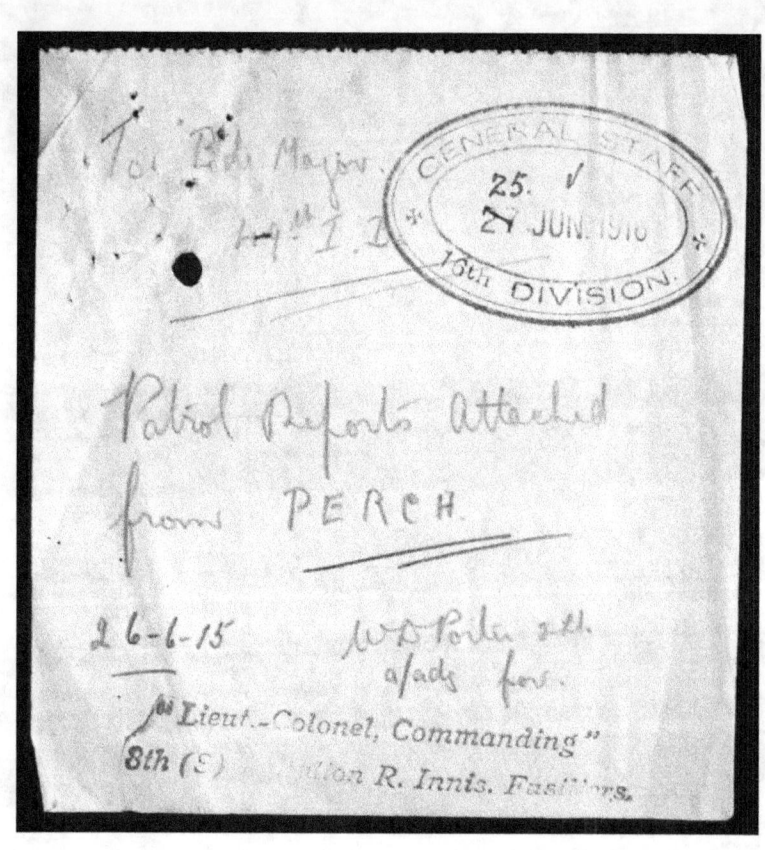

To Bde Major
              I.D

Patrol Reports Attached
from PERCH.

26-6-15   W D Porter 2Lt
           a/adj for.

    Lieut.-Colonel, Commanding
8th (S)   on R. Innis. Fusiliers.

SECRET & URGENT. S.134
H.Q. 49th Inf Bde

1. O.C. TROUT relieved by me this evening reports that SEAFORTH CRATER is not occupied & by all appearances is not at any time permanently occupied.

2. I am taking steps to verify this as soon as possible.

3. If this is the case I am inclined strongly to think that it would be tactically advisable to leave it as it is and hold & occupy it ourselves on the near lip — wiring it strongly — & if possible deny its occupation to enemy in more or like manner as they have at present done to us.

4. I could carry this out & operate elsewhere as originally intended.

"A" Form. Army Form C. 2121.
MESSAGES AND SIGNALS.

TO — PERCH Report by OC B Coy (No 1)

I examined the gaps made in the wire by the Artillery thoroughly through a telescopic periscope & I formed this opinion:—

There are two gaps in the wire immediately opposite Boyau 68. Each gaps about 1½ to 2 yds. wide and the wire between the two gaps is strong. The interval between the two gaps is about 15 yds. The wire in the gaps has been laid flat

Time 10.30 pm.   O.C. "B" Coy. PERCH.

"A" Form. Army Form C. 2121.
MESSAGES AND SIGNALS.

TO PERCH

Sender's Number: SB 26
Day of Month: 25th
AAA

I inspected the wire through a telescopic periscope & found there is a gap about 25 yds wide. The wire is lying loose on the ground in this gap.

From: O.C. B. Coy.
Time: 11.45

CONFIDENTIAL.

D.A.G.,
    Base.

        Reference your C.R.140/1342 of 10th instant.

        War Diary attached belongs to 8th. Royal Inniskilling Fusiliers, and has been amended accordingly.

        The matter has been suitably noticed with the unit concerned.

                            Major General,
                            Commanding 16th Division.

21st June, 1916.

PRISONERS.

which have
1 officer, 208 other ranks/passed through Corps Cage during
last 24 hours belong to following units:-

	Unit.	Officers.	Other ranks.
2nd Division.	4th Gren.	-	15
	33rd Fus.	-	38
	44th I.R.	-	35
7th Division.	393rd I.R.	-	25
	165th I.R.	1	18
11th Division.	51st I.R.	-	1
24th Division.	179th I.R.	-	8
35th Division.	176th I.R.	-	15
19th Landwr.Div.	388th Lw.I.R.	-	2
	38th Landstm.	-	5.
3rd Bav.Div.	23rd Bav.I.R.	-	12
1st Pioneer Bn.		-	4
25th Pioneer Bn.		-	9
1st F.A.R.		-	15
93rd F.A.R.		-	6
	TOTAL	1	208 o.r.

REPORT ON EXAMINATION OF PRISONERS.

1. **1st Pioneer Bn. (attd.2nd Division).** Prisoner of this battalion, belonging to the 2nd Field Coy., was taken in a dugout at WYTSCHAETE. Prisoner states his company consisted of three platoons. Two of these went up to the line every evening and, after repairing dugouts in WYTSCHAETE and doing other pioneer work, returned to their H.Q.

    RELIEFS. One platoon always remained at H.Q. Platoons therefore did 6 days in the line and 3 days out.

    HEADQUARTERS. Up to May 23rd the H.Q. of the battalion were in the huts surrounding PILLEGREMS FARM. After that date they were back near HOUTHEM.

    CASUALTIES. On May 23rd a direct hit on their quarters around PILLEGREMS FARM caused 18 casualties, 8 men being killed.

2. **2nd T.M. COY., (2ND DIVISION).** The H.Q. of the company were at WERVICQ. As is usual this company had four heavy and eight medium T.Ms. The personnel of the 2nd Coy. was 6 officers, 4 offizier stellvertreter, 4 Feldwebel and 260 men armed with carbines. Prisoner did not know of the exact location of the T.Ms. of his company but stated that the medium had been back in COMINES for some time, while the heavies were in position a little in front of WYTSCHAETE. They were placed in pairs about 80 yards apart.

/3. 401st........

Prsnrs. (contd. 2.).

3. **401st FERNSPRECH ABTEILUNG (Telephone Detachment).** Prisoner of this section which is attached to the 1st Guard Reserve Division states that they were in TOURCOING on 6th inst. They received orders in the evening to go up to the OOSTTAVERNE line and stand by there to repair the lines of the 2nd Division who had no special signal troops. These repair posts were formally occupied by battalion signallers but they were called up to the line on the night of the 6th and replaced by men from the 401st Telephone Detachment. Prisoner states that the 1st Guard Reserve Division came up to TOURCOING on the 2nd inst. They had suffered very heavy losses on the ARRAS front.

4. **165TH REGIMENT (7th DIVISION).** Prisoners of this regiment state that their orders were to drive the English out of the OOSTTAVERNE LINE. They claim that they did this on the night of the 7th but that the English returned the next morning and dispersed the 10th and 12th companies of the 165th regiment who were in the line. The division had been three days in MENIN. Great precautions seem to have been taken to prevent regiments from recognising one another.

    ROUTE OF APPROACH. MENIN - WERVICQ - GODSHUIS - KORENTJE. They crossed the canal in P 26 a and deployed shortly after.

    KORTEWILDE LINE. Prisoners state that they passed through the wire in front of this line at various points where it had been cut by our artillery. There are however a number of stretches of about 20 yards where the wire is in good repair. The trenches themselves are about 2 feet deep and badly damaged in places. Prisoners state that there were no troops in these trenches when they passed through them.

    COMPANY STRENGTH, DRAFTS AND LOSSES. The average company strength in the 165th regiment is stated to have been 150 trench strength. Prisoner of the 12th company estimated that his company had nearly 30 casualties on the way into the line. The 10th company have received drafts recently including a number of Active N.C.Os. and men who had been kept in Germany for training purposes. Prisoner was full of admiration for these men. Men of the 1918 class began joining the regiment at the end of January 1917.

5. **GENERAL.** Prisoners state that during the last fortnight the N.C.Os. have been given special practice in leading their men. The tactics most recently employed have been known as "English Tactics". By this they apparently meant advancing in two waves followed by sections in artillery formation. Prisoner of 10th company seems to know a great deal about the present training of officers in Germany.

---

1. **2nd SQUADRON, 10TH JAEGER ZU PFERDE.** The RITTMEISTER (captain) of this squadron who was captured in WYTSCHAETE had been seconded from his squadron to command one of the battalions of the 33rd regiment. This was at the end of March.

2. **33RD FUSILIER REGIMENT.** A prisoner belonging to a MINENWERFER ZUG of 33rd Fusilier Regiment states that he was back at rest near COMINES, when on the night of the 6th/7th he was called up with 15 others to take three mortars into the OOSTTAVERNE line at O 28. The ammunition never came up. Prisoner was for two years before the war with the 2nd Airship Bn. at BERLIN and knows a fair amount about Airship units.

/3. 51st REGIMENT ..

Psrs. (contd. 3).

3. 51st REGIMENT (11th Division). Prisoner knows that the whole division was alarmed but has not seen the other regiments in the line. He saw men of the 165th Regiment in the line.

   COMPANY STRENGTH, DRAFTS AND LOSSES. Prisoner's company (12th) has received a number of good men as drafts since leaving ARRAS. He states company trench strength was 162, but they suffered a number of casualties on their way up to the line.

4. GENERAL. Prisoner does not know the route used yesterday morning, but states that they detrained before reaching VERVICQ, and approached the line across country. Prisoner states that during the ARRAS show about 20 men per company were on leave for agricultural duties.

5. 393RD REGIMENT (7TH DIVISION). Prisoners of this regiment are very stupied and can give no information of tactical value. They state that they saw men of the 126th regiment 39th Division near MENIN.

6. 388TH LANDWEHR REGIMENT (19TH LANDWEHR DIVISION). Prisoner who belonged to 3rd Company states they were repairing roads in the OOSTTAVERNE area. Half the company was at OOSTTAVERNE and the other half at HOUTHEM. Reliefs took place every seven days.

   NOTE.
   Further reports on examinations of prisoners will be published with tomorrow's summary.

   -: ** :-

S E C R E T.

7th. R. Innis. Fus.
8th. R. Innis. Fus.
7th. R. Irish Fus.
8th. R. Irish Fus.

49th. Inf. Bde. No. S.O. 591 - 19/7/16.

Herewith one Copy of report on raid carried out by 8th. R. Innis. Fus. on the night of 15th/16th. July 1916.

Captain,
Brigade Major, 49th. Infantry Brigade.

Report on operations between 11 pm & 3.30 am 15/16-7-

Report of 2/Lt. Groombridge

At 10.55 pm I was at point "B" 30x S. of GORDON ALLEY. The R.E. Officer said he would join me there. When the mine went up the R.E. Officer had not returned from GORDON ALLEY so I reconnoitred the craters and found there were two craters each about 100x across and 40ft deep. The NORTH Crater was about 30x from our trench and the SOUTH crater about 50x. I returned towards point "B" and saw the R.E. Officer and his party on a mound more than 50x NORTH of the crater so I directed him to the craters. Then I returned & brought out my digging party. The R.E. Officer told me that his consolidating party had dumped his material somewhere & vanished so I took a party & went in search & found the material had been dumped on the mound where the R.E. Officer had first taken up his position so I brought the remaining material up to him. In the meantime the raiding and covering parties had gone out. The Consolidating and sapping parties for the SOUTH Crater had carried on without a hitch I believe.

About an hour after the commencement of operations the Germans attacked the far lip of the NORTH Crater & forced our covering party to retire to the rear lip. They occupied a small mound on the NORTH side of the crater about 50 yds. from the bombing post in course of construction. The enemy advanced round the NORTH side of the crater but was held up by the covering party from the mound. The mound was held by bombers until dawn when the bombing post & sap was completed. The enemy had a machine gun firing from the NORTH side which fired behind the mound.

The Consolidating party on the SOUTH Crater held the far lip successfully until the bombing post & sap on the SOUTH Crater was finished.

The bomb shelter on the NORTH crater did not appear to be put up in a firm manner. On entering the shelter, as soon as I put my foot on the bottom step, the first frame collapsed on my head.

All our casualties came from the enemy machine gun that was enfilading us from the north side.

16/7/16.

Report on Mine Explosion
Seaforth Craters and Raid

H.Q. 49th Inf Bde   17.7.16

I forward the report of (temp) Captain C.H. Godsland, O.C. Enterprise, on the operation carried out on the right front of Left Sub Section, toos Section at 11 pm of the 15th inst, under my command.

I attach my operation order as amended and plan of Artillery action.

In addition to the parties mentioned in the Operation Order 2 parties of 22 under a N.C.O. were detailed to assist in carrying out R.E. material from points 'B' & 'C'. Their orders were to carry out all remaining material to dump it immediately in rear of points selected for Bombing Posts on Crater lips and return to trenches.

The mines were fired precisely at 11 pm and the Raiding party and others as detailed acted as ordered.

~~The RE party~~ 175th Coy RE
Major Reynolds R.E. was in command of R.E. Operations ~~in~~ the construction of the two Bombing Posts and the providing of material for the same. His report has not been received by me. 2/Lt Hughes R.E. was responsible for the construction of Post on Right Crater (S1) and 2/Lt Hegarty RE on Left Crater (S2).

Raid   The Mine Explosion did little if any damage to enemy trenches. The Raiding Party had to make their way through undamaged wire. None of the Enemy (unless in Mine galleries or listening Posts) seem to have been injured by the Explosion. The Enemy seem to have been very much alive. I think this adds considerably to the credit of the small raiding party which was primarily a reconnaissance

particularly recommend him to notice. He personally inspected the operations at the close and satisfied himself as to the position. He holds the rank of Lieut in the (old) Reg. Army in this Regt and though long since recommended for promotion to the rank of Captain is still only a Temp Temp Captain in the Brigade.

Any further detailed recommendations I wd. ask leave to submit later as owing to the exigencies of service and disposition of the Battalion at the present it is difficult to do so at once with satisfaction.

The casualties suffered by all parties concerned in the operation were as follows :-

8th Munsters - killed or died of wounds 1 officer
9. OR̃ ~~wounded~~ 1 officer, 28. ORs
RE. - killed or died of wounds
3. ORs

~~Other~~ Arms. The action of the Artillery was Effective. The fire seems to have been well directed & must have caused considerable casualties besides damaging enemy works.

The T.M.B. & the Vickers & Lewis M.Gs. took up special positions and fired Effectively on the enemy's front & support line.

Enemy. The enemy's Artillery fire was not very heavy but rather severe for (approx) half an hour. It was ill-directed. His casualties from all causes must have been not inconsiderable.

17.7.16

H H Balfour Walton Lt Col
CO. 8th Munsters

S AnB (anal 11-1145
For "E" / S attack

11-5 Mine Brithitachs
      Area 1,3

12:30 Mine Ag at 7-5
      Bucks Bill Givenchy
      Extend Raid 5 Scot Rifles
      Hostile Say blown up? 2
      9 killed
      Main attack - 11-15
      to 9 wall about
      Ag b-14 Ag b-31.
      Noy Givenchy
      Whole 18th 2nd West ?
      & Cavalry Rgt hired
      for something as far
      as 3rd line, 43 Pris
      130-150 ? casualties
      own 12 killed 30 W?

Had 2/Lt Wray survived long enough to make a full report doubtless further information in detail as to enemy position wd have been forthcoming — as it is we took one prisoner on whom papers were found, a full pack and a great coat with shoulder straps bearing the No. 9 & also papers, 3 rifles, 3 rounds of SAA and some details are forthcoming about enemy trenches. I wish particularly to mention 2/Lt Wray i/c of Raiding party, Sergts Colston, Nelson (slightly wounded) and Slavin (severely wounded) and Pte Quinn (recently a Corpl but reduced & sentenced to 3 mths imp by F.G.C.M. and sentence suspended).

<u>Covering Parties</u>. These did very well. The left Crater (S.2)
<u>Bombg Post Squads</u> was at one time somewhat hard by pressed and had these occupying this crater not stuck to the business well in spite of rather severe losses the construction of this post and Sap might have been delayed. 2/Lt Wray's action in coming out again and taking charge of the defence of this position was most praise-worthy.

The Construction of the Bombing Posts and Saps was carried out successfully within the night. The precise position of the Bombproofs (as seen in daylight) in relation to the form taken by the craters and the somewhat inconspicuous features of former Explosions and to the line of enemy front in the distance about 14 BIS is not quite satisfactory but can easily be adjusted. The Saps were dug to a depth of (approx) 3' and sandbagged. The large amount of buried wire rendered this work very difficult indeed.

Major Reynolds RE made all his dispositions very effectively which largely contributed to the success of the work accomplished in a short time under some stress. I wish to bring his services to notice for approval.

Captain Goddard, OC Enterprise, conducted all the arrangements in a most satisfactory manner and I

CO's Copy

49th Infantry Brigade Raid Scheme
Left Sub Section. Loos Section

SECRET
URGENT

(1) **Objects.**
  (1) To form Bombing Posts on near lips of 2 craters to be blown under Seaforth Crater (referred to as S1 and S2 South and North respectively).
  (2) To carry out a modified raid on enemy's trenches behind the exploded craters in order to take advantage of the occasion.
    (a) to obtain prisoners
    (b) to obtain identifications and information.
    (c) to report on results of explosion on enemy garrison and trenches

(2) **Personnel**

		Officers	N.C.O	Men	R.E.
Party No 1.	Raiding Party. Left front line	1	3	18	
" No 2.	Covering Party S1 Right " "		2	12	
" No 3.	Covering Party S2 Left " "		2	12	
" No 4.	Bombing Post. S1 Right " "		1	6	
" No 5.	Bombing Post S2 Left " "		1	6	
" No 6.	Consolidation. S1 Right " " (RE)		1	4	1
" No 7.	Consolidation. S2 Left " "		1	4	1
" No 8.	Sap to crater. S2 Seaforth Way	1	2	25	5
" No 9.	Sap to crater S1 "	1	2	25	5
	Total of all Parties	3	15	112	12

(3) **Tasks**

No 1. Raiding Party. Starting point 'B' Left front line
Objective: to enter front line enemy trench, on enemy's side of craters in 3 parties, each consisting of 1 N.C.O and 6 men
One party to move up enemy front trench to Right; another to Left, one party in centre. All parties to enter at same place.

No 2. Covering Party for Crater S1. Starting point 'C' Right front line. Objective: to rush newly formed crater and occupy the far lip and SOUTH side in 2 Bomb parties to cover consolidation party and act as support to raiding party. On return of Raiding Party to retire on to Bombing Post and thence to return to trenches when ordered.

2.

<u>No.3. Covering Party for Crater S2</u>:— Starting point 'B' left front line. Objective: Same as No.2 in respect of Northern crater, occupying the NORTH side and the far lip.

<u>No.4. Party. Bombing Post for Crater S1</u>:— Starting point 'C' right front line. Objective: To occupy and hold near lips of Crater S1.

<u>No.5. Party. Bombing Post for Crater S2</u>:— Starting point 'B' left front line. Objective: To occupy and hold near lips of Crater S2.

<u>No.6 Party. Consolidation of Bombing Post on Crater S1</u>:— Starting point 'C' right front line. Objective:— Near lips of Crater S1, to assist R.E. in construction of bomb shelter, and to carry material out as required.

A

<u>No.7 Party. Consolidation of Bombing Post on Crater S2</u>:— Starting point 'B' left front line. Objective:— Same as above in respect of Crater S2.

<u>No.8 Party. Sap to Crater S1</u>:— Starting point 'A' in Seaforth Alley, thence by Seaforth Old Sap. Objective:— To line out from front trench to Crater S1 and dig sap to the Bombing Post on near lip.

A

<u>No.9 Party. Sap to Crater S2</u>:— Same as above in respect of Crater S2.

~~No.10 Party. Wiring of Sap ... S1~~ Dn

~~No.11 Party. Wiring of Sap ... S2~~ Dn

(4) <u>Tools and Material</u>. <u>Sign Boards</u> = 3 lids of Hales Grenade Boxes, painted white, with letters = A.B.C. on each in black, one letter on each board.
<u>Bomb Shelters</u> = The R.E. will supply tools and material and arrange transport to starting point.

3.

Sap Digging Parties 8&9:- 70 picks and 70 shovels.

~~Wiring Parties 10&11:- 36 ... posts at 18 per ...~~
~~725 yards barbed wire in 29 rolls of 25 yards ... stakes,~~
~~also 48 collapsible steel knife rests ... one~~
~~Raiding Parties 4 and 5 and Covering Parties 2 & 3. Each~~
~~...~~
~~... bottles S₁ & S₂ ...~~

Raiding Party:- 21 white cloth Armlets

(5) Stretcher Bearers
~~2 parties ... with 2 ... stretchers~~
~~follow out after Parties 4 and 5 respectively ...~~
~~... bottles S₁ and S₂, ... and await~~
~~...~~ A dressing Station will be established in the Right Coy's H.Q Dug-out in Support Trench between North St & Black Watch Alley.

(6) Bombs for Parties Nos 1, 2, 3, 4 & 5.

:- Each carrier of bomb parties to carry a bucket containing 20 Mills No 5 Grenades and every N.C.O and man to carry 6 Bombs in his pockets - ~~...~~

(7) Officers   O.C. Enterprise   Captain C. H. Godsland
              ~~...~~
              O.C. Raiding Party   ~~2/Lt ...~~
                                   2/Lt C. P. J. Wray.
              In charge of Party No 8. 2/Lt. ~~...~~ H. A. Green
              In charge of Party No 9. 2/Lt. G. W. Groombridge.

(8) Strength   Trench Strength of 3 Front Coys - } 8 Officers   222 O.Rs.
              D.C.A, less Signallers, S.B's & Runners }
              Total engaged in operations   - 3 Officers   127 O.Rs.
              (less above details)
              Remaining in 3 Front Coys   5 Officers   95 O.Rs.
              (less above details)

Probable date of operation night of 15/16 July

H. W. Mal...walton
Lt Col
14-7-16   C.O. PERCH

APPENDIX II

REPORT ON OPERATIONS CARRIED OUT ON 9TH SEPT., 1916.

1. On early morning of 9th inst., as leading Battalion of Brigade in Divisional Reserve, position was taken up in new trench from T.19.d.7.6. to T.19.a.8.5. Order from Right to Left, "A" "B" "C" "D" Coys. Battn. H.Q. T.19.a.9=3.

2. Orders were received that the Battalion was to be at disposal of 48th I.B., and that we would follow in close support of 8th R. Dublin Fus., in their advance on 2nd Objective, and assist in consolidation.

3. O.C. 8th Dublins wished to take full advantage of the creeping barrage from 1st Objective forward, and accordingly decided to advance immediately behind rear wave of 1st Munsters - Battalion taking 1st Objective in Rt. Sub-Section of 48th I.B. front - and to wait behind 1st Objective till 5.25 p.m.
Objective of 8th Dublins : T.14.c.5.4. to T.14.a.4.2.

4. In accordance with above my dispositions were made as follows:-
Battalion advanced in 8 waves on a 2 platoon front; first four waves consisting of 1 platoon each from "A" & "B" Coys., 2nd four waves consisting of 1 platoon each from "C" & "D" Coys. Men extended to 5 yards interval; 100 yards distance between waves.
Right flank directed - marching on T.14.c.5.4.
1st wave moved at 5.15 p.m.
Lewis Guns were placed on each flank of 3rd 4th, 7th & 8th waves.
Vickers Guns were on flanks of 5th wave.
Shovels were carried by men advancing.

5. Advance was carried out as ordered. 8th Dublins advanced from behind 1st Objective before 5.25 p.m., the waves of my Battalion went straight on and advancing through GINCHY reached final Objective at 5.50 p.m. On arrival it was found that the 8th Dublins had lost direction and that the line was occupied by Germans. On advancing, enemy shewed white flags but we rushed his trench causing him many casualties, and taking about 30 prisoners. We then advanced about 80 yards in front of the captured German trench, and dug in on a parallell line. Line held by 8th R. Innis. Fus., was from T.14.c.6½.5. to T.14.a.7.0. This line was reached about 5.50 p.m. and work of consolidation was at once commenced.
A connected line of Trench was dug, average depth 4'6", with 1' parapet. During the advance about 40 or 50 men of 7th R. Irish Fus. (support Battalion to 47th I.B.) got mixed with my men. They had two Lewis Guns with them and these were placed in position in front of centre of my line. Under their cover, some wire, both concertina and barbed, was put out for a distance of 25 yards.

6. Communication on our left flank, was established with 8th R. Dub. Fus. on arrival at line. They seemed to have lost most of their Officers, as a Seggt. Major was in charge of consolidation during the greater part of the night.
Communications Right flank - Touch gained with Troops of 47th Bde. (7th R. Irish Fus. attached) at about 8 p.m.

7. Enemy position - Patrol was sent out to discover enemy position, this patrol advanced 300 yards, and could find no trace of enemy. It is thought that he must have retired to his 3rd line.

8. Capt. Seaver, and Capt. Godsland, commanding "A" & "C" Coys., respectively, became casualties early in the advance. 2/Lt. (Tempy. Capt,) H.A. Green being senior Officer on the Spot, took command of the work of consolidation, which has been very effectively carried out. He, himself, was wounded but carried on, and directed work with great skill, rendering frequent reports as to situation, which must have been extremely valuable. He found out from R.E. that strong point at T.13.d.9.4. was not being carried on. He collected 12 men of 8th Dublins, and set them to work under R.E. Capt. Green's work and example had a splendid effect on his men and merits the greatest praise.

9. Our barrage was very effective, and on reaching final Objective,

2.

lifted on to line through T.14.a. Central. Enemy for-
on line just in front of GUILLEMONT. His shell fire on advance
of this Battalion was very ineffective, most of the casualties being
from Snipers, and Machine Gun fire.
Enemy made no attempt to counter attack, and was extremely quiet
throughout the night, and subsequently, until relief. Our Artillery
maintained heavy fire about 300 yards in front of our line from time
of gaining Objective onwards.

10. From Point T.14.c.6½.8 in our line, a good view of German 3rd Line
from about T.9.c.8½.3 to T.8.b.2.2. is obtained. Field of fire
from other parts of our line, about 400 yards.

11. Casualties:-
   Killed,   Lieut. Colonel H.P. Dalzell-Walton,
             2/Lieut. D.C. O'Connell, (4th Conn. Rangers attached).
             Lieut. T.J. Kennedy.

   Wounded, Capt. C. Seaver.
             Capt. C.H. Godsland.
             2/Lieut. H.V.L.A. Smith,
             2/Lieut. W.A. Campbell, (5th R. Irish Fus. attached.)
             2/Lt. L.W.L. Leader (4th Conn. Rangers attached).
             2/Lt. R.S. Purdy, (5th attd. 8th Bn.)
             2/Lt. E.W. McKegney, (5th attd. 8th Bn).

   Missing. 2/Lt. S.B. Coghill.

   Slightly
   wounded.
   (At Duty). Major A.J. Walkey.
              Capt. H.A. Green.

   Other Ranks. *Killed wounded & missing = 170*

   Present Strength:- Officers. 22   O.R. 422 *(includes detached)*

12. Lewis Guns:- 8 taken into Action.
                9 brought out of action,
                   (all serviceable).
                110 Magazines brought out of action.

10/9/16.

                                              A.J. Walkey
                                              Major,
                                    Commndg. 8th (S) Bn. R. Innis. Fus.

7th. R. Innis. Fus.
8th. R. Innis. Fus.
7th. R. Irish Fus.
8th. R. Irish Fus.
49th. T.M. Battery.
49th. M.G. Company.

16th. Div. No. 6520/1 (G). - 31/8/16.

49th. Inf. Bde. No. B.M.C. VIII/2261 - 1 /9/ 16.

Reference Sections 17 & 18 of 16th. Divnl. Standing Orders.

Officers Commanding units on arrival in a new area will at once report the arrival of their unit to the officers commanding the area and will at the same time inform him of the location of the Headquarters of their unit.

Similarly Commanders of Areas on arrival in their area will at once report to Divisional H.Qrs. the arrival and location of their H.Qrs.

Commanders of Areas will also report to Divisional H.Qrs. when all Units allotted to their area have arrived.

Captain,

Brigade Major, 49th. Infantry Brigade.

38/

C.C.
8th R Innis Fus.

B.M.C. VIII/2261

SECRET.   Copy No. 2.
               49th Infantry Brigade Order No. 52,   2/9/16.
                        ....
         Reference:- 1/10,000 Trench Map, Sheets LONGUEVAL, 57.c.s.w.3.
              and MARICOURT, 62.c.n.w.1.

1. The Fourth Army in conjunction with the French will renew the attack
    on Sept., 3rd at an hour to be notified later.

2. The XIV Corps is to clear GUILLEMONT and establish itself on the line:-
    Western edge of LEUZE WOOD - T.30.a.6.5.
         This attack will be carried out by the 5th Division on the right and
    20th Division on the left.
         Simultaneous attacks will be made by the French on the right of the
    5th Division, and by the XV Corps on the left of the 20th Division.

3. The dividing lines between formations in the attack will be as follows:-
    Between 5th Division and 20th Division - S.30.d.5.8½ - T.25.c.3½.2.
    Strong point at T.25.b.4.5. (inclusive to 20th. Division) - T.26.a.1.8. -
    W. corner of LEUZE Wood, (T.26.b.8.8½). (inclusive to 5th Division).

    Between 20th Division and Right Division of XV Corps.
    S.24.b.8½.8½. - T.19.b.2.5. - T.20.c.1.5. - T.20.a.6.5.

4. The objectives allotted to the 5th and 20th Divisions are at as follows
    and are shown on the attached map marked "A".

         5th Division   FALFEMONT FARM and trenches to
         Preliminary Objective.   the South of it up to point 48
         (Attack to commence at 6 a.m.)   (B.2.d.4.8.)

         1st Objective.
         (Attack to commence at Zero time).   German trenches in the road
                                                from B.1.a.8½.7½. to T.25.c.3½.5.
                                                (The trench junction at this
                                                latter point exclusive), also
                                                the dug-outs in the bank between
                                                T.25.c.5.6. and B.1.a.9.7.
                                                     The Southern face of the
                                                triangle between T.25.c.3½.8½.
                                                and S.30.b.7.1..

         2nd Objective.   German trenches from N.W. corner
                                                of FALFEMONT FARM to Trench
                                                Junction at T.25.b.1.4½ (exclusive)

         3rd Objective.   WEDGE WOOD - GINCHY ROAD up to
                                                T.26.a.1.7..

         Final Objective.   Western edge of LEUZE WOOD,
                                                gaining touch with the French,
                                                about SAVERNAKE WOOD.

         20th Division.

         1st Objective.   The German trenches in SUNKEN ROAD from T.25.a.
         (Attack to commence   3½.3. to T.25.a.2.7½ thence to the Eastern end
         at ZERO Time.)   of the QUARRY, thence German trench to T.19.c.
                                  9½.9. thence road to T.19.a.8½.1½.

         2nd Objective.   Trench Junction T.25.b.1.4½. (inclusive to 20th
                                  Division), thence SOUTH STREET, NORTH STREET
                                  to T.19.c.8½.8., buildings S. of GUILLEMONT -
                                  GINCHY Road at T.19.c.9.9 and T.19.c.9.1.,
                                  GINCHY - GUILLEMONT Road up to T.19.b.2.6. where
                                  touch will be obtained with the 7th Division.

2.

3rd Objective: WEDGE WOOD - GINCHY Road from T.26.a.1.7. to T.20.a.1.5. where touch will be obtained with the 7th Division, (XV Corps).

Final Objective. W. corner of LEUZE WOOD (T.26.b.8½.8½.) (exclusive) to T.20.a.6.5.., where touch will be obtained with 7th Division.

5.(a). The attack will be preceded by a bombardment of heavy artillery commencing at 8 a.m. on the morning of September 2nd. At intervals throughout the bombardment the ground will be searched by bursts of 18 pdr. fire.

(b). Fifty per cent of the Field Artillery guns in each Division will be employed for stationary barrages, and fifty per cent for creeping barrages.
Details of the stationary barrages are shown on the attached map marked "B".

(c) At zero an intense Field Artillery barrage will open on the first objective. This barrage will lift as shown on the attached map marked "B". At the same hour a creeping barrage will be opened one hundred yards in front of the Infantry and will advance at the rate of fifty yards per minute in front of the Infantry, until the objective is reached. When this barrage has passed two hundred yards beyond the objective it will become stationary.
Within the boundaries of GUILLEMONT Village the creeping barrage will advance at the rate of 100 yards per 4 minutes.
Whenever the creeping barrage reaches the stationary barrage, the stationary barrage will lift on to the next barrage line, i.e. the next colour in front of it on the map.
An intensive rate will be continued for fifteen minutes when fire will drop to two rounds a minute per gun.

(d). At the hour of zero, all heavy howitzers will lift from GUILLEMONT. Six inch howitzers will continue on the objectives in GUILLEMONT, one of GREEN STREET, HILL STREET, and the German trench line from T.25.a.8.? to WEDGE WOOD.

(e). At Zero plus 50 the Field Artillery barrage will again become intensive, and the Infantry will advance to their second objective, the same procedure as ordered in para (c) second will again be followed.
An intensive rate will be continued for fifteen minutes, when fire will drop to two rounds a minute per gun.

(f). The heavy howitzers and the six-inch howitzers will, after zero plus 50, not fire on any parts of the third objective except the CEMETERY and the WEDGE WOOD - GINCHY Road, between T.26.a.1.1, and T.20.a.1.5.

(g). At zero plus two hours the Field Artillery barrage will again become intensive, and the Infantry will advance to the third objective.
An intense rate of fire will be maintained for twenty five minutes.

(h). At zero plus two hours and forty five minutes in order to enable the Infantry to reach their final objectives the barrage will again become intensive, and the creeping barrage will advance at the rate of 50 yards per minute until it has passed two hundred yards beyond the final objective.
Details of the heavy artillery bombardment for this stage will be published separately.

6. The "Pusher" mines under the strong point at S.30.b.7.1 will be exploded at zero minus ten seconds, and the Flammenwerfer will open fire at the same hour, if in position.

7. Objectives when gained will be at once consolidated. Strong points will be formed as follows:-

5th Division. FALFEMONT FARM
T.25.c.4.8.
T.25.d.6.7.

30th Division.   THE QUARRIES..
                  T.19.a.5½.1.
                  Road Junction T.2.3.4½.
and elsewhere as Divisional Commanders may desire.

8. The No. 9 Sqdn. R.F.C. will have two contact aeroplanes in the air from zero until three and a half hours after zero; after that one contact aeroplane until dark on September 3rd.
   On September 4th they will detail one contact aeroplane from 5.50 a.m. to 8 a.m.

9. Flares will be lit as follows :-
   (a) On attaining each objective.
   (b) At 7 p.m. on September 3rd.
   (c) At 6 a.m. on September 4th.

10. The 49th Infantry Brigade Group will move to the Citadel tomorrow 3rd inst., as follows :-
    7th R. Irish Fus.,   march at 9 a.m.
    8th R. Irish Fus.,   "   " 9.20 a.m.
    7th R. Inniskilling Fus.,   "   " 9.40 a.m.
    8th R. Inniskilling Fus.,   "   " 10 a.m.

   The above Units without Transport will march across country to their destination.
   The following Units will march to the; CITADEL via the Main Road to Road Junction L.9.d.0.3, thence by road leading North to the CITADEL :-
    49th Inf. Bde. H.Q. Transport,   9 a.m.
    49th M.G. Coy.,   9.10 a.m.
    49th T.M. Battery,   9.20 a.m.
    157th Fd. Coy. R.E.   9.30 a.m.
    113th Fd. Ambulance.   9.50 a.m.
    144 Coy. A.S.C.   10 a.m.
    Transport 7th R. Irish Fus.,   10.20 a.m.
       "   8th "   "   "   10.30 a.m.
       "   7th Inniskillings   10.40 a.m.
       "   8th   "   10.50 a.m.

11. The 49th Bde. Group will be ready to move at 3 hours notice.
    Brigade H.Q. will close at 9 a.m. and will open at the CITADEL at the same hour.
    Advance parties will meet the Staff Captain at the Citadel at 8 a.m. 3rd inst..

12. Watches will be synchronized at 6 p.m., on September 2nd and at 9 a.m. on September 3rd.

13. Acknowledge.

                          (Signed). H.B.D. WILLCOX, Captain,
                          Brigade Major, 49th Infantry Brigade.

SECRET. Copy No. 12.

8th R. Innis. Fus. Operation Order No. 44. - 3/9/16.

1. In accordance with Bde. O.O. No. 52 of 3/9/16 Copy of which is attached, the Battalion will parade at 9.30 a.m. tomorrow on open ground S. of lines - formation Mass, facing N. - and will move off at 10 a.m.

2. Advance parties of 1 N.C.O. per Coy., and 1 N.C.O. for H.Q., Units will report 2nd in Command at Orderly Room at 7 a.m. Party will report to Staff Captain at CITADEL at 8 a.m.

3. Officers' kits will be carried down to Transport lines and will be loaded by 9 a.m. Mess Cart to be loaded by 9.30 a.m.

4. Transport will move in accordance with para 10 of Bde. Order.

5. Reveille tomorrow will be at 5.15 a.m.
    Breakfasts, 5.45 a.m.

6. Acknowledge.

                Capt. & Adjt.,
                8th R. Innis. Fus..

Copy No. 1 to O.C. "A" Coy.,
" " 2 " " "B" "
" " 3 " " "C" "
" " 4 " " "D" "
" " 5 " Signalling Officer.
" " 6 " B.L.G.O.
" " 7 " C.O.
" " 8 " 2nd in Command.
" " 9 " Transport Officer.
" " 10 " Quartermaster.
" " 11 " 49th I.B.
" " 12/13 Retained.

SECRET.   Copy No. 10

           8th R. Innis. Fus: Operation No. 45. 14-9-16
           ----

1. The Infantry and dismounted personnel of the Division will move
tomorrow by bus to Area - LONGPRE - AIRAINES - WORREL - HUPPY - ERONDELLE
(about 20 miles W.N.W. of AMIENS.).

2. Order of march of Brigade as follows:-
      Brigade H.Q.,
      157 Field Coy. R.E.,
      8th R. Irish Fus.
      8th R. Innis. Fus.
      7th R. Irish Fus.,
      7th R. Innis. Fus.,
      49th T.M.B.
      49 M.G.C.
      113 Field Ambulance.

3. Starting point:- Brigade Transport Lines.   Head of Column passes
starting point at 10.15 a.m.

4. Busses will be drawn up on LA NEUVILLE - VECQUEMONT ROAD, facing
West with tail of column at LA NEUVILLE.

5. 20 busses are allotted to the Battalion, which will be told off into
bus loads as follows:-
      1. Billeting party, 2/Lt. Palmgren, Interpreter, C.Q.M. Sgts.
         1 O.R. per Coy., 1 N.C.O. and 1 O.R. H.Q..
      2. Band.
      3. Signallers & Orderlies, O.R. Clerks, Post Cpl. H.Q. Servants
         and Cook, and M.O's Orderlies.
      4. Pioneers, Loaders, Tailors, Shoemakers, Water duty men,
         Butcher, and H.Q. Cooks.
      5. Guard and prisoners.
      6. H.Q. Officers.
      7. to 9, "A" Coy.,
      10 to 13 "B" Coy.,
      14 to 16 "C" Coy.,
      17 to 19 "D" Coy.,
      20 Kit.-
Busses accommodate 20 men.   Coy. Officers will go with their Coys.

6. The Battalion will parade at 9.30 a.m., on road outside Orderly Room
facing South, in order of bus loads from right to left.

7. Reveille tomorrow will be at 6.30 a.m. Breakfasts, 7.30 a.m.
Billets will be cleaned and all kits outside by 9 a.m.

8. As no facilities exist for carrying water, men must be warned that
they will only have the water in their water bottles for use until
arrival at destination.

9. O's. C. Coys., and Officers 1/c H.Q. Units will render certificates
that their billets have been left in a clean and sanitary condition,
and that the men's water bottles are full.

10. Acknowledge.
                                                    Capt. & Adjt.
                                                    8th R. Innis. Fus.
   Copy No. 1 to O.C. "A" Coy.,
      "   " 2 "   " "B" "
      "   " 3 "   " "C" "
      "   " 4 "   " "D" "
      "   " 5 " Signalling Officer.   Copy No. 8 to 49th I.B.
      "   " 6 " Quartermaster.   "   " 9/10 Retained.
      "   " 7 " 2/Lt. Palmgren.

SECRET.

7th. R. Innis. Fus.	157th. Coy. R.E.
8th. R. Innis. Fus.	144th. Coy. A.S.C.
7th. R. Irish Fus.	49th. M.G. Company.
8th. R. Irish Fus.	49th. T.M. Battery.
113th. Fd. Ambulance.	

49th. Inf. Bde. No. B.O. 52/2 - 3/9/16.

Reference 49th. Bde. Order No. 52 dated 2/9/16 :

Hour od Zero on September 3rd. will be 12 noon.
The French are attacking at the same hour.

The attack of FALFEMONT FARM by 5th. Division will be made at 9 a.m.

Acknowledge ~~by wire~~.

[signature] Captain,

Brigade Major, 49th. Infantry Brigade

9th R. Inns. Fus. O/o Order No. 46 – 1916.
September   Copy No

1. The Battalion will be relieved tonight by 12th LONDON REGT.

2. All spare bombs, ammunition, and Tools Etc will be handed over.

3. Relieving Coys will be guided from present Battn H.Q in main front line to the centre of the Support line. Support line will first be relieved and then the front line

4. On completion of relief Coys will retire independently, taking path towards present Battn H.Q. thence to H.Q. lately occupied in GUILLEMONT TRENCH, thence past S of ARROW HD COPSE in a direct line for S. Corner of TRONES WOOD. thence along road to SE Corner BERNAFAY wood where they should be met by guides from B Ech. who will guide them into DIV. RESERVE in BERNAFAY WOOD

O.C. 8th R. Innis Fus. S/842

1. Be prepared at H.Q. Battn. occupied in GUILLEMONT TRENCH to move with Battn. H.Q. at 10 pm. All your equipment etc to be with you there at that time.

2. Battn. on being relieved moves to DIVNL RESERVE in BERNAFAY WOOD

3. Acknowledge by bearer.

W E H Owen
Capt. Adjt

7.9.16   8th R. Innis Fus

5. Bde. HQ will be at S.28.b central on completion of relief.

6. Coy Commdrs will report completion of relief to present Batln HQ in person on passing through.

7. Completion of relief will be reported by Batln to present Bde HQ.

8. On arrival in BERNAFAY WOOD report will be made to Batln HQ.

9. Acknowledge.

7. 9. 16

W. H. Amos
Capt & Adjt
8th R. Innis Fus

1 A Coy
2 B .
3 C .
4 D .
5 HQ. 49th I.B.
6 Retained.

D Coy

Ref. O.O. 46 - 6th R Irish Regt. are taking over line from T.20.A.2.5 to 9thOH.Y. - WEDGE WOOD ROAD Exclusive.

Please arrange to have guides at Cross Roads T.20.B.2.5 at 10 pm to guide 6th R I Regt to this position.

Acknowledge

W E H Munn
Capt & Adjt
5th R Innis Fus

7·9·16

SECRET.

Copy No. 2....

49th. Infantry Brigade Order No. 52 - 2/9/16.

Reference :- 1/10000 Trench Map, Sheets LONGUEVAL, 57 C.S.W.3 and MARICOURT, 62.C. N.W. 1.

1. The Fourth Army in conjunction with the French will renew the attack on September 3rd. at an hour to be notified later.

2. The XIV Corps is to clear GUILLEMONT and establish itself on the line:- Western edge of LEUZE WOOD - T.20.a.6.5.
   This attack will be carried out by the 5th. Division on the right and 20th. Division on the Left.
   Simultaneous attacks will be made by the French on the right of the 5th. Division, and by the XV Corps on the left of the 20th. Division.

3. The dividing lines between formations in the attack will be as follows :-

   Between 5th. Division and 20th. Division - S.30.d.5.8½.- T.25.a.3½.2.- Strong point at T.25.b.1.5. (inclusive to 20th. Division) - T.26a.1.8. - W. corner of LEUZE Wood (T.26.b. (inclusive to 5th. Division).

   Between 20th. Division and Right Division of XV Corps - S.24.b.8½.8½. - T.19.b.2.6. - T.20.a.1.5. - T.20.a.6.5.

4. The objectives allotted to the 5th. and 20th. Divisions are at as follows, and are shown on the attached map marked "A".

5th. Division Preliminary Objective. (Attack to commence at 9 a.m.)	FALFEMONT FARM and trenches to the South of it up to point 48 (B.2.d.4.8.)
1st. Objective. (Attack to commence at zero time).	German trenches in the road from B.1.a.8½.7½. to T.25.a.3½.3. (The trench junction at this latter point exclusive), also the dug-outs in the bank between T.25.c.8.6. and B.1.a.9.7. The Southern face of the triangle between T.25.c.3½.8½. and S.30.b.7.1.
2nd. Objective.	German trenches from N.W. corner of FALFEMONT FARM to Trench Junction at T.25.b.1.4½ (exclusive)
3rd. Objective.	WEDGE WOOD - GINCHY ROAD up to T.26.a.1.7.
Final Objective.	Western edge of LEUZE WOOD, gaining touch with the French about SAVERNAKE WOOD.

P.T.O

(2)

20th. Division.

1st. Objective. The German trenches in SUNKEN ROAD from T.25.a.3½.3.
(Attack to to T.25.a.2.7½ thence to the eastern end of the
commence at zero QUARRY, thence German trench to T.19.c.2½.9. thence
time.) road to T.19.a.8½.1½.

2nd. Objective. Trench Junction T.25.b.1.4½. (inclusive to 20th.
Division), thence SOUTH STREET, NORTH STREET to
T.19.c.8.8., buildings South of GUILLEMONT - GINCHY
Road at T.19.c.9.9 and T.19.c.9.1., GINCHY -
GUILLEMONT Road up to T.19.b.2.6. where touch will
be obtained with the 7th. Division.

3rd. Objective. WEDGE WOOD - GINCHY Road from T.26.a.1.7. to T.20.a.
1.5. where touch will be obtained with the 7th.
Division. (XV Corps).

Final Objective. W. corner of LEUZE WOOD (T.26.b.8½.8½.) (exclusive)
to T.20.a.6.5., where touch will be obtained with
7th. Division.

5.(a) The attack will be preceded by a bombardment of heavy artillery
commencing at 8 a.m. on the morning of September 2nd. At intervals
throughout the bombardment the ground will be searched by bursts of
18-pdr. fire.

(b) Fifty per cent of the Field Artillery guns in each Division
will be employed for stationary barrages, and fifty per cent for
creeping barrages.
Details of the stationary barrages are shown on the attached map
marked "B".

(c)
At zero an intense Field Artillery barrage will open on the
first objective. This barrage will lift as shown on the attached map
marked "B". At the same hour a creeping barrage will be opened one
hundred yards in front of the Infantry and will advance at the rate
of fifty yards per minute in front of the Infantry, until the
objective is reached. When this barrage has passed two hundred
yards beyond the objective it will become stationary.
Within the boundaries of GUILLEMONT Village the creeping barrage
will advance at the rate of 100 yards per 4 minutes.
Whenever the creeping barrage reaches the stationary barrage, the
stationary barrage will lift on to the next barrage line, i.e. the
next colour in front of it on the map.
At intensive rate will be continued for fifteen minutes when
fire will drop to two rounds a minute per gun.

(d) At the hour of zero, all heavy howitzers will lift from
GUILLEMONT.
Six inch howitzers will continue on the objectives in GUILLEMONT,
east of GREEN STREET, HILL STREET and the German Trench line from
T.25.a.8.7½ to WEDGE WOOD.

(e) At Zero plus 50 the Field Artillery barrage will again become
intensive and the Infantry will advance to their second objective,
the same procedure as ordered in para (c) second will again be
followed.
An intensive rate will be continued for fifteen minutes, when
fire will drop to two rounds a minute per gun.

(f) The heavy howitzers and the six inch howitzers will, after zero
plus 50, not fire on any parts of the third objective except the
CEMETERY and the WEDGE WOOD - GINCHY Road, between T.26.a.1.1. and
T.20.a.1.5.

(g) At zero plus two hours the Field Artillery barrage will again become intensive and the Infantry will advance to the third objective.
An intense rate of fire will be maintained for twenty-five minutes.

(h) At zero plus two hours and forty five minutes in order to enable the Infantry to reach their final objectives the barrage will again become intensive, and the creeping barrage will advance at the rate of 50 yards per minute until it has passed two hundred yards beyond the final objective.
Details of the heavy artillery bombardment for this stage will be published separately.

6. The "pusher" mines under the strong point at S.30.b.7.1. will be exploded at zero minus ten seconds, and the flammenwerfer will open fire at the same hour, if in position.

7. Objectives when gained will be at once consolidated. Strong points will be formed as follows :-

5th. Division.   FALFEMONT FARM
                    T.25.c.4.8½.
                    T.25.d.8.7 .

20th. Division   THE QUARRIES.
                    T.19.a.5½.½.
                    Road Junction T.20.c.2.4½.
and elsewhere as Divisional Commanders may desire.

8. The No. 9 Sqdn. R.F.C. will have two contact aeroplanes in the air from zero until three and a half hours after zero; after that one contact aeroplane until dark on September 3rd.
On September 4th. they will detail one contact aeroplane from 5.30 a.m. to 8 a.m.

9. Flares will be lit as follows :-

    (a) On attaining each objective.
    (b) At 7 p.m. on September 3rd.
    (c) At 6 a.m. on September 4th.

10. The 49th. Infantry Brigade Group will move to the Citadel tomorrow 3rd. inst. as follows :-
    7th. R. Irish Fus.   march at 9 a.m.
    8th. R. Irish Fus.   do.   9.20 a.m.
    7th. R. Inniskilling Fus.   do.   9.40 a.m.
    8th. R. Inniskilling Fus.   do.   10 a.m.

The above Units without transport will march across country to their destination.
The following units will march to the Citadel via the main road to road junction L.9.d.0.3 thence by road leading North to the Citadel :-
    49th. Inf. Bde. H.Q. Transport   9   a.m.
    49th. M.G. Company.   9.10 a.m.
    49th. T.M. Battery.   9.20 a.m.
    157th. Field Coy. R.E.   9.30 a.m.
    113th. Field Ambulance.   9.50 a.m.
    144 Coy. A. S. C.   10   a.m.
    Transport 7th. R. Irish Fus.   10.20 a.m.
    "   8th.   "   "   10.30 a.m.
    "   7th. Inniskillings.   10.40 a.m.
    "   8th.   "   10.50 a.m.

11. The 49th. Bde. Group will be ready to move at 3 hours notice Brigade Headquarters will close at 9 a.m. and will open at the Citadel at the same hour.
Advance Parties will meet the Staff Captain at the Citadel at 9 a.m. 3rd. inst.

P.T.O.

12. Watches will be synchronized at 6 p.m. on September 2nd. and at 9 a.m. on September 3rd.

13. ACKNOWLEDGE.

[signature] Captain,

Brigade Major, 49th. Infantry Brigade.

Issued through Signals.

Copy No. 1 to 7th. R. Innis. Fus.
" 2 " 8th. R. Innis. Fus.
" 3 " 7th. R. Irish Fus.
" 4 " 8th. R. Irish Fus.
" 5 " 49th. M.G. Company.
" 6 " 49th. T.M. Battery.
" 7 " 157th. Field Coy. R.E.
" 8 " 113th. Field Ambulance.
" 9 " 144th. Coy. A. S. C.
" 10 " Bde. Signals.
" 11 " Bde. Transport Officer.
" 12 " Bde. Supply Officer.
" 13 " 16th. Division (G).
" 14 " 16th. Division (Q).
" 15 - 16 War Diary.
" 17 " Filed.

H.Q. 49th. Inf. Bde.

B/X/468.

Ref. your B.M.C. IX/2394, the following are a few points noted.

1. **Maintaining Direction.**
It is found that this can only be satisfactorily achieved by careful use of compass, unless some clearly defined mark can be held in sight throughout the advance.

2. **Recognition of Objective.**
As a guide to recognition of objective distance from starting point should be accurately measured off on the map, as objectives, especially trench lines, are rendered utterly unrecognizable by artillery preparation.

3. **System of Supply of Ammunition & Stores.**
This was not found entirely satisfactory. Dumps should be established as far forward as possible. It is suggested that a small dump should be established actually at Battn. H.Q., consisting of say, 15 boxes S.A.A., 20 boxes Mills Bombs and a small quantity of flares, Very Lights and Rockets. It is suggested that companies should each leave a small party of 1 L/Corpl. and 3 or 4 men at Battn. H.Q. These to be utilized for carrying forward ammunition and other stores required as soon as the objective has been gained. The arrangement worked on during operations, namely, of using Regtl. Police for carrying purposes failed, as it was found that police were fully occupied performing picqueting duties.

Sufficient use was not made of the ammunition of men who had become casualties. It would seem necessary to impress this more thoroughly on all ranks.

4. **Tools.**
The entrenching tool has proved utterly inadequate for consolidation purposes, especially when the ground is heavy. One Coy. of this Battn. advancing in close support of troops detailed to take the final objective carried shovels. The advantage thus gained was considerable. If opposition is met with shovels can be dropped, and be brought on by succeeding waves after the enemy has been ejected from his position. It is suggested that all waves of supporting troops should carry shovels - picks are not generally necessary as the ground is so pulverised by shell fire.

5. **Stokes Guns.**
These were not used in the attack on GINCHY on 9th. ult. A Stokes Gun on each flank of a Battalion advancing would be most useful for dealing with enemy machine guns in shell holes, or practically demolished emplacements. One enemy machine gun gave considerable trouble, and could easily have been knocked out by a Stkes Gun. It is realised that the ammunition supply is a difficult but a few rounds with each gun would be sufficient for the purpose indicated.

6. **Lewis Gun.**
These went forward on the flanks of 3rd. and 4th. waves of each Coy. This was found quite satisfactory. Here again ammunition supply is a dificulty as the gun team can only take forward with them about 24 magazines. It is suggested that all spare magazines in the Battn. should be collected, and kept loaded as a reserve at Battalion H.Q., and sent forward as required. It would be advantageous if a further supply of loaded magazines was available at Advanced Brigade Dumps, also if some spare parts were kept at the Advanced Bde. Dumps.

7. **Communications.**

Endeavour to maintain telephonic communication from Battn. H.Q. forward seems useless. It is suggested that Coy. Signallers should be grouped and used as orderlies. A relay system from Battn. H.Q. forward might be worth trying. Communication from Battn. H.Q. to Bde. Advanced Post has also to be done by orderly.

8. **Trenches.**

It was found that a great number of casualties were caused by men being buried in narrow trenches, as in the soft ground one H.E. shell blows in a very considerable length of trench.

9. **Miscillaneous.**

(a) It was found that the enemy still makes use of the white flag, and as soon as our parties get within range, throws bombs. It would seem necessary to warn all men against this before going into action as quite a number of casualties were caused by the enemy through use of this practice.

(b) It was also found that too many men were sent down with prisoners, and Regtl. Police had to be employed to regulate this.

8/10/16.

T. Boardman Major,
Commandg. 8th. R. Inniskilling Fusiliers.

49/16

WAR DIARY for month of JANUARY, 1917.

VOLUME 12

8th R. Inniskilling Fusiliers

Army Form C. 2118.

WAR DIARY
or
INTELLIGENCE SUMMARY.
(Erase heading not required.)

Instructions regarding War Diaries and Intelligence Summaries are contained in F.S. Regs., Part II. and the Staff Manual respectively. Title pages will be prepared in manuscript.

Place	Date January	Hour	Summary of Events and Information	Remarks and references to Appendices
LOCRE.	17/23		Battalion in Divisional Reserve DONCASTER HUTS. LOCRE.	contd
"	23rd		Battalion moved to front line and relieved 1/4. R. INNIS. fus in Right Subsection, WYTSCHAETE SECTOR. Dispositions:- B & C Coys front line. D & A coys Support and Reserve. Battalion HQ FORT VICTORIA.	contd
Front Line	23/26		Holding Rt. Subsection as above.	contd
"	26		B & C Coys in front line were relieved by A & D Coys. B & C Coys on completion of relief moved into Support & Reserve.	contd
"	26/29.		Holding 1st 14th Rt. Subsection as above	contd
"	29th		Battalion relieved by 6th. CONNAUGHT RANGERS. and on completion of relief moved into Divisional Corps Reserve WAKEFIELD HUTS. Battalion HQ at DRANOUTRE.	contd
			There was little activity on either side during this tour. Casualties - 1 O.R. killed.	contd
WAKEFIELD HUTS.	29/31		In Divisional Corps Reserve WAKEFIELD Huts. Battn HQ DRANOUTRE	contd
			The following Officers were taken on the strength of the Battn during the month
MAJOR W.E. ROTHWELL reported from 7th Bn. 12.12.16
CAPT. H.L. HORNBY. reported from General List 14.1.17
2/L. W.F. ELLIS. M.C. Jones 1.1.17
D.D. & L.   A.D.S.S./Form/C. 2118.

Army Form C. 2118.

WAR DIARY
or
INTELLIGENCE SUMMARY.
(Erase heading not required.)

Instructions regarding War Diaries and Intelligence Summaries are contained in F. S. Regs., Part II. and the Staff Manual respectively. Title pages will be prepared in manuscript.

Place	Date	Hour	Summary of Events and Information	Remarks and references to Appendices
			LIEUT. H. KEMP-ROBINSON, (5th. Ro. R. INNIS. Fus.) joined 25.1.17	
			2/LT. A.H. ROBBINS, joined Bn. on appointment from 1st. Artists Rifles 5.1.17	
			2/LT. W.J. MURPHY. Bn. R. Innis Fus. joined from 9th Bn. 30.1.17	
			The following officers were struck off the strength during the month	
			2/LT (T/CAPT.) PIERCE ⎫	
			2/LT J.F. WOODS ⎬ reported to 107 Inf. Bde. Hdqrs. a/o. A/77190 a/n. 1.17	
			2/LT H.W.L.A. SMITH ⎭	
			2/LT. T.E. FRIZELLE. ⎫ England (sick) 24.1.17	
			The following drafts were received during the month	
			4 O.R. from 16th I.B.D. 8.1.17	
			6 OR " 15.1.17	
			2 OR " 24.1.17	

Boardman
"Lieut.-Colonel, Commanding"
12th (S) Battalion R. Innis. Fusiliers.

WAR DIARY.

FOR MONTH OF FEBRUARY, 1917.

VOLUME 13

UNIT:- 8th Royal Inniskilling Fus.

Vol 13

Army Form C. 2118.

WAR DIARY
or
INTELLIGENCE SUMMARY.
(Erase heading not required.)

Instructions regarding War Diaries and Intelligence Summaries are contained in F.S. Regs. Part II. and the Staff Manual respectively. Title pages will be prepared in manuscript.

Place	Date February	Hour	Summary of Events and Information	Remarks and references to Appendices
WAKEFIELD HUTS	1/6th		In Divisional & Corps Reserve. WAKEFIELD HUTS, Batt. HQ DRANOUTRE.	#
	6th		Battalion relieved 6th Connaught Rangers & moved into Brigade Reserve, 2 Coys & HQ at DERRY HUTS, 2 Coys in KEMMEL CHATEAU.	#
DERRY HUTS & KEMMEL CHATEAU	8/10th		In Brigade Reserve. HQ, A & B Coys DERRY HUTS, C & D Coys in KEMMEL CHATEAU.	#
Front Line	10th		Battalion relieved 2 Coys 7th R.Innis.Fus in Left Sub-Section SPANBROEK SECTOR. Disposition from Coys in Front Line. HQ Fort VICTORIA. Two Coys 2nd Bn The Royal Irish Regt serve in Support & Reserve.	#
"	10/12th		Holding Left Sub-Section SPANBROEK SECTOR as above.	#
"	14th		Battalion relieved by 6th Connaught Rangers & on completion of relief moved into Divisional Reserve, KEMMEL SHELTERS. The situation throughout- the tour was very quiet.	#
KEMMEL SHELTERS	14/20th		In Divisional Reserve, KEMMEL SHELTERS.	#
"			Battalion relieved 7th Leinster Regt. & moved into Brigade Reserve, 2 Coys & HQ at DERRY HUTS, 2 Coys in KEMMEL CHATEAU.	#
DERRY HUTS & KEMMEL CHATEAU	22nd		In Brigade Reserve. Disposition - HQ, C & E Coys DERRY HUTS, A & B. Coys in KEMMEL CHATEAU	#
"	23/26		Battalion relieved 2 Coys 7th R.Innis.Fus in Left Sub section SPANBROEK SECTOR disposition from	#
Front Line	26th		Coys in Front Line. HQ Fort VICTORIA. Two Coys 7/8 R.Irish Fusiliers in Support & Reserve.	#
"	26/28th		Holding Left Sub-Section SPANBROEK SECTOR as above. Casualties 2 OR killed, 2 OR wounded	#

Army Form C. 2118.

WAR DIARY
or
INTELLIGENCE SUMMARY.
(Erase heading not required.)

Instructions regarding War Diaries and Intelligence Summaries are contained in F. S. Regs., Part II. and the Staff Manual respectively. Title pages will be prepared in manuscript.

Place	Date	Hour	Summary of Events and Information	Remarks and references to Appendices
	February		Lieut Kemp-Robinson R Innis Fus S.R., attached, left the Battalion on reposting to 1st Garrison Bn Hampshire Regt. (Auth AG No. A/345 dated 10.2.17) The following Officers joined during the month —	
			2/Lieut J. S. Irvine, R Innis. Fus, 4.2.17	
			2/Lieut A.L. Pacer, 4/R Innis.Fus (S.R.) 10.2.17	
			Lieut F Leathly 1st R Innis Fus 21.2.17	
			2/Lt W. Notley, on appointment 26.2.17	
			2/Lt A.J. Charlesworth 4/R Irish Regt (S.R.) 27/2/17	
			Troops joined the Battn during the month as under :—	
			5 O.R. from 6th 1.B.D. 4.2.17	
			5 O.R. " " " 27.2.17	
			1 O.R. Transferred from 1/5 R. Irish Fus. 12.11.16	
			1 O.R. Transferred from 22nd R.F. 23.2.17	
			Commanded S/R Rinniskilling Fusiliers	

2 MAR. 1917

WAR DIARY
FOR MONTH OF MARCH, 1917.

VOLUME 14

UNIT:- 8th Btn. R. Inniskilling Fus.

Army Form C. 2118.

WAR DIARY
or
INTELLIGENCE SUMMARY.
(Erase heading not required.)

Instructions regarding War Diaries and Intelligence Summaries are contained in F. S. Regs., Part II and the Staff Manual respectively. Title pages will be prepared in manuscript.

Place	Date MARCH	Hour	Summary of Events and Information	Remarks and references to Appendices
FRONT LINE	1/2nd		Holding left Sub-Section SPANBROEK SECTOR. Casualties 1 OR. killed, 1 OR. wounded.	
	2nd		Battalion relieved by 6th R. Irish Regt. on completion of relief moved into Divisional Reserve, DONCASTER HUTS.	
DONCASTER HUTS	2/19th		In Divisional Reserve DONCASTER HUTS	
	19th		Battalion relieved 2nd R. Dublin Fus. in left Sub-Section, KIERSTRAAT SECTION. Disposition – 'A' Coy. on left, 'D' Coy. on Right, 'C' Coy. S.P. 13 & VANKEEP, 'B' Coy. WATLING ST (Support) HQ YORK HOUSE	
FRONT LINE	19/23		Holding left Sub-Section as above. Casualties 1 OR. killed, 3 OR. wounded. The situation was quiet throughout the tour.	
	23rd		Battalion relieved by 7th R. Innis. Fus. on completion of relief moved into Brigade Reserve, BUTTERFLY FARM.	
BUTTERFLY FARM	23/29		In Brigade Reserve, BUTTERFLY FARM.	
	29th		Battalion relieved 7th R. Innis Fus. in left Sub-Section, VIERSTRAAT SECTION Disposition – 'C' Coy. left, 2 platoons 'B' Coy. on Right & 1 platoon VANKEEP, 'D' Coy. S.P. 13, 'A' Coy. WATLING ST (Support) H.Q. YORK HOUSE	
FRONT LINE	29/31st		Holding left Sub-Section as above. Casualties a wanted increase was shewed in our artillery activity during the tour.	

Army Form C. 2118.

WAR DIARY
or
INTELLIGENCE SUMMARY.
(Erase heading not required.)

Instructions regarding War Diaries and Intelligence Summaries are contained in F.S. Regs., Part II. and the Staff Manual respectively. Title pages will be prepared in manuscript.

Place	Date MARCH	Hour	Summary of Events and Information	Remarks and references to Appendices
			2/Lt I. M RATTRAY proceeded to ENGLAND to report to Secretary War Office & is struck off the Strength. Authy A.G's No. A/23276 dated 19/3/17	
			2/Lt W. D. Potter struck off the Strength of Batt 26/3/17. Authy 5215/2 (M.S.1 INDIA) 15 Cir. C. 19/3/17	
			2/Lt M. P. HANLON transferred to ENGLAND & struck off strength 14/3/17 reason - Sick - Authy. List No 696 dated 8/3/17	
			Lieut. D. J. WHITE, 4th R Innis. Fus, attd 2/R Batt proceeded to ENGLAND 1/3/17 & is struck off strength of Bn. Authy. A.G's. No. A/22707; dated 26/2/17	J.
			Lieut F. LEATHLEY, 1st R Innis. Fus. struck off Strength, 5/3/17 Authy A.G.'s DR020/2/106 dated 23/2/17 A.G's BASE CR.8174 - 24/2/17	
			2/Lt L.G.D. Macdougald transferred to ENGLAND, Sick, & struck off strength 22/2/17 Authy List No. 685 dated 25/2/17	
			2/Lt J. S. IRVINE R. Innis. Fus. transferred to ENGLAND, Sick, & struck off strength 20/2/17 Authy List No 683 dated 23/2/17	
			The following officers joined during the month -	
			2/Lt C D NEALON, Lt (CSR) Batt R. Innis. Fus.	5. 3. 17
			Lieut. W. A. Browne, " "	10. 3. 17
			2/Lt L.C. BROWN, on appointment	12. 3. 17
			" S. J. HENDERSON, 3rd R. Innis. Fus	
			" G. F. PATERSON, " "	18. 3. 17
			" J. S. CARRUTHERS " "	
			R. H. ROULSTONE	

WAR DIARY
or
INTELLIGENCE SUMMARY.

(Erase heading not required.)

Army Form C. 2118.

Place	Date	Hour	Summary of Events and Information	Remarks and references to Appendices
	MARCH		Drafts joined the Batt" during the month as under:—	
			4 OR. from 16th I.B.D. 4.3.17	
			16 OR. " 15th " 18.3.17	
			59 OR. " 8th " 19.3.17	
			52 OR. " 41st " 20.3.17	
			27 OR. " 38th " 20.3.17	
			3 OR. " 18th " 24.3.17	
			20 OR. " 17th " 26.3.17	
			23 OR. " 7th " 28.3.17	
			32 OR. " 8th " 28.3.17	
			10 OR. " 16th " 28.3.17	

M Baldwin
"Lieut.-Colonel, Commanding"
8th (S) Battalion R. Innis. Fusiliers.

— 1 APR. 1917

WAR DIARY FOR MONTH OF APRIL, 1917.

VOLUME:- 15

UNIT:- 8th R. Inniskilling Fus.

Army Form C. 2118.

WAR DIARY
or
INTELLIGENCE SUMMARY.
(Erase heading not required.)

Instructions regarding War Diaries and Intelligence Summaries are contained in F.S. Regs., Part II. and the Staff Manual respectively. Title pages will be prepared in manuscript.

Place	Date	Hour	Summary of Events and Information	Remarks and references to Appendices
	1917 APRIL			
FRONT LINE	1st		Holding left sub-sector VIERSTRAAT SECTOR. Disposition: 'C' Coy. left front: 2 Platoons 'B' Coy. right front & 1 Platoon VAN KEEP: D.Coy., S.P.13. 'A' Coy., WATLING ST (SUPPORT). Battn. HQ., YORK HOUSE. Casualties, 1 O.R. wounded.	apw
	1st.	8 p.m.	Battn. was relieved by 1st Bn. The Royal Munster Fusiliers, 47th Infantry Brigade. On relief, the Battn. moved into Divisional Reserve, BIRR BARRACKS, LOCRE.	apw
LOCRE	3rd.	2.30 p.m.	Enemy shelled our observation balloon, which was just overhead, with 10 cm. shells. Bursting high. No damage was caused.	apw
CLARE CAMP	7th.	6 p.m.	Bn. moved to CLARE CAMP (Canvas), relieving 7th R Inniskilling Fusiliers	apw
	7th/12th		Owing to recent drafts received, + new methods of warfare, the Bn. had to be considerably reorganised. The period at CLARE CAMP was spent in individual training, which was very much hampered by bad weather.	apw
	13th	9.30 a.m.	Commenced march with 48th Inf. Bde. to RECQUES Training Area, N.W. of ST. OMER	apw
HAZEBROUCK	13th	2.30 p.m.	Arrived in HAZEBROUCK area, + billeted there for night 13/14th.	apw
	14th	9.0 a.m.	Marched on from billets	apw
ARQUES	14th	2.30 p.m.	Arrived at ARQUES, + billeted there for night 14/15th	apw

T.134. Wt. W708—776. 500000. 4/15. Sir J.C. & S.

Army Form C. 2118.

WAR DIARY
or
INTELLIGENCE SUMMARY.
(Erase heading not required.)

(2)

Place	Date	Hour	Summary of Events and Information	Remarks and references to Appendices
	APRIL			
ARQUES	15th	9am	Marched out of billets.	agw
MENTQUE	15th	2.30pm	Arrived in MENTQUE: Bn was disposed as follows, during training period	
			Bn. HQ., A, C & D Coys, in MENTQUE.	
			B Coy in LA RONVILLE. Transport, CULEM.	
			The weather for the first two days of the march was good, but the last day was wet. There were few fallers-out considering that about half the Bn were composed of recent drafts, many of whom had had very little training. The transport animals arrived in good condition, & free from harness galls.	
MENTQUE	16/19		Platoon Training	agw
	20/21		Company Training	agw
	22/23		Battalion Training	agw
	24th		Brigade Assault at Arms: this was a most successful day, the weather was fine, & all concerned took a keen interest in the events. The Bn. won first place for Bayonet Fighting, & Guard Mounting, & taken competition being judged by the Divisional Commander.	agw
	25th		Battalion returned for Brigade Field Day.	agw

Army Form C. 2118.

WAR DIARY
or
INTELLIGENCE SUMMARY.
(Erase heading not required.)

(3)

Place	Date	Hour	Summary of Events and Information	Remarks and references to Appendices
MENTQUE	APRIL 26th		Brigade field Day. The general idea was an attack on the WYTSCHAETE RIDGE; Trenches etc., being marked out on the ground. Two Bns in front line, one in support, & one in Reserve. This Bn, being in support; supplied one company to each of the front line Bns, to act as "mop(p)ers-up", & escorts to prisoners. C Coy found carrying parties, & 'A' Coy constructed & manned 3 strong Points. Very successful work was carried out by signalling personnel with a contact aeroplane. The 2nd Army, 9th Corps, & 16th Divisional Commanders were present during the operation.	a/W
	27th		Battalion Training. Before going to Training Area, Platoons had been organised into 4 distinct sections, viz. Lewis Gunners, Bombers, Rifle Bombers, & Riflemen. Training was carried out in accordance with the most recent instructions, contained in the following publications:- SS 143 Instructions for training of Platoons for Offensive Action 1917 SS 144 Normal Formation for Attack SS 135 Training of Divisions for Offensive Action 1917	a/W

T.J.34. Wt. W708—776. 500000. 4/15. Sir J. C. & S.

WAR DIARY

Place	Date	Hour	Summary of Events & Information	Remarks & References
MENTQUE	APRIL 28th	11 am	Commenced march back to LOCRE with H.Q.th Inf. Bde.	a/pos
ARQUES	28th	5 pm	Arrived at ARQUES, & billeted there night 28/29th	a/pos
"	29th	10 am	Marched out from billets.	a/pos
HAZEBROUCK	29th	4 pm	Arrived at HAZEBROUCK, & billeted in that area night 29/30th	a/pos
"	30th	8 am	Marched out from billets.	a/pos
LOCRE	30th	10 pm	Arrived at LOCRE, & halted there until 5:30 pm, when the Bn. marched to WESTON CAMP, SCHERPENBURG, arriving there at 6.0 pm. Here the Bn. was under Canvas	a/pos
	30th	6.0 pm	The weather during the 3 days march was very hot, but as before, few fell out, & the transport animals finished in good condition. While passing through BAILLEUL, the Brigade was inspected by Corps Commander, 9th Corps.	

A.F. — C 2118

WAR DIARY (3)

Place	Date	Hour	Summary of Events & Information	Remarks & References
	APRIL 1		Lieut C.A. LEPETON, 1/8 K.R.R.F. (Atts) struck off strength whilst serving with T.M.B. Authority, A.G. G.H.Q. No. A/1049/170 d/- 29-3-17	agw
			2nd Lieut A.G. PORTER struck off strength pending Indian Commission. Authority M.S. to C-in-C. 51/1673 d/- 10-4-17	agw
			Capt H.L. HORNBY, granted sick leave & struck off strength 7-4-17 Authority, List No. 730	agw
			2nd Lt. R.F. CASEY joined the Bn 16-4-17	agw
			Capt. H.L. HORNBY rejoined from sick leave 23-4-17	agw
			Major W.E. ROTHWELL struck off strength with effect from 29-3-17 Authority M.S. to C-in-C. d/- 12-4-17	agw
			Drafts joined during month:-	
			3 O.R. from 16th I.B.D. 1-4-17	
			14 " " " " 5-4-17	
			28 " " " " 8-4-17	
			5 " " " " 11-4-17	
			4 " " " " 16-4-17	
			10 " " " " 18-4-17	
			3 " " " " 19-4-17	
			3 " " " " 21-4-17	

T. Boardman 2/Lt
for 2/Lt & A/Adjt
County 8/5th Bn R. Inniskilling Fus.

WAR DIARY:

VOLUME:- 16

FOR MONTH OF MAY, 1917.

UNIT:- 8th Ro Iniskilling Fusrs.

Army Form C. 2118.

WAR DIARY
or
~~INTELLIGENCE SUMMARY~~
(Erase heading not required.)

Refce MAP SHEET 28 S.W. Edition 5A 1/20.000

(I)

Place	Date	Hour	Summary of Events and Information	Remarks and references to Appendices
	1917			
WESTON CAMP. SCHERPENBURG	May 1	8.15pm	Marched out to relieve 7th Bn. South Lancs Regt. (Wildenloss) in Right Sub-section, DIEPENDAAL SECTOR, immediately N. of VIERSTRAAT - WYTSCHAETE ROAD. Distribution :- A. Coy. Right Front Line D. Coy. 1 Platoon in Lewis Guns, Left Front Line. " 2 Platoons in RESERVE. 9.1 a. C. Coy. 1 Platoon in SUPPORT, 1 in RESERVE BATTLE H.Q. at N.11 a. 00.10 B. Coy. in RESERVE Bn. Hq. N.10.d.20.90	aqw
FRONT LINE	2/5		Holding front line, as above. The hour was remarkably quiet. Casualties. 1 O.R. wounded.	aqw
RIDGE WOOD	night 5/6		Battn. was relieved by 7th R.INNIS. FUS. + on completion of relief moved into Bnge. avilsupport in RIDGE WOOD, N.5 a,b + c.	aqw
	7th	8.45pm	In punishment for enemy's shelling of back areas on previous nights, every gun in 2nd Army (up to 9.2 in calibre) opened fire for 5 minutes at intense rate. The enemy did not reply until 10.15 p.m., when he replied on the wood with 7.7 cm 10.5 cm + 15 cm shells. The Battn. at once moved into their emergency trenches	aqw

Army Form C. 2118.

WAR DIARY
or
INTELLIGENCE SUMMARY.
(Erase heading not required.)

II

Instructions regarding War Diaries and Intelligence Summaries are contained in F. S. Regs., Part II. and the Staff Manual respectively. Title pages will be prepared in manuscript.

Place	Date	Hour	Summary of Events and Information	Remarks and references to Appendices
RIDGE WOOD	1917 MAY 7th	10.15 pm	& although heavy shelling continued until about 10.50 pm, suffered only one casualty, 1 OR wounded.	
		11 pm	Our guns gave a repeat of their previous fire; there was some interchange firing on both sides throughout the night 7/8th.	agw
CURRAGH CAMP. SCHERPEN BURG.	9th	9 pm	The Batt. was being relieved by 7th Bn. Sherwood For[esters]. (19th Div.) when the enemy opened a violent bombardment of the whole front line system, DIEPENDAAL SECTOR	
		9.15 pm	at 9.15 pm endeavoure received to —— occupy the VIERSTRAAT SWITCH: D. Coy. having already been relieved, this forward position was taken up by A, B, & C Coys. These companies were withdrawn at about 11 pm, & relief proceeded with; the Bn. moving into CURRAGH CAMP. Casualties, 6/9th inclusive, 1 OR killed, 1 OR wounded, 1 OR wounded (at duty) 1 OR died in Hospital.	agw
	10th	2 am		
	10th	7 pm	Batt. marched out to relieve 1st Bn. Royal Munster Fus. in front line, left subsector, VIERSTRAAT SECTOR, on relief holding line as follows:— B. Coy. plus 2 L.G. of D Coy. Front line. C. Coy. SUPPORT (6 or 2 Lewis Guns) D. RESERVE LINE (CHINESE WALL) A. Coy. SP13 & VAN KEEP Bn. Hqrs. YORK HOUSE.	agw

Army Form C. 2118.

WAR DIARY
or
INTELLIGENCE SUMMARY.
(Erase heading not required.)

Instructions regarding War Diaries and Intelligence Summaries are contained in F. S. Regs., Part II. and the Staff Manual respectively. Title pages will be prepared in manuscript.

Place	Date	Hour	Summary of Events and Information	Remarks and references to Appendices
FRONT LINE	1917 MAY 10/14		Holding front line as detailed above. The tour was very quiet.	
	14th	9 p.m.	The Battn. was relieved by 7/8th R. Irish Fusiliers, & on relief, moved into Brigade Reserve at Butterfly Farm, N 19 a 6.9. No casualties	a/w
BUTTERFLY FARM	14/18		During this period, the Bn. was engaged on working parties. Casualties 2 OR. wounded.	a/w
RENMORE CAMP BRULOOZE	18th	5 p.m.	The Battn. moved from BUTTERFLY FARM, to RENMORE CAMP, where it was in Divisional Reserve.	a/w
Ditto	18th/31st		The Battalion was fully occupied with Working Parties. Nothing of incident occurred except on the evenings of 28th & 29th at 10 p.m. each night, when the enemy, during the shelling of our back areas, dropped a few shells into & around the camp. On the latter occasion wounding one man. On the night of the 28th, our transport lines on the LOCRE - BAILLEUL road were shelled, 9 two casualties were incurred :- 1 OR killed & 1 OR wounded, total of wounds other casualties, 18th/31st 1 OR killed & 4 OR wounded. End of Month	a/w

Army Form C. 2118.

WAR DIARY
or
~~INTELLIGENCE~~ SUMMARY.
(Erase heading not required.)

Instructions regarding War Diaries and Intelligence Summaries are contained in F.S. Regs., Part II. and the Staff Manual respectively. Title pages will be prepared in manuscript.

IV

Place	Date	Hour	Summary of Events and Information	Remarks and references to Appendices
	1917			
	MAY		Drafts joining	
			5 O.R. joined from 16th I.B.D. 4.5.17	Capt C.H.Godaland M.C. The Leinster Regt. joined on 6/5/17 & was posted to 'C' Coy, taking over command of that Coy. on 9/5/17
			5 " " 7.5.17	
			4 " " 10.5.17	
			21 " " 12.5.17	
			1 " " 11.5.17	Capt L.G.A. Constable MC joined 9/5/17 transferred to 'A' Coy.
			6 " " 14.5.17	
			25 O.R. transferred from London Regt. } 19-5-17 } having previously been attached to the Bn.	Capt. W.R. Magnus 12th Connaught Rangers (S.R) reported for duty 22.5.17 & was posted to B Coy.
			42 " " 28-5-17	
			1 O.R. reported from 7th R.Berwicks? 12.5.17	
			2 " joined from 16th I.B.D. 21.5.17	Capt F.C. Atkinson Fleming MC RAMC assumed duties of M.O. on 24/5/17
			3 " attached from London Regt. 21-5-17	
			18 " joined from 13th Kings Liverpools 26-5-17	
			25 " " 20th Lancashire Fus 26-5-17	
			19 " " 16th I.B.D. 31-5-17	

Army Form C. 2118.

WAR DIARY
or
INTELLIGENCE SUMMARY
(Erase heading not required.)

Place	Date	Hour	Summary of Events and Information	Remarks and references to Appendices
	1917 MAY		Departures	
			Capt G Buchanan R.A.M.C, returned to 10th F.A. for duty.	CJW
			2nd Lt J Ashurton granted extension of leave on medical grounds, & struck off strength. (Authy. 2nd Army No A/1717 of 11/5/17)	
			33 O.R. of London Regt (attached) despatched to Base Depot HAVRE 30/5/17	CJW
			Honours & Awards	
			No 43180 Pte McDonnell M, "D" Coy, awarded Serbian Order of the Cross of Karageorge: First Class, Gold Star with swords. London Gazette 21/4/17	CJW
			Mentioned in Despatches:- London Gazette 22/5/17	
			20681 Sgt McGarry J.	
			25125 " Nelson J.G.	
			26327 Pte Andrews W.	
			26348 " Ward P.	
			End of Month.	
			JMSmardeau Lt Col	
			Comdg 1st Bn R. Innis Killing Fus	CJW

T2134. Wt. W708—776. 50000m. 4/15. Sir J.C. & S.

WAR DIARY
or
INTELLIGENCE SUMMARY.
(Erase heading not required.)

HAZEBROUCK 5A
Affix Maps FRANCE 28. S.W.2 Edition 5A

Army Form C. 2118.

Instructions regarding War Diaries and Intelligence Summaries are contained in F.S. Regs., Part II. and the Staff Manual respectively. Title pages will be prepared in manuscript.

Place	Date	Hour	Summary of Events and Information	Remarks and references to Appendices
RENMORE CAMP.	1st & 2nd JUNE		In Divisional Reserve.	gw
BRULOOZE	2nd	9.45pm	"A" & "C" Coys marched out to relieve portions of 8th & 9th R. Dublin Fus in VIERSTRAAT SECTOR. On completion of relief the Bn. was disposed as follows:-	
			Brigade Support, LEFT SUBSECTION, VIERSTRAAT SECTOR. On completion of relief the Bn. was disposed as follows:-	
			Bn. Hq. THE FOSSE DUGOUT N 16 d 75.90	
			'A' Coy DONCASTER HUTS LOCRE	
			'D' " MACAW "	
			B " 1 Platoon FORT HALIFAX	
			" 1 " TOUCAN TRENCH	
			" 1 " YORK HOUSE	
			C Coy DONCASTER HUTS, LOCRE	gw
BDE SUPPORT	3rd & 4th		In support, as above: great artillery activity on our front, which did not provoke much retaliation. The enemy used gas shells intermittently in small numbers along the KEMMEL — VIERSTRAAT Road, causing us a few casualties.	
			Casualties 3/5th June 2 OR killed 24 OR wounded 1 Officer wounded (5th June) Capt H.L. HORNBY	gw

Army Form C. 2118.

WAR DIARY
or
INTELLIGENCE SUMMARY.
(Erase heading not required.)

Place	Date	Hour	Summary of Events and Information	Remarks and references to Appendices
VIERSTRAAT SWITCH — FRONT LINE	JUNE 4th	9 p.m.	The Bn. relieved the 2nd R. Irish Regt in the front line system, 'A' + 'C' Coys coming up from LOCRE. On completion of relief, the battalion was disposed as under:— Bn. Hq. S.P. 13. Left front line, VIERSTRAAT RD & CROWBAR TRENCH, 2 Platoons D Coy, with 4 Lewis Guns. Right front line, 1 platoon B. Coy, with 2 Lewis Guns. SHANNON TRENCH (Support) 1 platoon D. Coy, with 2 Lewis Guns. FERMOY TRENCH (Support) 2 platoons B. Coy, with 2 Lewis Guns. CHINESE WALL, SHANTUNG, 'A' Coy (less 3 Lewis Guns). S.P. 15, & VAN KEEP 3 Lewis Guns 'A' Coy. CHINESE WALL, SWATOW. C. Coy. HQ. B + D Coys, in WATLING ST, 'A' Coy, SP 13, C. Coy, BYRON FARM	AGW
	5th	3 p.m.	In conjunction with similar raids on the II Corps front, 2nd Lt Paterson (B.Coy) + 20 OR (B. Coy) left our lines at N24 a 65.90: they went along it to the north for some to enemy's front line at N24 a 45.95 under cover of an artillery barrage, "proceeded 70 yards; finding the trench practically non existant, & unoccupied. The party re entered our lines at 3.11 p.m. without casualty.	AGW
	5th	10.20 p.m.	The Battalion carried out a large raid; for particulars, see Appendix 'Y' attached	AGW

Army Form C. 2118.

WAR DIARY
or
INTELLIGENCE SUMMARY.
(Erase heading not required.)

Instructions regarding War Diaries and Intelligence Summaries are contained in F.S. Regs., Part II. and the Staff Manual respectively. Title pages will be prepared in manuscript.

Place	Date	Hour	Summary of Events and Information	Remarks and references to Appendices
FRONT LINE	June night 5/6th	1 am	After the raid referred to in last paragraph, the Bn. was relieved by 7th R. Innis. Fus. & 7/8 R. Irish Inns., & moved to DONCASTER HUTS, LOCRE, arriving there at 5 am. (6th)	AGW
DONCASTER HUTS, LOCRE	6th.		The day was spent in completing preparations for the attack on WYTSCHAETE RIDGE, 9 platoons were moving off to their various assembly positions from 4 pm onwards, the last of the Bn. clearing the camp about 10.30 pm.	AGW
FRONT LINE	7th. 8th. 9th.	3.10 am	Attack on WYTSCHAETE RIDGE: see Appendix "Z". Battalion having been withdrawn from front line, occupied old British front, support & reserve lines, as follows:— A & C Coys, old front & support lines from VIERSTRAAT RD to MAYO ST. B & D Coys. YUM-YUM TRENCH. Bn. Hq. BYRON FARM. The 49th Inf. Bde. was withdrawn from the line, & the bath. marched to DONCASTER HUTS, LOCRE, arriving there at about 5 pm. Casualties 6/9th June. 9 OR killed or died of wounds. 72 OR Wounded. 1 Officer wounded 2nd Lt P.J. Fahan.	AGW AGW AGW AGW
DONCASTER HUTS, LOCRE	9/10		The Battalion remained in LOCRE, & was employed in finding Working Parties	AGW

WAR DIARY
or
INTELLIGENCE SUMMARY.

(Erase heading not required.)

Army Form C. 2118.

(4)

Instructions regarding War Diaries and Intelligence Summaries are contained in F. S. Regs., Part II. and the Staff Manual respectively. Title pages will be prepared in manuscript.

Place	Date 1917	Hour	Summary of Events and Information	Remarks and references to Appendices
	JUNE			
LOCRE	13	6.35am	The Batt. marched out from LOCRE, with the remainder of the 49th Inf. Bde. to MERRIS area, arriving in billets about mid day.	CJW
MERRIS	16		Orders received to effect that 49th Inf. Bde. would move to CLARE CAMP near LOCRE on 17th.	CJW
CLARE CAMP	17	7.30am	The Battalion marched out from billets, arriving at CLARE CAMP about 11 am.	CJW
MERRIS	18th	5.0am	The Battalion marched back to MERRIS with 49th Inf. Bde., arriving there about 9 am.	CJW
EECKE	20th	7.25am	Marched out from billets at MERRIS, to EECKE, arriving there at 10 am.	CJW
BROXEELE	22nd	4.50am	" " " " EECKE to BRIXEELE Area " 10.30 am.	CJW
"	27/29		The 2nd Army Commander inspected the battalion on the march, when near ZUTYPEENE. The period now occupied with individual training, route marching, & training of specialists. The Divisional Commander inspected the Battn. at work on 28th June. "Transport."	CJW
ETRÉHEM & LEULINGHEM	30th		The Bn. marched to the TATINGHEM area, 2 Companies (B & D), being billetted in ETRÉHEM, 2 Companies (A & C) at LEULINGHEM, & Bn. Hq. at LEULINE.	CJW

Army Form C. 2118.

WAR DIARY
or
INTELLIGENCE SUMMARY.
(Erase heading not required.)

Instructions regarding War Diaries and Intelligence Summaries are contained in F. S. Regs., Part II. and the Staff Manual respectively. Title pages will be prepared in manuscript.

Place	Date	Hour	Summary of Events and Information	Remarks and references to Appendices
	1917 June		Drafts from 16th I.B.D. — 7/6/17, 4 O.R. 23/6/17 4 O.R.	
			9/6/17 20 O.R. 24/6/17 4 O.R.	AW
			29/6/17 7 O.R.	
			Strength - Officers. 2nd Lt R.C.G. HERMGES posted to 10th Bn R.Inniss.Fus, 8/5/17	
			Authority A.G. GHQ A/24589 d/ 4-5-17	
			Lt B.E. BUCKNALL, 3rd (S.R) Bn R Inniss Fus, struck off	
			establishment 7/3/17 Authority M.S. to C-in-C No. 9510 d/24/1/17	AW
			Command. Capt L.G.A. CONSTABLE M.C. relinquished command of 'A' Coy 11/6/17	
			& was reposted to D Coy on 23/6/17	
			2nd Lt W.G. GROOMBRIDGE took over command of 'A' Coy, 12/6/17	AW
			Promotions. Officers :- To be Temp. Captains :-	
			Temp 2nd Lt (A/Capt) H.A. GREEN. M.C	4.10.16
			Lieut (A/Capt) H. BRADLEY	30.10.16
			Temp Lieut (A/Capt) H.L. HORNBY	24-2-17
			To be Temp. Lieuts :-	
			2nd Lt W.G. GROOMBRIDGE	30-10-16
			C J COGGINS	24-12-16
			Temp 2nd Lt W.F. ELLIS. M.C	24-12-16
			Temp 2nd Lt Sir J.C. & S.		AW

Army Form C. 2118.

WAR DIARY
or
INTELLIGENCE SUMMARY.
(Erase heading not required.)

C.

Place	Date	Hour	Summary of Events and Information	Remarks and references to Appendices
	1917 June		Appointment of Officers. Temp Lt. W.G GROOMBRIDGE to be acting Captain whilst commanding a Company 11th. 23rd April 1917	GW
			Honours & Awards. Hon. Lieut & Quartermaster G. SEARLE awarded Military Cross King's Birthday Honours Gazette No 40366 Pte GLYNN. J awarded Military Medal	GW

3.7.17

R Walkey Major
Commdg. S.K.R Inniskilling Fus.

Army Form C. 2118.

2

WAR DIARY
INTELLIGENCE SUMMARY.
(Erase heading not required.)

Instructions regarding War Diaries and Intelligence Summaries are contained in F. S. Regs., Part II. and the Staff Manual respectively. Title pages will be prepared in manuscript.

Place	Date	Hour	Summary of Events and Information	Remarks and references to Appendices
	JULY			
ETRÉHEM	1–8		ETRÉHEM AREA – 2 Companies (B & D) & Transport being billeted in ETRÉHEM & 2 Companies	
LEULINGHEM			(A & C) at LEULINGHEM. Batt. HQ at LEULINE.	
RUBROUCK AREA	8th	6.10 am	Marched out from Bellah to RUBROUCK AREA arriving there about 10.20 am	
WINNIZEELE AREA	9th	5.10 am	Marched out from Bellah to WINNIZEELE AREA arriving there about 10 am.	
do.	9–26		This period was occupied with Battalion, Coy. & Platoon training, route marching, individual training etc. The Batt. was in Corps Reserve from 10th July	
HATOU No.2 AREA	26th	6.40 am	Marched to HATOU No.2 AREA arriving there 9 am.	
do.	26–28		HATOU No.2 AREA.	
REDROSE CAMP	30/31		Marched to REDROSE CAMP, BRANDHOEK AREA arriving about 1.15 am 31st	
BRANDHOEK AREA	31	9.35 pm	Moved to position of assembly immediately S.W. of VLAMERTINGHE. Echelon 'B' consisting of 3 Officers & 76 O.R. went back to Transport Lines situated about one mile E. of POPERINGHE	

Army Form C. 2118.
3

WAR DIARY
INTELLIGENCE SUMMARY.
(Erase heading not required.)

Instructions regarding War Diaries and Intelligence Summaries are contained in F. S. Regs., Part II. and the Staff Manual respectively. Title pages will be prepared in manuscript.

Place	Date	Hour	Summary of Events and Information	Remarks and references to Appendices
	July			
			Honours & Awards — 2/Li K.H. BORCHERDS, Connaught Rangers, attached, awarded CROIX DE GUERRE	
			Capt. H.L. HERREY, awarded the MILITARY CROSS	
			2/Li W. NOTLEY awarded the MILITARY CROSS	
			No. 21326 Pte CLANCY M. awarded the MEDAILLE MILITAIRE	
			The undermentioned NCO's & men awarded the MILITARY MEDAL	
			No. 40942 Sgt. Curtis R.E. No. 40981 Sgt. Wallen H.	
			No. 11584 Pte Bell H. No. 26325 Pte Weatherall A.	
			No. 40950 Pte Rowley H. No. 41302 Pte Davidson P.	
			No. 43825 Pte Munslowhite F.	A.
			Appointments, Officers — Lieut W.G. Groundridge to be Acting Capt. whilst Commdg. a Coy 11th – 23/4/17 & from 21st June '17	do
			Establishment, Officers — Major J.M. Wadmore struck off. Establishment of Bn with effect from 27.3.17	
			Aust Adj W.O. letter No. 1322 25/2 d/17.7.17	do
			Strength, Officers — Capt. & Adj. W.B.H. Mein M.C The Royal Scots, att'd, rejoined Bn. 19.7.17	
			2/Li W. Holley M.C. accepted as probationer for Indian Army. Struck off Strength Austly	do
			W.O. letter M.S.I. India No. 17898/2 d/17.7.17	

WAR DIARY

INTELLIGENCE SUMMARY.

Army Form C. 2118.

Place	Date	Hour	Summary of Events and Information	Remarks and references to Appendices
	July		Strength Officers — 1	
			Capt. C.H. Godsland M.C. accepted as probationer for Indian Army pending Regular Commission. Struck off Strength. Authy M.S. to C in C. No 570/165/19 of 9.7.17	
			Authy x 12 Corps AC/10/9 of 24.7.17 2/Lt A.L Pascoe granted Extention of Leave by W.O. & Struck off Strength 24.7.17	
			2/Lt J.A Hunter rejoined from Sick Leave 3.7.17	
			Lieut C.A. Le Patou rejoined from T.M.B. 7.7.17	
			Lieut W.Q. Brown to R.F.C. 7.7.17 Authy AG's No. D/20.29/2/167 of 23.5.17	G
			2/Lt W. Northfield England for Duty in at Cadet Officers 7/7/17	
			The following troops joined the Battn during the month —	
			100 OR from Cyclists Depot 24.7.17	
			84 OR from 18th TB. For Expol Bn. 27.7.17	
			4 OR " " 29.7.17	
			6 OR from 16th I.B.D. 1.7.17	
			10 OR do. 4.7.17	
			52 OR do. 7.7.17	
			3 OR do. 10.7.17	
			A.W.Allen Major	G
			for Lieut-Colonel Commanding 8th (S) Battalion Welsh Fusiliers	

49/16

War Diary
of
8th Bn. R. Innis. Fus.
for
August 1917.

49/16

WAR DIARY.

FOR MONTH OF AUGUST, 1917.

VOLUME 19

UNIT 8th R. Inniskilling Fusrs.

Amalgamated with
7th Battalion 23.8.17.

Army Form C. 2118.

WAR DIARY
or
INTELLIGENCE SUMMARY.

(Erase heading not required.)

Instructions regarding War Diaries and Intelligence Summaries are contained in F. S. Regs., Part II. and the Staff Manual respectively. Title pages will be prepared in manuscript.

Place	Date	Hour	Summary of Events and Information	Remarks and references to Appendices
VLAMERTINGHE No.3 Area H.10.a.b	1 Aug.		Battalion in bivouac	Ref. Map Sheet 28 N.W. 1/20000 b.A. Edition
do	1 Aug.	11.30 am	Battalion moved back to bivouac position in RED ROSE CAMP P.7.c.2.b.8.2 arriving about 1 p.m.	Edition do.
RED ROSE CAMP	2 Aug.		Battalion in Corps Reserve	do.
do	2 Aug.	1.10 pm	HQ A.C Coys moved to support of 47K 1.B in forward area, and were disposed as follows. HQ. LINDER F.M. I.4.b.1.0. A.C Coys HQ ORPHAN F.M. I.4.c.45.20.	do.
do	3 Aug.	5.30 pm	Bn. D Coys moved forward and occupied CAMBRIDGE TRENCH from I.5.a.35.65 to I.5.c.70.75	WTM do.
Forward Area	4 Aug.		Batln in dispositions as above. Intermittent shelling by Enemy at intervals throughout day and night. Very marked Enemy aerial activity 29 aeroplanes were observed over LANCER F.M I.4.b.1.0 about 7.30 pm	WTM do.
do	do	11.30 am	LT. COL. T.H BOARDMAN. D.S.O severely wounded - command of Bn passed to CAPT. W.E.H. MUIR M.C	WTM do.
do	5 Aug.	12.45 am	LT. COL. T.H BOARDMAN. D.S.O died of wounds at A.P. PETITE CHATEAU	WTM do.
do	do		Batln in dispositions as above. Situation quiet with slight Enemy shelling at intervals	
do	do	12 noon	MAJOR A.T. WALKEY M.C arrived from ECHELON B, and took over command of Bn from CAPT. W.E.H. MUIR M.C	
do	5 Aug.	9.15 pm	Batln moved forward to front line, and relieved 6th Bn. ROYAL IRISH REGIMENT.	

Army Form C. 2118. 3

WAR DIARY
or
INTELLIGENCE SUMMARY.

(Erase heading not required.)

Instructions regarding War Diaries and Intelligence Summaries are contained in F. S. Regs., Part II. and the Staff Manual respectively. Title pages will be prepared in manuscript.

Place	Date	Hour	Summary of Events and Information	Remarks and references to Appendices
	5 Aug.		Dispositions on completion of relief as under:-	Ref. Trench Maps FRESENBERG. 1/10.000.
			Battn. HQrs. SQUARE FM. C.30.b.85.85. 2 Platoons D Coy. from D.19.c.65.78 to D.19.c.90.45	
			C Coy. from D.19.c.90.45 to D.25.a.93.95. B Coy. from D.25.a.80.50	
			A Coy. from D.25.a.80.50 to D.25.c.85.90. 2 Platoons D Coy. Low FM. D.25.a.70.52.	
			The FRESENBERG- POTIZE RD was very heavily shelled by enemy 4.2s. and 5.9s during advance to	
			this position and a number of casualties were inflicted on us.	within do.
Front Line	6 Aug.		Holding line as above. Enemy shelled our positions continuously throughout the day,	do.
			SQUARE FM particularly receiving much attention. Enemy snipers were very active and all	
			movement by daylight was impossible. Our trenches & ludes shell holes and was in	
			very wet condition. Enemy aircraft active - One anti machine	
			CAPT. H. BROADLEY D Coy. Killed in action 2/Lt J.A. HUNTER wounded.	
do	6 Aug to 3.30 pm 2nd		R. DUBLIN Fus took over 100 yards trench from Right Coy. leaving Right of B C	within do.
			in head of S.E. corner of PRYST HOUSE.	within
do	7 Aug.		Holding front line - Enemy shelled our positions heavily during the day with 4.2". 5.9's	do
			and large calibre. Weather everywhere still very bad.	within
do	do	11 p.m.	Battalion was relieved by 7th R. INNIS. Fus. and on completion of relief about 2 am moved within	within

Army Form C. 2118.

WAR DIARY
or
INTELLIGENCE SUMMARY.
(Erase heading not required.)

Instructions regarding War Diaries and Intelligence Summaries are contained in F. S. Regs., Part II. and the Staff Manual respectively. Title pages will be prepared in manuscript.

Place	Date	Hour	Summary of Events and Information	Remarks and references to Appendices
			took to bivouac camp in VLAMERTINGE No 3 area. H 17 a. o. 9. Left and arrived in camp	Ref Sheet 28 N.W.1/20.000
H 17 a.o.9	Aug 8th		about 7 a.m. 8th August. The troops were in a much exhausted condition on arrival due to	Edn 6.a.
			the strain of holding a rough and very wet line, where shelters did not exist to keep out	aepm
			very severe weather conditions, and under continuous enemy shell fire.	
			Casualties from 1st to 8th August. Officers as rather on this Bn O.R. 20 killed & died of	do.
			wounds. 70 wounded. 7 missing.	
			Bath in Bivouac camp. Weather during this period was variable Time was spent in	do. aepm
			resting and refitting	
H 17 a. o. 9	Aug 14 8 p.m.		X Day. Battalion moved forward and relieved two Coys 6 1/2 Bn ROYAL IRISH REGT.	Ref FREZENBERG Shut 1/10.000
			in front line as follows:- C Coy from D 25 a. 75. 05 to D 25 a. 78. 50, with 1 platoon	
			in support. A Coy from D 25 a. 75. 50 to D 25 a. 80. 90. with 1 platoon in SUPPORT.	
			D/B Coys relieved two Coys. 2nd Bn ROYAL IRISH REGT. in support on FREZENBERG	
			RIDGE as follows:- D Coy from C 30 a. 90. 45 to C 30 d. 10.10. B Coy from	
			C 30 c. 60. 30 to I 6 a. 90. 90. Batln HQ. from	
Front Line	15 Aug		X Day. Batln occupying positions as above. The day was fairly quiet	aepm
	do.		the following preliminary moves took place:-	Provisional Orders to attack attached aepm

Army Form C. 2118.

WAR DIARY
or
INTELLIGENCE SUMMARY.
(Erase heading not required.)

Instructions regarding War Diaries and Intelligence Summaries are contained in F. S. Regs., Part II. and the Staff Manual respectively. Title pages will be prepared in manuscript.

Place	Date	Hour	Summary of Events and Information	Remarks and references to Appendices
Front line	15 Aug.	10 pm	(a). C. Coy. 7/8th. R. IRISH Fus. moved from VLAMERTINGE No.3 area, and occupied position about 50 yards W of Rd occupied by A.S Coy. 8/R.INNIS. Fus. D.8 Coy. 8/R.INNIS. Fus moved forward from Support to their assembly positions 100 yards W of front/own occupied by C. Coy. 7/8 R. IRISH Fus.	FREZENBERG Sheet 1/10.000
		11.30 pm	(b) Battn. H.Q. moved forward from Sq.root PM to Low PM D 25 a. 70. 52. All the above moves were completed by warm, and B" with attached Coy was in assembly position by 2.30 a.m. 10th inst. B" Strength 19 Offrs - 462 O.R. attd. Coy. 4 Offrs. 50 O.R. Final orders for attack are attached	Appendix II. Appendix III.
Front line	16 Aug	4.45 a.m	Z Day — At Zero Hour the B" advanced in accordance with plan. Report of operations is attached	
		9 pm	Advanced posts in neighbourhood of BORRY F'ms were withdrawn to original front line warm	
do	17 Aug	1 am	Battalion was relieved in front line by 6th. B" CONNAUGHT RANGERS, and moved back to support in CAMBRIDGE TRENCH I 5 a. 75.75 to I 5 a. 55. 05. B" HQ Dugout - I 5 a. 40. 40. Casualties 5 officers killed 6 Officers wounded 2 wounded missing 20 Officers Missing 40 O.R. killed 192 O.R. wounded 40 R wounded missing 93 O.R. missing	
Support	17 Aug		In positions as above.	
	17 Aug	9 pm	Battn moved back to VLAMERTINGE No 3 Area H 17 a. 0 9, arriving about 11 pm	Sheet 28 New war sheet 5a 1/20.000

T.134. Wt. W708—776. 500000. 4/15. Sir J.C. & S.

Army Form C. 2118.

WAR DIARY
or
INTELLIGENCE SUMMARY.
(Erase heading not required.)

Instructions regarding War Diaries and Intelligence Summaries are contained in F. S. Regs., Part II. and the Staff Manual respectively. Title pages will be prepared in manuscript.

Place	Date	Hour	Summary of Events and Information	Remarks and references to Appendices
H.17.a.0.9.	18 Aug.		In bivouac Camp VLAMERTINGHE No 3 area.	WD/m
	18 Aug.	5 pm	Bn marches to VLAMERTINGHE and Entrained; on completion of which moved by train to WATOU No. 3 Area, arriving about 8 p.m.	WD/m
WATOU No. 3 area.	18/20 Aug.		Bn in Camp - reorganizing and refitting.	WD/m
do.	20 Aug.	3.55 pm	Battalion marched to billets at GODWAERSVELDE arriving about 7 pm.	WD/m
GODWAERSVELDE	20/22 Aug.	-	Battalion in billets at do.	WD/m
do.	22 Aug.	4.35 am	Battalion marches to BRUINCHOVE, and Entrained on branch to VI Corps III Army.	WD/m
		8.31 am	Moved by train from BRUINCHOVE, and arrived at MIRAUMONT about 5 pm, detrained and marched to ACHIET-LE-PETIT arriving about 7 pm	WD/m
ACHIET-LE-PETIT	22 Aug.		Orders received that 7th + 8th Bn. R. INNIS Fus would amalgamate on 23rd Aug.	WD/m
do.	23 Aug.		The Battalion was amalgamated with 7th (S) Bn R. INNIS Fus, as the 7th/8th R. INNIS Fus under the command of Lt. Col. H. N. YOUNG D.S.O. Strength of Bn on amalgamation 15 Offrs. 431 O.R.	

T.1134. Wt. W708-776. 500000. 4/15. Sir J. C. & S.

Army Form C. 2118.

WAR DIARY
or
INTELLIGENCE SUMMARY.
(Erase heading not required.)

Instructions regarding War Diaries and Intelligence Summaries are contained in F.S. Regs., Part II. and the Staff Manual respectively. Title pages will be prepared in manuscript.

Place	Date	Hour	Summary of Events and Information	Remarks and references to Appendices
			Strength of Bn. at beginning of month. 29 Officers 810 O.R.	
			Strength on 28rd August 1917. 15 " 431 "	
			Officer casualties on 16.8.17 as under.	
			2/Lt. L.C. BROWN	
			2/Lt. R.R. CATHCART	
			2/Lt. A.B. BUCKWORTH } killed in action	
			2/Lt. C.D NEALON, with R.I. Rifles atto	
			2/Lt. G.H. PARLEY	
			Capt. W.R. MAGUIRE, with Connaught Rangers atto } wounded	
			Capt. L.G.A CONSTABLE, M.C.	
			2/Lt. R.H. ROULSTONE	
			2/Lt. R.E. PALMGREN	
			2/Lt. S.J. HENDERSON	
			2/Lt. R.V. POLLEY	
			Lieut. C.A LE PETON } wounded and missing	
			2/Lt. J.S. CARROTHERS	

Army Form C. 2118.

WAR DIARY
or
INTELLIGENCE SUMMARY.

(Erase heading not required.)

Instructions regarding War Diaries and Intelligence Summaries are contained in F. S. Regs., Part II. and the Staff Manual respectively. Title pages will be prepared in manuscript.

VII.

Place	Date	Hour	Summary of Events and Information	Remarks and references to Appendices
	August		2/Lt. L.G.D. MACDOUGALD	
			2/Lt. J.L. CHARLESWORTH. 4th R.I. Regt. atta } Missing	weath
			2/Lt. M.P.L. Cooper to be Ty. Lieut. London Gazette 2.8.17	
			Lieut. M.P.L. Cooper struck off strength (In England until to return) 14.8.17	100Am
			The following officers joined during month:-	
			2/Lt. R.R. CATHCART 2/Lt. G.H. FARLEY 2/Lt. J.G. DUFF.	
			2/Lt. M.B. BUCKWORTH 2/Lt. L.G.D. MACDOUGALD — all on 10.8.17	Appm
			The following drafts were received	
			10.8.17 — 11 O.R.	
			19.8.17 — 22 O.R.	
			End of Period	
			27.8.17.	

A. Walker
Lieut.-Colonel, Commanding
8th (S) Battalion R. Innis. Fusiliers.

[Stamp: 8TH (S) BATTALION 27 AUG 1917]

SECRET   Copy No. 8

"B" R. INNISKILLING FUSILIERS OPERATION ORDER NO. 91/1   25/4/17.

Reference Operation Order No. 91 of to-day's date.

1.   Zero hour for the Assault on the 1st. Objective will be 9.30 a.m.
     Battalion will parade in the same place as to-day ready to march off
     at Zero minus 1½ hours in the order H.Q., "B" "C" "A" "D" Coys.
     Transport will be parked in their various positions by 8.30 a.m.
     instead of 8 a.m.

2.   Watches will be synchronised as follows — A motor cyclist with
     Signal Time will visit all Units between 6 a.m. and 7 a.m. on the
     26th. Signalling Officer will arrange to have Signallers' watches
     checked.

3.   Steel helmets, Box Respirators and P.H. Helmets will be worn.

4.   ACKNOWLEDGE.

                                              S. Coggins.
                                                        2/Lieut.,
                                                        a/Adjutant..,
                                    "B" R. Inniskilling Fusiliers....

ISSUED FOR INSTRUCTIONAL PURPOSES ONLY.

SECRET.   Copy No. 15

"B" BATTN. ROYAL INNISKILLING FUSILIERS OPERATION ORDER NO. 91.

25/4/17

Ref. Sketch Map 1/10,000.

1. The X Division in conjunction with Division on either flank will make an attack on enemy's position on the YTSCHEATE RIDGE on the 26th. April 1917.

2. The X Division will attack with two Brigades in the line and one Brigade in Reserve. The 49th. Infantry Brigade will attack on the left and the Y Infantry Brigade on the right. The Z Infantry Brigade will be in Reserve.

3. The boundaries between the 49th. Infantry Brigade and the Infantry Brigade on either flank will be as follows:—
With the Infantry Brigade on the right
German Line at P.4.d.80.40 – P.11.a.20.70 – P.11.a.28.30. – P.11.c.62.42. – P.17.d.00.90.
With the Infantry Brigade on the Left.
German Line at P.5.d.60.55. – P.11.b.45.30. – P.11.d.60.65. – OBVIOUS AVENUE (Exclusive) to P.17.b.20.60. – ESTAMINET P.17.b.60.05.
These boundaries will be entered in red on Map already issued.

4. The Objectives allotted to the 49th. Infantry Brigade are as marked on map already issued –
1st. Objective in BLUE
Final Objective in BLACK.

5. There will be a pause of ten minutes at the line marked in GREEN to allow of attacks on either flank to get up, and a similar pause on the line marked in BROWN, that is 50 yards to S. of S.P. "C"

6. The attack on the 1st. Objective will be made by the R. Irish Fus. on the Right and the "A" R. Innis. Fus. on the Left

7. The Support Battalion "B" R. Innis. Fus. will be disposed as follows
(a) "B" Coy. will report to O.C. "A" R. Innis. Fus. to act as "Moppers up"
(b) "D" Coy. .. .. R. Irish Fus. .. ..
(c) "A" Coy. will construct S.Ps. "A" "B" & "C" and will carry up their own material. Tools to be drawn at the Dump at P.5.a.95.95. One Platoon to each S.P.
(d) "C" Coy. will provide the following Carrying Parties each consisting of a platoon.
    (1) Carrying Party for 49th. M.G.C.
    (2) .. .. .. 49th. T.M.B.
    (3) .. .. to Brigade Advanced Dump at P.11.a.90.55.
"C" Coy's. Lewis Guns will be left at Battn. H.Q.
As soon as these Units have carried out their duties they will assemble in WORTLEULINGHEM VILLAGE and report to Battn. H.Q.

8. The "A" R. Irish Regt. will be in Brigade Reserve.
After the 1st. Objective has been captured and consolidated the "A" R. Irish Regt. will advance and go through the "A" R. Innis. Fus. and R. Irish Fus. and will make the Attack on the Final Objective.

9. Both positions will be consolidated as soon as captured.

10. All watches will be synchronised at Zero minus 4 and at Zero minus 2 hours by Brigade Major. The Adjutant will bring two watches to Advanced Brigade H.Q. for the purpose.

2.

11. **HEADQUARTERS.**
Advanced Brigade H.Q., will be at P.5.a.80.70.
Reserve Battalion H.Q. at P.5.a.50.70.
Support Battalion H.Q. at P.5.a.20.50.
Right Battalion H.Q. at P.4.d.90.85.
Left Battalion H.Q. at CHALK PIT, P.5.a.80.30.

12. **ARTILLERY – GENERAL DESCRIPTION.**
A Bombardment of the enemy's positions will take place on V. W. X. Y days
The assault will take place Z day at Zero Hour.
The Heavy Artillery will bombard the crest of the Ridge and various selected points on enemy's front and do counter battery work.
The Field Artillery will form a Creeping Barrage along a line 100 yards short of the German Front Line.
A standing barrage on the German Support Trenches which will move forward on succeeding lines and S.P's as the creeping barrage progresses.
The creeping barrage will move forward at the rate of 100 yards in 4 minutes, pausing for 10 minutes 150 yards beyond the GREEN Line and then creep forward 150 yards beyond the BLUE line where it will remain, the rate of fire being reduced.
The Barrage will also pause for 10 minutes 150 yards beyond the BROWN Line.

13. **STRONG POINTS.**
As soon as the 1st. Objective has been carried, S.Ps. will be constructed
A At P.11. Central and
B At P.11.b.50.50.
and as soon as the Final Objective has been carried
C At B.17.b.10.70.

14. A Contact aeroplane will fly over the area of attack from Zero hour to Zero plus 2½ hours.
Flares will be lit by the leading infantry at the following hours or whenever the aeroplane asks for them by means of a succession of A's on a Claxton Horn or by a Very Light –
Zero plus 40 minutes
Zero plus 70 minutes
Zero for attack on Final Objective plus 20 minutes
Zero for attack on Final Objective plus 38 minutes.

15. A Dump of S.A.A. &c., will be formed at P.11.a.90.55.
Dumps of S.A.A. bombs and R.E. material will be formed at P.5.a.95.95 and P.4.b.90.25.

16. "B" & "D" Coys. will report to Battn. H.Q. of the Units to which they are to be attached at Zero minus 1 Hour.
Time and Order of march of Battalion from present Billets will be notified later.

17. Zero hour will be notified later.

18. **SIGNALLING ARRANGEMENTS.**
Communications will be maintained in accordance with "Forward Intercommunication in Battle".
TELEPHONE SERVICE.
Brigade Forward Station will advance with the last wave of the attack and will be established at P.11.a.63.99. Battn. Forward Posts should be established as near to this point as possible, and lines should be laid in to Brigade Forward Station as soon as this has been done.
As soon as the First objective has been reached Brigade Forward Station will move to P.11.a.98.40 and Battalion Forward Posts should again be established as near as possible and lines laid in.
D1 cable will be issued to Battalions for the Scheme if available and failing this enamelled wire should be used.

18 (contd). VISUAL.

Visual should be used direct where possible to prevent congestion at Brigade Forward Station.

Lamps will be issued to Battalions for Visual and Aeroplane Contact.

19. MEDICAL ARRANGEMENTS.

1. GENERAL IDEA.

(a). For the assault each Regtl. M.O. should have at his disposal, 1 N.C.O. and 8 Bearers R.A.M.C. from the Field Ambulance to assist the Regtl. Stretcher Bearers (Regtl. S.B's.) in clearing the area in front of the R.A.P.

(b). 10% of casualties are expected at each Objective. Of these 80% will probably be able to walk, 20% will require carriage.

Probable Fighting Strength -
- 1st Objective, 1200.
- "Moppers Up" and) Carrying Parties) 500
- 2nd Objective. 700.
- 2400.

giving total casualties with stretcher cases.

2. PREPARATIONS.

(a). Regtl. M.O's will prepare Casualty Labels in accordance with the figures in 1(b). Labels can be obtained if required from O.C. 112th F.A.

(b). Condemned First Field Dressings will, if available, be used Regimentally.

(c). The O.C. 112th F.A. will provide small Red Cross flags for marking the R.A.P's.

3. ORDERS FOR ASSAULT.

(a) The M.O's. R. Irish Fus. and "A" R. Innis. Fus. will establish R.A.Ps. close to their respective Battalion H.Q.

(b) The M.O. "B" R. Innis. Fus. will hold himself in readiness to establish an R.A.P? forward that Flank on which casualties are reported as heaviest.

(c) The M.O. "A" R. Irish Regt. will hold himself in readiness to move forward with his Battn.

(d) The following paras. will be considered as taking effect if permitted by hostile barrage.

(e) As soon as the first objective is captured and held and the R.A.Ps. clear of wounded, the M.O. R. Irish Fus. and "A" R. Innis. Fus. will move forward their R.A.Ps. to points close to the GREEN Line

(f) As soon as the 2nd. Objective has been captured and held the M.O. "A" R. Irish Regt. will establish his R.A.P?in the neighbourhood of the 1st. Objective.

20. Transport Officer will park 8 limbers to represent NORTH HOUSE ESTAMINET and HOUSES on road at Final Objective by 8 a.m.
Transport Officer will form by 8 a.m. on 26th. the following dumps
(i) 15 boxes S.A.A. and 15 boxes Bombs at P.5.a.95.95.
(ii) "   "   "   "   "   "   "   "   at P.4.b.90.25.
Half the Battalion's picks and shovels will be dumped at P.5.a.95.95 and other half at P.4.b.90.25.

21. The Drummers of the Brigade with their drums will represent the Creeping Barrage. They will report to Major Farmer at P.5.a.45.70. at 8.30a.m.

22 ACKNOWLEDGE.

J. Coggins
2/Lieut.,
a/Adjutant.,
"B" R. Inniskilling Fusrs......

Issued through Signals

```
Copy No.  1 to O.C. "A" Coy.
 "    "   2  "  "   "B"  "
 "    "   3  "  "   "C"  "
 "    "   4  "  "   "D"  "
 "    "   5  "  2nd in Command.
 "    "   6  "  Transport Officer.
 "    "   7  "  Medical Officer.
 "    "   8  "  Signalling Officer.
 "    "   9  "  R. Irish Fus.
 "    "  10  "  "A" R. Innis. Fus.
 "    "  11  "  49th M.G.Coy.
 "    "  12  "  49th T.M.B.
 "    "  13  "  H.Q. 49th I.B.
 "    "  14/15 Retained.
```

LH.

Second Army Q/1173/22.

II Corps.
VIII Corps.
IX Corps.
X Corps.
XIV Corps.
II ANZAC.

With reference the Second Army Traffic Map of 20/4/17.

The arrow near the letters N. O. in DRANOUTRE should be reversed as this portion of the road is a continuation of "Artillery Road", the traffic on which is from North to South.

G M Darell Major
DAQMG

A. H. Q.
27th May 1917.

Major-General,
D.A. & Q.M.G. SECOND ARMY.

Copies to all concerned.

LH.

49th. I.B. No. S.C.C.X1/108

2nd.R.Irish Regt.
7th. R.Innis. Fus.
6th. R.Innis. Fus. ✓
7/8th. R.Irish Fus.

    Herewith 1 copy of Second Army Traffic Map dated 20.4.17 together with a copy of Second Army letter G/1173/22 dated 27.5.1917.

    Please acknowledge receipt. ✓

3.6.17.

                                     Captain,
                     Staff Captain, 49th. Infantry Brigade.

S E C R E T.   49th. I.B. S.C.C. X1/100
_____   _____

2nd. R.Irish Regt.
7th. R.Innis., Fus.
8th. R.Innis. Fus.
7/8th. R.Irish Fus.
49th. M.G.Coy.

          Herewith Map (16th. Div. No.G/16/4)
of Traffic Routes, IX Corps Area.

    Please acknowledge.

                                            Captain,
26.5.17.   Staff Captain, 49th. Inf. Brigade.

SECRET.

2/Lieut. Polly.

8th. Royal Inniskilling Fusiliers

Reference Copy of Preliminary Instructions for Offensive Action given you to day after the heading, MOPPERS UP. Line 19. add:-

"Assembly Point WREN WAY S.or BIRR STREET behind "C"Coys. 1st Wave.

Please acknowledge.

[signature]

May May 23rd. 1917.

Lieut. & A/Adjutant.
7/8th. Royal Irish Fusiliers

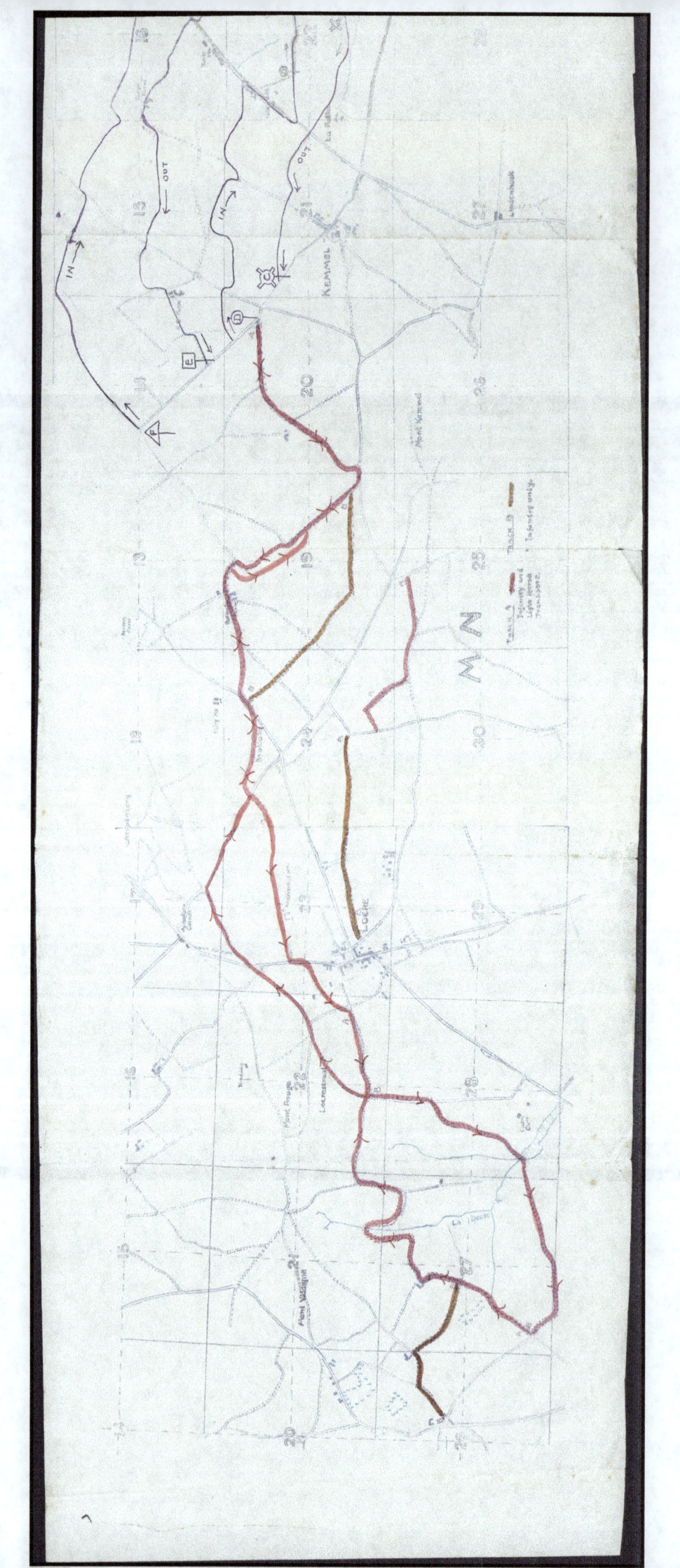

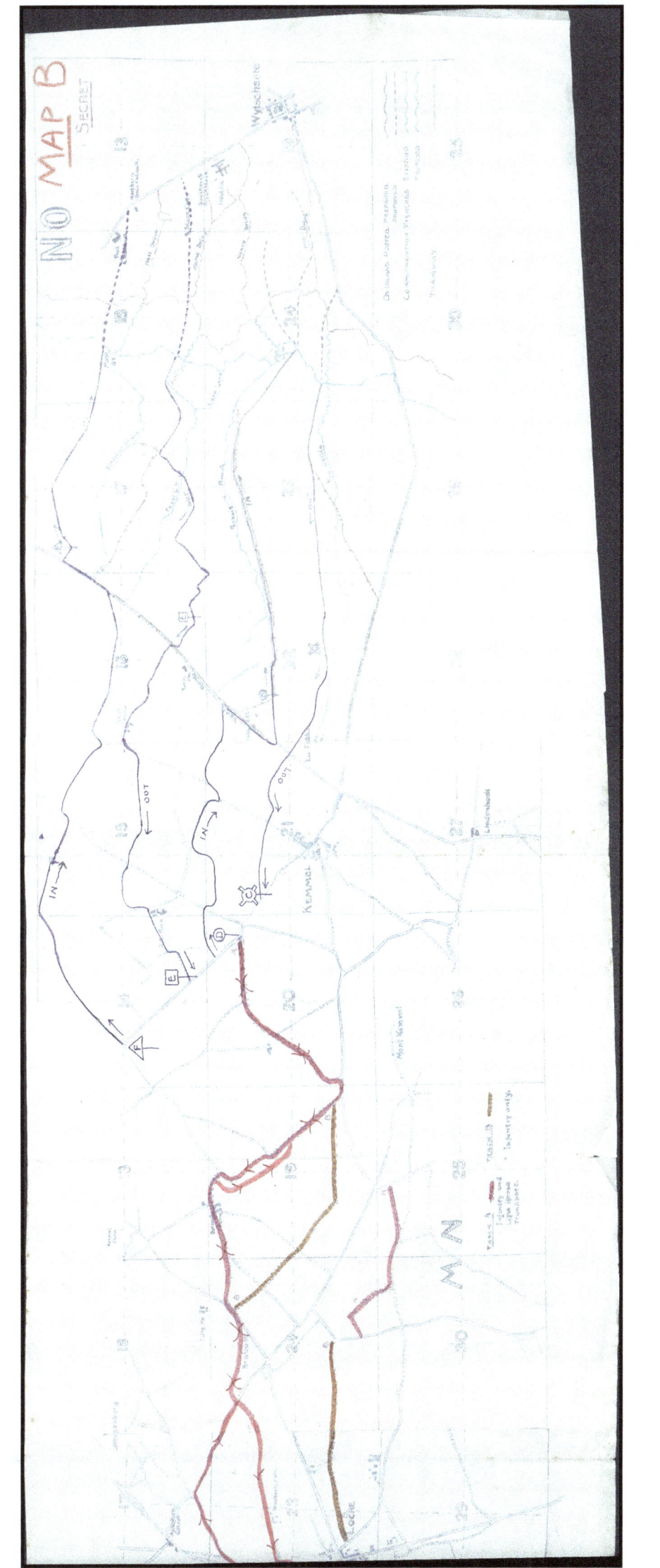

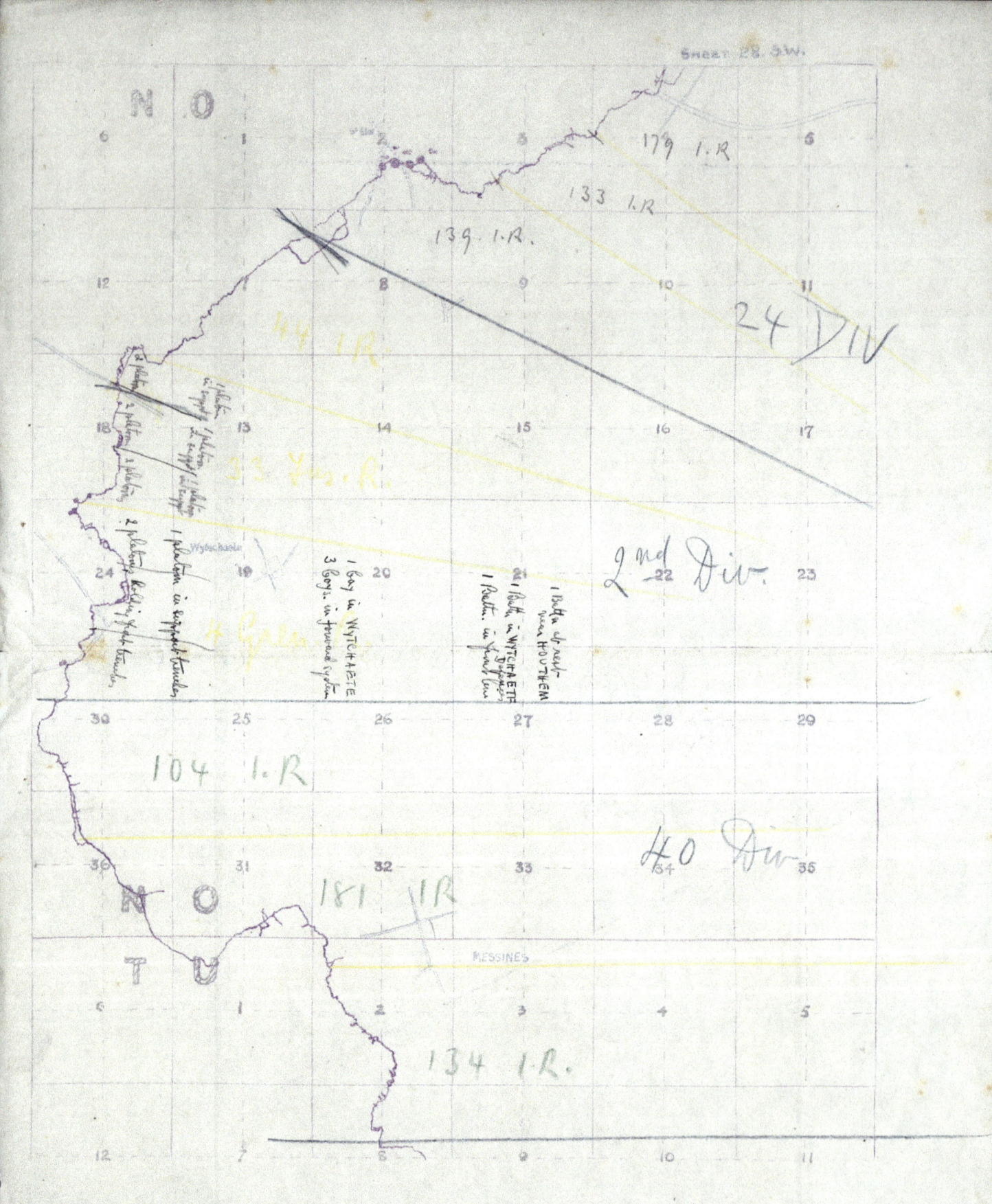

TRAFFIC ROUTES — IX CORPS —

Sheet 28. Scale 1:40,000

Legend:
- All traffic both ways ....
- Horse traffic both ways -----
- Lorry traffic one way →
- Horse traffic both ways ⇉
- Horse traffic only one way →
- Corps Boundary ....

IX Corps Topo Sec: 22.5.17
O.C.T.M.12

SECRET.   PRELIMINARY INSTRUCTIONS NO.1.   COPY.NO........
                    BY.
              Major.T.F.O'Donnell M.C.
         Commanding 7/8th.Royal Irish Fusiliers.   May 23rd.1917.

1. GENERAL PLAN.

The Attack on WYTSCHAETE RIDGE will be made by the 16th.Division with Divisions on either flank.
The attack by the 16th.Division will be made by:-
(a) 47th.Infantry Brigade on the Right.
    49th.Infantry Brigade on the Left.
    48th.Infantry Brigade in Reserve.

(b) The objectives allotted to the 7/8th.Royal Irish Fusiliers are:-
   (1) NANCY SUPPORT marked on Map by a series of Red Dashes.
   (2) RED LINE.
   (3) NANCY DRIVE, marked on Map by Series of Blue Dashes.
   (4) BLUE LINE.

(c) The Boundaries of the Battalion are:-
   (1) With the 47th.Infantry Brigade on the Right:-
       German Line at N.24.a.60.25.---North Corner of PETIT BOIS
       (N.24.b.4.9.)NORTH---WEST Corner BOIS DE WYTSCHAETE(N.24.b.75.80)
       ---South Corner of HOSPICE--- German Line N.of this Boundary
       is marked on Map by broad YELLOW LINE.

   (2) Left Boundary with the 7th.Royal Inniskilling Fusiliers is
       marked on Map with a PURPLE Line and is as follows:-
       N.17.b.80.00.---SHANNON TRENCH at N.18.a.32.00.---our Front Line
       at N.18.a.55.00.---German Front Line at N.18.a.80.75.---along
       a line 30.yards South of NAIL DRIVE----Southern Corner of
       UNNAMED WOOD--O.13.c.80.15;30.yards North of the Junction of
       OBVIOUS DRIVE AND NANCY DRIVE.This Boundary is shewn in purple.

TIME.   The following will be the times of Arrival and Departures from the various Coloured Lines.

         RED LINE   Arrive   0.35.
                     Depart. 1.05.
         BLUE LINE   Arrive   1.40.

ATTACK. The attack on the RED LINE will be made by "A"Coy.on the Right.
         "B" Coy on the Left.

         The Attack on the BLUE LINE will be by "C"Coys on the RIGHT
         and "D"Coy on the Left.
         Boundaries between Companies are:-
         Between "A" and "B"Coys. Point of Salient N.18.c.66.54,----
         German Front Line at N.18.d.27.18.---along a line running
         about 30.yards south of NAIL LANE to N.18.d.99.10.

         Boundaries between "C" and "D"Coys are:-
         N.18.d.99.10.---along a line running North of NAME DRIVE to
         NORTH Corner of the Hospice(Inclusive to Right Coy.)at
         O.19.c.84.95.
         Shown on attached Map by a thin Pencil Line.

WAVES   The Battalion will attack in four waves:-
         "A" and "B"Coys.first wave will occupy RED LINE.
         "A" and "B"Coys.second wave will occupy DOTTED RED LINE.
         "C" and "D"Coys First wave will occupy BLUE LINE.
         "C" and "D"Coys. Second Line will occupy Dotted Blue Line.

SHEET. 2.

ASSEMBLY POSITIONS.

"A" Company in front line from N.18.c.48.85. to point of Salient at N.18.c.67.55. Boundary between Platoons will be Bay.59 (N.18.c.57.43.) inclusive to left Platoon.

"B" Coy. in front line from Point of Salient at N.18.c.67.55. to N.18.d.55.00. (Bay.64.inclusive) Boundary between Platoons Bay 53. (N.18.c.54.80.) inclusive to left Platoon.

"C" Coy's first wave in WREN WAY from N.18.c.90.00. to BIRR TRENCH.
"C" Coy's Second Wave in Fermoy Trench from VAN KEEP to BIRR TRENCH.

"D" Coy's first wave in WREN WAY from BIRR TRENCH to CROWBAR TRENCH.
"D" Coy's Second Wave in FERMOY TRENCH from BIRR TRENCH to CROWBAR TRENCH.

MOPPERS UP.

One Company of the 8th. Royal Inniskilling Fusiliers will be attached to the Battalion to act as "Moppers-up."
Their Distribution and objectives are:-
1. Platoon in rear of First Wave
½ Platoon attached to "B" Coy. to "Mop-up" NANCY SUPPORT and along NAIL LANE up to and in BLACK COT.
Assembly Point in Front Line behind "B" Coy.

½ Platoon attached "A" Coy. to "Mop-up" dug outs at the junction of NAME SUPPORT and NAME DRIVE, NANCY SUPPORT. Assembly Point in Front Line behind "A" Company.

2. PLATOONS IN REAR OF 3rd. WAVE.
½ Platoon attached to "D" Coy. to "Mop-up" Dug outs round point O.13.c.72.15. Assembly Point in WREN WAY. N. of BIRR TRENCH behind "D" Coy's 1st. Wave.

1½ Platoons attached to "C" Coy. ½ Platoon to work along trench running S.E. from O.19.a.16.92. to dug outs at O.19.a.44.70. The One Platoon to go straight to the HOSPICE.
When these "Mopping Up" parties of the 8th.R.Innis Fusrs have completed their tasks, they will report the fact at Battalion H.Qrs.
Assembly Point - WREN WAY S of BIRR STRET behind C Coys 1st Wave

CARRYING PARTIES.

One Platoon 8th. Royal Innis Fusrs. will act as carrying party to the Battalion. Assembly Position in rear of Fourth Wave behind "D" Coy. in FERMOY TRENCH from BIRR TRENCH to CROWBAR TRENCH. This Party will carry shovels in first journey and loads of S.A.A., Bombs, Full Lewis Gun Magazines on subsequent journeys. All material will be dumped at BLACK COT. One Dump for S.A.A., one for Bombs, one for tools &c.
Dumps should be made about 20.yards apart so as to avoid the possibilit of all material being destroyed by the same shell.

VICKERS. Two.

The Vickers Guns will move behind the Fourth Wave, and will take up a favourable position in the neighbourhood of the BLACK COT from which to cover the advance on the BLUE LINE.
When the BLUE LINE has been taken, they will move forward to neighbourhood of the SOUTHERN BRICKSTACK, and assist in consolidating and in forming the Machine Gun Barrage for the attack on the GREEN and BLACK LINES.
They must be prepared to support the 3rd. and 4th. Waves at any point in the attack on the BLUE LINE, either by filling gaps in the assaulting waves, or by putting a barrage on any STRONG POINT. The two Guns will work conjointly.
Assembly Point will be in FERMOY TRENCH between BIRR TRENCH and CROWBAR TRENCH

(Continued on Page 3.)

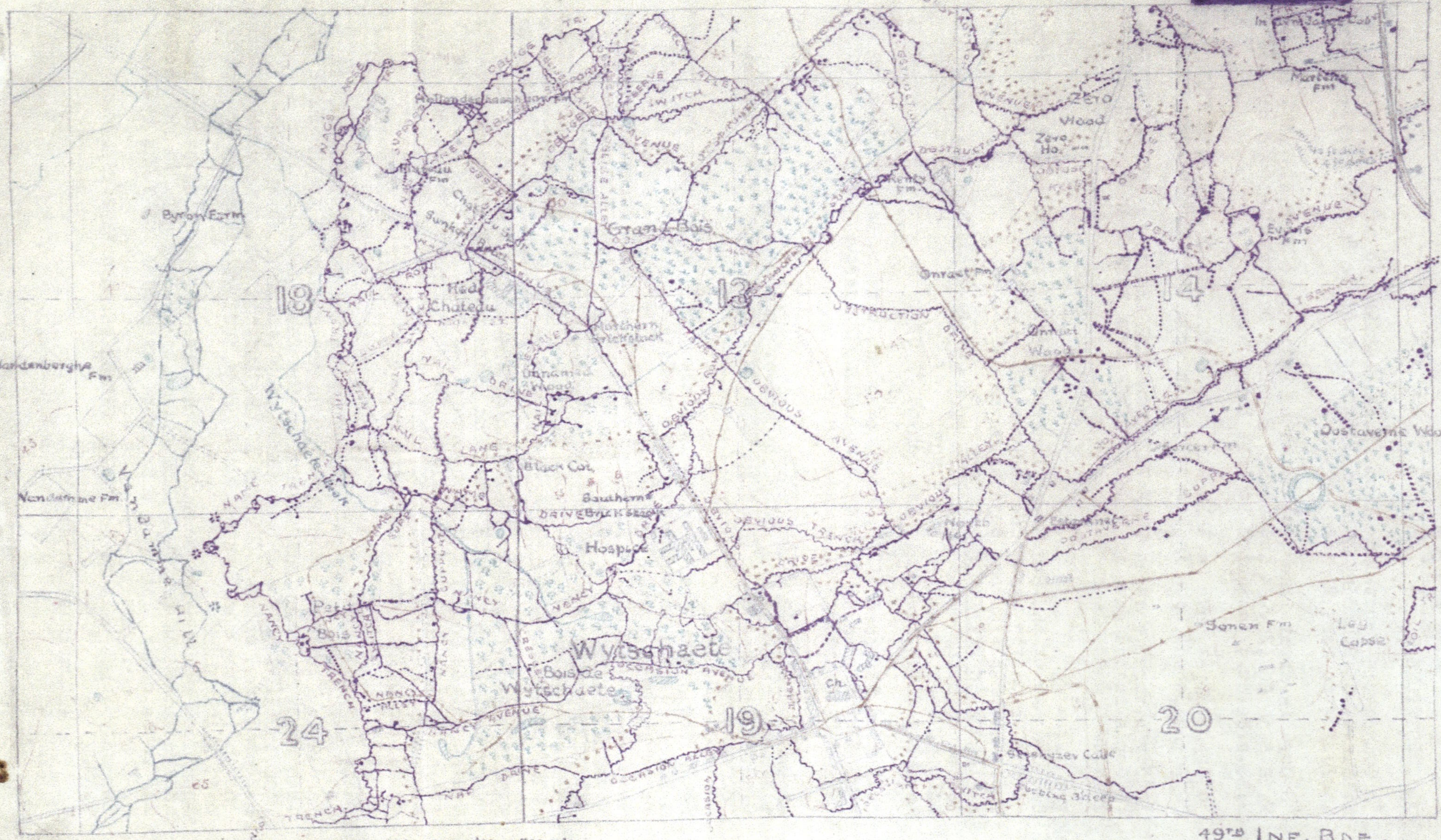

SCALE. 1/10,000. 100 0 100 200 300 400 500 yds.

49TH INF. BDE.

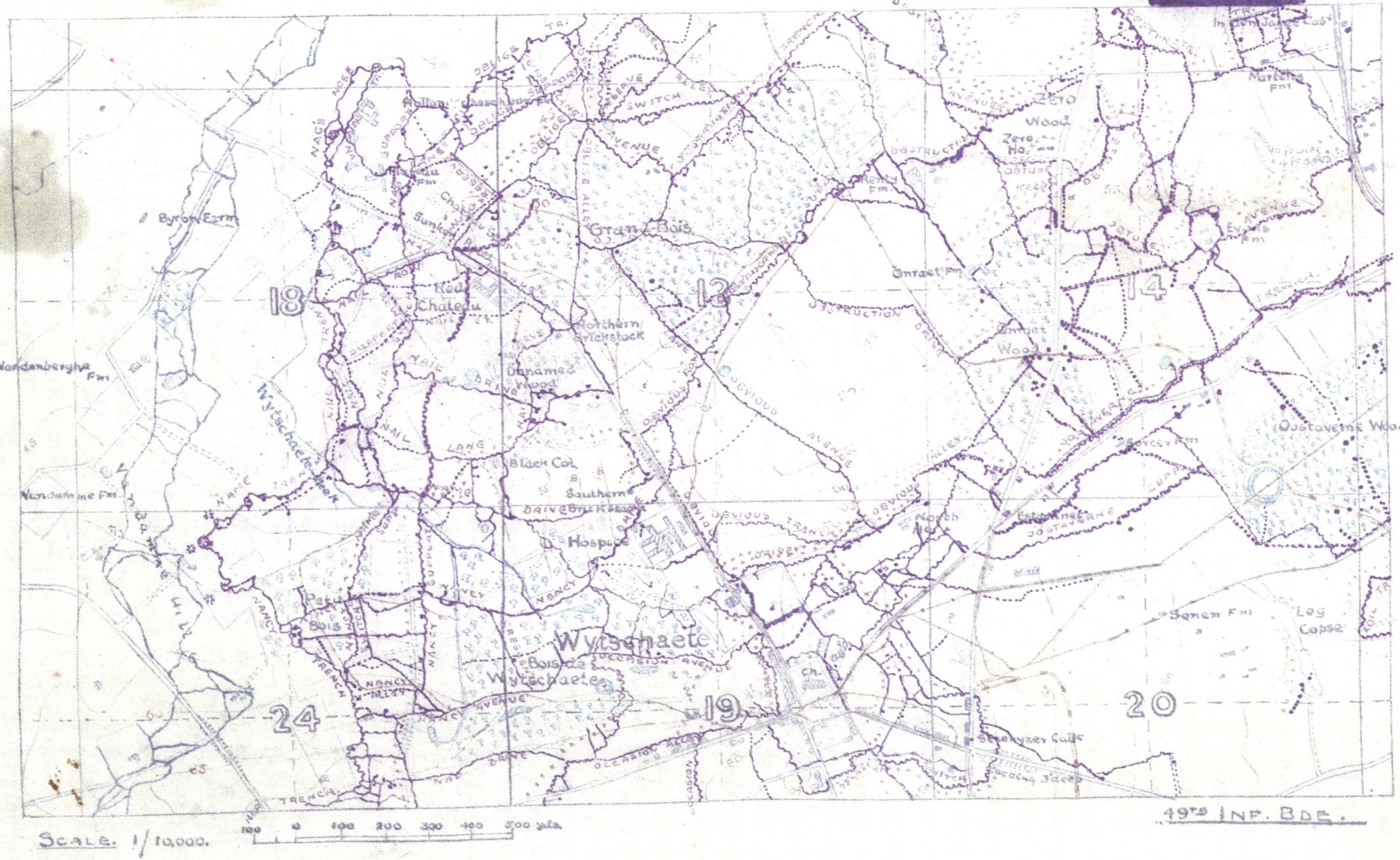

Grand Bois
Wytschaete
Bois de Wytschaete
Oostaverne Wood
Zero Wood
Onraet Wood
Unnamed Wood
Red Chateau
Northern Brickstack
Southern Brickstack
Hospice
Black Cot.
Byron Farm
Vandenberghe Fm
Vandamme Fm
Onraet Fm
Senen Fm
Leg Copse
North Ho.
Zero Ho.
Petit Bois
Wytschaete Beek
OBSTRUCTION
OBVIOUS TRENCH
OBVIOUS AVENUE
OCCASION AVENUE
OCCASION ALLEY
NANCY AVENUE
NANCY ALLEY
NAIL LANE
NAIL DRIVE
OBLIGE AVENUE
OBLIGE ALLEY
SWITCH
18
13
14
24
19
20
SCALE. 1/10,000.
100 0 100 200 300 400 500 yds.
49th INF. BDE.

Copy No 5

SECRET. 49th I.B. No. S.O.60
25th May, 1917.

49TH INFANTRY BRIGADE INSTRUCTIONS FOR THE OFFENSIVE.

These Preliminary Instructions are issued to give Commanding Officers an opportunity to study the possible Offensive and to make arrangements accordingly.

The Instructions are not complete and will be added to and amended from time to time.

These Instructions will on no account be taken in front of the VIERSTRAAT SWITCH and recipients are responsible that they are kept locked up.

ACKNOWLEDGE. ✓

                                                                    Captain,
Brigade Major, 49th Infantry Brigade.

Issued through Signals.

```
Copy No.  1 to  G. O. C.
   "      2      Staff Captain,
   "      3      2nd R. Irish Regt.
   "      4      7th R. Innis Fus.
   "      5      8th R. Innis Fus.
   "      6      7/8th R. Irish Fus.
   "      7      49th M.G. Company.
   "      8      49th T.M. Battery.
   "      9      Brigade Signal Officer.
   "     10      Bde. Intelligence Officer.
   "     11      16th Division.
   "     12      16th Division.
   "     13      47th Inf. Bde.
   "     14      48th Inf. Bde.
   "     15      57th Inf. Bde.
   "     16      177th Bde, R.F.A.
   "     17      157th Field Coy, R.E.
   "     18-19  War Diary.
         20     File.
```

SECRET.   Copy No. 5

49TH INFANTRY BRIGADE INSTRUCTIONS FOR THE OFFENSIVE.

GENERAL PLAN.

1. The Attack on the WYTSCHAETE RIDGE will be made by the 16th Division in conjunction with Divisions on either flank.

   (a) The 16th Division will attack with two Infantry Brigades in the line and one Infantry Brigade in Reserve.

   Right Attack.   47th Infantry Brigade.
                            156th Field Coy, R.E.
                            1 Company 11th Hants (Pioneers).

   Left Attack.   49th Infantry Brigade.
                            157th Field Coy, R.E.
                            1 Company 11th Hants (Pioneers).

   Divisional Reserve.   48th Infantry Brigade.
                            155th Field Coy, R.E.
                            11th Hants Pioneers (less 2 Coys).

   (b) The Boundaries between the 49th Infantry Brigade and the Brigades on either flank are as follows :-

   Right Boundary (with 47th Inf. Bde.)

   German Line at N.24.a.60.85 - North Corner of PETIT BOIS (N.24.b.4.9) - N.W. Corner of BOIS DE WYTSCHAETE (N.24.b.75.80) - South Corner of HOSPICE (O.19.a.70.70) - point where tramway crosses ST.ELOI - MESSINES road at O.20.a.20.30 - O.20.a.40.25.

   Left Boundary (with 19th Division).

   German line at N.18.b.23.53 - VIERSTRAAT-WYTSCHAETE Road (inclusive) to NORTHERN BRICKSTACK (O.13.c.32.88) - South Corner of GRAND BOIS (O.13.c.92.70) - OBVIOUS AVENUE (exclusive) - ESTAMINET Cross Roads (O.20.a.30.87).

   These Boundaries are shown in YELLOW on Map A.

   (c) The objectives allotted to the 49th Infantry Brigade and to the Infantry Brigades on either flank are shown as follows on Map A.

   1st Objective .... RED.
   2nd Objective .... BLUE.
   3rd Objective .... GREEN.
   4th Objective .... BLACK.

   (d) The following will be the times of arrival and departure from the various coloured lines :-

   RED LINE   Arrive 0.35.
                    depart 1.05.

   BLUE LINE   Arrive 1.40.
                    depart 3.40.

   GREEN LINE   Arrive 4.10.
                    depart 4.30.

   BLACK LINE   Arrive 4.40.

CONSOLIDATION AND STRONG POINTS.

2. With the exception of the GREEN LINE, all objectives denoted by coloured lines are to be consolidated as rapidly as possible after capture.

157th Field Company, R.E. will construct three Strong Points :-

    RED POST   O.13.c.15.90.
    BLACK POST O.13.c.40.25.
    OBVIOUS POST O.19.b.30.80.

The locations of these Strong Points are only approximate. Their exact positions will be decided on the spot. RED POST will be put in hand first.

As soon as the construction of a Strong Point is complete, the R.E. Officer in charge will report the fact to the Officer Commanding the Battalion in whose Area the Strong Point is, i.e.-

7th R. Innis Fus. in the case of RED POST.
7/8th R. Irish Fus. in the case of BLACK POST.
2nd R. Irish Regt. in the case of OBVIOUS POST.

The Battalion Commanders concerned will then detail one Platoon with its Lewis Gun to garrison the Strong Point. The R.E. Party will not leave a Strong Point until the Infantry Garrison takes it over.

Battalion Commanders of the three Assaulting Battalions are responsible that the work of consolidation is carried on as long as they remain in the line, and for handing it over to any troops by whom they may be relieved. It must be impressed on all ranks that no consolidation is to be considered complete until the position has been well wired.

As soon after its capture as possible, the wiring of the BLACK LINE will be carried out under R.E. supervision by parties of the 48th Infantry Brigade, specially detailed for this purpose.

The R.E. will search for and open up the following sources of water supply :-

    RED CHATEAU SUPPLY   N.18.b.80.28.
    HOSPICE SUPPLY.   O.13.c.3.2.
    On Road N. of WYTSCHAETE CHURCH O.19.b.80.35.

The following signboards will be prepared beforehand and placed in position by the R.E. as soon as possible :-

(a) IN and OUT boards on all Routes and Communication trenches.
(b) Direction Boards at road and trench junctions, and in the village of WYTSCHAETE.
(c) Boards and notices at the various Dumps, Farms, Strong Points and other important localities in the captured positions.

2.

(c) The attack on the RED and BLUE LINES will be made by the 7/8th R. Irish Fus. on the Right and the 7th R. Innis Fus. on the Left.

The Boundary between these two Battalions is as follows -

N.17.b.80.00 - SHANNON TRENCH at N.18.a.30.00 - our front line at N.18.a.55.00 - German front line at N.18.d.30.75 - along a line 30 yards south of NAIL DRIVE - Southern Corner of UNNAMED WOOD - O.13.c.80.15 20 yards north of the Junction of OBVIOUS DRIVE and NANCY DRIVE. This boundary is shown in PURPLE on Map A.

The attack on the GREEN and BLACK Lines will be made by the 2nd R. Irish Regt.

The 8th R. Innis Fus. will provide Moppers Up, Carrying Parties, etc.

CONSOLIDATION AND STRONG POINTS. 2.

With the exception of the GREEN LINE all lines will be consolidated after capture.

The 157th Field Coy. R.E. (under the orders of the C.R.E. 10th Division) will establish Strong Points to hold one Platoon as follows :-

See attached

(a) As soon as the BLUE Line has been captured.

Strong Point A at ....

Strong Point B at ....

(b) As soon as the BLACK Line has been captured.

Strong Point C at ....

As soon as the construction of a Strong Point is complete, the R.E. Officer in charge will report the fact to the Officer Commanding the Battalion in whose Area the Strong Point is. The Battalion Commander concerned will then detail one platoon with its Lewis Gun to garrison the Strong Point. The R.E. Party will not leave a Strong Point until the Infantry Garrison takes it over.

MOPPERS UP. 3.

One Company of the 8th R. Innis Fus. will be attached to the 7th R. Innis Fus. and one Company to the 7/8th R. Irish Fus. to act as "Moppers Up".

Special Parties of "Moppers Up" must be detailed for RED CHATEAU, UNNAMED WOOD, BLACK COT and the HOSPICE.

The 2nd R. Irish Regt. will provide their own "Moppers Up".

When the Mopping Up parties of the 8th R. Innis Fus. attached to the 7th R. Innis Fus. and 7/8th R. Irish Fus. have completed their task, they will report the fact to Battalion Commanders concerned, who will send them back to the 8th R. Innis Fus. assembly position in YUM YUM TRENCH, if he no longer requires them.

ACTION OF MACHINE GUNS. 4.

(1) Two guns of the 49th Machine Gun Company will be attached to each of the following Battalions :-

2nd R. Irish Regt.
7th R. Innis Fus.
7/8th R. Irish Fus.

They will work in pairs, each pair under a competent Machine Gun Officer, and in each case will accompany the final wave. These guns will not be used for indirect or barrage fire.

(ii) The general role of these guns will be :-

    (a) To protect the assaulting battalions against Counter-attacks during the assault.

    (b) After the capture of the BLUE and BLACK LINES to assist the consolidation by taking up positions to cover the ground in front of these lines.

    (c) To take advantage of good, fleeting targets in order to inflict loss on the enemy.

    (d) To cover the front of any gap which may occur in our lines.

(iii) The above tasks can best be carried out by the guns attached to the 7th R. Innis Fus. advancing on the line N.18.b.15.20 - N.18.b.60.05 - Northern edge of UNNAMED WOOD and eventually taking up a position in the vicinity of the NORTHERN BRICKSTACK.

    The guns attached to the 7/8th R. Irish Fus. should advance on the line N.18.d.20.55 - N.18.d.60.40 - Southern edge of UNNAMED WOOD and eventually taking up a position in the vicinity of O.13.c.70.15.

    The guns attached to the 2nd R. Irish Regt. should advance on the line O.13.c.80.20 - O.19.b.60.20 -eventually taking up a position in the vicinity of O.20.a.00.80.

(iv) In the event of the attack on either flank of any Battalion to which these guns are attached positions must at once be taken up to cover those flanks.

(v) Every effort must be made to get forward an adequate supply of ammunition for these six guns.

5.

ACTION OF STOKES MORTARS:

2 Mortars of the 49th Trench Mortar Battery will be attached to the 7th R. Innis Fus. and will move to a central position (To be chosen). These Mortars will be available to deal with opposition in RED CHATEAU, UNNAMED WOOD and OBVIOUS ROW as required.

2 Mortars will be attached to the 7/8th R. Irish Fus. and will move to a central position (To be chosen.) These Mortars will be available to deal with opposition in NAIL LANE, BLACK COT and the HOSPICE as required.

When the BLUE LINE has been captured the mortars attached to the 7th R. Innis Fus. and the 7/8th R.Irish Fus. will move to positions from which they can cover it.

For the attack on the BLACK LINE 2 mortars will be attached to the 2nd R. Irish Regt. They will move to a position of assembly at (to be chosen), and will be available to overcome opposition as required. When the BLACK LINE has been captured these two mortars will move to positions from which they can cover it.

The remaining two mortars will be kept in Reserve.

When the BLACK LINE has been captured the mortars attached to the 7th R. Innis Fus. and 7/8th R.Irish Fus. will again come under the orders of the O.C. 49th Trench Mortar Battery.

4.

6.

CARRYING PARTIES.

The 8th R. Innis Fus. will provide carrying parties as follows :-

D Party (a) One Platoon to 49th Machine Gun Company. Robbins
E Party (b) One Platoon to 49th Trench Mortar Battery. CARRUTHERS
B Party (c) One Platoon to 7th R. Innis Fus. HENDERSON
C Party (d) One Platoon to 7/8th R. Irish Fus. L C Brown
A Party (e) One Platoon to 2nd R. Irish Regt. NOTLEY

The Carrying Parties mentioned in (c), (d) and (e) above will move just in rear of the last wave of assaulting Battalions, and will carry shovels on the first journey and mixed loads of S.A.A., full Lewis Gun magazines, rifle grenades, bombs, etc. on the second and subsequent journeys. These stores will be dumped at places selected by Battalion Commanders.

All carrying parties will carry 150 rounds of S.A.A. 100 rounds of which will be dumped at the forward dumps before returning for another load of stores.

The final assembly position for parties of the 8th R. Innis Fus. after completing their various tasks will be YUM YUM TRENCH from the VIERSTRAAT ROAD to N.18.a.15.26.

7.

ASSEMBLY POSITIONS.

(a) 7/8th R. Irish Fus.

Front Line from N.18.c.40.15 to N.18.a.50.00.

WREN WAY from N.18.c.35.35 to CROWBAR TRENCH.

FERMOY TRENCH from VAN KEEP to WATLING STREET.

(b) 7th R. Innis Fus.

Front Line from N.18.a.50.00 to VIERSTRAAT ROAD.

SHANNON TRENCH from N.18.a.35.00 to the VIERSTRAAT ROAD.

(c) 2nd R. Irish Regt.

CHINESE WALL LINE from WATLING STREET to VIERSTRAAT ROAD.

(d) 157th Field Company, R.E. and 2 platoons 11th Hants, Pioneers SHANTUNG TRENCH from S.P.13 (exclusive) to WATLING STREET.

(e) 1 platoon 8th R. Innis Fus. and spare Stokes Mortar Personnel - CORK TRENCH from WATLING STREET to N.18.c.10.55.

5.

Battalions will arrange in detail the positions of their Platoons allowing for their Moppers Up, Carrying Parties, etc, and submit their plan to Brigade Headquarters.
Company Headquarters will be detailed to each Company. If no suitable dugouts are in existence, units will select positions and inform the Brigade who will have them built if possible.

POSITIONS OF HEADQUARTERS

8. 49th Infantry Brigade Headquarters & Left Artillery Group H.Q.

THE RIB. N.16.d.35.50.

<u>7/8th R. Irish Fus.</u>   S.P. 13.

<u>7th R. Innis Fus.</u>   Off YUM-YUM TRENCH (N.18.a.15.45).

<u>2nd R. Irish Regt.</u>   S.P.13.

<u>8th R. Innis Fus.</u>   KNOLL DUGOUTS (N.12.a.90.55).   S.P.13 about

<u>49th Machine Gun Coy.</u>   SWATOW TRENCH (N.17.d.80.90).

<u>49th Trench Mortar Battery.</u>   SWATOW TRENCH. N.17.d.80.90.

<u>157th Field Coy. R.E.</u>   THE RIB.

The Forward Command Post of the 2nd R. Irish Regt. for the attack on the BLACK LINE will be at the Brigade Forward Station.
The Brigade Forward Station will follow the last wave of the attack on the BLUE LINE and will be established about O.13.c.15.45.
When the BLACK LINE has been captured, communication will be extended forward to O.19.b.75.85.

COMMUNICATION TRENCHES.

9. The 49th Infantry Brigade has been allotted two main Communication Trenches -

WATLING STREET   (IN TRENCH).

THE FOSSE.   (OUT TRENCH).

5 Communication Trenches connect the CHINESE WALL LINE with the PARK LINE. They will be allotted as follows :-

<u>Right Battalion.</u>   THE FOSSE (to be constructed).
CHOW STREET.
CORK TRENCH.

<u>Left Battalion.</u>   CLARE STREET (to be constructed).
USNAGH STREET (under construction).

4 Communication Trenches connect the PARK LINE with the Front Line.
They will be allotted as follows :-

<u>Right Battalion.</u>   BIRR TRENCH (to be rebuilt).
CROWBAR STREET (to be rebuilt).

<u>Left Battalion.</u>   TARA STREET (to be rebuilt).
MAYO STREET.

6.

The following roads in the forward area have been allotted to the 16th Division :-

(a) KEMMEL - WYTSCHAETE Road (Suicide Road).

(b) V.C.Road.

Four cross country routes (two to each Brigade Area) leading forward from KIM ROAD to the neighbourhood of WYTSCHAETE are being prepared for wheeled traffic as far forward as our front line.

These tracks are lettered C, D, E and F. D and F will be reserved for IN (or Eastward) traffic; C and E for OUT (or Westward) traffic.

Within our own lines the above routes will be marked with posts as below, and are shown on Map B.

DRESS. 10. All officers will be dressed and equipped the same as the men. Sticks are not to be carried.

Fighting Order for all ranks :-

(a) Clothing, arms and entrenching tool as issued.

(b) Equipment as issued with the exception of the pack. Haversacks to be worn on the back, except for Lewis Gunners and Rifle Bombers, who will wear it at the side.

(c) Box Respirators and P.H.Helmets.

(d) Iron Rations, unexpended portion of the day's rations. Mess tin and cover.

(e) 120 rounds S.A.A. except Bombers, Signallers, Runners, Lewis Gunners and Rifle Bombers who carry 50 rounds.
Carrying Parties - 50 rounds S.A.A.

(f) Every man (except Bombing Sections) 2 Mills Bombs, one in each top pocket. These bombs will be collected into dumps as soon as the objective has been gained.

(g) Flares will be carried in the bottom pockets of the jacket.

NOTE. Machine Gun Company, T.M.Battery and Carrying Parties will not carry (f) and (g).

(h) 3 sandbags per man.

(i) 2 full waterbottles.

(j) Mopping Up Parties will carry one "P" Bomb in addition to 2 Mills Bombs.

(k) Bombing Sections will carry :-

(i) Bayonet men - 6 Mills Bombs.
(ii) Remainder of Section - 12 Mills Bombs per man.

7.

    (1) Rifle Bombers will carry <u>12</u> Hales No. 20 or 24.

    (m) Bombing Sections of Mopping Up Parties will carry 10 Mills Bombs and 1 "P" Bomb per man.

    (n) Lewis Gun Sections will carry 30 drums. All spare drums will be formed into dumps as far forward as possible, under Battalion arrangements.

Officers or Other Ranks equipped with Very Pistols will carry 6 ~~rounds of 1" Very Lights~~. [*"Red Signal cartridges"*] Battalions will indent for sufficient Bombs, etc, to complete them to the above establishments, and will issue to the men before proceeding into assembly positions.

The advisability of providing Mopping Up Parties with a proportion of electric torches or candles for use when searching dugouts, etc, should not be lost sight of.

The provisions laid down in "Instructions for the Training of Divisions for Offensive Action", page 60, Section XXXII are to be carried out.

11. In making references to times before or after which operations will commence, the following nomenclature will be adopted in future :-

    (a) <u>Referring to days.</u>

    "Z" day is the day on which operations take place.

    One day before "Z" .... "Y" day.
    Two days before "Z" .... "X" day.
    Three days before "Z" .... "W" day.
    Four days before "Z" .... "V" day.
    Five days before "Z" .... "U" day.

    Days before "U" day will be referred to as "Z" minus 6, "Z" minus 7, "Z" minus 8, etc.

    One day after "Z" .... "A" day.
    Two days after "Z" .... "B" day.
    Three days after "Z" .... "C" days.

    Days after "C" day will be referred to as "Z" day plus 4, "Z" plus 5, "Z" plus 6, etc.

    (b) <u>Referring to hours on "Z" day.</u>

    Zero is the exact time at which operations will commence, and times will be designated in hours and minutes plus or minus from Zero, even if they encroach on "Y" day.

    (c) In making references to times before and after which operations will take place the symbols + or - are not to be used. The word "PLUS" or "MINUS" is to be written in full.
In referring to times before or after Zero hour, the words "Zero plus ....." or "Zero minus ...." must be inserted, so as to prevent possible confusion with clock times.

12. <u>MAPS OF OUR TRENCHES.</u> No marked maps of any description of our own lines are to be taken in advance of Battalion Headquarters by any Officer, N.C.O or Man. Commanding Officers are held responsible for seeing that these orders are made known to all ranks and for seeing that they are enforced.

13. (a) In order to prevent leakage of information and to ensure that other methods of communication are practised all communication by telephone, except that mentioned in sub-para (e) and messages sent on the Buzzer will cease in advance of YORK ROAD until the hour of Zero.

   (b) The following methods of communication will be permitted in front of YORK ROAD :-

   > Pigeons.
   > Visual.
   > Runners.
   > Fullerphones for "S.O.S" Calls.
   > Rockets for "S.O.S" Calls.

   N.B. All Fullerphones in front of YORK ROAD will either be issued without handsets, or have the microphone removed from the speaking circuits.

   (c) Existing S.O.S. Lines from Batteries to Companies are to be abolished; the batteries are to be connected to Battalion Headquarters only.

   (d) Companies in the front line will be connected to Battalion Headquarters. Fullerphones only will be used on those lines and are not to be used except for S.O.S. calls.

   (e) For communication between Brigade Headquarters and the Headquarters of Battalions in the line one telephone may be retained in each Battalion Commander's dugout.
   The Battalion Commander will be held responsible for preventing the use of this telephone by any unauthorised person, and for ensuring that no message that could be of any use to the enemy is sent or received over it.

   (f) Until after Zero hour no message will be sent by pigeon which contains anything in the address "to" or "from", or in the body of the message, which would be of value if it fell into the hands of the enemy.

14. The scale of S.A.A., grenades, etc, to be issued in addition to those already in Divisional charge together with their distribution amongst Brigade and Battalion Dumps is given in Appendix A.

15. Reference S.S.135, Section XXX, the numbers therein laid down will be left behind when the unit goes into the attack.
   They will be accommodated at the 1st Line Transport Lines, and will rejoin their units when the latter come out of the line. It is, however, left to the discretion of the Brigadier to send forward any Officers or men should he consider it necessary to do so in order to maintain the efficiency of any particular unit. No Officer, N.C.O or man of those left behind will rejoin their unit without the authority of the Brigadier.
   Nominal Rolls of Officers being left behind will be sent to Brigade Headquarters.

16.
INFORMATION. Battalion and other Commanders are reminded of the necessity of impressing on all ranks under their Command of the utmost importance of sending back frequent reports on the situation, in order that higher authority may be informed and arrangements made in time to take advantage of success as well as to give efficient support.

17.
GAINING OBJECTIVES. The necessity of pushing forward to their objectives regardless of the progress of units on either flank, must be impressed on all ranks. It should also be made known to them that the care of the wounded is not their province, as special people are detailed for this purpose.

18.
ENEMY RUSES. All men should be warned against the probable misuse of white flags and signs of surrender by the enemy, who has been known to sham death and then shoot into the back of our assault.

The possibility of the enemy using other ruses, such as giving the order "Retire", must be impressed on all ranks.

Deep dugouts in the enemy's lines should be treated with caution owing to the possibility of their being mined.

19.
SYNCHRONIZATION OF WATCHES. Watches will be synchronized at 12 noon daily from 1st June, under arrangements to be made by the Signal Service.

20.
WIRE CUTTING. Wire cutting has now commenced and will be continued daily until "Z" day.

(a) The Brigade Intelligence Officer will arrange for one Battalion Intelligence Officer with a staff of observers to watch and report on daily the progress of the wire cutting on both front and back lines in the Brigade Area of Attack.

It will be the duty of the Brigade Intelligence Officer to keep in close touch with the Artillery: to inform the Battalion Intelligence Officer on duty where wire is being cut on that day; to receive reports from the Battalion Intelligence Officer on duty and to keep the G.O.C. and the three Assaulting Battalions informed as to the progress of the wire cutting; to notify the Infantry Brigade holding the line of any reconnaissance of the front line wire that he would like carried out at night, and to report the results of such reconnaissance to the Artillery.

(b) Arrangements will be made by the artillery, and Infantry in the line, to prevent the enemy, by gun and machine gun fire, from repairing his wire during the night.

(c). To enable patrols to examine the enemy's wire and to admit of raids being carried out, there will be no fire on the enemy's front line along the IXth Corps front between the hours named below :-

Night V/W	11 p.m. to 12 midnight.
Night W/X	10.30 p.m. to 11.30 p.m.
Night X/Y	12 midnight to 1 a.m.
Night Y/Z	11.30 p.m. to 12.30 a.m.

21. All Commanders down to Platoon Commanders will keep in touch throughout with the Commanders of similar formations on their flanks. They must know the disposition and action being taken by their neighbours, more particularly so when the units on their flanks belong to another Division.

[signed] Captain,
Brigade Major, 49th Infantry Brigade.

25th May, 1917.

SECRET

To OC 8th Inniskilly

I think your raiding party should be stronger, as you are going in on a 250 x yds front & to some depth which will mean flank guards. I consider strength should be more like 170 all ranks.

A L.G. should be with each on either flank

R Wilson Gour BS
2/6/17

SECRET.

2nd R. Irish Regt.
7th R. Innis Fus.
8th R. Innis Fus.
7/8th R. Irish Fus.
49th M.G. Company.
49th T.M. Battery.
Bde. Signal Officer.
16th Division (G).

49th Inf. Bde. No. S.O.69 – 25-5-17.

Herewith 2nd Edition of "49th Infantry Brigade Instructions for the Offensive" amended up to date.

Kindly return the "Instructions" already sent you with the exception of MAP A, which still holds good.

								   Captain,
				Brigade Major, 49th Infantry Brigade.

SECRET. 49th.I.B. No. S.C.C. 188/7

G.O.C.
Brigade Major.
16th Division Q.
2/R. Irish Regt.
7/R. Innis. Fus.
8/R. Innis. Fus.
7/8th R. Irish Fus.
49th M.G. Coy.
49th T.M. Battery.

With reference to Copy No...6.. of "49th Inf. Brigade Administrative Instructions for the Offensive", the following amendments are made therein:-

1. Rations. - para 2 (d). - Delete and substitute "(d) One days iron ration for all troops within a possible enemy barrage."

Para 2 (e) delete and substitute - "(e) Two complete days rations for all troops within a possible enemy barrage."

Delete from line 15 "Rations under (c) (d) and (e) etc., to "barrage" at end of line 3 on page 2, and substitute "Rations under (d) and (e) must be consumed by/of "A" day. Rations under (c) will be retained for consumption on a later date to be subsequently decided by the Corps Commander.

8 Prisoners of War.

Para 2., line 3, for "station" read "centre."

10 Salvage.

Add new paragraph:-

"3. In salving articles, perishable things, such as unboxed ammunition, fuzed grenades, food, etc., should be searched for and removed first."

Please ACKNOWLEDGE.

Bowen
Captain,
Staff Captain,
49th Infantry Brigade.

28.5.17.

R 15

SECRET.

Copy No. 6

49TH. INFANTRY BRIGADE.
ADMINISTRATIVE INSTRUCTIONS FOR THE OFFENSIVE.

o-o-o-o-o-o-o-o-

Herewith Copy No. 6 of 49th. Infantry Brigade Administrative Instructions for the Offensive.

It will be amended from time to time.

This copy will not be taken in front of the VIERSTRAAT SWITCH, and recipient is responsible that it is kept locked up.

ACKNOWLEDGE. ✓

K. Bowen.
Captain,

25 May, 1917.   Staff Captain, 49th. Inf. Brigade.

Issued through Signals.

Copy No. 1 O.O.C.
"   " 2 Brigade Major.
"   " 3 16th. Division "Q" (for information)
"   " 4 2nd. R.Irish Regt.
"   " 5 7th. R.Innis. Fus.
"   " 6 8th. R.Innis. Fus. ✓
"   " 7 7/8th. R.Irish Fus.
"   " 8 49th. M.G.Coy.
"   " 9 49th. T.M.Battery.
"   "10 War Diary.
"   "11 File.

One copy of Map B should be handed to Tpt. Officer who will be responsible for its safe keeping. K. Bowen.

One copy Map B. sent to T.O. under S/304 26/5/17

S/493
26 MAY 1917

STAFF CAPTAIN
49th INFTY. BRIGADE

SECRET.   Copy No. 6

49TH. INFANTRY BRIGADE.

ADMINISTRATIVE INSTRUCTIONS FOR THE OFFENSIVE.

Contents :-

1. RATIONS.
2. MEDICAL.
3. VETERINARY.
4. TRAFFIC and CROSS COUNTRY TRACKS.
5. WATER SUPPLY.
6. R.E. STORES.
7. BATTLE STRAGGLER POSTS.
8. PRISONERS of WAR.
9. REINFORCEMENTS.
10. SALVAGE.
11. STORAGE of SPARE KIT.

1. RATIONS.

1. Supplies will be drawn by train transport.

   Detail issues will be delivered from Refilling Points to unit transport lines by vehicles of the Divisional Train, and thence to units by regimental transport.

   Route from Transport Lines to be fixed by Division. Side roads and cross country tracks are to be used as far as possible.

2. In addition to
   (a) The Iron Ration on the man
   (b) The current day's ration

   Authority is given for the following rations to be held :-

   (c) One day's preserved meat and biscuit in supporting points for the maximum garrison.

   (d) One day's iron ration for all troops within a possible enemy barrage. ~~in the front line system at 1000 per Battalion. This number is calculated to cover men of Field Companies, Machine Gun Companies, and Trench Mortar Batteries in the Front Line.~~

   (e) Two day's preserved meat and biscuit for all troops inside a possible enemy barrage.

   ~~Rations under (c), (d) and (e) are to be consumed before zero.~~

   Rations under (d) & (e) must be consumed by end of 'A' day. Rations under (c) will be retained for consumption on a later date to be subsequently decided by the Corps Commander.

(1)

1. RATIONS.

1. Supplies will be drawn by train transport.

Detail issues will be delivered from Refilling Points to unit transport lines by vehicles of the Divisional Train, and thence to units by regimental transport.

Route from Transport Lines to be fixed by Division. Side roads and cross country tracks are to be used as far as possible.

2. In addition to

   (a) The Iron Ration on the man

   (b) The current day's ration

Authority is given for the following rations to be held :-

   (c) One day's preserved meat and biscuit in supporting points for the maximum garrison.

   (d) One day's iron ration for troops ~~in the~~ within a possible enemy barrage ~~front line system at 1000 per Battalion. This number is calculated to cover men of Field Companies, Machine Gun Companies, and Trench Mortar Batteries in the Front Line.~~

   (e) Two day's preserved meat and biscuit for all troops inside a possible enemy barrage.

~~Rations under (c), (d) and (e) are to be consumed before zero.~~

~~Arrangements will be made for the provision of cover from weather, and if possible from shell fire, of rations dumped in the forward area.~~

Storage for rations mentioned under para 2 (d) will be/ arranged ~~at or near~~ the Headquarters of the Battalions in whose charge they will be.

~~The rations referred to in para 2 (e) will not be drawn till~~ about 10 days before zero.

The object /

1. RATIONS. (Continued)

The object of permitting these dumps is to obviate the necessity for sending up rations during the bombardment when the enemy may put down a barrage.

3. RESERVE RATIONS AT STRONG POINTS AND FORTS.

	Map reference.	Iron Rations complete.	P.M. Tins.	Biscuit lbs.	Water Galls.
S.P. 13.	N.17.d.5.3.	Nil	48	50	50
S.P. 14.	N.18.a.3.6.	Nil	48	50	50
FORT HALIFAX	N.23.a.7.9.	Nil	24	25	25

4. RESERVE RATIONS AT BATTALION HEADQUARTERS.

"A" Battn.	-	1000	2000	2000	350
"B" "	-	1000	2000	2000	350

2. MEDICAL.

1. COLLECTION OF WOUNDED TO REGIMENTAL AID POSTS :-

By Regimental Stretcher Bearers aided by such T.U. men, Pioneers, Bandsmen, or others as may be detailed. Each unit is responsible for bringing it's own wounded back as far as it's own Aid Posts. If circumstances admit, such extra assistance as is possible, will be provided from Army or Corps Troops. Men detailed to assist Regimental Stretcher Bearers, whether from Army, Corps, or Divisional sources, will be held in readiness under Divisional arrangements at Brigade Headquarters where early information as to number of casualties will be available.

The Regimental Aid /

2. MEDICAL (Continued)

The Regimental Aid Posts on the present front are:-

In Right Bde. area
- N.23.d.0.4... and N.23.c.3.3...VIA GELLIA.
- N.23.a.9.7............. ROSSIGNOL ROAD.

In Left Bde. Area.
- N.17.d.3.5............ off WATLING STREET.
- N.17.d.2.3............ FOSSE.

Most of the Aid Posts average about 600 yards from the present front line, so the carry can be done in one relay. Later, in the event of a successful advance, on or beyond the present front line, fresh Regimental Aid Posts will be improvised, according to pre-arranged plan, and taking into consideration possible extension of tramways. The carry back from the new to the old Regimental Aid Posts would be done by Field Ambulance personnel under arrangements to be made by O's.C. Advanced Dressing Stations.

2. FROM REGIMENTAL AID POSTS TO ADVANCED DRESSING STATIONS :-

The present Regimental Aid Posts are all situated on Communication trenches, and on, or near Trench Tramways. Evacuations from these points to Advanced Dressing Stations will be done by R.A.M.C. personnel of the Field Ambulances. It will be done as much as possible by Trench Tramways, Rolling stock and Mules for traction to be provided by the Divisional Trench Tramway Officer.

The Advanced Dressing Stations are :-

KEMMEL BREWERY..........N.21.c.8.5..holding 100
LAITERIE................N.16.d.2.3..holding 50
PARRAIN FARM............N.28.b.70.95 holding 24 (lying)
KLEINE VIERSTRAATE......N.10.a.9.9..holding 64 (about)

These points are all placed so that both Communication trenches and Trench Tramways converge to them. They average 2,000 yards behind the front line. Here the wounded will be re-dressed if necessary, supplied with hot drinks/

MEDICAL (Cont'd).

with hot drinks and food, and taken by the Divisional Motor Ambulances to the Main Dressing Stations.

3. USE OF TRENCH TRAMWAYS.

Divisional Trench Tramway Officers will be accommodated in, or near, the Advanced Dressing Stations.

They will be responsible that Trolleys with Gate-ends for Stretchers, and mules to draw them are kept supplied to the Regimental Aid Posts, as fast as the number of casualties require, and as the circumstances permit.

4. MAIN DRESSING STATION.

LOCRE HOSPICE, M.29.b.65.90.

5. DIVISIONAL COLLECTING POST FOR WALKING WOUNDED.

M.24.d.3.8., on KEMMEL – BRULOOZE Road.

The broad gauge and Light Railways will be taken full advantage of in the evacuation of wounded. Wounded can, however, <u>only</u> be evacuated to or short of the point to which the rolling stock is returning in the normal course of events.

Returning Supply and Ammunition Trains will be used whenever available.

6. INCREASE OF STRETCHERS.

The total of Stretchers per Division will be increased prior to the operations to 1000. This figure will not include stretchers now on charge of Battalions, nor the present allotment of 21 wheeled stretchers per Division.

3. VETERINARY.

1. Mobile Veterinary Section will be located at M.26.b.9.7.

4. TRAFFIC AND CROSS COUNTRY TRACKS.

TRAFFIC.

1. As a general principle, horse drawn vehicles must be kept off motor routes whenever possible.

CROSS COUNTRY TRACKS.

2. Cross country tracks will be prepared by the Division from rear to front of the area for use by walking wounded, prisoners of war, reinforcements, and also by horse transport, as far as possible. Crossings over railways and through wire to be considered and prepared.

A tracing showing these tracks is attached marked "B".

5. WATER SUPPLY.

DRINKING WATER.

1. Water has been laid on by pipe to the trenches which should give a sufficient supply.

2. As the water carts of units will be in constant use daily it is hoped that extra water carts may be allotted by the Army, and placed under Corps control.

For use/

DRINKING WATER (Contd).

For use in event of a breakdown in any of the forward pipe line supplied these carts would be kept full at convenient centres such as DRANOUTRE, LOCRE, and LA CLYTTE, for use in case of necessity to deliver water to small dumps of petrol tins or tanks established on the line of the KEMMEL - VIERSTRAAT Road.

3. HORSE WATER.

No Horse watering places are to be established on roads. Arrangements must be made for each unit to water in its own line, or if this is not possible, tracks must be made across the fields from transport lines to horse watering places. Horses are not to be taken along or across main roads to water.

4. DRINKING WATER STATIONS IN BRIGADE AREA.

Number or Name.	Map Location.	Daily Supply in Gallons.	Remarks.
22	N.13.a.6.4.	2,500	
21	N.13.b.9.4.	5,000	
LOCRE	M.23.c.4.4.	4,000	
23	N.20.c.0.2.	1,000	

5. Water Stations exist at N.22.a.2.4., N.21.a.5.0. N.16.b.9.3. from the SCHERPENBERG Reservoir.

The SCHERPENBERG Supply is being extended from N.22.a.2.4. through N.23.Central and will eventually be carried up to WYTSCHAETE with a standpipe near IRISH HOUSE.

6. R.E. STORES.

Stores will be sent up by Light Railway to R.E. Farm (N.15.c.1.6) and N.16.d.5.8. and N.22.a.8.5. where there will be Divisional dumps. Thence they will be taken by Trench Tram to forward dumps in the trenches.

7. BATTLE STRAGGLER POSTS.

1. Divisional Straggler Posts and Collecting Stations will be established at N.15.c.2.3., N.21.c.8.6. KEMMEL. Collecting Station - BRULOOZE.

2. Each post will be provided with a copy of orders, an adequate supply of spare gas helmets, water and rations 100 First Field Dressings, and also a few empty grenade and S.A.A. Boxes.

3. A dug-out will be provided for each post.

4. A Medical Officer, detailed by the A.D.M.S., Reserve Division, will be on duty at each Collecting Station. 250 gas helmets will be supplied to these stations.

5. The Front Line Examining posts will act as Second Line of Straggler Posts.

6. Stragglers will not be given orders to rejoin their units. When a sufficient number have been collected to form a party, they will be marched to the Divisional Collecting Station, a special note being made of the names of men without arms. Then they will be returned, under escort, to their respective Brigade Headquarters with the ration parties after dark.

8 PRISONERS OF WAR.

1. A Divisional Collecting Station has been arranged at M.24.a. central.

Divisional Troops, after bringing prisoners to the Divisional Collecting Station will be immediately marched back to their units.

2. From Divisional Collecting Station prisoners will be marched back to the Corps Collecting Station, and thence to the Army Collecting Centre by detachments of Corps Troops.

3. Prisoners are to be marched by cross country tracks and are to be kept off roads as far as possible.

4. Copies of the following Army instructions are attached and are to be strictly observed,-
Orders for Guards over prisoners of War (8.A)
Orders for Officers or N.C.Os., in command of escorts to Prisoners of War (8.b).

8.a. ORDERS FOR GUARDS OVER PRISONERS OF WAR.

1. Any Sentry allowing a prisoner to escape will be severely dealt with, and no prisoner must be allowed the slightest loophole for escape.

2. Sentries and guards are not to talk to prisoners. Only A.P.M's., Staff Officers, Intelligence Officers, and Officer in charge may speak to them.

3. Prisoners will receive ordinary rations only, and soldiers are forbidden to give them tobacco, cigarettes, or food.

4. Soldiers are on no account to take any buttons, caps, or other articles from prisoners. German prisoners are not to be allowed to wear any article of English uniform.

5. Prisoners will be searched at once under proper arrangements in the presence of an officer.
   They are allowed to retain personal effects, decorations, badges, etc., unless they are required by General Staff. Documents, diaries, and orders found on them will be handed over to the General Staff without delay. They must be searched for knives, forks, or anything which might be used as a weapon or assist them to escape - such as a file. Their identity discs are not on any account to be taken from them.

6. No smoking is allowed.

7. Prisoners who give trouble will be separated from the others, and, if necessary, handcuffed.

8. Officer prisoners will be kept separate from the men and be very closely watched, as they may attempt to escape.

9. N.C.O's. should also be kept apart, and in small groups when possible.

10. Prisoners who have been interrogated are to be kept separate from the rest.

11. Prisoners are to be frequently counted. This will be more easily done at night if they are made to sleep in

in groups/

8.a. (Continued)

in groups of 5 or 10.

12. Men are to be conducted to the latrines or to get water in small parties of 3 or 4 at a time with a guard of 1 man to each pair of prisoners or a minimum guard of 3 men.

13. Prisoners will keep their places clean. Rations will be issued to them on parade and they will do their own cooking if any is wanted.

14. The escort of Prisoners of War should be from 15 per cent to 20 per cent of their strength under normal circumstances.

8.b. ORDERS FOR OFFICERS OR N.C.O's. IN COMMAND OF ESCORTS TO PRISONERS OF WAR.

1. Count your prisoners before taking them over or giving a receipt for them, also before starting after every halt.

2. Safeguard them on the march to .... where you will hand them over to .... and obtain a receipt, which should be handed over to ....

3. When handed over, demand a written receipt which you will give to the Officer i/c Prisoners of War Depot at .... on your return.

4. When on the march the escort should be in strength at head and rear of column, the flanks being lightly guarded.

5. Rifles of escort to be loaded. Any prisoner who attempts to escape should be shot. The escort should on no account be allowed to scatter in pursuit.

6. When halted neither Officers, N.C.O's., soldiers or civilians, are to be allowed to crowd round prisoners, they must be kept at a distance. No one is allowed to talk to the prisoners in the line of march, nor at any other time except :-

    Staff Officer.
    A.P.M's.
    Intelligence Officers.
    Officers i/c Prisoners.

7. Escorts are not to take buttons, caps, or other articles from prisoners, neither may they give the prisoners food or tobacco.

8. Officer prisoners will be kept separate from the non, and should be closely watched by an officer or N.C.O. who should march immediately behind them. N.C.O's. should also be kept apart when possible. Enemy deserters are to be kept separate and are not/to be allowed to communicate with other prisoners.

9. Any /

S.b. (Continued)

9. Any prisoners who have been examined by Intelligence Officers should be kept separated from those who have not.

10. Keep a sharp look for any prisoners attempting to get rid of papers while on the march. Any papers thrown away by prisoners to be collected and handed to the Intelligence Officers.

11. When documents and effects have been taken from prisoners and placed in labelled sandbags no prisoner is to carry his own bag.

---

9. REINFORCEMENTS.

1. Reinforcements for IX Corps will detrain at BAILLEUL.
2. Arrangements will be made by the Division for reinforcements to join their units with the Supply wagons, when required.

10. SALVAGE.

1. A Divisional Salvage Dump will be formed.
   The location of these Divisional Dumps on main roads and other places where empty vehicles pass will be arranged.
2. Every man of units returning from the trenches must bring away something salved with him, an extra rifle or pick and shovel, etc. Similarly every wagon or lorry going back empty is to be loaded with as much salved material as possible.
3. In salving articles, perishable things, such as unboxed ammunition, fuzed grenades, food, etc. should be searched for & removed first.

11. STORAGE OF SPARE KIT.

1. Arrangements have been made with the Town Major, BAILLEUL for accommodation for the storage of spare kit to be reserved as follows :-

    16th. Division....... 190 Rue de la Gare, BAILLEUL.

2. No ammunition, bombs or explosives are to be placed in these stores, on any account. The Division will arrange for the store to be properly partitioned off among various formations and units, and for notices to be put up showing the units, etc. to which/compartments are allotted.

    A Caretaker will be placed in charge of the store.

SECRET.   Copy No. 5.

G. O. C.
Staff Captain.
2nd R. Irish Regt.
7th R. Innis Fus.
8th R. Innis Fus.
7/8th R. Irish Fus.
49th M.G. Company.
49th T.M. Battery.
Brigade Signal Officer.
Bde. Intelligence Officer.
16th Division.
16th Division.
47th Inf. Bde.
48th Inf. Bde.
177th Brigade R.F.A.
157th Field Coy, R.E.

49th Inf. Bde. No. S.O.60 – 27-5-17.

Herewith Copy No 5 of "Appendix "D", 49th Infantry Brigade Instructions for the Offensive".

Kindly acknowledge receipt.

J. W. W. Willan Captain,
Brigade Major, 49th Infantry Brigade.

Appendix D

SECRET.   Copy No 5

49TH INFANTRY BRIGADE INSTRUCTIONS FOR THE OFFENSIVE.

1. The attached Tables show the loads to be carried by Carrying Parties of the 8th R. Innis Fus., attached to the three Assaulting Battalions.

2. In making references to the Carrying Parties to be supplied by the 8th R. Innis Fus. the following nomenclature will be adopted :-

   (i) The Platoon to be attached to 2nd R.Irish Regt. — *Molloy*
       "A" Carrying Party.

   (ii) The Platoon to be attached to 7th R. Innis Fus. — *Henderson*
       "B" Carrying Party.

   (iii) The Platoon to be attached to the 7/8th R.Irish Fus. — *L.C.Barron*
       "C" Carrying Party.

   (iv) The Platoon to be attached to the 49th M.G.Company. — *Robbins*
       "D" Carrying Party.

   (v) The Platoon to be attached to the 49th T.M.Battery. — *Carruthers*
       "E" Carrying Party.

   (vi) The unallotted Platoon. — *Corker*
       "F" Carrying Party.

3. The Staff Captain will issue detailed orders as to the drawing of the loads.

4. Loads to be carried on subsequent journeys will be decided by Battalion Commanders concerned according to their needs.

5. The guiding principles for the Carrying Parties attached to the three Assaulting Battalions will be :-

   (a) "B" and "C" Carrying Parties should establish two good dumps in the vicinity of the RED LINE.

   (b) "A" Carrying Party should carry their first load from our present front line. Subsequent loads should be drawn from the two dumps mentioned in (a).

6. "F" Carrying Party will carry 60 two gallon petrol tins of water from Advanced Brigade Dump No. 4 to the vicinity of the Brigade Forward Station - C.13.c.15.45.
   20 tins are allotted to each Assaulting Battalion.
   The Officer in Command of "F" Carrying Party will leave two reliable men in charge of the dump to issue the correct number of tins to each Assaulting Battalion.
   On completion of their task, "F" Carrying Party will return to the 8th R. Innis Fus. Assembly Position in YUM-YUM TRENCH and will hold itself in readiness to make further journeys if required.

7. If Battalion Commanders desire any modification in the loads laid down in the attached Tables, they will notify Brigade Headquarters as soon as possible.

"A" Carrying Party. Load for First Journey.

No. of men.	Details of Load.	Approx. weight of each man's load.	Shovels.	Sandbags.	S.A.A. Rounds.	Lewis Gun Drums.	S.O.S. Signals.
6.	13 shovels)Each 10 sandbags) 4 bandoliers)man.	55 lbs.	78	60	1200.		
6.	12 shovels)Each 10 sandbags) 4 bandoliers)man.	50 lbs.	72	60	1200.		
10.	12 L.G. Drums.)Each 10 sandbags) 4 bandoliers) 3 red cartridges 1½" 3 red cartridges 1"	50 lbs.		100	2000	120	60.
8.	13 L.G.Drums.)Each 10 sandbags.) 4 Bandoliers)man	55 lbs.		80	1600	104	
TOTALS 30.			150	300	6000	224	60.

NOTE :- "A" Carrying Party will be equipped with 30 YUKON PACKS.

"B" and "C" Carrying Parties. Loads for First Journey.

No. of men.	Details of Load.	Approx. weight of each man's load.	Shovels.	Sandbags	Rifle Grenades	Mills No 5 bombs.	S.A.A. Rounds.	Lewis Gun Drums.	S.O.S. Signals.
10 With YUKON PACKS.	15 shovels.) Each 10 sandbags.) 4 bandoliers)man.	65 lbs.	150	100			2000		
10 With YUKON PACKS.	1 box Rifle Grenades) Each 5 Lewis Gun Drums.) man. 10 sandbags.) 4 bandoliers.)	65 lbs.		100	200		2000	50.	
10 Without YUKON PACKS	2 boxes Mills) Each. No. 5.) 4 bandoliers.) man.	42 lbs.				240	2000		
TOTALS. 30			150	200	200	240	6000	50.	

NOTE :- "B" and "C" Carrying Parties will each be equipped with 20 YUKON PACKS.

"B" and "C" Carrying Parties. Loads for Second Journey.

No. of men.	Details of load.	Approx. weight of each man's load.	Shovels.	Sandbags.	Rifle Grenades.	Mills. No.1 5 Bombs.	S.A.A. rounds.	Lewis Gun Drums.	S.O.S. Signals.
10 With YUKON PACKS.	5 shovels) 10 sandbags.) Each 1 box Rifle) man. Grenades.)	65 lbs.	50	100	200.				
10 With YUKON PACKS.	15 L.G.Drums.) 10 sandbags.) Each 3 red cartridges) man. 1½") 3 red cartridges) 1")	62 lbs.		100				150	60
3 Without YUKON PACKS	8 L.G.Drums.) Each in canvas) man. buckets.)	34 lbs.						24.	
7 Without YUKON PACKS.	2 boxes Mills) Each No. 5 Bombs.) man.	40 lbs.				168.			
TOTALS 30			50	200	200	168		174	60

NOTE :- "B" and "C" Carrying Parties will each be equipped with 20 YUKON PACKS.

"A" CARRYING PARTY. LOAD FOR FIRST JOURNEY.

No. of men.	Details of Load.	Approx. weight of each man's load.	Picks.	Shovels.	Sandbags.	S.A.A. rounds.	Lewis Gun Drums.	S.O.S. Signals.
6	9 shovels 10 sandbags.) each 4 bandoliers.) man 3 picks.	55 lbs	18	54	60	1200.		
6	9 shovels 10 sandbags.) each 4 bandoliers.) man. 3 picks.	55 lbs	18	54	60	1200		
10	12 L.G.Drums. 10 sandbags. 4 bandoliers.) each 3 red cartridges) man. 12. 5 red cartridges 1.	50 lbs.			100	2000	120	60.
8	13 L.G.Drums.) each 10 sandbags.) 4 bandoliers.) man.	55 lbs.			80	1600	104	
TOTALS 30			36	108	300	6000	224	60.

NOTE :- "A" Carrying Party will be equipped with 30 YUKON PACKS.

"B" AND "C" CARRYING PARTIES. LOAD FOR SECOND JOURNEY.

No. of men.	Details of load.	Approx. weight of each man's load.	Picks.	Shovels.	Sandbags.	Rifle Grenades.	Mills No. 5 bombs.	S.A.A. rounds.	Lewis Gun Drums.	S.O.S. Signals.
10 With YUKON PACKS.	8 shovels.) 10 sandbags.) each 4 picks.) man.	65 lbs.	40	80	100					
10 With YUKON PACKS.	15 L.G. Drums.) 10 sandbags.) 3 rod cartridges) each 12") 3 red cartridges) man. 1"	62 lbs.			100				150	60
3 Without YUKON PACKS.	8 L.G. Drums.) each in canvas buckets) man.	34 lbs.							24.	
7 Without YUKON PACKS.	2 boxes Mills) each No. 5 bombs.) man.	40 lbs.					168			
TOTALS. 30			40	80	200		168		174.	60

NOTE :- "B" and "C" Carrying Parties will each be equipped with 20 YUKON PACKS.

"B" AND "C" CARRYING PARTIES. LOAD FOR FIRST JOURNEY.

No. of Men.	Details of Load.	Approx. Weight of each man's Load.	Picks.	Shovels.	Sandbags.	Rifle Grenades.	Mills No.5 bombs.	S.A.A. rounds	Lewis Gun Drums.	S.O.S. Signals.
10 With YUKON PACKS.	5 picks. 10 shovels.)each 10 sandbags.)man. 4 bandoliers.	65 lbs.	50	100	100			2000		
10 With YUKON PACKS.	1 box Rifle Grenades.)each 5 L.G. Drums.)man. 10 sandbags.) 4 bandoliers.)	65 lbs.			100	200		2000	50	
10 Without YUKON PACKS.	2 boxes Mills) each No.5) 4 Bandoliers.) man.	42 lbs.					240	2000		
TOTALS. 30.			50	100	200	200	240	6000	50.	

NOTE :- "B" and "C" Carrying Parties will each be equipped with 20 YUKON PACKS.

S E C R E T.　　　　　　　　　　　　　　　　　　　　Copy No 5

G. O. C.
Staff Captain.
2nd R. Irish Regt.
7th R. Innis Fus.
8th R. Innis Fus.
7/8th R. Irish Fus.
49th M.G. Company.
49th T.M. Battery.
Bde. Signal Officer.
Bde. Intelligence Officer.
16th Division.
16th Division.
47th Inf. Bde.
48th Inf. Bde.
58th Inf. Bde.
177th Bde. R.F.A.
157th Field Coy. R.E.

49th Inf. Bde. No. S.O.60 - 28-5-17.

Herewith Copy No 5 of "49TH INFANTRY BRIGADE INSTRUCTIONS FOR THE OFFENSIVE", Paras. 22 to 32.

Appendix "E" will be forwarded later.

In para. 10 "DRESS", page 7 of Instructions already issued, for "6 rounds of 1" Very Lights" read "6 one inch Red Signal Cartridges".

Kindly Acknowledge.

　　　　　　　　　　　　　　　　　　　　　　　　Captain,
　　　　　　　　　　　Brigade Major, 49th Infantry Brigade.

S E C R E T.

Copy No 5

49TH INFANTRY BRIGADE INSTRUCTIONS FOR THE OFFENSIVE.

(CONTINUED).

22. All Mines in the 16th Division Front will be exploded at Zero Hour.
   If the explosion of any of the above mines has not taken place by Zero plus 15 seconds it is to be understood that it will not take place at all.

   "Instructions to Troops in connection with the firing of Large Mines" will be forwarded to all concerned.

23. Danger Areas are being marked under Divisional arrangements. Notice Boards will be put up in all subways.

24. No telescopic rifles are to be taken forward in the Attack. They are to be kept at Quartermaster's Stores for use later when required.

25. To prevent congestion of ordinary traffic during the movement of troops, Battalions will march at 500 yards interval.

26. It is most important that every precaution should be taken to prevent bayonets from flashing in the moonlight should there be a Moon when units are moving to their Positions of Assembly.

27. In the event of hostile aeroplanes flying low over our lines to ascertain whether our trenches are more strongly manned than usual, all ranks will remain still and will not look up.
   Such aeroplanes are to be dealt with by Anti-aircraft Lewis and Machine Guns. Each Battalion in the line maintaining 4 Lewis Guns for this purpose.

28. In order to assist the Artillery in locating our own Infantry, distinguishing flags will be carried on the scale of not less than 2 per platoon. Strict orders are to be issued against planting these flags in the ground in order to avoid mistakes which might be caused by flags left behind in evacuated positions.
   The flags will be provided under Divisional arrangements. At the time of issue all concerned will receive full details as to their size and colour and the way in which they should be carried.

29. The "S.O.S" Signal will remain RED Signal Cartridges as at present.

30. The following R.E. Dumps will be established in the Forward Area :-

   RESERVE DUMP   R.E.FARM (N.15.c.1.5).

   INTERMEDIATE DUMP   QUEBEC VILLA (N.16.d.5.8).

   Advanced Dumps.   (1) N.17.d.2.2.

                       (2) WATSONVILLE (N.17.d.6.7.

As soon as possible a dump will be formed at NORTHERN BRICKSTACK

31. In order to avoid casualties, the whole of the Infantry detailed for the Assault of the RED and BLUE Lines should get rapidly across NO MAN'S LAND. As few troops as possible will be left in our own front and support lines.

32. Appendix E is given as a guide to the form in which narratives of the Operations should be forwarded to Brigade Headquarters.

JWDWillcox Captain,
Brigade Major, 49th Infantry Brigade.

28-5-17.

SECRET.

G. O. C.
2nd R. Irish Regt.
7th R. Innis Fus.
8th R. Innis Fus.
7/8th R. Irish Fus.
49th M.G. Company.
49th T.M. Battery.
16th Div. (G).
47th Inf. Bde.
48th Inf. Bde.
58th Inf. Bde.
177th Bde, R.F.A..

49th Inf. Bde. No. S.O.60 - 27-5-17.

Herewith Copy No ..5.... of "Appendix"C", 49th Infantry Brigade Instructions for the Offensive".

Kindly acknowledge receipt.

Willem Captain,
Brigade Major, 49th Inf. Brigade.

Appendix C.

SECRET.

Copy No 5

SIGNAL INSTRUCTIONS FOR THE OFFENSIVE.

The general system is based on S.S.148 ("Forward Intercommunication in Battle").

BURIED CABLE.

There will be one Cable Head in each Attacking Brigade Front. Cable Head of 49th Infantry Brigade will be at the head of subway at N.24.a.50.70.

BRIGADE FORWARD STATION.

This will be situated at O.13.c.15.45.
Three metallic pairs will be laid between this point and Cable Head, of which two will be for the use of the Artillery and one for the Infantry.

BATTALION FORWARD POSTS.

These should be established as near as possible to the Brigade Forward Station to avoid unnecessary maintenance of lines.
The following appear to be the best positions :-

Right Battalion. 7/8th R. Irish Fusiliers.

In NAIL RESERVE about O.13.c.10.32.

Left Battalion. 7th R. Innis Fus.

In NAIL DRIVE about O.13.c.00.55.

2nd R. Irish Regt. in OBVIOUS ALLEY about O.19.b.75.85.

Battalion Forward Party will consist of :-

    Battalion Signal Officer.
    1 Signal Clerk.
    1 N.C.O. Signaller.
    8 Signallers (for visual and telephone).
    6 Runners.
    2 additional Runners per Relay Post.
    1 Pigeoner.
    4 Riflemen (to assist in carrying stores).
    Power Buzzer Squad (if required).

Equipment to be carried :-

    2 Lucas Lamps.
    4 folding signalling shutters.
    2 telescopes - signalling.
    4 signalling flags.
    2 D.III telephones.
    1 Fullerphone.
    1 4 x 5 Buzzer exchange.
    2 ½ mile lengths D.3 cable.
    Aeroplane signalling equipment.
    2 pairs pigeons.
    Stationery.

Before these parties start they must know exact position of Forward Posts. Arrangements should be made to point this out beforehand from the front line trenches.

When the post has been established, exact location should be reported at once to Brigade Forward Station, Flank Battalions and Companies.

It should be marked by BLUE and WHITE Flag.

PERSONNEL IN RESERVE.

As many men as possible should be left in Reserve.

TELEPHONE SYSTEM.

The Communications of a Battalion are shown in accompanying sketch. No other lines will be laid without sanction of Brigade Signal Officer.

F.O.O's may lay lines through Battalion Forward Posts to the Brigade Forward Station. When these lines are laid the Battalion concerned will be responsible for their maintenance between Battalion Forward Posts and Brigade Forward Station. All Lines must be maintained.

Care should be taken to impress upon all officers the necessity of NOT speaking on the telephone unless absolutely necessary. Telegrams are a much quicker method of communication and monopolise the lines much less.

VISUAL.

Battalion Forward Posts should get into touch with their Companies as soon as possible.

The Brigade Receiving Station will be established at N.16.d.95.75. Battalion Headquarters and Brigade Forward Station will work to this Station which will show an open light periodically.

Battalion Forward Posts will work to Brigade Forward Station.

Visual messages should be as short as possible. Messages in "B.A.B" Code are quicker than any others.

Company H.Q. Signal Detachments should carry a fold up Signalling Shutter and Lamp.

RUNNERS.

System of Runners will be arranged by Battalion Signal Officers between -

(a) Battalion H.Q. and Brigade H.Q.
(b) Battalion Forward Post and Brigade Forward Station.
(c) Companies and Battalion Forward Posts.

No Runners should be despatched with a message which can be sent by other means. Runners should be kept fresh in case of Emergency.

PIGEONS.

There will be a daily supply of -

4 pairs per Battalion. i.e. -
2 pairs for Headquarters.
2 pairs for Battalion Forward Post.

Refilling point for Battalions will be Brigade Forward Station.
Every effort must be made to return empty baskets to refilling point.
Care must be taken to show clearly -

    a. Hour and place of despatch of message.

    b. Address to and from.

CODE CALLS.

From Zero Hour onwards Position Calls (such as F.E.7) cease to exist and NAME CODES (KI, AK, BK, CK, DK) will be used.
Position Calls of Forward Posts will be Code of H.Q. of formations preceded by letter A. e.g. -

    AKI.   AAK.   ABK.

Companies will take call of the Battalion followed by letters A, B, C and D to denote the Company.

POWER BUZZER.

These will not be issued to AK, BK, and DK, as their [AK-DK] Forward Posts will be close to Brigade Forward Station. One will be issued to CK.
There will be two Amplifiers.

    a. N.17.d.7.2.

    b. O.13.c.15.45.

A Power Buzzer will be installed at N.17.d.7.2 for the purpose of working forward to Brigade Forward Station. Power Buzzer Calls will be exactly the same as those used in Aeroplane Contact work, Brigade Forward Station being U1.

AEROPLANE CONTACT.

This will be used at Battalion Headquarters and at Brigade Forward Station.

WIRELESS.

Instructions will be issued later.

INSTRUMENTS.

All instruments must be carefully tested and adjustments made. Every man will be held responsible that the instrument he is using is in good order.

LAYING OF LINES.

Every use should be made of enemy trenches and natural cover when laying lines.
Lines between Battalion H.Q. and Battalion Forward Posts should be laid up to the front line before Zero Hour and cable should be ready to lay immediately required.

RESERVES.

The Signallers and Runners of the 8th R.Innis Fus. will reinforce Brigade and Battalions if necessary.

LINES TO FORWARD STATION.

Units wishing to lay lines to Brigade Forward Station should report at once :-

    a. How many they require.
    b. Exact location of their Station.

INDENTS.

Indents for cable and other material should be submitted immediately.

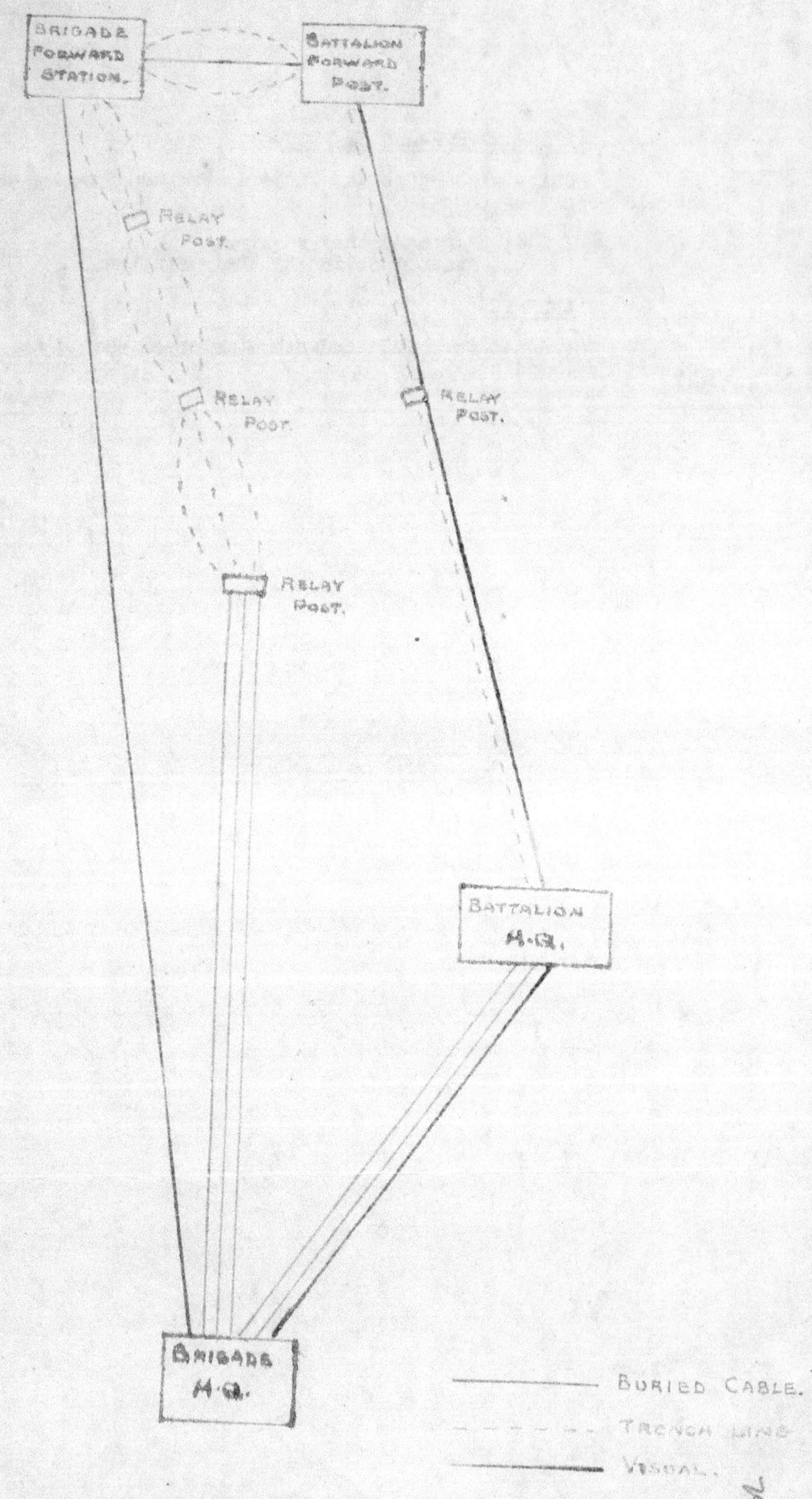

SECRET.
==========

Copy No 5......

G. O. C.
Staff Captain.
2nd R. Irish Regt.
7th R. Innis Fus.
8th R. Innis Fus.
7/8th R. Irish Fus.
49th M.G. Company.
49th T.M. Battery.
Bde. Signal Officer.
Bde. Intelligence Officer.
16th Division.
16th Division.
157th Field Coy, R.E.

49th Inf. Bde. No. S.O. 60 - 30-5-17.

Herewith Copy No 5... of "Appendix E, 49th Infantry Brigade Instructions for the Offensive".

Kindly acknowledge.

[signature] Captain,
Brigade Major, 49th Infantry Brigade.

S E C R E T.

Appendix E.

Copy No 5

49TH INFANTRY BRIGADE INSTRUCTIONS FOR THE OFFENSIVE.

Guide to the Form in which Narrative of Operations should be forwarded to Brigade Headquarters.

(a) Composition of Unit, including any attached troops. Name of Commander.

(b) Disposition of Unit at Zero.

(c) Brief plan of the operation, giving objectives, boundaries, etc.

(d) Account of the action itself.

(e) Any comments that may be useful in assigning reasons for the success or failure of the action.

(f) Rough sketch maps :-

   (i) To show dispositions at Zero, boundaries and objectives.

   (ii) To show positions reached.

N.B.

The narrative of Operations must be kept up for future teaching. It is most important that accounts be accurate, otherwise the lessons deduced are false.

S E C R E T.

Copy No 5.....

G. O. C.
Staff Captain.
2nd R. Irish Regt.
7th R. Innis Fus.
8th R. Innis Fus.
7/8th R. Irish Fus.
49th M.G. Company.
49th T.M. Battery.
Bde. Signal Officer.
Bde. Intelligence Officer.
16th Division.
16th Division.
47th Inf. Bde.
48th Inf. Bde.
58th Inf. Bde.
177th Bde., R.F.A.
157th Field Coy, R.E.

49th Inf. Bde. No. S.O. 60 - 31-5-17.

Herewith Copy No 5..... of paras. 33 to 35 of 49TH INFANTRY BRIGADE INSTRUCTIONS FOR THE OFFENSIVE.

Para. 2 of Instructions already issued is cancelled, an amended Copy of Para. 2 is attached.

After Para. 30 insert "As soon as feasible a Dump will be formed at NORTHERN BRICKSTACK."

ACKNOWLEDGE.

[signature] Captain,
Brigade Major, 49th Infantry Brigade.

SECRET.   Copy No 5

49TH INFANTRY BRIGADE INSTRUCTIONS FOR THE OFFENSIVE.

(CONTINUED).

33.   As soon as possible after Zero it is proposed to carry forward the following Communication Trenches, etc, to the captured positions. This work will be carried out by the R.E. and Pioneers.

(a) Communication Trenches.

The FOSSE - BIRR TRENCH via NAME TRENCH - NAME DRIVE.
To be used for OUT Traffic.

WATLING STREET - MAYO STREET via NAIL DRIVE.
To be used for IN Traffic.

(b) Overland Routes.

Route E via BLACK COT for OUT Traffic.
Route F via RED CHATEAU and NORTHERN BRICKSTACK for IN traffic.

34.   Liaison between Artillery and Infantry.

Four Advanced Intelligence Officers will be detailed to each attacking Infantry Brigade from the Groups covering the Brigade. One of these officers will be allotted to each Battalion in the Attack. He and his party will remain with Battalion Headquarters until the GREEN LINE is reached, after which he will be free to move forward to obtain visual observation.

The duties of these Advanced Intelligence Officers will be to collect information as to the tactical situation from various sources, such as Battalion Commanders, personal observation or any other possible means. In addition, they will act as F.O.O's if required to observe fire.

35.   Liaison between Infantry and Engineers.

Brigade and Battalion Signal Officers should accept for transmission messages dealing with R.E. and Pioneer questions whenever the situation admits of this being done.
Such messages will be reduced to a minimum.

49th. I.B. No. S.C.S. XI/102

S E C R E T.

2/R. Irish Regt.
7/R. Innis. Fus.
8/R. Innis. Fus.
7/8th R. Irish Fus.
49th M.G. Coy.
49th T.M. Battery.
Brigade T.O.
Brigade O.M.S.
Brigade Signal Officer.

With reference to para 10 (b) of 49th Brigade S.C. 60 dated 25.5.17. Packs will be left at the Transport Lines of units. They will be distinctly marked on the bottom side with the No. Name, Company, and Regiment of the owner. e.g.—

Each pack will contain only Government property. Private effects of soldiers should be placed in a bag which should be tied securely, labelled or marked with the owners No. Name, Company, and Regiment as above, and attached to the pack.

Bowen
Captain,
Staff Captain,
49th Infantry Brigade.

31.5.17.

APPENDIX "A".

COMPANY ORDER.
by
CAPTAIN W. L. C. MOORE BRABAZON, COMMANDING
"A" COY., 2nd. BATTALION, THE ROYAL IRISH REGIMENT.

1.

OFFICERS. Lieut. P. L. BLAKE will act as O.C. Company during operations, 2/Lieuts. TROUGHTON and GIFFIN will accompany him.

2.

CARRYING PARTIES. The 8th. R. Innis. Fus. will act as carrying parties and will bring forward S.A.A. and shovels to forward dumps made by O.C.Company in GREEN LINE.

3.

LEWIS GUNS. The Lewis Guns of "A" Company will be attached to "B" Company (Support) and be for disposal as ordered by O. C. "B" Company.

4.

ORDER OF BATTLE. The Battalion order of battle is as follows for the attack on the GREEN and BLACK LINES :-

"C" Company   Right Front Company.
"D" Company   Left Front Company.
"B" Company   In Support.
"A" Company   MOPPERS-UP.

5.

ASSEMBLY POINT. The Battalion Assembly Position will be CHINESE WALL from WATLING STREET to the VIERSTRAAT ROAD and will be drawn up as laid down in para. 6.

"A" Company will be disposed as follows :-

2/Lieut. TROUGHTON and 60 other ranks will be drawn up in rear of "C" Company.

2/Lieut. GIFFIN and 40 other ranks in rear of "D" Company.

Company H.Qrs. (Lieut. BLAKE, C.S.M. and 3 Runners) in centre of Right Sector.

Each man will carry a rifle, the requisite amount of S.A.A. and bombs, rifle grenades, sandbags and in addition 3 "P" bombs per man.

Officers - 2 bombs and 2 "P" bombs each.

6.

ACTION. The Company will move forward behind their respective front line companies, first wave Zero plus 2.30 - in groups as detailed below, in artillery formation till reaching the BLUE LINE when they will break up and go for their respective areas and trenches and mop-up, moving 10 yards in rear of leading wave - great care being taken over the dug-outs - picquet each entrance till sure that each dug-out is empty.

7.

O's. C. Sectors will detail parties to conduct prisoners back to the BLUE LINE and hand them over to Battalion holding it, these men will return with mixed loads of S.A.A., bombs, etc., drawn from forward dumps.

2.

8.

HEAD-QUARTERS.   Battalion H.Qrs. will be S.P.13.
For the attack on BLACK LINE H.Q. will advance to 0.13.c.15.45.
Company H.Q. will advance down OBVIOUS TRENCH and as soon as possible take up a position in a dug-out in O.19.b.75.65. - afterwards when ground between GREEN and BLACK LINES is cleaned up advancing to house in O.20.a.20.50.

9.

DISPOSITIONS.   Right Sector.   2/Lieut. TROUGHTON.)
                                 Sgt. HANRAHAN.
                                 RUNNER.   ) Sector H.Qrs.
                                 SERVANT.

               Left Sector.   2/Lieut. GIFFIN.
                                 Sgt. BRYANT.
                                 RUNNER.   ) Sector H.Qrs.
                                 SERVANT.

The Coy. Sector for mopping-up is OBVIOUS AVENUE - Jn. OBVIOUS TRENCH - ESTAMINET (NORTH HOUSE incl.) on Left, and a line from right of HOSPICE to dump on BLACK LINE at O.20.a.40.15. - approximate dividing line OBVIOUS TRENCH to Junction with OBVIOUS DRIVE then to House at O.20.a.20.50. - BLACK LINE.

RIGHT SECTOR.

Sgt. MARTIN and 10 men will work between OBVIOUS TRENCH and DRIVE.

Cpl. KAVANAGH and 10 men bomb and clear dug-outs in OBVIOUS DRIVE.

Cpl. HARNETT and 10 men between OBVIOUS DRIVE and Brigade on right clearing shell holes and dug-outs.

On reaching the ruined houses O.19.b.50.50. Sgt. KEOGH and Cpl. KINSELLA and 20 men will advance and thoroughly clear the houses of any pockets of the enemy and the 5 sections continuing on through GREEN to BLACK LINE.

O.C.Right Sector has 1 section Sgt. BEAL and 10 men for emergency.

LEFT SECTOR.

Cpl. MC.CARTHY and 10 men to work down OBVIOUS AVENUE.
Cpl. DOWLING and 10 men to work down OBVIOUS TRENCH.
Sgt. BROWN and 10 men to work between the two trenches.
At the Jn. Cpl. WHITNEY then goes forward and helps clean up NORTH HOUSE and dug-outs to GREEN LINE and the houses on the road in front of BLACK LINE.

9.

MEDICAL OFFICER.   Battalion Aid Post S.P.13 - Advanced Aid Post in dug-out of OBVIOUS DRIVE O.19.b.20.65.

10.

CONSOLI-DATION.   After completion of the mopping-up to the BLACK LINE Company will place themselves under the orders of Senior Officer for consolidating BLACK LINE, S.P's. and houses.

---------------oOo---------------

APPENDIX "B".

COMPANY ORDERS
by
CAPTAIN R. A. BELEMORE, COMMANDING, "B" COY.,
2nd. BATTALION, THE ROYAL IRISH REGIMENT.

---

1. "B" Company will act as Support Company to "D" and "C" Companies on the attack on the GREEN and BLACK LINES.

2. Nos. 5 and 6 Platoons will support "D" Company on the left and Nos. 7 and 8 Platoons will support "C" Company on the right.

3. Lieut. PALMER will be in command of Nos. 5 and 6 Platoons and 2/Lieut. DONOVAN will be in command of Nos. 7 and 8 Platoons.
   Special attention will be paid to any enemy resistance passed by the front line, namely strong points and machine gun nests, etc.

4. "B" Company will not take part in the actual attack on the GREEN LINE unless the forward companies are held up, in which case support will be rendered as required.

5. The Company will help "D" and "C" Companies in reaching the final objective, and remain there with them when it is gained.
   No..... Platoon will garrison Strong Point C when constructed.

6. The Company will move forward from the BLUE LINE in 2 waves of platoons, about 200 yards distance. The first wave of "B" Company will be about 250 yards in rear of leading companies. /100 /150
   Support to "C" and "D" Companies will be under the initiative of platoon commanders if the Company Commander is not present to give orders.

---oOo---

APPENDIX "C".

COMPANY ORDERS
by
**CAPTAIN P. J. G. GORDON RALPH, COMMANDING, "C" COMPANY,
2nd. BATTALION, THE ROYAL IRISH REGIMENT.**

---

1. "C" Company is the Right Assaulting Company.
   Nos. 9 and 10 Platoons in the first wave.
   Nos. 11 and 12 Platoons in the second wave.
   Nos. 9 and 11 Platoons on the right in each case.
   LEFT boundary OBVIOUS TRENCH.
   No. 10 Platoon will detail 1 N.C.O. and 4 bombers to deal with opposition in this trench and keep touch with "D" Company.

2. Moppers-up; 1 Platoon of "A" Company will follow the second line of the first wave and mop-up OBVIOUS DRIVE and trenches in rear.
   Only moppers-up will take back prisoners and will hand them over to troops in BLUE LINE.

3. On reaching BLACK LINE all platoons will consolidate the front line which will be held at all costs.

4. All men going back to BLUE LINE for any purpose whatever will carry up S.A.A. or bombs, etc., on the return journey.
   The C.S.M. will be responsible that this ammunition is dumped in a central place on the BLACK LINE and be responsible for its issue.

5. No. 9 Platoon will direct and 2 N.C.O's. will be detailed to look after the direction.

6. No. 11 Platoon will obtain connection with troops on our right at GREEN LINE and BLACK LINE.

7. During the attack Company H.Qrs. will be in front of the centre of the second wave and on the BLACK LINE in the centre of the Company during consolidation. All reports will be sent to these points.

8. Platoon Commanders will render progress and situation reports every half hour.

---oOo---

APPENDIX "D".

COMPANY ORDERS
by
CAPTAIN J. I. COTTER, COMMANDING, "D" COY.,
2nd. BATTALION, THE ROYAL IRISH REGIMENT.

---

1. "D" Company will attack the GREEN and BLACK LINES on the left, Nos. 14 and 15 Platoons leading and Nos. 13 and 16 Platoons in close support.

2. The leading platoons will go forward and leave the final clearing up and inspecting of dug-outs to troops coming behind, keeping as close to the Artillery barrage as possible.

3. Nos. 13 and 16 Platoons will support and join front line platoons as convenient, sending their Lewis Guns up with the forward platoons at the earliest convenient moment.

4. No. 13 Platoon will find a bombing party of 1 Sgt. and 4 bombers and 4 riflemen to move up OBVIOUS AVENUE and to keep contact with 19th. Division on left.

5. The C.S.M. will see that all men keep with their Platoons and will move in the centre of last wave of attack.

6. During the attack from the GREEN to the BLACK LINE all platoons will go forward together and occupy the most convenient position on or about the BLACK LINE.

---oOo---

APPENDIX "E".

COMMUNICATIONS

As soon as the Battalion moves forward to the BLUE LINE, the Signallers will move forward and establish a station at Battalion H.Q. as near the Brigade Advanced station as possible in O.13.c.15.45.

A line will then be laid up to, or as near as possible to, the front line (i.e. BLUE LINE).

When the attacking troops move forward to their final objective the Battalion Forward Station will go forward and establish itself in OBVIOUS ALLEY about O.19.b.75.85.

They will then be in communication with Battalion H.Q. and advanced Brigade station.

Communication will be established with all Companies and also the Battalions on the flanks.

There will be a Relay Post both of linesmen and runners near the BLUE LINE about O.13.c.7.5.

This however will be established later according to the nature of the ground.

RUNNERS.   There must be 12 H.Q. Runners in addition to the Company Runners.

6 at Battalion Forward Station.
2 at Relay Post.
4 at Battalion Headquarters.

All the partially trained signallers should be attached to the signallers. They could be used as runners if necessary or could, if required, replace casualties in the Signallers.

Communication forward of Battalion Forward Station will be by visual where possible, or by runners where visual is not possible.

AEROPLANE CONTACT.
Will be at Battalion Headquarters.

It is most important that all lines be maintained as visual signalling has not proved a success.

---------------oOo---------------

APPENDIX "F".

CARRYING PARTY.

The platoon of the 8th. R. Innis. Fus. will follow the last wave in the attack.

The loads to be carried will be as per attached schedule.

These loads will be carried by the platoon of the 8th. R. Innis. Fus. as far as the BLACK LINE.

This carrying party will then go back and on its second and subsequent journeys will bring up mixed loads of ammunition, etc., and deposit them at the dumps formed about the BLUE LINE.

---------------oOo---------------

Carrying Party Loads for 1st Journey.

No. of men.	Details of Load.	Approx. weight of each man's load.	Shovels.	Sandbags.	S.A.A. Rounds.	Lewis Gun Drums.	S.O.S. Signals.
6.	13 Shovels) Each 10 Sandbags) 4 Bandoliers) man.	55 lbs.	78.	60.	1200.		
6.	12 Shovels) Each 10 Sandbags) 4 Bandoliers) man.	50 lbs.	72.	60.	1200.		
10.	12 L.G. Drums) 10 Sandbags) 4 Bandoliers) Each 3 Red Cart- ridges 1g") man. 3 Red Cart- ridges 1")	50 lbs.		100.	2200.	120.	60.
8.	13 L.G. Drums) Each 10 Sandbags) 4 Bandoliers) man.	55 lbs.		80.	1600.	104.	
TOTALS 30.			150.	300.	6000.	224.	60.

Note:- "A" Carrying Party will be equipped with 30 YUKON PACKS.

Secret — Operation Order No. 30 Copy No. 4
by
Lieut Colonel H.G. Gregorie, DSO., Commanding
2nd Battn. The Royal Irish Regt.

Amendments.

Para 6 for "228 yards to N. 18. a. 27. 15."
        read "228 yards to N. 18. a. 27. 65."
Para 12 4th. line for "O. 20. a. 80. 00."
        read "O. 20. a. 00. 80."

2/6/17.   H.G. Gregorie
                                           Lieut Colonel.
        Commanding 2/The Royal Irish Regt.

Issued at 4 pm.
Copy No. 1 War Diary   No. 9 O.C. "B" Coy
      2 G.O.C. 49th Inf. Bde.   10. O.C. "C" Coy
      3 G.O.C. 48th Inf. Bde.   11. O.C. "D" Coy
      4 8th R. Innis. Fus.   12. Intelligence Offr.
      5. 49th T.M. Batty.   13. Signalling Offr.
      6. 49th T.M. Batty.   14. Medical Offr.
      7. Second in Command   15. Chaplain
      8. O.C. "A" Coy   16. File
          No. 17 Spare.

OPERATION ORDER No. 80
by
LIEUT. COLONEL H. G. GREGORIE, D.S.O., COMMANDING,
2nd. BATTALION, THE ROYAL IRISH REGIMENT.

Reference Trench Map   The Field.
Sheet 28 S.W. 2. Ed. 5.A. 1/10,000.   29-5-1917.

Copy No. 4

GENERAL PLAN.

1. The Attack on the WYTSCHAETE RIDGE will be made by the 16th. Division in conjunction with Divisions on either flank.

(a) The 16th. Division will attack with two Infantry Brigades in the line and one Infantry Brigade in Reserve.

Right Attack.   47th. Infantry Brigade.
                       156th. Field Coy., R.E.
                       1 Company 11th. Hants (Pioneers)

Left Attack.   49th. Infantry Brigade.
                       157th. Field Coy., R.E.
                       1 Company 11th. Hants (Pioneers).

Divisional Reserve.   48th. Infantry Brigade.
                       155th. Field Coy., R.E.
                       11th. Hants Pioneers (less 2 Coys)

(b) The Boundaries between the 49th. Infantry Brigade and the Brigades on either flank are as follows :-

Right Boundary (with 47th. Inf. Bde.)

German Line at N.24.a.60.85. - North Corner of PETIT BOIS (N.24.b.4.9.) - N.W. Corner BOIS DE WYTSCHAETE (N.24.b.75.80.) - South Corner of HOSPICE (O.19.a.70.70.) - point where tramway crosses ST. ELOI - MESSINES road at O.20.a.20.30. - O.20.a.40.25.

Left Boundary (with 19th. Division.)

German Line at N.18.b.23.53. - VIERSTRAAT-WYTSCHAETE Road (inclusive) to NORTHERN BRICKSTACK (O.13.c.32.80.) South Corner of GRAND BOIS (O.13.c.92.70.) - OBVIOUS AVENUE (exclusive) - ESTAMINET Cross Roads (O.20.a.30.87.)

These Boundaries are shewn in YELLOW on Map A.

(c) The objectives allotted to the 49th. Infantry Brigade and to the Infantry Brigades on either flank are shewn as follows on Map A.

        1st. Objective.............RED.
        2nd. Objective.............BLUE.
        3rd. Objective.............GREEN.
        4th. Objective.............BLACK.

(d) The following will be the times of arrival and departure from the various coloured lines :-

        RED LINE   Arrive 0.35.
                        depart 1.05.

        BLUE LINE   Arrive 1.40.
                        depart 3.40.

        GREEN LINE   Arrive 4.10.
                        depart 4.20.

        BLACK LINE   Arrive 4.40.

(e) The attack on the RED and BLUE LINES will be made by the 7/8th. R. Irish Fus. on the Right and the 7th. R. Innis. Fus. on the Left.

The Boundary between these two Battalions is as follows -

N.17.b.80.00. - SHANNON TRENCH at N.18.a.32.00. - our Front line at N.18.a.55.00. - German front line at N.18.d.20.75. - along a line 30 yards south of NAIL DRIVE - Southern Corner of UNNAMED WOOD - O.13.c.80.15. 20 yards north of the Junction of OBVIOUS DRIVE and NANCY DRIVE. This Boundary is shewn in PURPLE on Map A.

The attack on the GREEN and BLACK Lines will be made by the 2nd. R. Irish Regt.

The 8th. R. Innis Fus. will provide Moppers Up, Carrying Parties, etc.

CONSOLIDATION AND STRONG POINTS.

2. With the exception of the GREEN LINE all lines will be consolidated after capture.

The 157th. Field Coy. R.E. (under the orders of the C.R.E. 16th. Division) will establish Strong Points to hold one Platoon as follows :-

(a) As soon as the BLUE Line has been captured.

Strong Point A at ....

Strong Point B at ....

(b) As soon as the BLACK Line has been captured.

Strong Point C at ....

As soon as the construction of a Strong Point is complete, the R.E. Officer in charge will report the fact to the Officer Commanding the Battalion in whose Area the Strong Point is. The Battalion Commander concerned will then detail one platoon with its Lewis Gun to garrison the Strong Point. The R.E. Party will not leave a Strong Point until the Infantry Garrison takes it over.

MACHINE GUNS.

3. (i) Two guns of the 49th. Machine Gun Company will be attached to each of the following Battalions :-

2nd. R. Irish Regt.
7th. R. Innis Fus.
7/8th. R. Irish Fus.

They will work in pairs, each pair under a competent Machine Gun Officer, and in each case will accompany the final wave. These guns will not be used for indirect or barrage fire.

(ii) The general role of these guns will be :-

(a) To protect the assaulting battalions against Counter-attacks during the assault.

(b) After the capture of the BLUE and BLACK LINES to assist the consolidation by taking up positions to cover the ground in front of these lines.

(c) To take advantage of good, fleeting targets in order to inflict loss on the enemy.

(ii) To cover the front of any gap which may occur in our lines.

(iii) The above tasks can best be carried out by the guns attached to the 7th. R. Innis Fus. advancing on the line N.18.b.15.20. - N.18.b.60.05. - Northern edge of UNNAMED WOOD and eventually taking up a position in the vicinity of the NORTHERN BRICKSTACK.

The guns attached to the 7/8th. R. Irish Fus. should advance on the line N.18.d.20.55. - N.18.d.60.40. - Southern edge of UNNAMED WOOD and eventually taking up a position in the vicinity of O.13.c.70.15.

The guns attached to the 2nd. R. Irish Regt. should advance on the line O.13.c.80.20. - O.19.b.60.80, - eventually taking up a position in the vicinity of O.20.a.00.80.

(iv) In the event of the attack on either flank of any Battalion to which these guns are attached positions must at once be taken up to cover these flanks.

(v) Every effort must be made to get forward an adequate supply of ammunition for these six guns.

4.

STOKES MORTARS.
2 Mortars of the 49th. Trench Mortar Battery will be attached to the 7th. R. Innis. Fus. and will move to a central position (to be chosen). These Mortars will be available to deal with opposition in RED CHATEAU, UNNAMED WOOD and OBVIOUS ROW as required.

2 Mortars will be attached to the 7/8th. R. Irish Fus. and will move to a central position (to be chosen). These Mortars will be available to deal with opposition in NAIL LANE, BLACK COT and the HOSPICE as required.

When the BLUE LINE has been captured the Mortars attached to the 7th. R. Innis. Fus. and the 7/8th. R. Irish Fus. will move to positions from which they can cover it.

For the attack on the BLACK LINE 2 Mortars will be attached to the 2nd. R. Irish Regt. They will move to a position at X(to be chosen)X and will be available to overcome opposition as required. When the BLACK LINE has been captured these two mortars will move to positions from which they can cover it.

of assembly

The remaining two mortars will be kept in Reserve.
When the BLACK LINE has been captured the mortars attached to the 7th. R. Innis. Fus. and 7/8th. R. Irish Fus. will again come under the orders of the O.C. 49th. Trench Mortar Battery.

5.

CARRYING PARTY.
The 8th. R. Innis Fus. will provide one platoon to act as a carrying party for the 2nd. R. Irish Regt.
This carrying party will be employed in carrying shovels on its first journey and mixed loads of S.A.A., full Lewis Gun magazines, rifle grenades, bombs, etc., on its second and subsequent journeys.

X CHINESE WALL near "B" Coys. H.Q. X

4.

6.

ASSEMBLY POSITIONS. The assembly position of the Battalion will be the CHINESE WALL LINE from WATLING STREET to VIERSTRAAT ROAD. This line is allocated as follows:-

From Junction of
CHINESE WALL and
WATLING STREET
for a distance
of 265 yards to
N.18.a.07.23.   "C" Coy. with attached party of "A" Coy. and "A" Coy. H.Q.

From N.18.a.07.23.
for a distance of
228 yards to
N.18.a.27.15.   "B" Coy. with attached party of "A" Coy Lewis Gunners.

From N.18.a.27.15.
for a distance of
171 yards to
Junction of CHINESE
WALL and VIERSTRAAT-
WYTSCHAETE ROAD.   "D" Coy. with attached party of "A" Coy.

7.

POSITIONS OF HEAD-QUARTERS.

49th. Infantry Brigade Headquarters & Left Artillery Group H.Q.	THE RIB N.16.d.35.50.
7/8th. R. Irish Fus.	S.P.13.
7th. R. Innis. Fus.	Off YUMYUM TRENCH N.18.a.15.45.
2nd. R. Irish Regt.	S.P.13.
8th. R. Innis. Fus.	KNOLL DUG-OUTS N.22.a.90.55.
49th. Machine Gun Coy.	SWATOW TRENCH. N.17.d.80.90.
49th. Trench Mortar Battery.	SWATOW TRENCH.
157th. Field Coy. R.E.	THE RIB.

The Brigade Forward Station will follow the last wave of the attack on the BLUE LINE and will be established about O.13.c.15.45.

When the BLACK LINE has been captured communication will be extended forward to O.19.b.75.85.

The Forward Command Post of the 2nd. R. Irish Regt. for the attack on the BLACK LINE will be at the Brigade Forward Station.

8.

ORDER OF BATTLE. The Battalion will be disposed as follows for the attack upon the GREEN and BLACK LINES :-

"C" Company   Right Front Company.
"D" Company   Left Front Company.
"B" Company   In Support.
"A" Company   MOPPERS-UP.

The Boundary line between "C" and "D" Companies is as follows :-

O.13.c.78.12.   The Junction of NANCY DRIVE, SUNKEN ROAD and
  to   OBVIOUS ROW.
O.19.b.25.90.   OBVIOUS TRENCH.
  to
O.19.b.50.70.   Trench Junction OBVIOUS DRIVE - OBVIOUS ALLEY.
  to
O.20.a.25.57.   Road Junction.

5.

The Officer Commanding "A" Company will dispose of his Lewis Guns in such a manner as to support the attack of "C" and "D" Companies with special reference to covering their flanks. These guns during the advance will be near "B" Company's H.Q.

ACTION.

9. The Battalion will leave the CHINESE WALL at ZERO hour plus 2.30. in artillery formation. In the event of an enemy barrage on our front and support lines, the communication trenches leading as far as our front line will be used. It will arrive at the RED LINE at ZERO plus 3.00 and depart at ZERO plus 3.15 for the BLUE LINE. It will attack from the BLUE LINE at ZERO plus 3.40.

For detailed action of the several Companies see Appendices "A", "B", "C" and "D".

MOPPERS UP.

10. The position of the Moppers-Up in the Attack will be about 10 yards behind the second line of the first wave.

Moppers-up will be detailed to conduct prisoners back to the BLUE LINE where they will hand them over to the Battalions holding it and will return to the front line at once with mixed loads of ammunition drawn from forward dumps. No other men are to be detailed to conduct prisoners back.

Deep dug-outs must be treated with caution, especial regard being given to the possibility of their having two or more exits or being connected with other works by subterranean passage or of their being mined.

STRONG POINT GARRISON.

11. The Officer Commanding "B" Company will hold a platoon in readiness to occupy Strong Point "C" when the R.E. Officer shall report it ready for occupation.

MACHINE GUNS ATTACHED TO BATTALIONS.

12. The two guns of the 49th. Machine Gun Company will assemble at........................ and will move forward with the Support Company until the BLACK LINE has been reached when they will be posted at C.20.a.80.C0.

STOKES MORTARS ATTACHED TO BATTALIONS.

13. The two mortars of the 49th. Trench Mortar Battery will assemble at .... and will move forward with the Support Company. They will be utilised for overcoming local centres of resistance at the instance of the Officers Commanding "C" and "D" Companies. On the Battalion reaching the BLACK LINE they will be posted at C.20.a.25.72.

FORWARD DUMPS AND SUPPLY OF SHOVELS AND AMMUNITION.

14. The 8th. R. Innis. Fus. will establish two ammunition dumps in the BLUE LINE which will be available for the 2rd. R. Irish Regt. Shovels and ammunition will be carried forward from the BLUE LINE by ... Platoon of the 8th. R. Innis Fus. and will be left at advanced dumps to be established by the Officer Commanding "A" Company.

15.

DRESS AND EQUIPMENT.

All officers will be dressed and equiped the same as the men. Sticks are not to be carried.

Fighting Order for all ranks :-

(a) Clothing, arms and entrenching tool as issued.

(b) Equipment as issued with the exception of the pack. Haversacks to be worn on the back except for Lewis Gunners and Rifle Bombers, who will wear it at the side.

(c) Box Respirators and P.H.Helmets.

(d) Iron Rations, unexpended portion of the day's rations. Mess tin and cover.

(e) 120 rounds S.A.A. except Bombers, Signallers, Runners, Lewis Gunners and Rifle Bombers who carry 50 rounds. Carrying Parties - 50 rounds S.A.A.

(f) Every man (except Bombing Sections) 2 Mills Bombs, one in each top pocket. These bombs will be collected into dumps as soon as the objective has been gained.

(g) Flares will be carried in the bottom pockets of the jacket.

NOTE. Machine Gun Company, T.M. Battery and Carrying Parties will not carry (f) and (g).

(h) 3 sandbags per man.

(i) 2 full water bottles.

(j) Mopping Up Parties will carry one "P" Bomb in addition to 2 Mills Bombs.

(k) Bombing Sections will carry :-

   (i) Bayonet men - 6 Mills Bombs.
  (ii) Remainder of Section - 12 Mills Bombs per man.

(l) Rifle Bombers will carry 12 Hales No. 20 or 24.

(m) Bombing Sections of Mopping Up Parties will carry 10 Mills Bombs and 1 "P" Bomb per man.

(n) Lewis Gun Sections will carry 30 drums. All spare drums will be formed into dumps as far forward as possible, under Battalion arrangements.

Officers or Other Ranks equipped with Very Pistols will carry 6 one inch red signal cartridges.

WATER SUPPLY. ADVANCED WATER DUMP.

16. No reliance can be placed upon finding drinkable water behind the enemy's present front lines. A small supply only of drinking water can be secured to supplement the water carried by themen. Five petrol tins (containing 2 gallons each) will be issued to each Company after Zero plus 4.40 at a point in the vicinity of the Brigade Forward Station O.13.c.15.45. Any further supplies which may be made available will be issued from the same point.

ENEMY RUSES.

17. All men should be warned against the probable misuse of white flags and signs of surrender by the enemy who has been known to sham death and then shoot into the back of our assault.

The possibility of the enemy using other ruses, such as giving the order "Retire", must be impressed on all ranks.

COMMUNICATIONS.

18. Arrangements made by the Signalling Officer for communication from front to rear and to the flanks, apart from communication by H.Q. and Company runners, are detailed in Appendix E.

MEDICAL ARRANGEMENTS.

19. A Battalion Aid Post will be established in the existing Aid Post at N.17.d.30.50.

An advanced Battalion Aid Post will be established in the dugout just off OBVIOUS DRIVE at O.19.b.20.63.

A reserve of 25 additional Stretcher Bearers will be kept near the Brigade advanced post at O.13.c.15.45. at the disposal of the Medical Officer.

All Stretcher Bearers during the advance will carry water in petrol tins for use of the Medical Officer at the Aid Posts and for the Battalion generally.

FLAGS FOR PLATOONS.

20. In order to assist the Artillery in locating our own Infantry, distinguishing flags will be carried on the scale of not less than 2 per platoon. Strict orders are to be issued against planting these flags in the ground in order to avoid mistakes which might be caused by flags left behind in evacuated positions.

The flags will be provided under Divisional arrangements. At the time of issue all concerned will receive full details as to their size and colour and the way in which they should be carried.

"S.O.S." SIGNAL.

21. The "S.O.S." Signal will remain RED Signal Cartridges as at present.

Lieut. Colonel,

Commanding, 2nd. Battalion, The Royal Irish Regiment.

Issued at _____ p.m. 30-5-1917.   *12 noon 2/6/17*

Copy No. 1. War Diary.   No. 9. O. C. "B" Company.
        2. H.Q., 49th. I. Bde.   10. O. C. "C" Company.
        3. H.Q. 48th I. Bde.   11. O. C. "D" Company.
        4. 8th. R. Innis. Fus.   12. Intelligence Officer.
        5. 49th. M. G. Coy.   13. Signalling Officer.
        6. 49th. T. M. Batty.   14. Medical Officer.
        7. Second-in-Command.   15. Chaplain.
        8. O. C. "A" Company.   16. File.
                    No. 17. Spare.

Officer Commanding 7th. Royal Inniskilling Fusiliers
" " 8th. Royal Inniskilling Fusiliers

Reg. No. T.O./160/VI.

Herewith Sheets No.8.&.9.of Operation Orders No.I.

Please acknowledge.

W.H. Stitt. Capt. adj.
for Lieut.Colonel.

June 4th.1917.

Commanding 7/8th.Battalion Royal Irish Fusiliers

SECRET

S/307.

ORDERS FOR RAID.

Ref. Map OOSTTAVERNE Part of Sheet 28, 1/5,000

1. A raid will be carried out by the 8th. R. Innis. Fus., on the night of 5/6th. June 1917. Zero hour will be notified later.

2. Raiding Party "C" Coy. 8th. R. Innis. Fus. approximately 100 strong and two Officers, 2 N.C.Os. and 12 O.R., R.E.
   O.C, Enterprise Capt. C.H. Godsland M.C.

3. <u>RAID AREA.</u>

   Northern Boundary N.18.b.20.28 - N.18.b.60.15
   Southern Boundary N.18.d.14.70 - N.18.d.50.75
   Eastern Boundary N.18.b.60.15 - N.18.d.50.75

4. <u>OBJECT.</u> To damage enemy works and personnel, M.G. Emplacements, dugouts &c., and to capture prisoners and to obtain information regarding the state of enemy trenches.

5. <u>METHOD OF ATTACK.</u> The raiding party will be divided into two waves with distance about 50 yards.
   First Objective German Front Line taken by 1st. Wave.
   Second Objective NAIL SWITCH taken by 2nd. Wave.
   Each wave will do its own mopping up. Special parties will be told off for blocking purposes in German Front Line and NAIL SWITCH and also to deal with NAIL ROW. R.E. Party will proceed with 2nd. Wave and will be responsible for carrying out demolitions.

6. <u>ACTION OF ARTILLERY.</u> Wire will be out in the whole raid area previous to raid.
   A. 18-pounders at Zero
   (1) Barrage on German Front Line from N.18.b.20.85 - N.24.a.65.95
   (2) Box Barrage along N.18.b.20.53. - N.18.b.77.23. - N.18.d.80.58 - N.18.d.20.55.
   (3) At Zero plus two minutes
       Barrage on front line from N.18.b.22.50 - N.18.d.20.55. will lift and jump to N.18.b.55.36. - N.18.d.50.57.
   (4) At Zero plus 6 minutes.
       Barrage on NAIL SWITCH (as above) will lift to N.18.b.77.23. - N.18.d.80.58.
   (5) The box barrage will remain on until all raiding party are reported back.
   (6) Feints at Zero to Zero plus 15 minutes.
       N.24.b.00.40 - N.24.d.00.57.
       BOIS QUARANTE.
   B. Heavy Artillery. and
      To commence at Zero/continue until raiding party reported back.
   (1) NAG AVENUE from N.18.b.80.20. - O.13.c.30.85.
   (2) NAIL RESERVE from O.13.c.30.85. - N.18.d.85.22.
   (3) NANCY SUPPORT to N.24.b.60.56
   (4) Selected targets CHATEAU SPUR and NAG SUPPORT.

7. <u>ACTION OF STOKES.</u>

   To commence at Zero and continue until all raiding party back.
   (1) N.18.b.20.85 - N.18.b.20.40.
   (2) N.18.d.20.61 - N.18.c.75.00.

8. <u>ACTION OF MACHINE GUNS.</u>

   O.C. 49th. M.G. Company will arrange to carry out fire, commencing at Zero, on the following targets - NAG SUPPORT SUNKEN ROAD, CHATEAU SPUR, GRAND BOIS, UNNAMED WOOD, BLACK COT, Southern end of NAIL SWITCH.

withdrawal.

9. H.Q. of O.C. Enterprise and Medical Arrangements will be notified later.

10. **Signals and communications**

Messages from Enemy Lines to O.C. Enterprise will be sent by runner. O.C. Enterprise will be in communication with Batt. H.Q. (S.P. 13) by telephone. Signal to return to our lines will be 3 Golden Rain Rockets fired in quick succession.
Watches will be synchronised at Batt. H.Q. at Zero minus 6 hours and minus two hours.

11. Probable duration of raid, 1 hour.

12. Prisoners and Articles brought from enemy lines will be sent direct to Batt. H.Q.

13. Orders concerning special action of Lewis Guns, Return of Prisoners and any special equipment will be issued later.

1 /6/ 17.

Lieut. Colonel.
Commanding.....
8th. R. Inniskilling Fusiliers.....

S E C R E T.
Reference Map   Copy No. 17
Trench
MYTSCHAETE 1:10,000

LEFT GROUP OPERATION ORDER No. 56

1. A Raid by the 8th R. Innis. Fusrs will take place on the night 5th/6th June 1917.
2. Zero hour will be notified later.
3. Raid area:-
   N. Boundary   N 18 b 20 25 to N 18 b 60 15
   S. Boundary   N 18 d 14 75 to N 18 d 50 75
   E. Boundary   N 18 b 60 15 to N 18 d 50 & 75
4. Batteries will fire as follows:-
   Zero to zero plus 2.
   C/177   N 18 b 22 65 to N 18 b 19 25
   A/177   N 18 b 19 25 to N 18 b 16 00
   B/177   N 18 b 16 00 to N 18 d 15 70
   402nd Bty RFA N 18 d 15 70 to N 18 d 19 30

   Zero plus 2 to zero plus 7.
   C/177   N 18 b 59 58 to N 18 b 60 20
   A/177   N 18 b 60 20 to N 18 b 60 00
   B/177   N 18 b 60 00 to N 18 d 59 68
   402nd Bty RFA N 18 d 59 68 to N 18 d 38 35

   At zero plus 7 C/177, A/177, B/177 and 402nd Bty RFA cease fire.
5. Rate of fire for batteries mentioned in para 4, 4 rounds per gun per minute. 100% A
6. Zero to zero plus 2.
   C/59   N 18 a 25 55 to N 18 b 60 35
   B/59   N 18 b 60 35 to N 18 b 60 15

   Zero plus 2 onwards.
   C/59   N 18 b 22 65 to N 18 b 72 52
   B/59   N 18 b 72 52 to N 18 b 00 25
7. Zero onwards.
   "D" Bty RHA   N 18 d 00 15 to N 18 d 98 75
   A/59   N 18 d 98 75 to N 18 d 77 43
   18-pdr Bty Right Group N 18 d 77 43 to N 18 d 19 30
   D/177 1 gun PLATEAU FARM N 18 b 45 60
          2 guns PLATEAU SPUR N 18 b 85 50 searching along the spur to
                                 N 18 a 60 30
          1 gun ROUTER N BRICKSTACK
          2 guns CANADA WOOD
   D/59   1 gun GLASGOW
          1 gun N 18 d 50 10
          2 guns HUN PRINCE N 18 a 70 05 to N 18 d 40 80
8. 18-pdr batteries mentioned in para 6 & 7 will fire 4 rounds per gun per minute for first five minutes and afterwards 2 rounds per gun per minute with occasional bursts of 4 rounds per gun per minute for 1 minute. 50% A 50% AX
9. 4.5" Hows. mentioned in para 8 will fire 2 rounds per gun per minute for the first 10 minutes and afterwards 1 round per gun per minute with occasional bursts of 2 rounds per gun per minute for 3 minutes.
10. Watches will be synchronised at zero minus 2 hours
11. Acknowledge

4.6.17   Adjutant, Left Group   Lieut RFA

Copy No 1 to A/177   Copy No 7 to C/59   Copy No 13 Left Subgroup
   "   " 2 " B/177   "   " 8 " D/19   "   " 14 16th D.A.
   "   " 3 " C/177   "   " 9 " "D" Bty RHA "   " 15 49th Inf.Bde
   "   " 4 " D/177   "   " 10   402nd Bty RFA " " 16 Liaison Off.
   "   " 5 " A/59   "   " 11   " " 17 O.C. 8th Innis.
   "   " 6 " B/59   "   " 12   Right Group   " " 18 War Diary Fusrs
                                                   " " 19 File

SECRET.   Copy No.....

8th. R. INNISKILLING FUSILIERS. OPERATION ORDER No. 103 - 4/6/17.
BY LIEUT. COLONEL. T.H. BOARDMAN D.S.O.

Reference Maps FRANCE 28 S.W. Edition 5A. 1/20,000
OOSTTAVERNE 1/5,000.

GENERAL PLAN.

1. The attack on WYTSCHAETE RIDGE will be made by the 16th. Division in conjunction with Divisions on either flank.
   The Attack by the 16th. Division will be made by
   47th. Infantry Brigade on the RIGHT.
   49th.   "   "   " LEFT.
   48th.   "   "   in RESERVE.

2. Battalions of 49th. Inf. Bde. will be disposed as follows :
   7th. R. Innis. Fus.   LEFT
   7/8th. R. Irish Fus. RIGHT.
   These two Battalions will carry out the attack on the RED and BLUE Lines.
   2nd. Battalion The Royal Irish Regt. will pass through, and attack GREEN and BLACK Lines.
   8th. R. Innis. Fus. will provide Moppers Up and Carrying Parties for the three Attacking Battalions, 49th. M.G.C. and 49th. T.M.B.
   "B" & "D" Coys. will act as Moppers Up and will be attached to 7th. R. Innis. Fus. and 7/8th. R. Irish Fus. respectively. Full details as to their work is laid down in Appendices "A" & "B".
   "A" & "C" Coys. will provide Carrying Parties, and details as to their work are shown in Appendix "C".
   Having completed their task and reported to Units to which they are attached, Coys. and Platoons of 8th. R. Innis. Fus. will reassemble in YUMYUM TRENCH.

3. The various Boundaries and objectives are marked as follows on Map already issued (OOSTTAVERNE)

   (a) Boundaries.
       Red dotted Lines, Northern and Southern, 49th. Inf. Bde.
       Blue dotted lines, Dividing line between 7th. R. Innis. Fus. and 7/8th. R. Irish Fus.
   (b) Objectives.
       1st. Objective RED
       2nd. Objective BLUE
       3rd. Objective GREEN
       4th. Objective BLACK
   (c) The following will be the times of arrival at and departure from the various objectives :

	Arrive	Depart
RED LINE	0.35	1.05
BLUE "	1.40	3.40
GREEN "	4.10	4.20
BLACK "	4.40	-

4. Positions of Headquarters.

   49th. Infantry Brigade and Left Artillery Group   THE RIB
                                                      N.16.d.35.50.
   7/8th. R. Irish Fus.   S.P. 13
   7th. R. Innis. Fus.   Off YUMYUM TRENCH N.18.a.15.45.
   2nd. R. Irish Regt.   S.P. 13.
   8th. R. Innis. Fus.   S.P. 13 at first and afterwards
                                                      N.18.a.15.45.
   49th. M.G.C.   SWATOW TRENCH N.17.d.80.90.
   49th. T.M.B.   "   "   "   "
   157th. Field Coy. R.E. THE RIB.

7. Continued.
6.
   (a) One day after "Z" .... "A" Day.
       Two days after "Z" .... "B" Day.
       Three days after "Z" .... "C" Day.
       Days after "C" Day will be referred to as "Z" plus 4 "Z" plus 5, "Z" plus 6 &c.

   (b) Referring to hours on "Z" Day
       Zero is the exact time at which operations will commence, and times will be designated in hours and minutes plus or minus from Zero, even if they encroach on "Y" Day.

   (c) In making references to times before and after which operations will take place assembles + or - are not to be used. The word plus or minus is to be written in full.
       In referring to times before or after Zero Hour, the words "Zero plus ...." or "Zero minus ......" must be inserted, so as to prevent possible confusion with clock time.

8. No marked maps .... of any description of our own lines will be taken in advance of Bn. H.Q. by any Officer N.C.O., or Man. All maps so marked will be handed in to Battn. H.Q. at once.

9. Information.

   Unit Commanders will send reports to Bn. H.Q. at every half hour from Zero onwards.

10. All ranks except stretcher bearers are strictly forbidden to leave their work in order to assist wounded.

11. All men should be warned against the probable misuse of white flags and signs of surrender by the enemy, who has been known to sham death and then shoot into the back of our assault.
    The order "Retire" must be absolutely ignored.
    Deep dug-outs in enemy lines are on no account to be entered, except with permission from Officer. Before clearing a dugout containing a number of the enemy, a sufficient number of men must be present to act as escort.

12. Watches will be synchronised at 9 a.m. 12 Noon and 6 p.m. daily, under arrangements to be made by Signal Officer.

13. All Commanders down to Platoon Commanders will keep in touch throughout with the Commanders of similar formations on their flanks. They must know the disposition and action being taken by their neighbours, more particularly so when the Units on their flanks belong to another Division.

14. All mines in the 16th. Division Front will be exploded at Zero Hour. If the explosion of any of the above mines has not taken place by Zero plus 15 seconds it is to be understood that it will not take place at all.
    "Instructions to troops in connection with the firing of large mines" will be forwarded to all concerned.

15. Danger areas are being marked under Divisional arrangements. Notice Boards will be put up in all subways.

16. No telescopic rifles are to be taken forward in the attack. They are to be kept at Quartermaster's Stores for use when required.

17. To prevent congestion of ordinary traffic during the movement of troops, Battalions will march at 500 Yards distance.

18. It is most important that every precaution should be taken to prevent bayonets from flashing in the moonlight should there be a moon when Units are moving to their positions of assembly.

"B" AND "C" CARRYING PARTIES. LOAD FOR FIRST JOURNEY.

No. of Men.	Details of Load.	Approx. weight of each man's load.	Picks.	Shovels.	Sandbags.	Rifle Grenades.	Mills No.5 Bombs	S.A.A. Rounds.	L.G. Drums	S.O.S. Signals
10 WITH YUKON PACKS.	3 picks. 10 Shovels. } Each 10 Sandbags. } Man. 4 bandoliers.	65 lbs.	30	100	100			2000		
10 WITH YUKON PACKS.	1 Box Rifle Grenades) 5 L.G. Drums. } Each 10 Sandbags. } Man. 4 Bandoliers.	65 lbs.			100	200		2000	50	
10 WITHOUT YUKON PACKS.	2 Boxes Mills } Each No.5. } Man 4 Bandoliers.	42 lbs.			200		240	2000		
TOTALS 30.			30	100	200	200	240	6000	520	

NOTE :- "B" & "C" Carrying Parties will each be equipped with 20 YUKON PACKS.

"B" AND "C" CARRYING PARTIES. LOAD FOR FIRST JOURNEY.

No. of Men.	Details of Load.	Approx. weight of each man's load.	Picks.	Shovels.	Sandbags.	Rifle Grenades.	Mills No.5 Bombs	S.A.A. Rounds.	L.G. Drums	S.O.S. Signals
10 WITH YUKON PACKS.	3 picks. ⎫ 10 Shovels. ⎬ Each 10 Sandbags. ⎪ Man. 4 bandoliers. ⎭	65 lbs.	30	100	100			2000		
10 WITH YUKON PACKS.	1 Box Rifle Grenades ⎫ Each 5 L.G. Drums. ⎬ Man. 10 Sandbags. ⎪ 4 Bandoliers. ⎭	65 lbs.			100	200		2000	50	
10 WITHOUT YUKON PACKS.	2 Boxes Mills ⎫ Each No.5. ⎬ Man 4 Bandoliers. ⎭	42 lbs.					240	2000		
TOTALS 30.			30	100	200	200	240	6000	50	

NOTE :- "B" & "C" Carrying Parties will each be equipped with 20 YUKON PACKS.

Report of Raid carried out by 8th Bn. R. Inniskilling Fus.
on the night of 5th June '17

1. For Disposition & Size of Raiding Party see Orders for Raid. S/3/14 dated 3rd June 1917.

2. The first wave consisting of 'C' Coy. crept out over the parapet & moved off at ZERO, followed by the 2nd Wave consisting of 'A' Coy.

3. The following is the Time TABLE of events as received at Raid HQ. BYRON FARM.

   10.32 p.m. 2/Lt. Cooper arrived at Left Front TRENCH
   10.38 "   Capt. Hornby arrived at NAIL SWITCH
   10.43 "   Capt. Hornby reported wounded.
   10.46 "   2/Lt. Robbins entered R. Front Line unopposed.
   10.55 "   2/Lt. Cooper reported "Cleared LEFT FRONT up to NAIL Switch
   10.58 "   4 German prisoners sent on to Brigade HQ.
   11.1   "   2/Lt. Robbins reported having cleared R. Front up to NAIL SWITCH.
   11.15 "   All in except Capt. HORNBY.
   11.40 "   Capt. HORNBY reported in.

4. Information concerning German Front Line

   Generally this hardly exists & there was no sign of occupation none of the officers of 'C' Coy. who entered the Front Line saw any Germans. A certain number of dugouts were found but they had not been occupied & in some cases were waterlogged. There is practically no wire except a few scattered concertinas & there is a certain amount of wire near the willows about N.18.d.00.72. The going in No Mans Land was found to be quite good. NAG & NAIL Row are practically obliterated & unoccupied.

5. Information concerning NAIL SWITCH.
   At the NORTH END this trench was found to be in better order than was expected & there are still some dugouts which are intact. The Southern end of the line is badly damaged & was difficult to recognise. The wire in front of the front line has practically disappeared

All the prisoners were obtained from this line. Nine of them coming out from one dugout, five of whom were killed in returning to our front line.

6. <u>Number of prisoners taken</u>   Four arrived at our Front Line.

7. No machine gun emplacements were found which were not already blown in.

8. <u>Casualties</u>   1 officer wounded, 13 O.R. wounded.

9. <u>General</u>   Very few Very Lights were put up in the Raid Area. Those that were put up came from GRAND BOIS & the SOUTHERN end of PETIT BOIS

The moment barrage started a red light bursting into two red balls was sent up from UNNAMED WOOD & shortly afterwards from GRAND BOIS.

There was practically no M.G. fire

The enemy sent over "minen jars" from near the crest of the ridge onto NAIL SWITCH

There was practically no artillery retaliation on our Front Line. What there was being on SOUTH of the BATTN. frontage

The moral of the prisoners taken appeared to be distinctly poor.

T.M.Boardman. Lt.Col.
Commdg 9th R. Inniskilling Fus.

ATTACK ON WYTSCHAETE RIDGE – 7th. June 1917.

8th. R. Inniskilling Fusiliers Preliminary Report on Operations from ZERO to Midnight June 7/8th.

... ...

1. Disposition of Battalion at Zero See Battalion Operation Orders No. 103 dated 4/6/17 Paragraph 4, Appendices A, B, & C,.

2. No. of Officers and O.R. going into Action – Officers 22 O.R. 481

3. Names of Officers going into Action and their Appointment :

Lt. Colonel.	T.H.	Boardman D.S.O.	C.O.
Capt.	H.A.	Green M.C.	2nd. in Command.
2/Lieut.	C.J.	Coggins	Adjutant.
2/Lieut.	W.C.	Groombridge	B.L.G.O.
2/Lieut.	K.H.	Borcherds	Intelligence Officer.
2/Lieut.	W.E.	Ellis M.C.	Signalling Officer.
Captain	F.C.	Atkinson-Fleming M.C.	M. O. Attached. R.A.M.C.

"A" Coy.

Captain	L.G.A.	Constable M.C.	Company Commander.
2/Lieut.	W.	Notley	O.C. "A" Carrying Party.
2/Lieut.	S.J.	Henderson	" "B" " "
2/Lieut.	L.C.	Brown	" "C" " "

"B" Coy.

Captain	W.R.	Maguire	Company Commander.
Lieut.	W.A?	Browne	Mopping Up Blue Line. 7th. R. Innis. Fus.
2/Lieut.	C.D.	Nealon	.. .. Red Line.
2/Lieut.	G.F.	Paterson	.. ..

"C" Coy.

Captain	F.W.	Martin	Company Commander.
2/Lieut.	M.P.L.	Cooper	O.C. "F" Carrying Party
2/Lieut.	A.H.	Robbins	.. "D" " "
2/Lieut.	J.S.	Carruthers	.. "E" " "

"D" Coy.

Captain	H.	Broadley	O.C. Company & Police Post CHINESE WALL.
2/Lieut.	R.E.	Palmgren	Mopping Up BLUE Line 7/8th. R.I.F.
2/Lieut.	R.V.	Polley	Mopping up HOSPICE
2/Lieut.	R.H.	Roulstone	.. .. RED Line 7/8th. R.I.F.

4. Approximate Time Table of Events. Timed from Battalion Headquarters

7 a.m.	No. 15 Platoon returned to YUM YUM Trench) "D" Coy.
8.30 a.m.	No. 13 & 14 Platoons " ")
8 a.m.	"B" Coy. retruned to YUMYUM Trench
9 a.m.	Battn. H.Q. changed from S.P. 13 to BYRON FARM N.18.a.3.4.
10 p.m.	Battalion distributed as follows :

Headquarters BYRON FARM
"A" & "C" Coys. OLD Front and Support Line from VIERSTRAAT Road to MAYO Trench.
"B" & "D" Coys. YUMYUM Trench.
"A" & "C" Coys. Carrying Parties worked up to 9.30 p.m. assisted by parties from "B" & "D" Coys. & German Prisoners.

5. Action of Moppers Up

(a) "B" Coy. attached 7th. R. Innis. Fus. All the trenches mopped

Para. 5 continued.

(mopped) up in this Sector were completely demolished, the dugouts knocked in, and the wire non existant. No opposition was encountered and the prisoners taken were quite content to be taken. No special difficulty was found in the SUNKEN ROAD. Some difficulty was found in maintaining direction owing to the dense dust, and also in recognising the various objectives. A machine gun was taken from a battered dugout.
    Approximate number of prisoners taken 150.
    Approximate number of casualties suffered 1 Officer Wounded, 1 O.R. killed, 25 O.R. wounded, 5 O.R. Missing.

(b) "D" Coy. attached 7/8th. Battn. R. I. F. The experience of this company closely resembles that of "B" Coy.. They were temporarily disorganized by the mine explosion in the PETIT BOIS Salient and a concrete Lewis Gun was buried and lost. Also one man was wounded. Many strong dugouts were encountered but in all cases they had been badly damaged. The HOSPICE was found to be very badly damaged and no prisoners were taken here. All prisoners were found in shell holes and were in a semi dazed condition. One light machine gun was removed. Approximate number of prisoners taken 120.
    Approximate number of casualties 2 O.R. Killed, 11 O.R. wounded, 1 O.R. Missing.

6.   Record of Carrying Parties

(a)   Battalion Carrying Parties lettered "A" "B" & "C".
   "A" Carrying Party attached 2nd. R. Irish Regt.
   Material carried from POLL Trench to BLACK Line 104 shovels, 36 picks, 3.000 rounds S.A.A., 60 S.O.S. Signals, 128 L.G. Drums, 300 Sandbags.   Materials carried from UNNAMED WOOD to BLACK Line 40 petrol tins full of water.

   "B" Carrying Party attached 7th. R. Innis. Fus.
   Material carried from MAYO STREET Dump to RED Line 540 shovels, 180 picks, 204 bandoliers, 75 L.G. Drums, 60 Boxes Mills No. 5. Number of journeys – nine.

   "C" Carrying Party attached 7/8th. R. Irish Fus.
   Materials carried from FERMOY Trench to centre UNNAMED WOOD 200 Shovels, 60 picks, 8 Boxes S.A.A., 6 Boxes Rifle Grenades, 240 L.G. Magazines, 16 coils barbed wire, 10 Boxes Mills No. 5, 200 sandbags. Number of journeys – Six.
Approximate number of Casualties of "A" "B" & "C" Carrying Parties 12 O.R. Wounded, 1 O.R. Missing.

(b)   Carrying Parties attached to M.G. Coy., T.M. Battery.
   "D" Party attached to M.G.C.
   Material carried from YORK ROAD to BLACK COT 32 Boxes S.A?A.
   Material carried from WATSONVILLE to BLACK COT 68 Boxes S.A.A. Afterwards all S.A.A. at BLACK COT was carried to NORTH HOUSE (BLACK Line). This party did not finish carrying before 9.30 p.m.

   "E" Party attached to T.M. Battery.
   Number of Stokes Shells from MAYO STREET to RED CHATEAU and on to GREEN Line, 500. Number of Journeys – five.
   Number of Stokes Shells from WATSONVILLE to HOSPICE – 540. Number of journeys – six.

   "F" Carrying Party
   Number of water tins carried from FOSSE to BLACK COT, 80. This party also carried from MAYO STREET to UNNAMED WOOD 50 Boxes Mills, 20 Boxes S.A.A., 10 shovels. In addition to above wiring material was carried by large party of German prisoners.
   "D" Coy. supplied a carrying party of 25 and "B" Coy. one of 20, to Brigade. The Battalion also supplied 12 extra stretcher bearers to Advanced Aid Post UNNAMED WOOD.
   Approximate number of casualties "D" "E" & "F" Parties 14 O.R. wounded.

7. Regulation of Prisoners.

Captain Broadley established a chain of Police Posts along CHINESE WALL to regulate the dispatch of prisoners to the Brigade and to prevent stragglers working their way back from their Units. Approximate number of prisoners passing through to these posts was as follows :
4.45 a.m.   40 ,   5.30 a.m. 68,   6.20 a.m. 225, 9.20 a.m. 391
3 p.m.   445.

8. Casualties (as known to date of writing this) ~~to-day's date~~ 12th. June) 1 Officer wounded, 3 O.R. killed, 62 O.R. wounded, 7 O.R. missing.

9. Supply of Rations, Water &c.,

This was quite satisfactory, the rations coming up by pack transport.

10. Communications.

No difficulty was found in keeping in touch with the Brigade. Communication with Companies was maintained by runners.

11. Medical Arrangements.

The Regimental M.O. and stretcher bearers were attached to 7/8th. R. I. F. and went forward to Advanced Aid Post near BLACK COT at 4 a.m. Regimental Band worked under Brigade arrangement from 4 a.m. 7th. June to 5 a.m. 8th. June.

8 /6/ 17.

A.J. Walkey, Major
for Lieut. Colonel.,
Commanding.....,
8th. R. Inniskilling Fusiliers.......

REPORT OF RAID CARRIED OUT BY

8th R. INNISKILLING FUSILIERS, 49th INF. BDE. on

the night 15th/16th July.

(vide attached sketch).

----

1.   The object of this raid and the composition of the Parties engaged are given in Appendix.

    In addition to the parties detailed in Appendix, two parties each of 22 men under a N.C.O. assisted in carrying material from points 'B' & 'C' to the sites selected for the Bombing Posts.

2.   At 11.0 p.m. on the night 15th/16th July, two mines were successfully exploded.

    Two craters were formed separated by a mound. The explosion did little damage to the enemy's trenches.

    The near lip of the South crater was about 40 yards and that of the North crater about 20 yards from our line.

    The North and South Craters were approximately 60 yards and 80 yards wide respectively.

3.   Simultaneously with the blowing of the mines our Artillery formed a barrage on the enemy Support and Communication trenches and front line trenches on either flank. (see sketch).

    Our trench mortars opened fire on selected points in the enemy's line at M.6.b.7.4. and N.1.a.2.4. whilst our machine guns swept the enemys parapets.

    Our artillery fire was accurate and our Trench Mortars and Machine guns maintained a well directed fire.

4.   The Raiding Party was divided into three squads each consisting of 1 N.C.O. & 6 men, called right, centre and left squads respectively.

    The party left our trenches at 11.0 p.m. from point 'B' and entered the German trenches at 'Z'. They were only able to reach the trenches by making their way through undamaged wire.

(a) The Right Squad was to move along the enemy's front trench to the right, bombing dug-outs as they advanced and was to hold point 'X' for ten minutes to enable the officer to reconnoitre.

    This squad bombed from point of entry to the junction of the enemy sap and front line at Y.

    A dug-out was found and was bombed, the leading bayonet man was here killed.

    The squad then advanced to point X.

    The squad encountered a small party of the enemy which was bombed and after a short fight our bombers retired slowly.

    Whilst retiring a wounded German was encountered and captured.

    This squad withdrew to our lines by an old German Sap having been in the trenches for 35 minutes.

(b) The Centre Squad was to advance up the communication trench in rear (S.E.) of SEAFORTH Crater, for 120 yards.

    This squad bombed dug-outs in the front line between the point of entry and the communication trench.

    On entering the communication trench they were met by a party of the enemy and a short fight ensured during which the N.C.O. in command and two men were wounded.

    This squad then returned to our lines by SEAFORTH Crater having remained in the German trenches 35 minutes.

(c) The Left Squad was to move to the left along the enemy's front line for 120 yards.

    This squad found the trenches blown in and also

encountered....

encountered a strong party of the enemy which was immediately engaged.

The squad was forced back and the enemy came out over his parapet and attempted to get in rear of this squad, but this manoeuvre was frustrated by our left covering party and the enemy was driven back into his trenches.

The left squad then retired on to our left Covering Party which held up the enemy for a time but had to retire to the near lip of the new crater after 20 minutes, with a loss of one N.C.O. and two men wounded.

5. The Officer Commanding the Raiding Party, led the three squads over and having started them towards their objectives he carried out an examination of the German trenches.

He returned with the right and centre squads to our lines but on learning that the left squad had not returned and that the left covering party had been forced back he again went out to ascertain the situation.

On reaching the scene of operations he found a fierce fight in progress. He thereupon organized the left covering Party and the left squad and succeeded in driving the enemy from the far lip of the new crater.

This party of the enemy considerably outnumbered our left squad and Covering Party and it was entirely due to the officers timely intervention and determined action that the hostile party was not only driven back but was dispersed.

It was whilst organizing this counter-attack that the Officer was struck by a bomb which unfortunately killed him.

6. The parties of the enemy which were met with put up a very determined resistance especially the party encountered by the left squad.

It would appear that the enemy were prepared for a raid and had established strong bombing posts either in his communication trench or at the junction of his support and communication trench.

Rifle Grenades and Aerial Torpedoes were the chief causes of our casualties.

The enemy's artillery fire was ill directed and not severe.

7. The parties detailed for consolidation carried out their work successfully and by 3.0 a.m. the saps to the new Craters and Bombing Posts on the near lips of the craters had been constructed.

The saps were dug to a depth of 3 feet and were sandbagged.

The large amount of buried wire met with rendered the construction of the saps a matter of some difficulty.

8. Our casualties amounted to :-

8th R. Inniskilling Fusiliers.

Killed or Died of wounds.	1 Officer.	9 Other Ranks.
Wounded.	1 Officer.	28 Other Ranks.

Royal Engineers.

Killed or Died of wounds.	-	3 Other Ranks.
Total.	2 Officers.	40 Other Ranks.

No estimate of the casualties inflicted on the enemy is obtainable but it may be assumed that his casualties from all causes were not inconsiderable.

9.   The Officer Commanding the Raiding Party at the time of his return to our trenches with the Right and Centre Squads gave the following information as regards the enemy trenches:-

    (i)   Depth - 15 feet.

    (ii)   Width - 8 feet at the top, 4 feet at bottom.

    (iii) Revetment - Rabbit wire and sandbagged in places.

    (iv)   Drainage - Nil. Spoil from mines covered up the floor of the trench.

    (v)   Trench was boarded, but boards covered with spoil.

    (vi)   Empty recesses in front wall of fire trench evidently intended for S.A.A. or Bombs.

    (vii) All dug-outs had at least two entrances and were built in pairs.

    (viii) Dug-outs about 25 feet deep.

    No further details are forthcoming as the Officer left to organize the counter-attack mentioned in para 5 before further information could be obtained from him.

SECRET.

SKETCH.

Scale of Yards

B.182	——	4 - 18 prs.
C. 77	——	5 - "
C.182	——	6 - "
B.180	——	4 - "
A.180	——	4 - "
4·5 Hows.	●	
60 Prs.	○	

ORDERS FOR RAID.   SECRET.

Reference Map OOSTTAVERNE Part of Sheet 28. 1/5000

1. A raid will be carried out by the 8th. Battalion R. Inniskilling Fusiliers on the night of 5/6th. June 1917. Zero Hour will be 10 p.m.

2. Raiding Party will be drawn from "A" & "C" Coys. 8th. R. Innis. Fus and will consist of 4 Officers and approximately 170 Men.
O.C. Enterprise Capt. C.H. Godsland M.C.

3. RAID AREA.
   Northern Boundary   N.18.b.20.28 - N.18.b.60.15.
   Southern Boundary   N.18.d.14.70 - N.18.d.50.75.
   Eastern Boundary   N.18.b.60.15 - N.18.d.50.75.

4. OBJECT. To damage enemy personnel, works, &c., to capture prisoners and to obtain information regarding the state of the enemy trenches

5. OBJECTIVES.   1st. Objective   German Front Line.
                 2nd. Objective   NAIL SWITCH.

6. METHOD OF ATTACK. The raiding party will attack in 2 waves, the first wave consisting of "C" Coy. will take the first objective, the second wave consisting of "A" Coy. will take the second objective. Distance between waves will be 30 yards and each wave will consist of 1 line.

First Objective. O.C. "C" Coy. will arrange to provide the following parties.
   (1) 3 Blocking Parties consisting of 1 N.C.O. and 4 men each to block the following points, N.18.b.20.28, N.18.d.20.78, N.18.d.14.70.
   (2) A Mopping Up Party of 1 N.C.O. and 8 for NAG ROW.
   (3) A Mopping Up Party of 1 N.C.O. and 8 who will work in a Northerly direction along SUPPORT ROW.
   (4) A Left Flank Party of 1 N.C.O. and 4 along Northern Raid Boundary.
   (5) Two Lewis Guns along BECK at N.18.b.12.32.
   (6) A Right Flank Party of 1 N.C.O. and 4 along Boundary between Support Line and NAIL SWITCH.
   (7) Two Lewis Guns along BECK at N.18.d.05.75.
   (8) A Prisoner Collecting Station of 1 N.C.O. and 4 Men near Sap at N.18. Central.

2/Lieut. Cooper will be responsible for the Northern Part of 1st. Objective to N.18.d.20.95.

2/Lieut. Robbins will be responsible for the Southern Part of 1st. Objective.

Second Objective. O.C. "A" Coy. will arrange to provide the following parties.
   (1) Blocking Party for North end of NAIL SWITCH of 1 N.C.O. and 8 Men.
   (2) Blocking Party for South end of NAIL SWITCH of 1 N.C.O. and 4 Men.
   (3) Right Flank Party posted about N.18.d.60.75 and consisting of 1 Lewis Gun and 1 N.C.O. and 4 Men.
   (4) A Prisoner Collecting Station of 1 N.C.O. and 4 Men at N.18.d.60.90.

Capt. Hornby will be responsible for the 2nd. Objective and will have with him 2/Lieut. Notley.

All Lewis Gun Teams will consist of 2 Men each, extra magazines being carried up by Assaulting Troops and dumped.

7. ACTION OF ARTILLERY.   See Appendix " A "

8. ACTION OF STOKES MORTARS.
To commence at Zero and continue until all raiding party are back
   (1) To fire on SUNKEN ROAD from N.18.b.22.52 to N.18.b.70.28.
   (2) N.18.d.24.58 - N.18.d.20.20.

APPENDIX "C".

DETAIL OF CARRYING PARTIES.

Party.	To whom attached.	Position of Assembly.	2nd & Subsequent loads drawn from	Carried to.
"A" 2/Lt. Notley's Platoon.	2nd R. Irish Regt.	CHINESE WALL NORTH. N.18.a.07.23 – N.18.a.27.25.	2 Dumps in Vicinity of RED LINE.	1st Journey BLACK LINE. 2nd etc., from RED LINE to BLACK LINE.
"B" 2/Lt. Henderson's Platoon.	7th R. Innis. Fus.	USNAGH STREET, near junction with SHANNON TRENCH.	Battn. Dump near junction of MAYO STREET – WATLING STREET SUPPORT.	RED LINE at point to be selected by O.C. 7/R. Innis. Fus.
"C" 2/Lt. L.C. Brown's Platoon.	7/8th R. Irish Fus.	Rear of 4th Wave behind "D" Coy. in FERMOY TRENCH from BIRR TRENCH to CROWBAR TRENCH.	Battn. Dump at junction of BIRR TRENCH with FERMOY TRENCH.	BLACK COT.
"D" 2/Lt. Robbins' Platoon.	49th M.G.C.	PIONEER PM To report 24 hours before ZERO with 1 day's rations. Afterwards half Platoon to N.17.b.50.05. half Platoon to N.16.b.99.40.	Composition of loads:- (1) 3 Belt boxes, (2) 1 box S.A.A. (3) 2 tins water. Picks shovels & sandbags with each load.	(1). Behind Ridge in RED LINE due E. of BLACK COT (2). At junction of OBVIOUS TRENCHES. (3) NORTH HOUSE RIDGE.(10 guns).
"E" 2/Lt. Carruthers Platoon.	49th T.M.B.	Half Platoon FERMOY TRENCH. (for 7/8th R.I.F). Half Platoon 150 yds. N. of MAYO St. in front line (for 7th R. Innis. Fus.).	Load:- Each men to carry 2 sandbags each containing 3 shells.	Follow Stokes Gun Teams.
"F" 2/Lt. Cooper's Platoon.	3 Assaulting Battalions.	CORK TRENCH from WATLING ST. to N.18.c.10.55.	No. 4 Advanced Brigade Dump.	Bde. Forward Station O.13.c.15. 45.

SCHEME FOR 3" STOKES BOMBARDMENT TO ASSIST RAID ON NIGHT 5TH/6TH.

No. of Gun.	Position	Time	Rate.	Total	Target
I	N.18.c.45.18	From Zero to Zero plus 3 mins.	All fire at rate of 25 rounds per minute.	246	N.18.d.20.20 to 22.35.
II	N.18.c.58.60			246	N.18.d.22.48 to 40.40.
III	N.18.a.78.38	From Zero plus 3 mins. to Zero plus 60 mins.	All fire at rate of three rounds per minute.	246	N.18.b.70.28 to 48.39.
IV	N.18.a.78.40			246	N.18.b.43.40 to 22.52.

GRAND TOTAL ... ... 984 Rounds.

(Sd.) St. G.H.L. Clarke, Capt.,
O.C., 49th. T.M. Battery.

4.6.17.

S E C R E T.   Copy No. 15.

RIGHT GROUP OPERATION ORDER No. 10.
BY
Lieut. Colonel., L.E.S. WARD D.S.O., R.F.A. Commdg.,

Ref. Map 1/10.000 WYTSCHAETE Trench Map.

1. A raid by the 8th. Royal Inniskilling Fusiliers, 49th. Inf. Brigade will take place to-night 5th. June.

2. ZERO Hour will be 10.20 p.m.

3. The Left Group provides the supporting Artillery.

4. Right Group, less K.49, will carry out a dummy raid at the same hour.

5. Creeping and Standing Barrages will be as laid down in Right Group O.O. No. 7 dated 3.6.17.

6. Howitzer batteries (D/180 and D/113) will not take part. C/58 and B/177 will be engaged with the Left Group.

7. The dummy raid will finish at ZERO plus 15 minutes.

8. The rate of fire will be two rounds per gun per minute.

9. Watches will be synchronised under arrangements by the Adjutant, 180th. Brigade R.F.A.

10. Operation Order No. 8 will not now be published.

11. ACKNOWLEDGE.

5.6.17.   (Sd.) L.E:S. Ward, Lt. Col., R.F.A.,
                                            Commanding Right Group.

SECRET.

Copy No. 17.

Reference Trench Map
WYTSCHAETE 1:10.000.

LEFT GROUP OPERATION ORDER NO. 56.

1. A raid by the 8th. R. Innis, Fus. will take place on the night 5th/6th. June 1917.
2. Zero hour will be notified later.
3. Raid Area :-
   N. Boundary N.18.b.20.28. to N.18.b.60.15
   S. Boundary N.18.d.14.70. to N.18.d.50.75
   E. Boundary N.18.b.60.50. to N.18.d.50.75.
4. Batteries will fire as follows :
   Zero to zero plus 2
   C/177   N.18.b.22.65   to   N.18.b.19.26
   A/177   N.18.b.19.26   to   N.18.b.16.00.
   B/177   N.18.b.16.00   to   N.18.d.15.70.
   402nd. Bty. RFA N.18.d.15.70   to   N.18.d.19.30.
   Zero plus 2 to Zero plus 7.
   C/177   N.18.b.60.58   to   N.18.b.60.20
   A/177   N.18.b.60.20   to   N.18.b.60.00
   B/177   N.18.b.60.00   to   N.18.d.50.68.
   402nd. Bty. RFA N.18.d.50.68   to   N.18.d.38.35
   At zero plus 7 C/177, A/177, B/177 and 402 Bty. RFA cease fire.
5. Rate of fire for batteries mentioned in para. 4, 4 rounds per gun per minute 100 % A.
6. Zero to zero plus 2.
   C/59   N.18.b.20.58   to   N.18.b.60.35
   B/59   N.18.b.60.35   to   O.13.a.00.15
   Zero plus 2 onwards.
   C/59   N.18.b.22.65   to   N.18.b.72.52.
   B/59   N.18.b.72.52   to   O.13.a.00.15
7. Zero onwards.
   "Z" Bty. RHA   O.13.a.00.15   to   N.18.d.98.75
   A/59   N.18.d.98.75   to   N.18.d.77.43
   1 18-pdr. bty. Right Group N.18.d.77.43 to N.18.d.12.30
   D/177   1 gun PLATEAU FARM N.18.b.49.60
           2 guns CHATEAU SPUR N.18.b.85.50 searching along the spur to O.13.a.00.30.
           1 gun NORTHERN BRICKSTACK.
           2 guns UNNAMED WOOD.
   D/59   1 gun BLACK COT
           1 gun N.18.d.50.19.
           2 guns NAME DRIVE N.18.d.70.05 to N.18.d.40.18.
8. 18-pdr. batteries mentioned in paras. 6 & 7 will fire four rounds per gun per minute for first five minutes and afterwards 2 rounds per gun per minute with occasional bursts of 4 rounds per gun per minute for 1 minute. 50 % A 50 % AX.
9. 4.5" Hows. mentioned in para. 6 will fire 2 rounds per gun per minute for the first 10 minutes and afterwards 1 round per how. per minute with occasional bursts of 2 rounds per how. per minute for 3 minutes.
10. Watches will be synchronised at Zero minus 2 hours.
11. ACKNOWLEDGE.

4.6.17.

(Sd.) R.H. Jobson   Lieut. RFA
Adjutant, Left Group.

ORDERS FOR RAID.   SECRET.

S/314

Reference Map OOSTTAVERNE Part of Sheet 28. 1/5000

1. A raid will be carried out by the 8th. Battalion R. Inniskilling Fusiliers on the night of 5/6th. June 1917. Zero Hour will be ~~10 p.m.~~ 10.20

2. Raiding Party will be drawn from "A" & "C" Coys. 8th. R. Innis. Fus and will consist of 4 Officers and approximately 170 Men.
    O.C. Enterprise Capt. C.H. Godsland M.C.

3. RAID AREA.
    Northern Boundary N.18.b.20.28 - N.18.b.60.15.
    Southern Boundary N.18.d.14.70 - N.18.d.50.75.
    Eastern Boundary   N.18.b.60.15 - N.18.d.50.75.

4. OBJECT. To damage enemy personnel, works, &c., to capture prisoners and to obtain information regarding the state of the enemy trenches

5. OBJECTIVES.   1st. Objective   German Front Line.
                  2nd. Objective   NAIL SWITCH.

6. METHOD OF ATTACK. The raiding party will attack in 2 waves, the first wave consisting of "C" Coy. will take the first objective, the second wave consisting of "A" Coy. will take the second objective. Distance between waves will be 30 yards and each wave will consist of 1 line.
First Objective. O.C. "C" Coy. will arrange to provide the following parties.
    (1) 3 Blocking Parties consisting of 1 N.C.O. and 4 men each to block the following points, N.18.b.20.28, N.18.d.20.78 N.18.d.14.70.
    (2) A Mopping Up Party of 1 N.C.O. and 8 for NAG ROW.
    (3) A Mopping Up Party of 1 N.C.O. and 8 who will work in a Northerly direction along SUPPORT ROW.
    (4) A Left Flank Party of 1 N.C.O. and 4 along Northern Raid Boundary.
    (5) Two Lewis Guns along BECK at N.18.b.12.32.
    (6) A Right Flank Party of 1 N.C.O. and 4 along Boundary between Support Line and NAIL SWITCH.
    (7) Two Lewis Guns along BECK at N.18.d.05.75.
    (8) A Prisoner Collecting Station of 1 N.C.O. and 4 Men near Sap at N.18. Central.
2/Lieut. Cooper will be responsible for the Northern Part of 1st. Objective to N.18.d.20.95.
2/Lieut. Robbins will be responsible for the Southern Part of 1st. Objective.
Second Objective. O.C. "A" Coy. will arrange to provide the following parties.
    (1) Blocking Party for North end of NAIL SWITCH of 1 N.C.O. and 8 Men.
    (2) Blocking Party for South end of NAIL SWITCH of 1 N.C.O. and 4 Men.
    (3) Right Flank Party posted about N.18.d.60.75 and consisting of 1 Lewis Gun and 1 N.C.O. and 4 Men.
    (4) A Prisoner Collecting Station of 1 N.C.O. and 4 Men at N.18.d.60.90.
Capt. Hornby will be responsible for the 2nd. Objective and will have with him 2/Lieut. Notley.
All Lewis Gun Teams will consist of 2 Men each, extra magazines being carried up by Assaulting Troops and dumped.

7. ACTION OF ARTILLERY. See Appendix " A "

8. ACTION OF STOKES MORTARS.
To commence at Zero and continue until all raiding party are back
    (1) To fire on SUNKEN ROAD from N.18.b.22.52 to N.18.b.70.28.
    (2) N.18.d.24.58 - N.18.d.20.20.

- 2 -

9. ACTION OF MACHINE GUNS.
To commence at Zero and continue until all Raiding Party are in.
M.G. SUPPORT to SUNKEN ROAD, CHATEAU SPUR, UNNAMED WOOD, BLACK COT.
Southern End of NAIL SWITCH from N.18.d.50.55. - N.18.d.40.50.

10. WITHDRAWAL.
(1) When the parties under Capt. Hornby, 2/Lieuts. Cooper and Robbins have completed their task, these Officers will send each 3 runners each to O.C. Enterprise to report completion of task. Battalion Signal Officer will detail 2 Signallers to report to Capt. Hornby with Lucas Signalling Lamp. The signal on lamp that task is completed will be a succession of dashes.
(2) Recall Signal will consist of Golden Rain Rockets fired in quick succession from front line.
(3) "C" Coy. will not withdraw until "A" Coy. have passed through them.
(4) The Lewis Guns of "C" Coy. will cover the withdrawal of "C" Coy.
(5) B.L.G.O. will arrange Lewis Guns in our Front Line to cover withdrawal.

11. H.Q. of O.C. Enterprise will be at BYRON FARM which is in direct communication with Brigade H.Q.
Watches will be synchronised at Battn. H.Q. (S.P. 13) at Zero minus 6 hours and minus 2 hours.
O.C. Enterprise will arrange to have sufficient Orderlies with him to be able to send messages forward.

12. The M.O. will arrange to have an Advanced Dressing Station near BYRON FARM. The Stretcher Bearers of "A" & "C" Coys. will not go over with their Coys. but will be under the orders of the M.O.

13. DISTINGUISHING MARKS. "A" Coy. will wear Yellow Arm Bands, "C" Coy. will wear no Arm Bands.

14. Probable Duration of Raid, 1 Hour.

15. EQUIPMENT. All ranks will be lightly equipped carrying rifle and bayonet and two bombs in pocket. Special Bombing Parties will be provided with Bombing Waistcoats.

16. O.C. Enterprise will take steps to see that no one taking part in the raid has any maps, papers &c., in his possession.

17. All papers and other articles that may be of use for purposes identification must be removed from dead Germans and brought back.

18. Prisoners and all articles brought from enemy lines must be sent direct to Battn. H.Q.

T.M.Boardman
Lieut. Colonel.,
Commanding......,
8th. R. Inniskilling Fusiliers...

3/6/17.

- 2 -

9. ACTION OF MACHINE GUNS.
To commence at Zero and continue until all Raiding Party are back. MAG SUPPORT to SUNKEN ROAD, CHATEAU SPUR, UNNAMED WOOD, BLACK COT. Southern End of NAIL SWITCH from N.18.d.50.55. - N.18.d.40.30.

10. WITHDRAWAL.
   (1) When the parties under Capt. Hornby, 2/Lieuts. Cooper and Robbins have completed their task, these Officers will send back 3 runners each to O.C. Enterprise to report completion of task Battalion Signal Officer will detail 2 Signallers to report to Capt. Hornby with Lucas Signalling Lamp. The signal on lamp that task is completed will be a succession of dashes.
   (2) Recall Signal will consist of Golden Rain Rockets fired in quick succession from front line.
   (3) "C" Coy. will not withdraw until "A" Coy. have passed through them.
   (4) The Lewis Guns of "C" Coy. will cover the withdrawal of "C" Coy.
   (5) B.L.G.O. will arrange Lewis Guns in our Front Line to cover withdrawal.

11. H.Q. of O.C. Enterprise will be at BYRON FARM which is in direct communication with Brigade H.Q.
   Watches will be synchronised at Battn. H.Q. (S.P. 13) at Zero minus 6 hours and minus 2 hours.
   O.C. Enterprise will arrange to have sufficient Orderlies with him to be able to send messages forward.

12. The M.O. will arrange to have an Advanced Dressing Station near BYRON FARM. The Stretcher Bearers of "A" & "C" Coys. will not go over with their Coys. but will be under the orders of the M.O.

13. DISTINGUISHING MARKS. "A" Coy. will wear Yellow Arm Bands, "C" Coy. will wear no Arm Bands.

14. Probable Duration of Raid, 1 Hour.

15. EQUIPMENT. All ranks will be lightly equipped carrying rifle and bayonet and two bombs in pocket. Special Bombing Parties will be provided with Bombing Waistcoats.

16. O.C. Enterprise will take steps to see that no one taking part in the raid has any maps, papers &c., in his possession.

17. All papers and other articles that may be of use for purposes of identification must be removed from dead Germans and brought back.

18. Prisoners and all articles brought from enemy lines must be sent direct to Battn. H.Q.

Lieut. Colonel.,
Commanding.....,
8th. R. Inniskilling Fusiliers...

3/6/17.

"B" & "C" CARRYING PARTIES. LOAD FOR SECOND JOURNEY.

No. of Men.	Details of Load.	Approx. weight of each man's load.	Picks.	Shovels.	Sandbags.	Rifle Grenades.	Mills No. 5 Bombs.	S.A.A. Rounds.	L.G. Drums	S.O.S. Signals.
10 WITH YUKON PACKS.	8 Shovels) Each 10 Sandbags) Man. 4 Picks.)	65 lbs.	40	80	100					
10 WITH YUKON PACKS.	15 L.G. Drums) 10 Sandbags.) Each 3 Red Cartridges) Man. ½" 3 Red Cartridges) 1"	62 lbs.			100				150	60
3 WITHOUT YUKON PACKS.	8 L.G. Drums in Canvas Buckets (each Man)	34 lbs.							24	
7 WITHOUT YUKON PACKS.	2 Boxes Mills No. 5 Bombs. (Each Man)	40 lbs.					168			
TOTALS. 30			40	80	200		168		174	60

NOTE :- "B" & "C" Carrying Parties will each be equipped with 20 YUKON PACKS.

"B" AND "C" CARRYING PARTIES. LOAD FOR FIRST JOURNEY.

No. of Men.	Details of Load.	Approx. weight of each man's load.	Picks.	Shovels.	Sandbags.	Rifle Grenades.	Mills No.5 Bombs	S.A.A. Rounds.	L.G. Drums	S.O.S. Signals
10 WITH YUKON PACKS.	3 picks. 10 Shovels. } Each 10 Sandbags. } Man. 4 bandoliers. }	65 lbs.	30	100	100			2000		
10 WITH YUKON PACKS.	1 Box Rifle Grenades } Each 5 L.G. Drums. } Man. 10 Sandbags. } 4 Bandoliers. }	65 lbs.			100	200		2000	50	
10 WITHOUT YUKON PACKS.	2 Boxes Mills } Each No.5. } Man 4 Bandoliers. }	42 lbs.				200	240	2000		
TOTALS 30.			30	100	200	200	240	6000	50	

NOTE :- "B" & "C" Carrying Parties will each be equipped with 20 YUKON PACKS.

"A" CARRYING PARTY. LOAD FOR FIRST JOURNEY.

No. of Men.	Details of Load.	Approx. weight of each man's load.	Picks.	Shovels.	Sandbags.	S.A.A. Rounds.	Lewis Gun Drums.	S.O.S. Signals.
6	9 Shovels } each 10 Sandbags } man. 4 bandoliers 3 picks.	55 lbs.	18	54	60	1200		
6	9 Shovels } each 10 Sandbags } man. 4 bandoliers 3 picks.	55 lbs.	18	54	60	1200		
10	12 L.G. Drums } each 10 Bandbags. 4 bandoliers. 3 Red Cartridges. ½" 3 Red Cartridges. 1" } man.	50 lbs.			100	2000	120	60
8	13 L.G. Drums } Each 10 Sandbags. } Man. 4 bandoliers.	55 lbs.			80	1600	104	
TOTALS. 30			36	108	300	6000	224	60

NOTE :- "A" Carrying Party will be equipped with 30 YUKON PICKS.

NO. 103. - APPENDIX

INSTRUCTIONS FOR CARRYING PARTIES.

1. (a) The 70 Yukon Packs ("A" Party 30 "B" & "C" Parties 20 each) are at No. 4 Main Brigade Bomb Dump POLL TRENCH and are in charge of the Brigade Bomb Dump Keeper.
   (b) The Brigade Bombing Officer is responsible for their safe custody and protection from weather.

2. Bombs, S.A.A., Red Signal Cartridges, Shovels and petrol tins will be obtained from No. 4 Main Dump. Lewis Gun Drums filled from Units concerned.

3. 2nd. R. Irish Regt. on receipt of instructions will deliver to No. 4 Main Brigade Dump 224 filled Lewis Gun Drums in canvas bags. The 7th. R. Innis. Fus. and 7/8th. R. Irish Fus. will each deliver to No. 4 Main Brigade Dump when instructed 50 filled Lewis Gun Drums. The remaining 174 filled drums belonging to these two Units will be delivered by them on Y/Z Night, to their Battalion Dumps in Support Line being placed in charge of Bomb Store Keepers.

4. "A" "B" & "C" Carrying Parties on Y Day will pick up their respective loads and carry same up to their assembly positions.

5. "B" & "C" Carrying Parties after completing their first carry will unload their packs at the forward dumps to be specified by Battalion Commanders, and will then return to the Battalion Dumps in Support Line, of the Units to which they are attached and load up for the second journey from there. Position of the Forward Dumps as soon as determined are to be notified by O.Cs. 7th. R. Innis. Fus. and 7/8th. R. Irish Fus. to O.Cs. 2nd. R. Irish Regt. and 8th. R. Innis. Fus. Forward Dumps will be in the vicinity of the RED LINE.

6. "A" Carrying Party will unload at place to be detailed by O.C. 2nd. R. Irish Regt. and returned under his instructions for any further supplies that may be required, obtaining same from the Forward Dumps established by "B & "C" Carrying Parties.

7. ON "Y" Night "F" Carrying Party will collect from No. 4 Main Brigade Dump 60 two gallon petrol tins which they will fill with water at YORK ROAD Water Tanks N.16.b.9.3. and carry to No. 4 Advanced Brigade Dump N.17.d.8.8. placing same in charge of Store Keeper.

8. On "Z" Day "F" Carrying Party will carry up these tins to Brigade Forward Station about O.13.c.15.45. The allitment of water will be 20 Tins to each of the three Assaulting Battalions. O.C. "F" Carrying Party will leave two reliable men in charge of the dump to issue the correct number of tins to each Battalion. On completion of their task "F" Carrying Party will return to the 8th. R. Innis. Fus. assembly position in YUMYUM TRENCH and will hold itself in readiness to make further journeys if required.

9. Parties A B & C will move in rear of last wave of Battalions for which they are carrying.

10. On conclusion of the various tasks "A" "B" & "C" Carrying Parties will bring back all the Yukon Packs with them to their final assembly positions in YUMYUM TRENCH.

11. Dumps formed in the German Lines are to be marked with a board 1 foot square lettered " D " in black on a white ground. This mark must be notified to all concerned.

---oOo---

APPENDIX "B".

"B" Coy. 8th R. Innis. Fus. Mopping Up for 7th R. Innis. Fus.

Party.	Position in Advance.	Assembly Position.	Coy. to which attached.	Work.	Final Task.
Nos. 1 & 2 Sects. No. 4 Platoon.	—	—	—	—	—
"A". Platoon Sergeant of No. 4 Platoon.	3rd Line.	Front Line.	"A" & "B".	No. 1 (Right). Ground up to NAIL SWITCH (inclusive). No. 2 (Left). Special attention to SUNKEN ROAD.	Complete Mopping Up of NAIL SWITCH.
Nos. 3 & 4 Sects. No. 4 Platoon.	—	—	—	Love Streigne to NAIL SWITCH until relieved by "A".	
"B". No. 5 Section. No. 5 Platoon. 2/Lt. Nealon.	4th Line.	Front Line.	"A" & "B".	No. 3 (Right). Mop up RED CHATEAU line. No. 4 (Centre). No. 5 (Left). No. 5 Special attention SUNKEN ROAD.	Assist "C" Party if necessary.
Nos. 6, 7, & 8 Sects. No. 5 Platoon. "C". 2/Lt. Paterson.	9th Line.	Support Line.	"C" & "D".	No. 6 (Right). NAIL DRIVE. " 7 (Centre). RED CHATEAU. " 8 (Left). SUNKEB ROAD.	RED LINE
Nos. 9,10, 11, & 12 Sections. "D". No. 6 Platoon. Lt. Browne.	13th Line.	Support Line.	"C" & "D".	No. 9 (Right) " 10 (Right Centre.) " 11 (Left Centre). " 12 (Left.).	BLUE LINE.

Assembly Positions Yellow letters on black.
O.C. Moppers Up on capture of RED LINE at Bn. H.Q. in RED LINE.

APPENDIX "A".

"D" Coy. 8th R. Innis. Fus. Mopping up for 7/8th R. Irish Fus.

Party.	Position in Advance.	Assembly Positions.	Coy. to which attached.	Work.	Final Task.	Remarks.
A	1 & 2. Sects. No. 13. Platoon. i.e. 3rd Platoon. Sergt. 17.O.R.	Rear of 1st Wave.	Front Line from N.18.c.48.25 to point of Salient at N.18.c.67.55	"A" Coy., RIGHT.	Dugouts junction of NAME SUPPORT & NAME DRIVE, NANCY SUPPORT.	RED LINE.	
B	3 & 4 Sects. No. 13. 2/Lieut. Houlehan. 17.O.R.	Rear of 1st Wave. i.e. 3rd Honestone. Line.	Front Line N.18.c.67.55 to N.18.c.55.00.	"B" Coy., LEFT.	NANCY SUPPORT and along NAIL LANE up to & including BLACK COT.	RED LINE.	"A" & "B" party go over together.
C	5 & 6 Sects. No. 14. 2/Lieut. Palmgren. 17.O.R.	Rear of 3rd Wave. i.e. 5th Line.	WREN WAY, N. of BIRR TRENCH behind 1st Wave of "D" Coy.	"D" Coy. LEFT.	DUGOUTS round point O.13.c.72.15 (rear of BLUE LINE).	BLUE LINE.	
D	7 & 8 Sects. No. 14. 2/Lieut. 17.O.R.	Rear of 3rd Wave. i.e. 8th Line.	WREN WAY S. Rear of BIRR TRENCH, behind "C" Coy. 1st Wave.	"C" Coy. RIGHT.	Trench running S.E. from O.19.a.10.92 to DUGOUTS at O.19.a.44.70. From RED to BLUE LINES.	BLUE LINE.	"C" & "D" party go over together.
E	No. 15. 2/Lieut. Polley. 34 O.R.	Rear of 3rd Wave. i.e. 9th Line.	DITTO.	"C" Coy. RIGHT.	HOSPICE.	BLUE LINE.	

SECRET.   Copy No. 15.

8th. R. INNISKILLING FUSILIERS. OPERATION ORDER No. 103 - 4/6/17.
BY LIEUT. COLONEL. T.H. BOARDMAN D.S.O.

Reference Maps FRANCE 28 S.W. Edition 5A. 1/20,000
                OOSTTAVERNE 1/5,000.

GENERAL PLAN.

1. The attack on WYTSCHAETE RIDGE will be made by the 16th. Division in conjunction with Divisions on either flank.
   The Attack by the 16th. Division will be made by
   47th. Infantry Brigade on the RIGHT.
   49th.   ..   .. LEFT.
   48th.   ..   ..   in RESERVE.

2. Battalions of 49th. Inf. Bde. will be disposed as follows :
   7th. R. Innis. Fus.   LEFT
   7/8th. R. Irish Fus.   RIGHT.
   These two Battalions will carry out the attack on the RED and BLUE Lines.
   2nd. Battalion The Royal Irish Regt. will pass through, and attack GREEN and BLACK Lines.
   8th. R. Innis. Fus. will provide Moppers Up and Carrying Parties for the three Attacking Battalions, 49th. M.G.C. and 49th. T.M.B.
   "B" & "D" Coys. will act as Moppers Up and will be attached to 7th. R. Innis. Fus. and 7/8th. R. Irish Fus. respectively. Full details as to their work is laid down in Appendices "A" & "B".
   "A" & "C" Coys. will provide Carrying Parties, and details as to their work are shown in Appendix "C".
   Having completed their task and reported to Units to which they are attached, Coys. and Platoons of 8th. R. Innis. Fus. will reassemble in YUMYUM TRENCH.

3. The various Boundaries and objectives are marked as follows on Map already issued (OOSTTAVERNE)

   (a) Boundaries.
       Red dotted Lines, Northern and Southern, 49th. Inf. Bde.
       Blue dotted lines, Dividing line between 7th. R. Innis. Fus. and 7/8th. R. Irish Fus.
   (b) Objectives.
       1st. Objective RED
       2nd. Objective BLUE
       3rd. Objective GREEN
       4th. Objective BLACK
   (c) The following will be the times of arrival at and departure from the various objectives :

		Arrive	Depart
RED	LINE	0.35	1.05
BLUE	..	1.40	3.40
GREEN	..	4.10	4.20
BLACK	..	4.40	-

4. Positions of Headquarters.

   49th. Infantry Brigade and Left Artillery Group   THE RIB
                                                      N.16.d.35.50.
   7/8th. R. Irish Fus.   S.P. 13
   7th. R. Innis. Fus.   Off YUMYUM TRENCH N.18.a.15.45.
   2nd. R. Irish Regt.   S.P. 13.
   8th. R. Innis. Fus.   S.P. 13 at first and afterwards
                           N.18.a.15.45.
   49th. M.G.C.   SWATOW TRENCH N.17.d.80.90.
   49th. T.M.B.   ..   ..   ..
   157th. Field Coy. R.E. THE RIB.

4. (contd).

The Forward Command Post of the 2nd R. Irish Regt., for the attack on the BLACK LINE will be at the Brigade Forward Station.
The Brigade Forward Station will follow the last wave of the attack on the BLUE LINE and will be established about O.13.c.15.45.
When the BLACK LINE has been captured, communication will be extended forward to O.19.b.75.85.

5. COMMUNICATION TRENCHES.

The 49th Inf. Bde. has been allotted two Main Communication Trenches –
    WATLING STREET (IN TRENCH).
    THE FOSSE   (OUT TRENCH).
Five Communication Trenches connect the CHINESE WALL LINE with the PARK LINE. The will be allotted as follows :-
Right Battalion, THE FOSSE, CHOW STREET, AND CORK TRENCH.
Left Battalion, CLARE STREET & USNAGH STREET.
Four Communication Trenches connect the PARK LINE with the Front Line, they will be allotted as follows:-
Right Battalion, BIRR TRENCH & CROWBAR STREET (both to be rebuilt).
Left Battalion, TARA STREET (to be rebuilt), MAYO STREET.
The following roads in the Forward Area have been allotted to the 16th Division,
  (a). KEMMEL → WYTSCHAETE ROAD (SUICIDE ROAD).
  (b). V.C. ROAD.
Four Cross-country routes (two to each Brigade Area) leading forward from KIM ROAD to the neighbourhood of WYTSCHAETE are being prepared for wheeled traffic, as far forward as our front line.
These tracks are lettered "C" "D" "E" & "F". "D" & "F" will be reserved for IN or Eastward traffic; "C" & "E" for OUT or Westward traffic.

6. DRESS.

All Officers will be dressed and equipped the same as the men; sticks are not to be carried.
Fighting Order for all ranks:-
(a). Clothing, Arms and Entrenching Tool, as issued.
(b). Equipment as issued with the exception of the pack. Haversacks to be worn on the back, except for Lewis Gunners, Rifle Bombers and carrying parties, who will wear it at the side.
(c). Box Respirators and P.H. Helmets.
(d). Iron Rations, unexpended portion of the day's rations, Mess tin and cover.
(e). 120 rounds S.A.A. except Bombers, Signallers, Runners, Lewis Gunners and Rifle Bombers who carry 50 rounds.
Carrying parties, 50 rounds, S.A.A.
(f). Every man (except bombing sections), two Mills Bombs, one in each top pocket. These bombs will be collected into dumps as soon as the Objective has been gained.
(g). Moppers Up and Carrying Parties will not carry flares, nor will carrying parties carry (f).
(h). Three sandbags per man for Moppers Up only.
(i). Water Bottle, full.
(j). Mopping Up parties will carry one "P" Bomb in addition to two Mills Bombs.
(k). Bombing Sections will carry:-
  (1). Bayonet Men 6 Mills Bombs.
  (2). Remainder of Section, 12 Mills Bombs per man.
(l). Bombing Sections of Mopping Up Parties will carry 10 Mills Bombs and 1 "P" Bomb, per man.

7. In making reference to times before or after which operations will commence, the following Nomenclature will be adopted in future :-
(a). Referring to days –
"Z" Day is the day on which operations take place.
One day before "Z".................... "Y" day.
Two days before "Z".................... "X" "
Three days before "Z".................. "W" "
Four days before "Z"................... "V" "
Five days before "Z"................... "U" "

Days before "U" day will be referred to as "Z" minus 6, "Z" minus 7, "Z" minus 8 etc..

- 3 -

7. Continued.

   (a) One day after "Z" .... "A" Day.
       Two days after "Z" .... "B" Day.
       Three days after "Z" .... "C" Day.
       Days after "C" Day will be referred to as "Z" plus 4 "Z" plus 5, "Z" plus 6 &c.

   (b) Referring to hours on "Z" Day
       Zero is the exact time at which operations will commence, and times will be designated in hours and minutes plus or minus from Zero, even if they encroach on "Y" Day.

   (c) In making references to times before and after which operations will take place assembles + or − are not to be used. The word plus or minus is to be written in full.
       In referring to times before or after Zero Hour, the words "Zero plus......" or "Zero minus ......" must be inserted, so as to prevent possible confusion with clock time.

8. No marked maps .... of any description of our own lines will be taken in advance of Bn. H.Q. by any Officer N.C.O., or Man. All maps so marked will be handed in to Battn. H.Q. at once.

9. Information.

   Unit Commanders will send reports to Bn. H.Q. at every half hour from Zero onwards.

10. All ranks except stretcher bearers are strictly forbidden to leave their work in order to assist wounded.

11. All men should be warned against the probable misuse of white flags and signs of surrender by the enemy, who has been known to sham death and then shoot into the back of our assault.
    The order "Retire" must be absolutely ignored.
    Deep dug-outs in enemy lines are on no account to be entered, except with permission from Officer. Before clearing a dugout containing a number of the enemy, a sufficient number of men must be present to act as escort.

12. Watches will be synchronised at 9 a.m. 12 Noon and 6 p.m. daily, under arrangements to be made by Signal Officer.

13. All Commanders down to Platoon Commanders will keep in touch throughout with the Commanders of similar formations on their flanks. They must know the disposition and action being taken by their neighbours, more particularly so when the Units on their flanks belong to another Division.

14. All mines in the 16th. Division Front will be exploded at Zero Hour. If the explosion of any of the above mines has not taken place by Zero plus 15 seconds it is to be understood that it will not take place at all.
    "Instructions to troops in connection with the firing of large mines" will be forwarded to all concerned.

15. Danger areas are being marked under Divisional arrangements. Notice Boards will be put up in all subways.

16. No telescopic rifles are to be taken forward in the attack. They are to be kept at Quartermaster's Stores for use when required.

17. To prevent congestion of ordinary traffic during the movement of troops, Battalions will march at 500 Yards distance.

18. It is most important that every precaution should be taken to prevent bayonets from flashing in the moonlight should there be a moon when Units are moving to their positions of assembly.

19. In the event of Hostile Aeroplanes flying low over our lines to ascertain whether our trenches are more strongly manned than usual, all ranks will remain still and will not look up.
Such Aeroplanes are to be dealt with by Anti-Aircraft, Lewis and Machine Guns, each Battalion in the line maintaining four Lewis Guns for this purpose.

20. In order to assist the Artillery in locating our own Infantry, distinguishing flags will be carried on the scale of not less than two per Platoon. Strict orders are to be issued against planting these flags in the ground in order to avoid the mistakes which might be caused by flags left behind, in evacuated positions. The flags will be provided under Divisional arrangements. At the time of issue all concerned will receive full details as to their size and colour and the way in which they should be carried.

21. The S.O.S. Signal will remain RED Signal Cartridges as at present.

22. The following R.E. Dumps will be established in the Forward Area :-
RESERVE DUMP   R.E. FARM, N.15.c.1.5.
INTERMEDIATE DUMP QUEBEC VILLA, N.16.d.5.8.
ADVANCED DUMPS   (1). N.17.d.2.2.
                   (2). WATSONVILLE. N.17.d.6.7.
As soon as feasible a Dump will be formed at NORTHERN BRICKSTACK.

23. In order to avoid casualties the whole of the Infantry detailed for the assault of the RED & BLUE LINES should get rapidly across NO MANS LAND. As few troops as possible will be left in our own front and support lines.

24. The wearing of captured German Headdress, Uniform or Equipment is strictly forbidden.

25. After taking the BLACK LINE troops will be pushed forward to establish themselves on a more advanced line.

26. (a). The New Objective will be known as THE OOSTTAVERNE LINE. The portion allotted to IXth Corps extends from O.28.b.5.2. to O.16.c.4.2.
(b). The 33rd Inf. Bde. and 68th Field Coy. R.E. from the 11th Division will be attached to the 16th Division for the purpose of this advance.

27. TANKS. One Section of Tanks (four tanks) has been allotted to the 16th Division for the advance from the BLUE to the BLACK LINE. Four Sections of Tanks and any others which can be rallied have been allotted to the 16th Division for the advance from the BLACK LINE to the OOSTTAVERNE LINE.
Details as to the employment of these Tanks will be issued later to all concerned.
It must be impressed on all ranks in the Infantry that the Tanks are there to assist their advance if possible, but that they must never for a moment suppose that success depends on their presence. The men must never wait for the Tanks but must push on to their Objective irrespective of whether they come up or not. There is a great danger of the attack being held up if this is not thoroughly realised by all ranks. On no account must men gather around the Tanks.

28. S.A.A. & BOMB LIMBERS, of Regimental and M.G.Coy. Transport and all Mobile Reserves of tools will be ready loaded up by ZERO Hour and Brigaded under arrangements to be made by the Staff Captain. They are not to be unloaded without orders from Brigade H.Q.

29. Position of Lewis Machine Guns will be as follows:-
"A" Coy. 4 Guns with Teams and all magazines in YUMYUM Trench.
"B" "   1 Gun and team with 15 magazines with 13th line 7th R. Innis. Fus. and 3 guns with Nos. 1 of each in YUMYUM Trench.
"C" "   4 Guns with teams and all magazines in YUMYUM TRENCH.
"D" "   4 Guns with teams, carrying 15 magazines per team to report to B.L.G.O. 7/8th R. Irish Fus.
Remainder of magazines of guns going into action will be dumped in YUMYUM TRENCH.

30. **Police Arrangements.**

Police Posts will be formed along CHINESE WALL Line to direct Stragglers to the Battn. Assembly Trenches and to prevent escorts to prisoners being too large.

31. Acknowledge

                         S.J. Walker Major
                         for Lieut. Colonel.,
                                   Commanding....,
              8th. R. Inniskilling Fusiliers.....

Issued through Signals :

```
Copy No.  1 to O.C. "A" Coy.
  "   "   2  "   "  "B"  "
  "   "   3  "   "  "C"  "
  "   "   4  "   "  "D"  "
  "   "   5  .. Signalling Officer.
  "   "   6  .. Intelligence Officer.
  "   "   7  .. B. L. G. O.
  "   "   8  .. Medical Officer.
  "   "   9  .. H. Q. 49th. Inf. Bde.
  "   "  10  .. O. C. 2nd. R. Irish Regt.
  "   "  11  ..    "   7th. R. Innis. Fus.
  "   "  12  ..    "   7/8th. R. Irish Fus.
  "   "  13  .. 49th. M. G. C.
  "   "  14  .. 49th. T. M. B.
  "   "  15  .. War Diary.
  "   "  16/17 Retained.
```

APPENDIX 'Z'

Attack on Wytschaete

7th June 1917

Operation Order No. 103
Report on Operations
Maps (2)

War Diary
June 1917

SECRET.   Copy No.....

8th. R. INNISKILLING FUSILIERS. OPERATION ORDER No. 103 – 4/6/17.
BY LIEUT. COLONEL. T.H. BOARDMAN D.S.O.

Reference Maps FRANCE 28 S.W. Edition 5A. 1/20,000
                OOSTTAVERNE 1/5,000.

GENERAL PLAN.

1. The attack on WYTSCHAETE RIDGE will be made by the 16th. Division in conjunction with Divisions on either flank.
 The Attack by the 16th. Division will be made by
    47th. Infantry Brigade on the RIGHT.
    49th.   "   "   " " LEFT.
    48th.   "   "   in RESERVE.

2. Battalions of 49th. Inf. Bde. will be disposed as follows :
    7th. R. Innis. Fus. LEFT
    7/8th. R. Irish Fus. RIGHT.
 These two Battalions will carry out the attack on the RED and BLUE Lines.
 2nd. Battalion The Royal Irish Regt. will pass through, and attack GREEN and BLACK Lines.
 8th. R. Innis. Fus. will provide Moppers Up and Carrying Parties for the three Attacking Battalions, 49th. M.G.C. and 49th. T.M.B.
 "B" & "D" Coys. will act as Moppers Up and will be attached to 7th. R. Innis. Fus. and 7/8th. R. Irish Fus. respectively. Full details as to their work is laid down in Appendices "A" & "B".
 "A" & "C" Coys. will provide Carrying Parties, and details as to their work are shown in Appendix "C".
 Having completed their task and reported to Units to which they are attached, Coys. and Platoons of 8th. R. Innis. Fus. will reassemble in YUMYUM TRENCH.

3. The various Boundaries and objectives are marked as follows on Map already issued (OOSTTAVERNE)

(a) **Boundaries.**
    Red dotted Lines, Northern and Southern, 49th. Inf. Bde.
    Blue dotted lines, Dividing line between 7th. R. Innis. Fus. and 7/8th. R. Irish Fus.

(b) **Objectives.**
    1st. Objective RED
    2nd. Objective BLUE
    3rd. Objective GREEN
    4th. Objective BLACK

(c) The following will be the times of arrival at and departure from the various objectives :

	Arrive	Depart
RED LINE	0.35	1.05
BLUE "	1.40	3.40
GREEN "	4.10	4.20
BLACK "	4.40	–

4. **Positions of Headquarters.**

49th. Infantry Brigade and Left Artillery Group	THE RIB N.16.d.35.50.
7/8th. R. Irish Fus.	S.P. 13
7th. R. Innis. Fus.	Off YUMYUM TRENCH N.18.a.15.45.
2nd. R. Irish Regt.	S.P. 13.
8th. R. Innis. Fus.	S.P. 13 at first and afterwards N.18.a.15.45.
49th. M.G.C.	SWATOW TRENCH N.17.d.80.90.
49th. T.M.B.	" " " "
157th. Field Coy. R.E.	THE RIB.

Odd Spare Sheets
of O.O. 103
(Offensive)

"A" CARRYING PARTY. LOAD FOR FIRST JOURNEY.

No. of men.	Details of load.	Approx. weight of each man's load.	Picks.	Shovels.	Sandbags.	S.A.A. rounds.	Lewis Gun Drums.	S.O.S. Signals.
6.	9 shovels) 10 sandbags)each 4 bandoliers)man. 3 picks)	55 lbs.	18.	54.	60.	1200.		
6.	9 shovels) 10 sandbags)each 4 bandoliers)man. 3 picks)	55 lbs.	18.	54.	60.	1200.		
10.	12 L.G. Drums) 10 sandbags) 4 bandoliers)each 3 red cart-)men. ridges 1") 3 red cart-) ridges 1")	50 lbs.			100.	2000.	120.	60.
8.	13 L.G. Drums)each 10 sandbags) 4 bandoliers)man.	55 lbs.			80.	1500.	104.	
TOTALS 30.			36.	108.	300.	6000.	224.	60.

NOTE :- "A" Carrying Party will be equipped with 30 YUKON PACKS.

SECRET.   S.O/I/5.

~~A Coy~~   ~~2nd in Command~~
~~B "~~   ~~49th Infy Bde~~
~~C "~~   B Coy 8th R.Innis Fus
D "   ~~8th R.Innis Fus~~

Herewith Instructions for the Offensive and Appendixes.
S.O/I.6/4.6.17 and Appendix (C) d/4.6.17.
These instructions are on no account to be taken E of the VIERSTRAAT SWITCH.
Those not forwarded to you are struck out.
ACKNOWLEDGE.

                    acTaggart   Captn & Adjutant.

4. 6. 17.

SECRET. Copy No. 17

G.O/I. d/4.6.17.

INSTRUCTIONS FOR THE OFFENSIVE
(continuation of)

4. 6. 17.

32. DUMPS.

(a) There will be an advanced R.E. Dump at WATSONVILLE (N.17.d.6.7.).

As soon as feasible an R.E. Dump will also be formed at the NORTHERN BRICKSTACK.

(b) The Battalion Dump will be in the immediate vicinity of the "U" of UNNAMED WOOD vide Trench Map OOSTAVERNE part of Sheet 28 1/5000 or WYTSCHAETE 28 S.W. 2. Ed 5 A.

33. (a) After the BLACK line (the Brigades 4th Objective) has been captured, Troops will be pushed forward to establish themselves on more advanced lines.
This new Objective will be known as the OOSTAVERNE LINE.

(b) The 33 Infy Bde and the 98th Field Coy R.E. from the 11th Divn being attached to the Division for the purpose of this advance.

34. ARTILLERY ACTION ON "Z" DAY UP TO THE TAKING OF THE BLACK LINE:
Vide para I c and e above and Map A.

(a) Action previous to Assault.
Previous to the assault there will be no intense bombardment - night firing and Artillery work generally will be carried as usual until Zero hour. It is essential that there should be no alteration in the rate or volume of fire previous to Zero hour, and that everything should appear normal.

(b) Action at Zero.
At Zero all guns will open at their maximum rate of fire, and the Infantry will form up under the 18 pdr creeping barrage.

(c) BARRAGE arrangements:
The barrages will consist of:
(i) A Creeping barrage of 18 pdr shrapnel moving in advance of the Infantry at average lifts of 100 yards. The times of lift and pauses in the Creeping barrage up to the BLACK LINE are shown on Map C.

(ii) Standing barrages of 18 pdrs, 4.5 howitzers, medium and heavy howitzers, which will be established on successive trenches, Strong points, etc within the limits of safety of each gun or howitzer.
These barrages have been arranged in depth so as to ensure that all ground which commands the line of advance of our Infantry is kept under fire from Zero onwards.

(d) Protective Barrages.
During the periods of consolidation of the RED, BLUE and GREEN LINES, the creeping barrage will form a protection barrage 150 yards in front of our Infantry. Fire will not be kept on the same points the whole time, but a system of searching and sweeping will be employed, so that all enemy movement in the area will be stopped.

(e) Protective Barrage in front of the BLACK LINE.
The Protective Barrage in front of the BLACK LINE will be placed 300 yards in front of our Infantry. The Infantry holding the BLACK line will push out their patrols as far as the barrage permits.

INSTRUCTIONS FOR THE OFFENSIVE
(continuation of)   continued.

35. TANKS.

One section of TANKS (4 Tanks) have been allotted to the 16th Division for the advance from the BLUE to the BLACK LINE.

Four sections of Tanks and any others which can be rallied have been allotted to the 16th Division for the advance from the BLACK LINE to the OOSTAVERNE LINE.

Details as to the employment of these tanks will be issued later to all concerned.

It must be impressed on all ranks in the Infantry that the Tanks are there to assist their advance if possible, but that they must never for a moment suppose that success depends on their presence. The men must never wait for the Tanks but must push on to their Objective irrespective of whether they come up or not. There is a great danger of the attack being held up if this is not thoroughly realized by all ranks.

36. EMPLOYMENT OF TUNNELLING COYS ON DUGOUTS AND ROADS.

A party of 3 Officers and 30 Other ranks from 250th Tunnelling Company provided with the necessary maps of enemy trenches will reconnoitre captured dugouts as soon as the Objective is reached.

This party will mark habitable dugouts with the number of men which can be accommodated in them and will carry out repairs to other Dugouts as required.

No dugouts until inspected and noted by this party as habitable are on any account to be occupied by anyone.

37. CONTACT PATROLS.

Aeroplanes for contact patrols will be R.E. 8 type and will be specially marked by a black flap attached to the rear of each lower plane. Photographs are being issued.

38. Two contact aeroplanes will be in the air at the same time. One watching the area South of VYTSCHAETE and the other VYTSCHAETE and the area north of the Village.

Contact patrols will fly over the line and call for flares at the following hours, and any hours subsequent to these hours at which special aeroplanes may be ordered.

Troops will also be prepared to put out flares at any other time if the aeroplanes calls for them.

By 7th R.Innis Fus   { Zero plus 45 minutes
                     { Zero plus 2 hours

39. Aeroplanes will call for flares and WATSON Fan by sounding a Claxton Horn and firing a "Very" white light, or by giving either of these two signals.

40. Green flares will be used. They should be lit in bunches of three each about 30 yards apart.

WATSON Fans will be used in conjunction with flares, The Fans should be turned over every two seconds and not quicker, that is, the white side will be exposed to the aeroplane for 2 seconds and the dark side for two seconds, and so on. An issue of Fans will be made as they become available.

41. No aeroplanes will be in the air before Zero.

42. X Corps contact aeroplanes will be distinguished by three broad white bands on the fuselage and also by a black board on the lower left plane.

II Anzac contact aeroplanes will be distinguished by two black streamers on the lower right hand plane.

43. The Code call for Liaison between the Battalion and Aircraft will be U.N.

A.C. Argent.
Captn & Adjutant.

Copy No 1 File   6 Bde for information.
        2 A Coy   7 2nd in Command   9 8th R.INNIS. (for information
        3 " "   8)   10. M.G
        4 C " "   to) not issued.   11. T.M   4.6.17.

SECRET;   Copy No. 9

APPENDIX C to S.O/I.

MOPPERS UP.   Sheet 3
(continuation of).

4.6.17.

9. The Battalion Dump will be in the immediate vicinity of the U in UNNAMED WOOD.

10. No 6 Platoon will take with them their L/G and 15 L/G drums.
    The remaining L/G's of the Company with their Nos I will not be required and will proceed direct to their Battalion assemble position in YUM YUM TRENCH.

11. All "Moppers Up" will carry one "P" Bomb in addition to two Mills Bombs.

12. Bombers of bombing sections will carry 10 Mills Bombs and one "P" Bomb per man.

13. Rifle Grenadiers will carry bombs in lieu of Rifle Grenades.

14. All Bombs remaining on completion of their tasks will be dumped at the Battalion Dump prior to their marching off to their own Battn assembly position in YUM YUM TRENCH.

15. ACKNOWLEDGE.

                                    A.C. Tarbet
                                    Captn & Adjt.

Copy No 1 File
       2 A Coy
       3 B "
       4 C "
       5 D "
       6 Bde for information.
       7 2nd in Command.
       8 B Coy 8th R.Innis Fus.
       9 8th R.Innis Fus for information.
      10)
      to) not issued.
      15)

SECRET.

ACCOMMODATIONS AND ARRANGEMENTS IN S.P. 13.

Attached is a rough plan showing where Headquarters of units will be accommodated.

So as to ensure that these arrangements are properly carried out and that unauthorised people do not overcrowd the dugouts the following will command the dugout.

1st. Lieut. Col. WELDON, D.S.O. until he moves out.

2nd. Lieut. Col. GREGORIE, D.S.O. until he moves out.

3rd. Lieut. Col. BOARDMAN, D.S.O. until the dugout is taken over by the 48th Bde. H.Q. when Lt. Col. BOARDMAN will move to the Battn. H.Q. near BYRON FARM.

The Brigade Signal Officer will arrange that the signallers of the 8th R. Innis Fus. Signals will man the signal office at S.P.13 until relieved by 48th Bde. Signallers.

The Brigade Forward Station Party and the 7/8th R. Irish Fus. Forward Post will form up just before Zero outside Eastern Entrance marked Z. As soon as the mines have gone up they will move down using entrance Z through the Tunnel. The staircase to entrance Z will be kept clear.

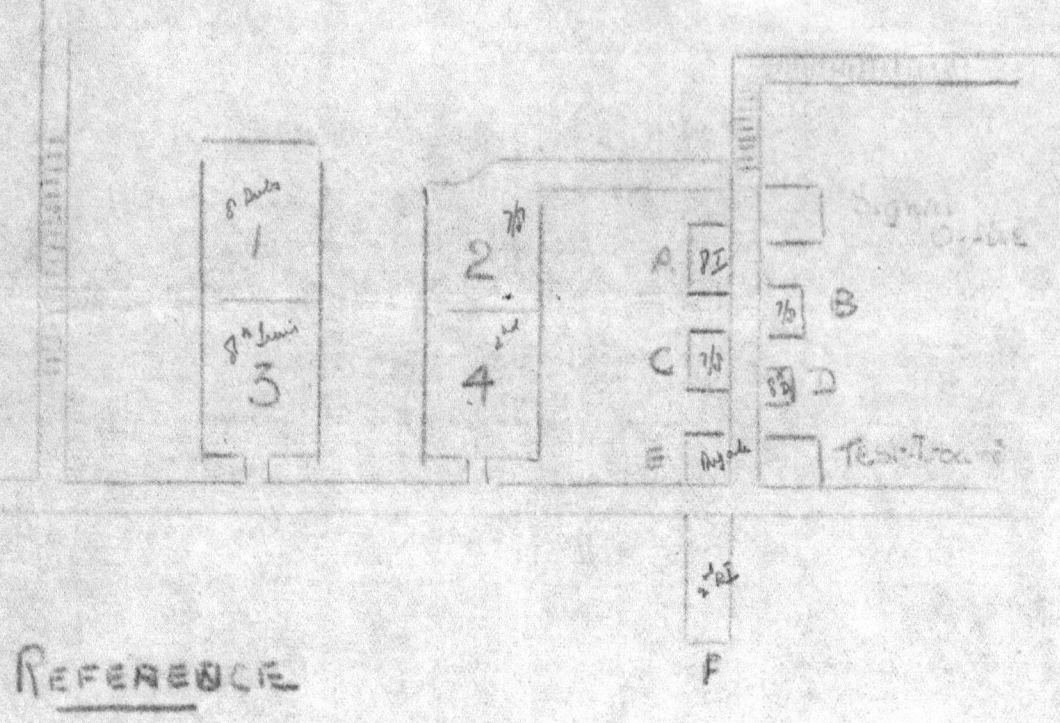

REFERENCE

2. 7/8th Roy Irish. Fus.
4. 2nd Roy Irish Regt.
3. 8th Roy Innis. Fus
1. 8th Roy. Dublin Fus.

A   Sig: & Runners of 8th R Innis Fus
B }   "   "   7/8 R Irish Fus
C }
D   "   "   8 Roy Dublins
E   Brigade Signals
F   "   "   2nd Roy Irish Regt.

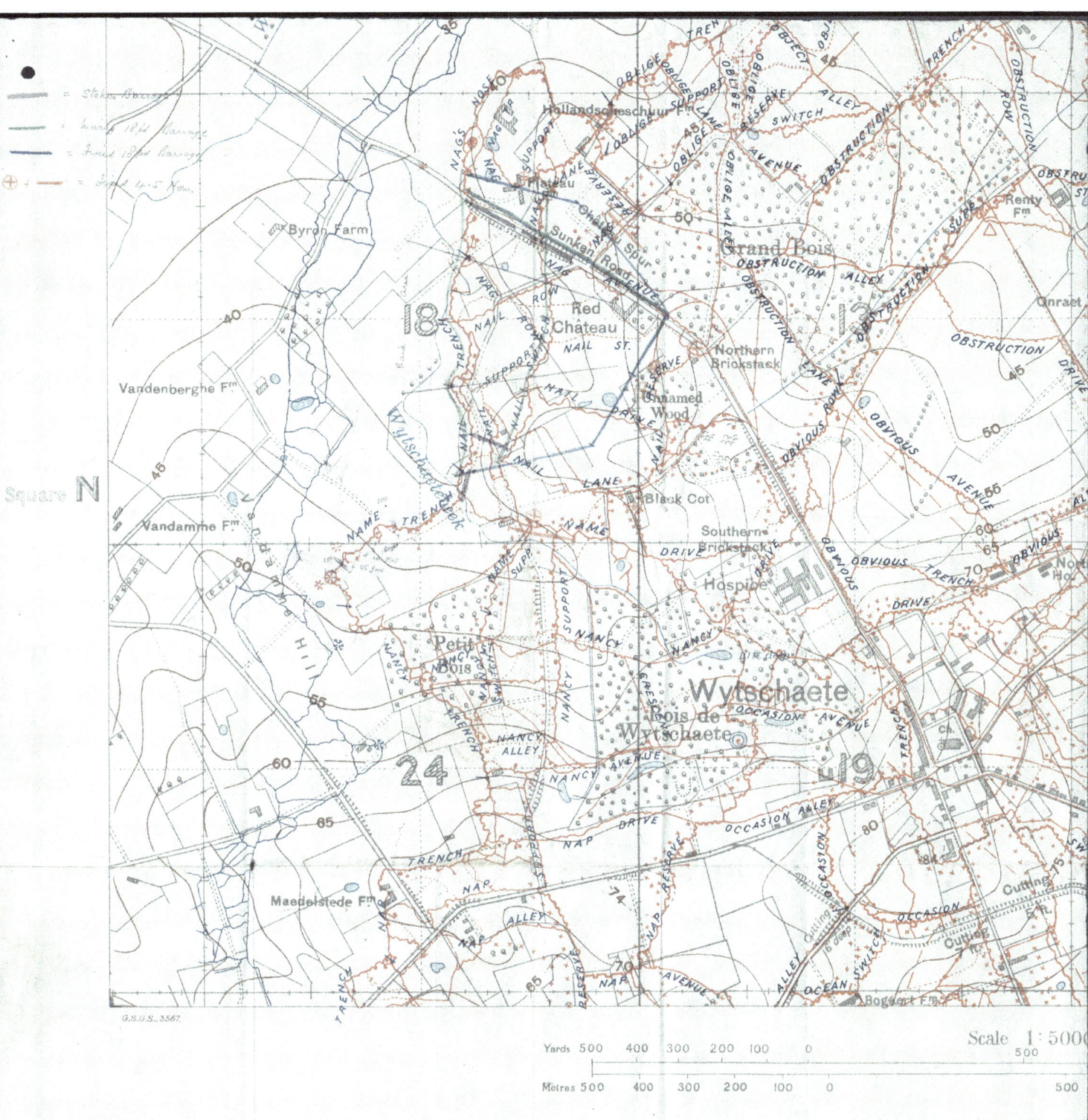

WAR DIARY.

FOR MONTH OF JUNE, 1917.

VOLUME :- 14

UNIT :- 8è Battn. R. Inniskilling Fusrs.

Report of Raid carried out by 8th. Bn. R. Inniskilling Fusrs. on the night of 5th. June 1917.
---

1. For disposition and size of Raiding Party see Orders for Raid S/314 dated 3rd. June 1917.

2. The first wave consisting of "C" Coy. crept over the parapet and moved off at Zero followed by the 2nd. Wave consisting of "A" Coy.

3. The following is the Time Table of events as received at Raid H.Q. BYRON FARM.

10.32	p.m.	2/Lieut. Cooper arrived at Left FRONT TRENCH.
10.38	p.m.	Capt. Hornby arrived at NAIL SWITCH.
10.43	p.m.	Capt. Hornby reported wounded.
10.46	p.m.	2/Lieut. Robbins entered R. FRONT LINE unopposed.
10.55	p.m.	2/Lieut. Cooper reported "Cleared Left Front & up to NAIL SWITCH.
10.53	p.m.	4 German Prisoners sent on to Brigade H.Q.
11.1	p.m.	2/Lieut. Robbins reported having cleared R. Front up to NAIL SWITCH.
11.15	p.m.	All in except Capt. HORNBY.
11.40	p.m.	Capt. Hornby reported in.

4. Information concerning GERMAN FRONT LINE.

   Generally this hardly exists and there was no sign of occupation none of the Officers of "C" Coy. who entered the Front Line saw any Germans. A certain number of dug-outs were found but they had not been occupied and in some cases were waterlogged. There is practically no wire except a few scattered concertinas and there is a certain amount of wire near the willows about N.18.d.00.72. The "going" in No Man's Land was found to be quite good. NAG & NAIL ROW are practically obliterated and unoccupied.

5. Information concerning NAILTSWITCH.

   At the North End this trench was found to be in better order than was expected and there are still some dug-outs which are intact. The Southern End of the Line is badly damaged and was difficult to recognise. The wire in front of the whole line has practically disappeared. All the prisoners were obtained from this line nine of them issuing from one dug-out. five of whom were killed in returning to our front line.

6. <u>Number of Prisoners taken</u> Four arrived at our Front Line.

7. No Machine Gun Emplacements were found which were not already blown in.

8. <u>Casualties.</u> 1 Officers wounded. 13 O.Rs wounded.

9. Very few Very Lights were put up in the Raid Area. Those that were put up came from GRAND BOIS and the Southern end of PETIT BOIS. The moment barrage started a red light bursting into two red balls was sent up from UNNAMED WOOD and shortly afterwards from GRAND BOIS. There was practically no Machine Gun Fire.
   The enemy sent over "rum jars" from near the crest of the ridge into NAIL SWITCH.
   There was practically no artillery retaliation on our Front Line - what there was being on South of Battalion frontage.
   The moral of the prisoners appeared to be distinctly poor.

Lieut. Colonel.,
Commanding.....
8th. R. Inniskilling Fusiliers........

SECRET.

List of Machine Gun Emplacements, Strong Points etc in enemy's line opposite VIERSTRAAT SECTOR suggested for treatment by Heavy Artillery.

STRONG POINTS.

Knockedout (handwritten next to N.18.b.95.20)

	Confirmed.	Suspected.
N.18.b.95.20		S
N.24.b.35.32.	C	
b.6.7.		S
O.13.c.64.25.		S
O.19.a.5.3.	C	
a.43.70.	C	
b.70.88.	C	
c.25.60.		S
c.25.90.		S
WYTSCHAETE DEFENCES.	C	

o.19.b.80.65 (handwritten)
10.58 (handwritten)

O.P's.

	Confirmed.	Suspected.
N.18.d.3.7.		S
d.36.12.		S
N.24.b.3.1.		S
O.13.c.10.60.		S
a.75.60.		S
O.19.b.48.44.		S
b.45.00.		S
b.27.50.	C	
b.68.86.	C	
b.08.50.		
b.79.65.		S
b.60.58.	C	
b.45.58.		S
b.43.24.		S
c.8.8.	C	
d.28.92.		S
d.0.4.		S
d.4.9.	C	
d.35.90.		S
O.25.a.45.65.		S

Concrete Structure (handwritten)
N24 b. 00. 44
O. 13. C. 00 13 (under construction)

MACHINE GUN EMPLACEMENTS.

	Confirmed.	Suspected.	
N.18.b.24.47.		S	
b.90.25.	C		reported destroyed 14/5/1
b.53.41.	C		
d.4.4.		S	
d.75.92	C		
d.98.17.		S.	
d.31.45.	C		
d.18.25.	C		
N.24.a.95.40.		S.	
b.18.24.	C		
b.06.40.	C		
b.32.33.		S	
b.6.8.		S	
b.61.48.	C		
b.62.19.	C		
b.54.68.	C		
c.85.34.		S	
c.92.37.		S	
d.19.59.		S	
d.26.82.	C		
d.31.90.		S	
d.45.60.		S	
d.30.59.	C		
d.52.57.	C		
O.13.a.58.10.		S	
c.18.53.		S	
c.25.80.		S	
c.00.09.	C		
c.20.98.		S	
c.15.45.	C		
d.34.97			
O.19.c.90.54.	C		
c.78.82.	C		
d.36.63.	C		
d.40.55.	C		
d.07.35.		S	
d.12.57.	C		

HEADQUARTERS

	Confirmed.	Suspected.
Battn. O.19.a.4.6.	C	
b.3.1.		S
O.20.d.2.3.	C	
O.25.b.20.25.	C	
Coy. N.18.b.65.20.		S
d.95.25.		S
d.45.15.	C	
N.24.b.61.27.		S
O.13.c.25.98.	C	
O.25.a.95.95.	C	

DUG-OUTS.

	Confirmed.	Suspected.	
N.18.d.2.6.	C		
d.21.14.		S	
d.95.25.	C		Group.
N 18 d 57.77			
N.24.a.80.64.		S	
b.5.0.	C		
b.8.5.		S	
b.25.50.	C		
b.62.75.		S	
b.94.85.		S	
b.85.02.	C		
b.61.38.		S	
b.85.63. b60.15	C		
b.3.3. b 74.85	C		
NANCY SUPPORT	C		
N.24.c.82.45.	C		
c.85.55.	C		
c.92.37.		S	
d.53.73.		S	
d.80.73.	C		
O.13.a.55.22.	C		
OBVIOUS ROW	C		
O.19.a.4.6.	C		
a.45.32.	C		
a.5.0.	C		
a.28.13.		S	
a.04.47.	C		
c.80.83.	C		
d.62.90.	C		
d.9.9. houses	C		
a.26.56			
N.24b.95.45	C		

BLUE CLAY.

	Confirmed.	Suspected.
N.18.b.54.49.	C	
b.55.39.	C	
b.60.35.	C	
b.80.27.	C	
N.24.b.87.02.	C	
b.85.04.	C	
b.88.56.	C	
b.1.6.	C	
O.19.c.21.64.	C	

TELEPHONE EXCHANGE.

O.25.a.95.95.	C	
O.26.a.4.5.	C	

DRESSING STATION.

O.26.a.32.79.	C	

DUMPS.

	Confirmed.	Suspected.	
N.18.b.58.62.		S	Small
N.24.b.92.52.	C		Small
O.19.a.55.90.	C		
b.03.55.		S	
b.30.73.		S	
c.51.62.	C		
c.95.35.		S	
O.20.a.2.4.	C		
a.4.1.	C		

SECRET   49th I.B.

8/R. Innis. Fus.

(a) Will you kindly arrange for Lt C.D. NEALON, to be at No 4 Main Brigade Bomb Dump (N.17.a.15.25) just off WATLING STREET) at 10 a.m. tomorrow.

       The 2/R. Irish Regt. has been detailed to hand over to him 224 filled Lewis Gun drums at that hour. These form part of the load carried on Yukon Packs by "A" Carrying Party.

(b) Reference Appendix "A" re "Carrying Parties" of Administrative Instructions for the Offensive para 1 (b) Kindly arrange for this party of 1 N.C.O. and 12 men to be at No 4 Main Brigade Bomb Dump (off WATLING STREET at N.17.a.15.25) at 10-15 a.m. tomorrow. They should arrive report on arrival there to Lt C.D. NEALON.

       Will you please inform him of this and instruct him that this party will be loading "A" Carrying Party's Yukons at that time.

                                    Bowen.
                                          Captain,
                                        Staff Captain,
4-6-17   49th Infantry Brigade.

S E C R E T   49th I.B. Q. 42

2/R. Irish Regt. & T.O.
7/R. Innis. Fus. & T.O.
8/R. Innis. Fus. & T.O.
7/8th R. Irish Fus. & T.O.
Brigade T.O.
Asst. Staff Captain.

1. At 8 a.m. on the night of "Y/Z" days, 8 pack animals from each Battalion Section of the Brigade Pack Transport Coy. will be formed up at a spot just South of junction of "CHEAPSIDE" and LA CLYTTE - KEMMEL Road at N.30.d.9.5.

2. Each animal will carry 8 petrol tins filled with water, and will be in possession of its nosebag with food, hay net, water bucket, gas helmet etc.

3. The Transport Officer of the 8/R. Innis. Fus. will command this party of 32 animals. Each battalion Section will be under a N.C.O.

4. Four men, to act as guides will accompany this party and will be used as follows:-

On arrival at the spot detailed above 2 will be sent to Brigade Headquarters THE RIB, N.16.d.5.5. to report to Staff Captain, so that they will be available to convey orders. The remaining two will be for emergency.

5. The remainder of the Pack Transport Coy. will be kept ready at Brigade Transport Lines for other purposes e.g. carriage of rations etc.

Acknowledge

Bowen
Captain,
Staff Captain,
49th Infantry Brigade.

5-6-17-

S E C R E T.

49th. I.B. No. S.C.C.X1/110

2nd. R.Irish Regt.
7th. R.Innis. Fus.
8th. R.Innis. Fus.
7/8th. R.Irish Fus.
49th. M.G.Coy.

        To-morrow 6th. instant all Transport will be packed ready to move at half an hour's notice.

    Rations to-morrow night and succeeding night will be taken up by means of pack transport.

                                           Captain,

5.6.17.   Staff Captain, 49th. Inf. Brigade.

SECRET.   S.O/I/6.

~~2222~~

~~No 3 Platoon A Coy 8th R.Innis Fus.~~
~~O.C. 8th R.Innis Fus.~~
~~49th Infy. Bde.~~

1. The Battalion Dump for Lewis Gun Drums etc etc will be in SHANNON TRENCH at its junction with USNAGH STREET.

2. The Battalion forward Dump will be as already stated in S.O/I. d/4.6.17 and in the immediate vicinity of the U in UNNAMED WOOD.

   Please instruct all and everyone of your carrying party as to the exact location of these points.

3. Please acknowledge.

                                    A.E Taggart
                                              Captn & Adjutant.

5. 6. 17.

S E C R E T.

S P E C I A L O R D E R.

The big day is very near.

All our preparations are complete, and the Divisional Commander wishes to express his appreciation, and his thanks, to all the Officers and Men who have worked so cheerfully, and so well.

The 16th. Division is fortunate in having had assigned to it the capture of the stronghold of WYTSCHAETE.

Every Officer and Man - Gunners, Sappers, Pioneers, R.A.M.C., A.S.C. and Infantrymen of historic Irish Regiments - knows what he has to do.

Let all do their best, as they have always done, continuing to show the same courage and devotion to duty which has characterized the 16th. (Irish) Division since it landed in France, and it will be our proud privilege to restore to Little Belguim, the "White Village", which has been in German hands for nearly three years.

W.B. Hickie,
Major-General,

June 5th. 1917.   Commanding 16th. (Irish) Division.

SECRET

49th I.B. No. Q-47

2/R. Irish Regt. and T.O.
7/R. Innis. Fus. and T.O.
8/R. Innis. Fus. and T.O.
7/8 R. Irish Fus. and T.O.
49th M.G. Coy. and T.O.
Brigade Transport Officer.
Brigade Q.M.S.
Asst. Staff Captain.
49th T.M. Battery.

The following points regarding issue of rations on "Z" day and afterwards are published:-

1. As soon as Rations are loaded at the Transport Lines on the Battalion Pack animals, a wire will be sent by Brigade Transport Officer to Brigade Headquarters stating time they will leave the Transport Lines.
They will then proceed via Track "F" East of KEMMEL - LA CLYTTE Road to the YORK Road end of WATLING STREET J.16.b.9.3.

2. Each Battalion will send down two intelligent guides to Brigade Headquarters, to report to Staff Captain, who They should know exactly the position of their Battalion H.Q. These guides will then be able to lead their pack animals to their Battalion Headquarters.

3. Two runners from the Transport Lines will be sent when ordered by Brigade Transport Officer to Advanced Divisional Headquarters, at SCHERPENBERG, and to report there at 10 a.m. on Zero day. These runners will be sent back to the Transport Lines with any information that can be given about the position of the troops.

✓ Acknowledge.

6-6-17.

Captain,
Staff Captain,
49th Infantry Brigade.

SECRET

49th I.B. No. Q. 48

2/R. Irish Regt. and T.O.
7/R. Innis. Fus. and T.O.
6/R. Innis. Fus. and T.O.
7/8th R. Irish Fus. and T.O.
Brigade T.O.
Asst. Staff Captain.

Reference 49th Infantry Brigade Q 42 dated 5-6-17, re 8 pack animals from each Battalion for carriage of water, 1 additional animal from each Battalion will be sent to Brigade Headquarters, THE RIB, N.16.d.4.5. at 9 a.m. on "Z" day.

These animals will be equipped in addition to its hay-net, food, etc., with harness traces etc. so as to be available for hauling tramway trucks. The drivers of these animals should be in possession of 2 strong ropes, for use as an addition to the traces, each about 6 to 8 feet long.

ACKNOWLEDGE.

Bowen
Captain,
Staff Captain,
49th Infantry Brigade.

6-6-17

2nd. R. Irish Regt.
7th. R. Innis. Fus.
8th. R. Innis. Fus.
7/8th. R. Irish Fus.
49th. T.M. Battery.

49th. Inf. Bde. No. S.M. 121 - 6/6/17.
---

20 of these slow fuzes will be in the Stokes Dump at junction of CROWBAR TRENCH and SHANNON TRENCH.

Captain.

Brigade Major., 49th. Inf. Bde.

INSTRUCTIONS FOR THE DEMOLITION OF HOSTILE GUNS WITH 3" STOKES TRENCH MORTAR BOMBS AND SPECIAL SLOW FUZE.

1. The slow fuze consists of a length of Bickford Fuze with a fuze lighter fixed to one end, and a No. 8 Detonator crimped to the other end. The time of burning of the fuze is
ONE AND A HALF MINUTES.
The fuzes are packed in tins containing 10 fuzes and 4 spare fuze lighters. The contents are labelled on each tin. Care must be taken when crimping the detonator on to the Bickford fuze to leave a space of ¼ inch between the end of the Bickford fuze and the fulminate.

2. The bombs are the ordinary 3" Stokes bombs WITHOUT THEIR FUZES OR COMPONENTS.

3. To demolish a hostile gun -

   (a) Open the breech, place the bomb in the breech of the gun, with the cartridge container forward, as far as it will go.
   (b) Insert the detonator end of the slow fuze into the gaine tube of the bomb, and press it gently home.
   (c) When the gun has thus been prepared, withdraw the safety pin from the fuze lighter and press the cap down, at the same time turning it round. As soon as the fuze is lit, take cover.

If several guns are to be demolished together, the bombs must be first placed in position, fuzes inserted and fuze lighters lit simultaneously.

NOTE.
(1) In taking cover the party should spread out and warn off any approaching troops. The fragments may carry 300 yards.

(2) If the breech cannot be opened -

   (a) In the case of a field gun place the bomb between the gun and the seat (so that it touches the gun) on the muzzle side of the shield.
   (b) In the case of any larger gun, place the bomb just inside the muzzle, taking care that the bomb does not slide down the bore.

DEMOLITION PARTY.

A demolition party consists of 1 N.C.O. and 2 men. The N.C.O. carries 2 Stokes Bombs and 1 tin of slow fuzes. Each man carries 4 Stokes Bombs in 2 sandbags.

The men should be practised in their duties before being sent into action.

2nd R. Irish Regt.
7th R. Innis Fus.
8th R. Innis Fus.
7/8th R. Irish Fus.
49th M.G.Company.
49th T.M.Battery.
Staff Captain.
Bde. Signal Officer.

49th Inf. Bde. No. B.O. 139/1 - 6-6-17.

ZERO HOUR is ...3.10.A.M... night. 6th/7th June

ACKNOWLEDGE BY WIRE. ✓

J B D Willan Captain,
Brigade Major, 49th Infantry Brigade.

HEAD-QUARTERS No. Q 51 49TH BRIGADE   SECRET

3/R. Irish Regt.   and T.O.
7/R. Innis. Fus.   and T.O.
8/R. Innis. Fus.   and T.O.
7/8th R. Irish Fus.   and T.O.
49th M.G. Coy.   and T.O.
Brigade T.O.
Asst. Staff Captain.
Brigade Q.M.S.
------------------------:—

      Tomorrow being "Z" day, the orders laid down in Q 42, dated 5th., Q 47 and Q 48 dated 6th inst. will be carried out.

Acknowledge.

[signature]
Captain,
Staff Captain,
49th Infantry Brigade.

6-6-17

SECRET.　　　　　　　　　　　　　　　　　　Copy No. 5.

G.O.C.
Staff Captain.
2nd R. Irish Regt.
7th R. Innis Fus.
8th R. Innis Fus.
7/8th R. Irish Fus.
49th M.G. Company.
49th T.M. Battery.
Bde. Signal Officer.
Bde. Intelligence Officer.
16th Division.
16th Division.
47th Inf. Bde.
48th Inf. Bde.
58th Inf. Bde.
177th Bde, R.F.A.
157th Field Coy, R.E.

49th Inf. Bde. No. S.O. 60 - 6-C-17.

Herewith Copy No. 5 of 49th INFANTRY BRIGADE INSTRUCTIONS FOR THE OFFENSIVE, paras. 42 to 49.

Please ACKNOWLEDGE receipt. ✓

[signature] Captain,
Brigade Major, 49th Infantry Brigade.

SECRET.

S E C R E T.   Copy No........

49TH INFANTRY BRIGADE INSTRUCTIONS FOR THE OFFENSIVE.

(CONTINUED).

42. ACTION ON THE CAPTURE OF THE BLACK LINE.

(a) The BLACK LINE should be completely in our hands by Zero plus 5 hours. The portion held by the 16th Division will be consolidated by the 47th and 49th Inf. Bdes. with the assistance of wiring parties from the 48th Inf. Bde. working under the C.R.E.

(b) The 47th and 49th Inf. Bdes. will push forward patrols to the Protective Barrage, which will be established 300 yards in advance of the BLACK LINE.

(c) The OOSTAVERNE LINE will be subjected to a heavy bombardment from Zero plus 5 hours until the approach of our attacking infantry, and a number of field guns will be brought forward into previously selected positions.

43. ADVANCE TO THE MAUVE LINE.

(a) At Zero plus 5 hours 30 minutes the barrage will creep forward at the rate of 100 yards every 3 minutes and pile up on the line ROAD JUNCTION O.27.d.6.9 - O.21.central - O.15.d.1.7 until Zero plus 6 hours 30 minutes, when it will cease unless recalled by the S.O.S. Signal.

(b) At Zero plus 5 hours 30 minutes cavalry patrols will move forward within the limits of the barrage, and the 36th, 16th and 19th Divisions will push forward strong patrols, which will establish themselves on the line O.27.d.2.9 - Railway Junction O.21.c.6.1 - OIL TRENCH - eastern side of OOSTAVERNE WOOD.
This line will be known as the MAUVE LINE.

The portion of the MAUVE LINE allotted to the 16th Division is from Railway Junction at O.21.c.6.1 on the right (where it joins hands with the 36th Division) to junction of railway and OIL TRENCH at O.21.a.2.8 on the left (where it joins hands with the 19th Division).
47th and 49th Inf. Bdes. will each push forward two strong patrols of not less than 50 men each, and accompanied by Lewis Guns, which will establish themselves on the MAUVE LINE. The boundary between Brigades will be a straight line from the point of junction between brigades on the BLACK LINE (O.20.a.40.85) to the south end of LEG COPSE and thence along the WAMBEEK to the MAUVE LINE.
It is the intention of the Divisional Commander, as soon as circumstances permit, to move forward troops from the 48th Inf. Bde. in Reserve to hold and complete

the consolidation of the MAUVE LINE within the divisional boundaries, taking this line over from the patrols of the 47th and 49th Inf. Bdes., which will then rejoin their brigades. The 155th Field Coy, R.E. will be placed at the disposal of G.O.C. 48th Inf. Bde. to assist in this consolidation.

(c) Four sections of Tanks, with any others that can be rallied, will co-operate in this advance and in the subsequent advance to the OOSTAVERNE LINE.

44. SUBSEQUENT ADVANCE TO THE OOSTAVERNE LINE.

(a) There will be a new Zero hour for the advance from the MAUVE LINE.
At NEW ZERO the II ANZAC, IXth and Xth Corps will advance to the attack of the OOSTAVERNE LINE preceded by an artillery barrage.

(b) In the case of the IXth Corps, the advance will be made by the 33rd Inf. Bde. and 68th Field Coy, R.E. under the command of G.O.C. 16th Division.

(c) At New Zero minus 15 minutes the barrage will form up again on the line O.27.d.6.9 - O.21.central - O.15.d.0.7.

(d) By New Zero the 33rd Inf. Bde. will, having deployed behind the MAUVE LINE, be closed up to the barrage ready to advance to the attack of the OOSTAVERNE LINE.

(e) At New Zero the barrage followed by the infantry will creep forward at the rate of 100 yards every three minutes and pile up on ODIOUS - ODOUR - ODONTO TRENCHES. Under cover of this advance the IXth Corps Cavalry Regt., IXth Cyclist Battalion and 19th Motor Machine Gun Company, should previous reconnaissance prove the ground suitable, will move forward to positions of assembly east of the WYTSCHAETE - MESSINES Ridge.

(f) At New Zero plus 20 minutes barrage lifts onto the Support trench.
At New Zero plus 35 minutes barrage lifts from support trench and forms protective barrage 300 yards to the east of it.

(g) The line captured will be consolidated and prepared to resist counter-attacks.

(h) At New Zero plus 1 hour 5 minutes the barrage ceases and, if opportunity offers, Cavalry patrols will be pushed through to reconnoitre and prepare the way for the Corps Mounted Troops.

(i) For the purpose of keeping direction and being in close touch with the Corps on either flank, the following houses or farms on each boundary on and east of the MAUVE LINE will be objectives for both the 33rd Inf. Bde. and the flank units of the neighbouring Corps :-

Between 33rd Inf. Bde. and II Anzac Corps.

Farm O.27.d.2.9.	Consolidated by 33rd Inf.Bde.
Farm O.28.c.2.9.	Consolidated by II Anzac Corps.
Farm O.28.b.7.1.	ditto.

Between 33rd Inf. Bde. and Xth Corps.

    Farm O.15.d.7.5.   Consolidated by X Corps.
    Farm O.16.c.4.2.   ditto.

45.   To carry out the plan laid down in para. 43 (b) the O.C. 7/8th R. Irish Fus. will, after taking the BLUE LINE, at once reform 1 Company, reinforced if necessary from other Coys. to not less than 4 platoons of 32 men each with 6 Lewis Guns and additional signallers, to carry out the advance from 2nd R. Irish Regt's outpost line in front of the BLACK LINE to the MAUVE LINE, where they will establish themselves in posts until relieved by the 48th Inf. Bde.

    Arrangements must be made to supply the Company before advancing with flares, S.A.A and Lewis Gun Drums.

    The O.C. 2nd R. Irish Regt. will arrange to keep up communication with this Coy. during its advance, and report on progress of the advance.

    The O.C. 2nd R. Irish Regt. will also detail a Strong Post of about 1 Platoon to be formed at SONEM FARM O.20.b.10.45. as soon as the Company of 7/8th R. Irish Fus has advanced East of it, for purpose of facilitating communication and for taking over, or assisting in collecting of prisoners and passing them to the rear, and also to form a strong supporting point half way to the MAUVE LINE.

46.   When it has been decided to proceed with the advance to the OOSTAVERNE LINE, orders to this effect will be sent direct to G.O.C. 33rd Inf. Bde. who will move to positions of assembly as follows :-

Brigade Headquarters.

    H.Q. 33rd Inf. Bde. to S.P.13 DUGOUTS, where the Brigadier will be in close touch with G.O.C. 48th Inf. Bde. (Infantry Brigade in Divisional Reserve.

47.

HEADQUARTERS.

(a) When the two Battalions of the 48th Inf. Bde. which are accommodated in the VIERSTRAAT SWITCH move forward to the CHINESE WALL LINE, H.Q. 48th Inf. Bde. will be prepared to advance to S.P.13 DUGOUTS. This will be about the time when the advance from the BLUE to the BLACK LINE begins.

(b) From this time S.P. 13 DUGOUTS will be reserved for H.Q. 48th and 33rd Inf. Bdes.

(c) After the capture of the BLACK LINE, when the Field Artillery begin to advance, the battalion headquarter dugouts in S.P. 13 will be reserved for the use of artillery group headquarters.

48. **CAPTURED GUNS.**

The following will be the policy to be observed in dealing with hostile guns west of the OOSTAVERNE LINE.

Enemy guns which may be of use to us will be saved. The gun teams should be killed and the Breech Mechanism with any removable sight removed if necessary. Destruction by explosives is not to be resorted to unless it is evident that the OOSTAVERNE LINE cannot be gained and held. In this case the officer on the spot must use his own judgment as to destroying the guns. Explosives for this purpose will be taken forward by the Field Coys. attached to the 33rd and 48th Inf. Bdes.

Breech blocks and sights removed from the guns will be retained near the guns by the parties who remain in charge of them until it becomes evident that no use can be made of the guns by us, in which case parts removed will be carried back to Battalion Headquarters or destroyed.

R.A.personnel is to be told off ready to be sent up to man the guns if required.

49. **SMOKE CANDLES.**

No smoke from smoke candles will be used on the IXth Corps front on "Z" day.

SECRET.

49th I.B. No. Q55

Second-in- Command 2/R. Irish Regt.
   do   do   7/R. Innis. Fus.
   do   do   8/R. Innis. Fus.
   do   do   7/8th R. Irish Fus.
Quartermaster 2/R. Irish Regt.
   do   7/R. Innis. Fus.
   do   8/R. Innis. Fus.
   do   7/8th R. Irish Fus.
Major E.W.P. UNIACKE.

     The personnel of ("B" Echelon) left behind by units will rejoin their Battalion in and around the VIERSTRAAT SWITCH tonight.

     The senior Officer will report to Brigade Headquarters on arrival.

Bowen.

Captain,
Staff Captain,
49th Infantry Brigade.

7-6-17

SECRET. COPY No. 12

8th. R. INNISKILLING FUSILIERS OPERATION ORDER No. 109 - 29/6/17.

Ref. (1/40,000 SHEET 27
(1/100,000 HAZEBROUCK 5 A.
(1/20,000 SHEET 27 A. S.E.

1. The 49th. Infantry Brigade will march to the TATINGHEM AREA on 30th. June.

2. ORDER OF MARCH. - 7th. R. Innis. Fus., 8th. R. Innis. Fus., 2nd. R. Irish Regt., 7/8th. R. Irish Fus., 49th. I.B. H.Q., 49th. M.G.C., 49th. T.M.B. 144th. Coy. A.S.C., 113th. F.A.

3. The Starting Point for the Battn. will be the Cross Roads G.27.b.9.4. The Batta. will be formed up along the road running East of this point in the order H.Q., B, D, C, A Coys. ready to move off by 6 a.m.

4. ROUTE. ST. MOMELIN - ST. OMER - ST. MARTIN-AU-LAERT to destination ETREHEM and LEULINGHEM.

5. Intervals of 500 yards will be maintained between Battalions.

6. 2/Lieut. A.H. Robbins will proceed mounted at sufficient distance in front of the Battn. to give warning to Traffic Control.

7. Battn. Transport, including Baggage Wagons., will accompany Battn.

8. A motor lorry will be available for conveyance of men's packs. Each Coy. will detail one man to act as loading party and these men will be responsible for packs until lorry arrives.

9. Usual halts will be observed.

10. DRESS. Skeleton marching order, haversack carried on back, All mess-tins /mugs, &c., to be carried inside haversack. Only brakesmen will march behind vehicles. Lewis Guns and magazines will be carried on limbers.

11. Brigade H.Q. will close at BUYSSCHEURE at 6 a.m. and will open at TATINGHEM on arrival.

12. Watches will be synchronised by all Officers between the hours of 6 p.m and 8 p.m. to-day at Orderly Room.

13. O.C. "B" Coy. will detail one platoon to stay behind and make sure that the billets of Battn. are left in a clean and proper condition. Transport Officer will make his own arrangements.

14. ROUTINE. Reveille 3.30 a.m. Breakfast 4.15 a.m. Officers' valises to be outside billets at 4.30 a.m. Mess Cart and Maltese Cart packed by 5.30 a.m.

15. ACKNOWLEDGE.

Lieut.,
a/Adjutant.,
Issued through Signals :   8th. R. Inniskilling Fus.

Copy No. 1 to O.C. "A" Coy.
"   " 2 " "   "B" "
"   " 3 " "   "C" "
"   " 4 " "   "D" "
"   " 5 .. Signalling Officer.
"   " 6 .. Medical Officer.
"   " 7 .. Quartermaster.
"   " 8 .. Transport Officer.
"   " 9 .. 2/Lieut. A.H. Robbins.
"   " 10 .. R. S. M.
"   " 11 .. H.Q. 49th. I.B.
"   " 12/13 Retained.

SECRET.

SECOND ARMY BARRAGE MAP.
June, 1917.

CORPS BOUNDARY ——
DIVISIONAL BOUNDARY ●●●●●●

(SPECIAL) 1:10,000 MAP 8150/2.

Scale 1:10,000

CONVERSION TABLE
MINUTES — HOURS.

61 mins	1 hour 1 min		
62	2		
63	3		
64	4		
65	5		
67	7		
69	9	220 mins	3 hours 40 mins.
70	10	224	44
71	11	228	48
72	12	230	50
73	13	232	52
77	17	234	54
82	22	236	56
85	25		
90	30	240	4 hours 0 mins.
91	31	244	4
100	40	245	5
104	44	246	6
105	45	248	8
108	48	249	9
110	50	250	10
115	55	255	15
116	56	264	24
118	58	272	32
119	59	275	35
120	3 hours 0 mins.	284	44
122	2	288	48
125	5		5 hours 0 mins.
127	7	304	4
129	9	318	18
131	11	323	23
132	12	326	26

19th DIV.

16th DIV.

36th DIV.

OOSTTAVERNE LINE

DOTTED BLACK LINE

IX CORPS GREEN LINE

X CORPS GREEN LINE

BLACK LINE

BLUE LINE

RED LINE

G/16/8

2/R.I. No. O.R. A

8th Royal Inniskilling Fus.

                Reference Operation Order No. 30,
    dated 29-5-1917.

                Schedule for "A" Carrying Party
    is cancelled and the attached Schedule is substituted.

The Field.   Lieut.Colonel,
4-6-1917.   Commanding, 2nd. Battalion, The Royal Irish Regt.

This is in accordance with our Schedule

a/w o/y

SECRET: Copy No. 9

S.O/I.

INSTRUCTIONS FOR THE OFFENSIVE
(continuation of).

Sheet 8

I.6.17.

20. All mines on the 16th Divisional front will be exploded at "Zero" hour.

21. Bayonets will not be fixed until the assembly position is reached. Every precaution is to be taken to prevent Bayonets from flashing in the moonlight.

22. Smoking is to be discouraged owing to the danger of "the striking of matches" or Cigarette ends being observed.

23. All ranks are to be ordered not to look up at hostile aeroplanes, whilst in their assembly positions, and no movement is to take place whilst hostile aeroplanes are in a position to notice that our trenches are far more heavily manned than usual.

24. Distinguishing flags to assist the Artillery in locating our own Infantry will be carried on a scale of not less than 2 per platoon. These flags will be supplied under Divisional arrangements, when further instructions will be issued.
Implicit orders are to be given personally by an Officer to each man to whom a flag is given to carry that on no account is the flag to be planted in the ground as this might be the cause of serious mistakes should a position have to be evacuated.

25. In order to minimise casualties, every wave and line will cross NO MAN'S LAND as quickly as possible. Care however must be taken to ensure that waves and lines do not lose their formations and become hopelessly mixed.

26. Communication trenches,
Vide para 12 above.

As soon as possible after Zero, the R.E. and Pioneers will continue the following trenches into the captured position:-

    (a) THE FOSSE - BIRR TRENCH via NAME TRENCH & NAME DRIVE.

    (b) WATLING STREET - MAYO STREET via NAIL DRIVE.

    (a) will be used as an OUT trench.
    (b) " " " " IN trench.

27. Strong Points,
Vide Para 16 above.

A Strong Point within the Battalion area will be established in the best position there is for it in the vicinity of O.13.c.15.90, (RED POST).

The O.C. B Coy will previous to the attack detail a platoon from the 1st Wave to garrison it.
The Commander and all ranks of this platoon must be instructed to this effect and must be ready to move into it as soon as the R.E. have finished work thereon.

The Commander of this platoon will get in touch with the R.E. working on this S.P. immediately they commence to work and inform them that his platoon has been told off as the garrison and where it is.

~~The O.C. B Coy will similarly warn one of the platoons on the left of his Company previous to the attack that it may have to be sent up to relieve D Coy platoon.~~
~~This platoon however will not move without direct orders from Bn. H.Q.~~

Other Strong Points are being established about O.13.c.40.25, BLACK POST - Garrison 7/8th R.I.F.
O.19.b.30.80. OBVIOUS POST, 2nd R.I.R.

Sheet No. 9

INSTRUCTIONS FOR THE OFFENSIVE
(continuation of)   (continued.

28. Troops on Left Flank.
    Vide para I c. above.

    The 58th Infy Bde, 19th Div'n are attacking on the immediate left of the Battalion.

    A Battalion of the Wiltshire Regt attacking up to the continuation of the RED LINE.

    "A"   "   "   Welsh Regt attacking from the RED LINE to the BLUE LINE.

    Another "   "   Welsh Regt attacking from the BLUE LINE to the GREEN LINE.

29. The O.C. B and D Coys will, to ensure that proper connection is maintained with the troops on their left (vide para 28 above); each order the section on the left (or N) of their lines and waves to cross the boundaries laid down in para 2 c. above, from the very commencement of their advance and to move forward at a distance of about 15 yards to the left or N of it.

    The O.C's of the Battalions on our left are similarly being asked to send sections to cross our left or Northern boundary and to advance at about 15 yards to the South of it.

    The boundaries of the Battalion will thus overlap each other and the various lines and waves will be interlocked.

30. ACKNOWLEDGE.

                                        O. C. Taggart
                                            Captn & Adjt.

Copy No 1 File
         2 A Coy
         3 B "
         4 C "
         5 D "
         6 Brigade
         7 A Coy 8th R.Innis Fus
         8 B "   "   "   "
         9 8th R.Innis Fus
        10 M.G.
        11 T.M.
        12 7/8th R.I.F. for Information.

I.4.17.

SECRET:

APPENDIX. C. to S.O/I. d/30.5.17.

Ref: MAP: WYTSCHAETE. 28.S.W.2. Ed 5 A.

"MOPPERS UP".

1. "B" Coy (Captn Green, M.C.) 8th R.Innis Fusrs will be attached to the Battalion as "Moppers Up".

    This Company is organised as follows:-

    No 4 Platoon (2/Lieut Healen) and approximately 32 O.R's.
    " 5   "   ("   Patterson) "   "   35 "
    " 6   "   ("   Browne)   "   "   36 "

2. DISTRIBUTION:

    A party Nos 1 & 2 Sectns under Sectn Comdrs will form the 3rd line.
    B "   3.4 & 5 "   "   No 4 Plat Comr "   "   4th   "
    C "   6.7 & 8 "   "   5   "   "   "   9th   "
    D "   9.10.11.& 12. "   "   6   "   "   "   13th "

    See also para 5 of S.O/I. d/30.5.17.

3. ASSEMBLY POSITIONS:

    The various lines of "Moppers Up", vide para 2 above, will assemble in the trenches of the waves which they follow.
    See also para 6 of S.O/I. d/30.5.17 and Appendix G.

4. BOUNDARIES:

    The Boundaries on the South and North will be those within which the Battalion is operating, vide para 2 c of S.O/I.d/30.5.17.

5. DUTIES:

    Attention is directed to Section IV, para 4 of S.S.135 "Instructions for the Training of Divisions for the Offensive".

    A PARTY.

    The German front line will probably have ceased to exist.
    The portion of it between MAG ROW and HAIL ROW is known to be waterlogged.

    No 1 section will be responsible for Mopping up the ground as far as NAIL SWITCH inclusive.

       Its Boundary on the left or N, being HAIL ROW to its junction with MAG ROW and thence MAG ROW to NAIL SWITCH.

    No 2 section will be responsible for Mopping up the ground as far as NAIL SWITCH.

       Its Boundary on the Right or S, being the Northern boundary of No 1 section.

    Special attention being paid to the SUNKEN ROAD.

    On completion of their duty they will take over the Mopping up of B party in NAIL SWITCH.

    B PARTY:

           No 3 section will be on the Right.
           " 4   "   "   " in " Centre.
           " 5   "   "   " on " Left.

    This party will move straight up to NAIL SWITCH where it will almost immediately be relieved by A party.
       It will then "Mop Up" to the RED CHATEAU LINE i.e. the

APPENDIX C (continued). Sheet 2.

continuation of NANCY SUPPORT.

No 5 section paying particular attention to the SUNKEN ROAD.

This party on completion of its duty will move forward to the assistance of "C" party at the discretion of its Commander, should it appear necessary.

C PARTY:

       No 6 section will be on the Right.
       " 7 " " in " Centre.
       " 8 " " on " Left.

No 6 section will pay special attention to NAIL DRIVE.
" 7 " " " " " " THE RED CHATEAU.
" 8 " " " " " " THE SUNKEN ROAD.

D PARTY:

       No 9 section will be on the Right.
       " 10 " " " " Centre.
       " 11 " " " Left "
       " 12 " " " Left "

6. The O.C. the "Moppers Up" will generally supervise the work of the "Moppers Up" and will issue such further instructions to the various parties as detailed above as may be necessary.

   A copy of all such instructions to be forwarded in the first place to Bn H.Q's (7th R.Inn's Fus).

On the capture of the RED line, his position will be in the immediate vicinity of the advanced Bn H.Q's.
He will not withdraw the various parties from their areas or allow them to be withdrawn without previous ~~reference~~ reference to the senior Officer present at advanced Bn H.Q's.

7. The Commanders of the various parties will report to the O.C. "Moppers Up" on completion of their tasks and await his instructions.

8. On Orders being given for the Moppers Up or any one party of them to withdraw they will proceed to the 8th R.Inn's Fusrs assembly position in YUM YUM TRENCH where they will again come under the orders of the O.C. 8th R.Inn's Fusrs.

Copy No 1 File
      2 A Coy
      3 B "
      4 C "
      5 D "
      7 2nd in Command
      8 B Coy 8th R.Inn's Fus.
      9 8th R.Inn's Fus for information.
      6 49th Bde " "

30.5.17.

49th.I.B. No. S.C.C. IX/188/11.

SECRET.

2/R. Irish Regt.
7/R. Innis. Fus.
8/R. Innis. Fus.
7/8th R. Irish Fus.

With reference to para 1 of Section 2 "MEDICAL" of 49th Infantry Brigade Administrative Instructions for the Offensive, the G.O.C. directs that a party of 10 men be detailed from your bandsmen and drummers etc., to act as auxiliary Stretcher Bearers. These will proceed up to the line on Battalions moving thereto, and will be assembled in MACAW TRENCH, N.16.d.5.4. to N.16.d.9.7. on 'Y' Day.

Captain,
Staff Captain,
49th Infantry Brigade.

1.5.17.

Officer Commanding

8th. Royal Inniskilling Fusiliers

    Herewith Operation Orders No.1. Copy No.14. Sheets one to seven. Addition will be made to these orders from time to time so they have not been closed.

    Should any of the additions affect you they will be forwarded. Please acknowledge.

June 2nd.1917.

W.H. Stitt Capt. Adj
for Lieut.Colonel.

Commanding 7/8th.(S)Battalion Royal Irish Fusiliers

SECRET. COPY. NO. 14

OPERATION ORDERS. NO. 1

REFERENCE MAPS. FRANCE 28. S.W. Ed. 5.a. and MAPS attached.   2 JUN 1917

o-o-o-o-o-o-o-o-o-o-o-o-o-o-o-o-o-o-o-o-o-o-o-o-o-o-o-o-o-o-o-o-o-o-o-o-o-o-o-o-o

1. GENERAL PLAN.

The attack on WYTSCHAETE RIDGE will be made by the 16th. Division with Divisions on either flank.
The attack by the 16th. Division will be made by:-
(a) 47. Infantry Brigade on the RIGHT.
   48th. Infantry Brigade on the LEFT.
   49th. Infantry Brigade in RESERVE.

(b) The objectives allotted to the 7/8th. Royal Irish Fusiliers are:-
   (1) NANCY SUPPORT marked on Map by a series of Red Dashes.
   (2) RED LINE.
   (3) NANCY DRIVE, marked on Map by series of Blue Dashes
   (4) BLUE LINE.

(c) The Boundaries of the Battalion are:-
   (1) With the 7th. Leinster Regiment on the Right.:-
   German Line at N.34.a.60.85.-----North Corner of PETIT BOIS.
   (N.34.b.4.9.) NORTH--WEST Corner BOIS DE WYTSCHAETE (N.24.b.75.80.)---
   South Corner of HOSPICE. This Boundary is marked on Map by broad YELLOW LINE.

   (2) Left Boundary with the 7th. Royal Inniskilling Fusiliers is marked on Map with a PURPLE LINE and is as follows:-
   N.17.b.80.00.-----SHANNON TRENCH at N.18.a.32.00.-----our Front Line at N.18.a.55.00.-----German Front Line at N.18.d.20.75.---along a line 30 yards South of NAIL DRIVE------Southern Corner of UNNAMED WOOD----O.13.c.80.15., 20 yards North of the Junction of OBVIOUS DRIVE and NANCY DRIVE. This Boundary is shewn in PURPLE.

TIME.

The following will be the times of Arrival and Departure from the various Coloured Lines.

   RED LINE. Arrive Plus 0.35.
              Depart. Plus 1.05.
   BLUE LINE Arrive Plus 1.40.
2nd. Royal Irish Regiment will attack the Green and Black Lines passing through the BLUE LINE at Plus 3.40.

ATTACK.

The attack on the Red Line will be made by "A" Company on the Right "B" Company on the Left.

The Attack on the Blue Line will be by "C" Coy. on the Right and "D" Coy. on the Left.

Boundaries between Companies are:-
Between "A" and "B" Coys'. Point of Salient N.18.c.68.54.-----German Front Line at N.18.d.27.18.-----along a line running about 30 yards South of NAIL LANE to N.18.d.99.10.

Boundaries between "C" and "D" Coy. are:-
N.18.d.99.10.-----along a line running North of NAME DRIVE to NORTH CORNER of HOSPICE (Inclusive to Right Coy.) at N.19.a.64.93.
Shewn on attached Map by Thin Pencil Line.

WAVES.

The Battalion will attack in four waves:-
"A" and "B" Coys first wave will occupy RED LINE.
"A" and "B" Coys second wave will occupy DOTTED RED LINE (NANCY SUPORT)
"C" and "D" Coys first wave will occupy BLUE LINE.
"C" and "D" Coys second wave will occupy DOTTED BLUE LINE.

(Continued on Sheet 2.)

SHEET...2.

II. ASSEMBLY POSITIONS.

"A" Coy. in front line from N.18.c.48.25. to point or Salient at N.18.c.67.55. Boundary between Platoons will be Bay 39.(N.18.c.57.43.) inclusive to Left Platoon.

"B" Coy. in front line from Point or Salient at N.18.c.67.55. to N.18.a.55.00.(Bay.64.inclusive) Boundary between Platoons Bay 53. N.18.c.54.80.) inclusive to Left Platoon.

"C" Coy's. first wave in WREN WAY from N.18.c.30.00. to BIRR TRENCH.
"C" Coy's. second wave in FERMOY TRENCH from VAN KEEP to BIRR TRENCH.

"D" Coy's. first wave in WREN WAY from BIRR TRENCH to CROWBAR TRENCH.
"D" Coy's. second wave in FERMOY TRENCH from BIRR TRENCH to CROWBAR TRENCH.

III. MOPPERS UP.

"D" Company of the 8th. Royal Inniskilling Fusiliers will be attached to the Battalion to act as "Moppers Up." This Coy. consists of three platoons.

PLATOON	STRENGTH.	COMMANDER	ATTACHED TO
(a) ½.No.13.	17.O.Ranks.	2/Lieut.Roulstone.	"A"Coy.7/8th.
(b) ½.No.13.	17.O.Ranks.	ditto...	"B"Coy.7/8th.
(c) ½.No.14.	17.O.Ranks.	2/Lieut.Palmgreen.	"D"Coy.7/8th.
(d) ½.No.14.	17.O.Ranks.	ditto...	"C"Coy.7/8th.
(e) No.15.	34.O.Ranks.	2/Lieut.POLLEY.	"C"Coy.7/8th.

(a) Party will "Mop.Up" dug outs at the junction of NAME SUPPORT and NAME DRIVE, NANCY SUPPORT. Assembly Point in front line behind "A"Coy.
(b) Party will "Mop Up" NANCY SUPPORT and along NAIL LANE up to and in BLACK COT. Assembly Point behind "B"Coy.
(c) Party will "Mop Up" dugouts round point O.13.c.79.15. Assembly Point in WREN WAY, N. of BIRR TRENCH behind "D"Coys. first wave.
(d) Party will "Mop Up" trench running S.E. from O.19.a.10.92. to dugouts at O.19.a.44.70.
(e) Party will go straight to HOSPICE. (d) and (e) Parties will assemble in WREN WAY, S. of BIRR TRENCH behind "C"Coy's. first waves.
When these parties have completed their tasks they will report the fact to the Companies to which they are attached and then to Battalion Headquarters.

IV. CARRYING PARTIES.

One Platoon of the 8th. Royal Inniskilling Fusiliers consisting of 35.O.Ranks under 2/Lieut.BROWN will act as carrying party. Assembly position in rear of Fourth Wave behind "D"Coy. in FERMOY TRENCH from BIRR TRENCH to CROWBAR TRENCH. This party will carry any material from Battalion Dump at Junction BIRR TRENCH with SHANNON TRENCH up to BLACK COT where dumps will be established, at least 20.yards apart under the R.S.M.

V. VICKERS GUNS.

The Two Vickers Guns under Lieut.A.G.MAY 49.M.Gun Co. will move behind the Fourth Wave, and will take up a favourable position in the neighbourhood of the BLACK COT from which to cover the advance on the BLUE LINE.
When the BLUE LINE has been taken, they will move forward to neighbourhood of the SOUTHERN BRICKSTACK, and assist in consolidating and in forming the Machine Gun Barrage for the attack on the GREEN and BLACK LINES.
They must be prepared to support the 3rd. and 4th. waves at any point in the attack on the BLUE LINE, either by filling gaps in the assaulting waves, or by putting a barrage on any strong point. The two guns will work conjointly.
Assembly Point will be in FERMOY TRENCH between BIRR TRENCH and CROWBAR TRENCH.

(Continued on Sheet 3.)

S H E E T. 3.

VI. STOKES' GUNS.

Stokes' Guns under 2/Lieut. TAYLOR 49.T.M.Bty. will move behind the 4th. Wave to the neighbourhood of BLACK COT and cover the advance of the 3rd. and 4th. Waves by firing on the HOSPICE, and on any STRONG POINTS or Machine Guns that may offer resistance or hold up the advance.
As soon as the BLUE LINE is taken, the Guns will be brought to a position in rear of NANCY DRIVE so as to help the consolidation of the BLUE LINE and the HOSPICE by firing on the STRONG POINT S.W. of the HOSPICE at O.19.b.10.60. The two guns will work conjointly. Assembly Trench will be FERMOY TRENCH between VAN KEEP and WATLING STREET H.Qrs. in a dugout at..............

VII. CONSOLIDATION.) STRONG POINTS.)

All lines will be consolidated after capture. Strong Points will be constructed by the 157.Field.Co.R.E. to hold one Platoon and Vickers Gun.
  RED POST .. O.13.a.35.90.
  BLACK...... O.13.c.40.25.
  OBVIOUS.... O.19.b.54.80.

As soon as the construction of a Strong Point is complete, the R.E. Officer in charge will report the fact to the Officer Commanding the Battalion in whose area the STRONG POINT is. In which case, a platoon of "A" or "B" Coys' may be detailed with its Lewis Gun to occupy the Strong Point.

VIII. POSITIONS OF HEADQUARTERS.

49th. Infantry Brigade Headquarters also Left Artillery Group H.Q.

THE RIB N.16.d.35.50.	
7/8th. Royal Irish Fusiliers	S.P.13.
7th. Royal Inniskilling Fusiliers.	YUM YUM TRENCH (N.18.a.15.45.)
2nd. Royal Irish Regiment.	S.P.13.
8th. Royal Inniskilling Fusiliers.	THE FOSSE N.16.d.8.8.
49th. Machine Gun Company.	S.P.13.
49th. Trench Mortar Battery.	SWATOW TRENCH.
157 Field Company R.E.	THE RIB.

POSITIONS OF COMPANY HEADQUARTERS.

"A" Coy's H.Q. in a dugout front line at..................

"B" Coy's H.Q. in a dugout in front line at..................

"C" Coy's H.Q. in a dugout in FERMOY TRENCH at N.18.c.7.30.

"D" Coy's H.Q. in a dugout at Junction WATLING STREET and FERMOY TRENCH
                    N.18.c.3.72. ? ? ? ? ?

Attached T.M's in a dugout in FERMOY TRENCH at N.18.c.8.36.

Attached M.Guns in a dugout in WATLING STREET N.18.c.8.36.

H.Qrs. "Moppers Up" will be at Battalion Headquarters in S.P.13.
The Forward Command Post of the 2nd. Royal Irish Regiment for the attack on the BLACK LINE will be at Brigade Forward Station. The Brigade Forward Station will follow the last wave of the attack on the BLUE LINE and will be established about O.13.c.15.45.
When the BLACK LINE has been captured the Brigade Forward Station will move forward to O.19.b.75.85.

(Continued on Sheet 4.)

IX. COMMUNICATION TRENCHES.

49th. Infantry Brigade are allotted Two Communication Trenches.
- WATLING STREET. (In Trench.)

  THE FOSSE. (Out Trench.)

As soon as possible after ZERO the following Communication Trenches will be made by the R.E. and Pioneers.
(a) THE FOSSE----BIRR TRENCH via NAME TRENCH ----NAME DRIVE to be used for OUT traffic.
(b) WATLING STREET----MAYO STREET via NAIL DRIVE. To be used for IN traffic.

The Communication Trenches connecting the CHINESE WALL LINE with the PARK LINE are allotted the BATTALION:-
- THE FOSSE   (To Be Constructed)
- CHOW STREET............"B" and "D" Coys and "Moppers Up".
- CORK TRENCH............"A" and "C" Coys and "Moppers Up".

The Communication Trenches connecting the PARK LINE with the Front Line are allotted:-
- BIRR TRENCH............"A" and "C" Coys and "Moppers Up"
- CROWBAR TRENCH........."B" and "D" Coys and "Moppers Up"

Two Overland Routes for Transport are being prepared.

(a) N.17.a.15.65.------N.17.a.50.70.-----N.17.b.00.80.----N.17.b.90.60.
    N.18.a.75.45.

(b) LAITERIE. N.16.d.48.10.----N.17.c.42.35.-----N.17.c.60.10.NORTH of
    S.P.13.-------by BIRR TRENCH.

X. DEFENSIVE FLANKS.

LATERAL COMMUNICATIONS.
Communication must be kept up with either flank. If it is found that any portion of a Company Line is more advanced than that on a flank, defensive flanks consisting of one or more Lewis Guns must be put out at once to cover the gap between the lines. In the same way, should the line on any Company's flank be more advanced, the Company is responsible that communication is established with the people on his flank and that the gap is covered with one or more Lewis Guns.

XI. DRESS.

All Officers will be dressed and equipped the same as the men. Sticks are not to be carried. Fighting Order for all ranks:-
(a) Clothing, Arms and entrenching tool as issued.
(b) Equipment as issued with the exception of the pack.
    Haversacks to be worn on the back except for Lewis Gunners and Rifle Bombers. *who will carry it at the side*
(c) Box Respirators and P.H. Helmets.
(e) Iron Rations, unexpired portion of day's rations. Mess tin and Cover.
(f) 120 rounds of S.A.A. except Bombers (   ) signallers, runners.
    Lewis Gunners and Rifle Bombers who carry 50 rounds. Carrying Parties 50 rounds S.A.A.
(g) Every men to carry two Mills' Bombs, one in each top pocket. These bombs will be collected into dumps as soon as the objective has been gained.
(h) Flares will be carried in the bottom pocket of the jacket.
    NOTE. Machine Gun Coy., Trench Mortar Battery and Carrying Parties will not carry g. and h.
(i) Three Sandbags per man.
(j) One Water Bottle full of Cold Tea.
(k) Bombing Sections will carry:-
    Bayonetman Six No.5.per man. (Mills')
    Remainder of Section Twelve No.5. Grenades per man.
(l) Rifle Bombers will carry 12.Wales Grenades or 13 No.34.Grenades

(Continued on Sheet 5.)

SHEET. 5.

XI DRESS (Contd.)
(m) All Lewis Gun Sections will carry 30 Drums (All spare drums will be brought to BLACK COT DUMP by carrying party (vide para IV.)

XII. TIME.
In making references to times before or after which operations commence the following nomenclature will be adopted in future:-

(a) Referring to days.
"Z" Day is the day on which operations take place.
One day before "Z" Day................"Y" Day.
Two days before "Z" Day...............ced "X" Day.
Three days before "Z" Day.............."W" Day.
Four days before "Z" Day..............."V" Day.
Five days before "Z" Day................"U" Day.
Days before "U" Day will be referred to as "Z" minus 6, "Z" minus 7, "Z" minus 8. etc.

(b) Referring to hours on "Z" Day.

ZERO is the exact time at which operations will commence, and times will be designated in hours and minutes plus or minus from ZERO, even if they encroach on "Y" Day.

XIII. ZERO.
ZERO HOUR WILL BE.................................

"Z" DAY WILL BE ....JUNE 1917.

XIV. MAPS.
No marked Maps of any description of our lines are to be taken in advance of Battalion Headquarters by any Officer N.C.O. or man. Company Commanders are held responsible that these orders are made known to all ranks, and will return such maps to Orderly Room before going into the line, at the same time rendering a certificate, certifying that none of these maps remain in their possession.

XV. SIGNALLING.
(a) In order to prevent leakage of information and to ensure that other methods of information are practiced all communications by telephone except that mentioned in Sub-para (d) and messages sent on the buzzer will cease in advance of YORK ROAD until the hour of ZERO.

(b) The following methods of communication will be permitted in front of YORK ROAD.:-

    PIGEONS.
    VISUAL.
    RUNNERS.
    FULLERPHONES FOR "S.O.S" CALLS.
    ROCKETS FOR "S.O.S." CALLS.

N.B.
All Fullerphones in front of YORK ROAD will either be issued without hand sets, or have the microphones removed from the speaking circuits.

(c) Existing "S.O.S." Lines from Batteries to Companies are to be abolished; the Batteries are to be connected to Battalion Headquarters only.

(d) Companies in the Front Line will be connected to Battalion Headquarters Fullerphones only will be used on these lines and are not to be used except for "S.O.S" Calls.

(e) For Communication between Brigade Headquarters and the Headquarters of Battalions in the line, one telephone may be retained in each Battalion Commanders' Dugout.

(f) Until after ZERO hour no message will be sent by pigeon which contains anything in the address "TO" or "FROM", or in the body of the message, which would be of value if it fell into the hands of the enemy.

SHEET. 6.

15. SIGNALLING (Continued)
- (g) Two hours before ZERO, Companies will send one runner to Battalion H.Qrs.(S.P.13.) to report to Signal Officer. These runners will remain with Battalion Headquarters until the Battalion Forward Post is established in BLACK COT.
- (h) Battalion Forward Post will be marked with a Blue and White Flag.
- (i) As soon as Battalion Forward Post is established, all messages should be sent there
- (j) Battalion Forward Post will move forward after fourth wave.
- (k) CODE CALLS From ZERO hour onwards position calls (such as F.E.17) cease to exist and NAME CODES (A.K.,B.K., C.K.,D.K.,) will be used.
  Companies will take call of Battalion followed by letters A,B,C,D, to denote the Company.
  e.g. D.K.N. = "A" Coy.
  D.K.B. = "B" Coy. and so on.
- (l) Messages will be carried by all runners in the right hand breast pocket.
- (m) In cases of important messages such as "Objectives have been taken" etc. Companies should send two runners, with a few minutes interval between them

XVI. MEDICAL.
The REGIMENTAL AID POST will be FOSSE N.17.d.2.3. Wounded will be collected and brought to Regimental Aid Post by Regimental Stretcher Bearers, Bandsmen, etc. and such others as may be detailed. Later, in the event of a successful advance, fresh Regimental Aid Posts will be improvised according to pre-arranged plan.
The carrying back from New to Old Regimental Aid Post will be done by Field Ambulance Personnel.
Advanced Dressing Stations will be at:-
KEMMEL BREWERY N.21.c.8.5.
LAITERIE N.16.d.2.3.
PARRAIN FARM N.28.b.70.95.
Walking wounded will proceed direct to BRULOOZE CORNER

XVII. CROSS COUNTRY TRACKS.
Cross Country Tracks as shewn on Maps already issued will be used by walking wounded, prisoners of war, reinforcements and horse transport as far as possible.

XVIII. BAYONETS.
It is most important that every precaution should be taken to prevent bayonets from flashing in the moonlight, should there be a moon when units are moving to their places of assembly.

XIX. AIRCRAFT.
In the event of hostile aeroplanes flying over our lines to ascertain whether our trenches are more strongly manned than usual, all ranks will remain still and will not look up. Such Aeroplanes are to be dealt with by Anti-aircraft, Vickers or Lewis Guns. The Battalion Lewis Gun Officer will arrange for 4.L.G's to be maintained for this purpose.

XX. MINES.
All Mines on the 16th. Division Front will be exploded at ZERO hour If the explosion of any of the above mines has not taken place by ZERO plus 15 seconds, it is to be understood that it will not take place at all.
Danger Areas are being marked. Notice Boards will be put up in all Sub-ways.

XXI. "S.O.S."
The S.O.S. Signal will remain, RED signal cartridges as at present.

XXII. NO MAN'S LAND.
In order to avoid casualties, the whole of the Infantry detailed for the assault of the RED and BLUE lines should get rapidly across "NO MAN'S LAND." As few troops as possible being left in the front and support lines.

SHEET. 7.

XXIII. DUMPS.
Dumps formed in the German Lines are to be marked with the following distinguishing marks (lettering Black on White ground.)

```
         12"
    +----------+
    |          |
12" |    D.    |
    |          |
    +----------+
```

XXIV. PRISONERS OF WAR.
A Divisional Collecting Station has been arranged at M.24.a.central & Divisional Troops after troops to the collecting stations will be immediately marched back to their units. Prisoners are to be marched by cross country tracks and are to be kept off the road as far as possible. Sentries and Guards are not to talk to prisoners.
Prisoners will receive ordinary rations only and soldiers are forbidden to give them tobacco, cigarettes or food.
Soldiers are on no account to take any buttons, caps or other articles from prisoners. Any German Documents etc. picked up are to be immediately sent to Battalion Headquarters.
Officer Prisoners to be kept separate from the men.
Escort should not exceed 20% of the number of prisoners.
It is the duty of the "Moppers Up" to take back prisoners and not that of the Battalion carrying out the assault.
Carrying Parties returning for more stores and slightly wounded walking cases should be used where possible.

XXV. SUNRISE.
All Officers will carefully watch when the sun rises each morning, as the sun can be used as means of judging direction.

XXVI. WATER.
The R.E. will search for and open up the following sources of water supply:-

    RED CHATEAU   N.18.b.80.20.

    HOSPICE.   O.13.c.3.8.

On road N. of WYTSCHAETE CHURCH at O.19.b.20.35.
On no account will the water from the wells be drunk until passed fit to drink by the R.E.
60. Petrol Tins of Drinking Water are being carried to the vicinity of O.13.c.15.45., 20 of these tins will be issued to this Battalion.

APPENDIX "A"

Copy 6

SECRET

49th INFANTRY BRIGADE ADMINISTRATIVE INSTRUCTIONS FOR THE OFFENSIVE.

Instructions for Carrying Parties.

(Ref. S.O. 69 dated 25-5-17 Page 4, para 6 and Appendix "B")

1. (a) The 8/R. Innis. Fus. will be responsible for seeing that the full complement of 70 Yukon Packs (now in possession) (i.e. "A" Party 30, "B" & "C" Parties 20 each) are delivered at No. 3 Main Brigade Bomb Dump (N.16.c.9.1a) by a date which will be given later. They will be placed in charge of the Brigade Bomb Dump keeper there. *"A" delivered 3/6/17 SEE MIKE ccc 203*
(b) On receipt of further instructions the 8th R. Innis Fus will detail a party of 1 N.C.O. and 6 men to pack these YUKON PACKS for the 1st journey in accordance with the attached Schedule and leave them at the Brigade Dump all packed. *(New Dump N 17 a 15.35 Poll Tr)*
(c) The Brigade Bombing Officer is responsible for the safe custody and protection from weather. *amendt 4/6/17*

2. Bombs, S.A.A, Red Signal Cartridges, shovels and petrol tins will be obtained from No. 3 Main Dump. Lewis Gun Drums filled from units concerned.

3. 2nd R. Irish Regt. on receipt of Instructions will deliver to No. 3 Main Brigade Dump 324 filled Lewis Gun Drums in canvas bags.
The 7th R. Innis Fus and 7/8th R. Irish Fus. will each deliver to No. 3 Main Brigade Dump when instructed - 50 filled Lewis Gun drums. The remaining 174 filled drums belonging to these two units will be delivered by them on Y/Z night, to their Battalion Dumps in Support Line, placing them in charge of the Bomb Store Keepers.

4. "A", "B", "C". Carrying Parties on Y day will pick up their respective loads and carry same up to their assembly positions.

5. "B" and "C" Carrying Parties after completing their first carry will unload their packs at the forward dumps to be specified by the Battalion Commanders, and will then return to the Battalion Dumps in support line, of the units to which they are attached and load up for the second journey from there.
The position of the Forward Dumps as soon as determined are to be notified by the O.C's of the 7th R. Innis Fus and 7/8th R. Irish Fus. to the C.O's of the 2nd R. Irish Regt and 8th R. Innis Fus.

6. "A" Carrying Party will unload at place to be detailed by the C.O. 2nd R. Irish Regt. and return under his Instructions for any further supplies that may be required obtaining same from the Forward Dumps established by "B" and "C" Carrying Parties.

7. On "Y" night "F" Carrying Party will collect from No. 3 ~~Brigade~~ Main Brigade Dump 60 two-gallon petrol tins which they will fill with water at YORK ROAD water tanks, N.16.b.9.3, and carry to No. 4 Advanced Brigade Dump, N.17.d.8.8, placing same in charge of Store Keeper.

8. On "Z" day "F" Carrying Party will carry up 60 petrol tins filled with water from No. 4 Advanced Brigade Dump and carry same as far as the Brigade Forward Station about O.13.c.15.45. The allotment of water will be 20 tins to each of the 3 Assaulting Battalions.

9. On conclusion of the various tasks "A", "B" and "C" Carrying Parties will bring back all the YUKON PACKS with them to their final Assembly Positions.

10. ACKNOWLEDGE. ✓

W. Bowen
Captain,
Staff Captain, 49th Infantry Brigade.

2-6-17.

Copy No. 1 to G.O.C.
" 2 Staff Captain.
" 3 Brigade Major.
" 4 2nd R. Irish Regt.
" 5 7th R. Innis Fus.
" 6 8th R. Innis Fus.
" 7 7/8th R. Irish Fus.
" 8 49th M.G. Company.
" 9 49th T.M. Battery.
" 10-11 War Diary.
" 12 File.
" 13 Asst. Staff Captain.
" 14 Bde. Bombing Officer.

"A" CARRYING PARTY. LOAD FOR FIRST JOURNEY.

No. of men.	Details of Load.	Approx. weight of each man's load.	Picks.	Shovels.	Sandbags.	S.A.A. rounds.	Lewis Gun Drums.	S.O.S. Signals.
6	9 shovels 10 sandbags.) each 4 bandoliers.) man 3 picks.	55 lbs	18	54	60	1200.		
6	9 shovels 10 sandbags.) each 4 bandoliers.) man. 3 picks.	55 lbs	18	54	60	1200		
10	12 L.G.Drums. 10 sandbags.) each 4 bandoliers.) 3 red cartridges) man. 1½ 3 red cartridges 1"	50 lbs.			100	2000	120	60.
8	13 L.G.Drums.) each 10 sandbags.) 4 bandoliers.) man.	55 lbs.			80	1600	104	
TOTALS 30			36	108	300	6000	224	60.

NOTE :- "A" Carrying Party will be equipped with 30 YUKON PACKS.

"B" AND "C" CARRYING PARTIES. LOAD FOR FIRST JOURNEY.

No. of Men.	Details of Load.	Approx. weight of each man's load.	Picks.	Shovels.	Sandbags.	Rifle Grenades.	Mills No. 5 bombs.	S.A.A. rounds	Lewis Gun Drums.	S.O.S. Signals.
10 With YUKON PACKS.	3 picks. } each 10 shovels.} man. 10 sandbags. 4 bandoliers.	65 lbs.	30	100	100			2000		
10 With YUKON PACKS.	1 box Rifle Grenades.} each 5 L.G. Drums. } man. 10 sandbags. 4 bandoliers.	65 lbs.			100	200		2000	50	
10 Without YUKON PACKS.	2 boxes Mills } each No. 5 } man. 4 Bandoliers.	42 lbs.					240	2000		
TOTALS 30			30	100	200	200	240	6000	50	

NOTE :- "B" and "C" Carrying Parties will each be equipped with 20 YUKON PACKS.

"B" AND "C" CARRYING PARTIES. LOAD FOR SECOND JOURNEY.

No. of men.	Details of load.	Approx. weight of each man's load.	Picks.	Shovels.	Sandbags.	Rifle Grenades.	Mills No. 5 bombs.	S.A.A. rounds.	Lewis Gun Drums.	S.O.S. signals.
10 With YUKON PACKS.	8 shovels.) 10 sandbags.)each 4 picks.)man.	65 lbs.	40	80	100					
10 (10) With YUKON PACKS.	15 L.G.Drums. 10 Sandbags. 3 rod cartridges)each 1½") 3 red cartridges)man. 1"	62 lbs.			100				150	
3 Without YUKON PACKS.	8 L.G. Drums.)each in) canvas buckets)man.	34 lbs.							24.	
7 Without YUKON PACKS.	2 boxes Mills)each No. 5 bombs.)man.	40 lbs.					168			
TOTALS. 30			40	80	200		168		174.	60

NOTE :- "B" and "C" Carrying Parties will each be equipped with 20 YUKON PACKS.

Appendix A.

49TH INFANTRY BRIGADE INSTRUCTIONS FOR THE OFFENSIVE.

1. The attached Table shows the distribution of S.A.A., Grenades, etc. amongst Brigade and Battalion Dumps.

2. S.A.A. and Bomb. Limbers of Regimental and Machine Gun Company Transport and all mobile reserves of tools will be ready loaded up by Zero Hour and Brigaded under arrangements to be made by the Staff Captain. They are not to be unloaded without orders from Brigade Headquarters.

3. Dumps formed in the German Lines are to be marked with the following distinguishing mark (lettering black on a white ground).

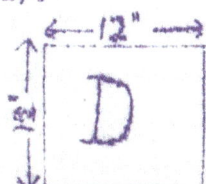

The above distinguishing mark is to be notified to all concerned.

4. In addition to the Reserves on Limbers, machine guns employed for barrage fire will be in possession of the following amount of ammunition at Zero Hour :-

    3500 rounds belted at the gun.

    8000 rounds at the belt filling depot.

    8500 rounds in reserve dumps.

5. K. and K.N. ammunition will be reserved for machine guns as far as possible.

6. The Brigade Bombing Officer is responsible for the supply of grenades to the Battalion Stores.

TABLE SHOWING SCALE OF S.A.A, GRENADES, &c, TO BE KEPT AT BRIGADE AND BATTALION DUMPS.

Position of Dump.	S.A.A. Boxes.	No. 5 Mills	Rifle Grenades No.20 & 24.	No. 23.	Stokes.	Flares No. 2 Green Red. 1½"	Cartridges Green. 1½"	Signal Rod. 1"	Rif.Gren. signals for night use.	F Grenades.	Smoke Candles.	H.S.K. Very Green Lights.	1" D.I
Main Bde.Dump No. 3. N.16.c.9.3.	30	1200	-	-	700	100	60	39	100		375	50	600
Main Bde. Dump No. 4. N.17.a.15.25.	30	1200	-	-	700	100	60	39	100		375	50	600
Adv. Bde. Dump No. 3. N.17.d.55.15.	50	1000	80	36	400	200	60	-		54			600
Adv. Bde. Dump No. 4. N.17.d.70.80	50	1000	80	36	600	200	60			54			600
Battalion Dump N.18.c.22.12.	35	800	80	24		100							300
Battalion Dump N.18.a.40.10.	35	800	60	48		100							300
Stokes Dump. N.18.c.30.90.					600								

TABLE SHOWING SCALE OF S.A.A., GRENADES, &c, TO BE KEPT AT BRIGADE AND BATTALION DUMPS IN ADDITION TO THE AMOUNTS ALREADY HELD BY THE BRIGADE IN THE LINE.

Position of Dump.	S.A.A. Boxes	S.A.A. No. 5 Hills Nos.20 & 24.	Rifle Grenades No.23	Stokes	Flames	Very Lights No. 2 Green 1 inch D.I	Cartridges 1 inch Red	Signal Green 1½"	Signal Red 1½"	Signal Green 1"	Signal Red 1"	Rifle Grenade Signals for night use.	P. Grenades	Smoke Grenades	M.S.K. Candles
Adv.Div. Dump. N.21.a.1.9.	300	8000	10,000	5000	6000	2000	5000	400	200	100	100	200	200	500	100
Bde. Dump No. 3. N.16.D.5.5.	50	2000	1500	1000	700	200	600	50	25	25		75	100	375	75
Bde. Dump No. 4. N.17.a.15.25.	50	2000	1500	1000		200	600	50	25	25		75	100	375	75
Adv.Bde. Dump No.3 N.17.d.55.15	50	2000	1500	500	400	200	800	100	50	50		50	50		
Adv.Bde. Dump No.4 N.17.d.70.80	50	2000	1500	500	600	200	800	100	50	50		50	50		
Battalion Dump. N.18.c.45.30.	50	1250	1000	500		150	200.								
Battalion Dump. N.18.a.65.15.	50	1250	1000	500		150	200.								
Trench Mortar Dump. N.18.c.50.80.					500										

SECRET.   Copy No ...6...

AMENDMENTS TO APPENDIX "A" of 49th INFANTRY BRIGADE ADMINISTRATIVE INSTRUCTIONS FOR THE OFFENSIVE.

1. Reference Appendix "A" of 49th Infantry Brigade Administrative Instructions for the Offensive - "Carrying Parties" the following notes and amendments will be made:-

Note. - Para 1 (b) - the Brigade Dump referred to therein will be No 4 Main Brigade Bomb Dump (N.17.6.15.25) and not No 3 Main Brigade Bomb Dump.

2. Para 2 - "For No.3 Main Brigade Bomb Dump" read "No. 4".

3. Para 3 - For "No 3 Main Brigade Dump" read "No 4" in (two places.)

4. Para 7 - For "No 3 Main Brigade Dump" read "No 4"

Appendix A
Altered accordingly
apd

4-6-17

Captain,
Staff Captain,
49th Infantry Brigade.

Appendix B.

ACTION OF DIVISIONAL MACHINE GUNS.

1. The following machine guns will be at the disposal of the Division for covering and barrage fire :-

47th Machine Gun Coy. (less 6 guns).	10 guns.
49th Machine Gun Coy. (less 6 guns).	10 guns.
48th Machine Gun Coy.	16 guns.
33rd Machine Gun Coy.	8 guns.
	Total	44 guns.

2. The machine guns allotted for covering and barrage fire will be divided into three categories :-

    (a) Guns to establish a creeping barrage, either direct, enfilade or oblique, in front of the Artillery barrage. The object of this barrage is to catch the enemy rushing back from the Heavies or sheltering in shell holes or ditches between the trenches.

    (b) Guns detailed for fire on selected targets, such as Strong Points, cuttings or ravines.

    (c) Guns to sweep all ground in front and rear of the enemy's main line of resistance from the commencement of the attack. All guns will be given a protective barrage line in order to cover the pauses at the intermediate objectives.

3. The zone of fire allotted to the Division is as follows :-
    From line MAP DRIVE (inclusive) - HILL 84 (inclusive) - STEENYZER CABARET (inclusive).
    To line RED CHATEAU - Junction of OBVIOUS AVENUE with OBVIOUS ROW - House at C.14.d.30.50.

4. Guns told off to form the Creeping M.G.Barrage will lift in conformity with the creeping Artillery barrage. The line of the lowest bullets of the M.G.Barrage will be 200 yards in front of the Artillery Barrage line.

5. The following targets are also to receive treatment from the Machine Guns placed at the disposal of the Division:-

    (a) Railway cutting south of HILL 84.

    (b) The area between PETIT BOIS and BOIS DE WYTSCHAETE.

    (c) The eastern edge of the BOIS DE WYTSCHAETE and up to the edge of the village.

    (d) UNNAMED WOOD.

    (e) Junction of OBVIOUS Trenches west of NORTH HOUSE.

6. To carry out the above tasks, the M.G's at the disposal of the Division from each Brigade will be grouped together. The Group Commanders will be under the control of the Divisional Machine Gun Officer (D.M.G.O.) During the actual operations this officer will be located at THE RIB (N.16.d.35.50), where he will be in communication with each Group and with Divisional Headquarters.

7. The allocation of Zones and tasks to the various Groups will be as follows :-

   (a) **47th and 49th Inf. Bde. Groups.**

   From Zero Hour until the RED LINE is reached these groups will search for 250 yards Eastwards from a line running due north from the KEMMEL - WYTSCHAETE Road at O.19.d.00.85 to the junction of OBVIOUS AVENUE and OBVIOUS ROW about O.13.d.00.70. The area behind WYTSCHAETE WOOD and the junction of all the OBVIOUS trenches near NORTH HOUSE to receive particular attention.

   From Zero plus 35 minutes till the advance from the BLUE LINE begins at Zero plus 3 hours 40 minutes, creep forward and keep up a slow rate of fire on the line WYTSCHAETE CHURCH - NORTH HOUSE. When the advance from the BLUE LINE begins fire should be intensified and the range gradually increased until the protective barrage line, i.e. 300 yards East of BLACK LINE, is reached. As soon as the BLACK LINE is reached, six guns of each Group will move forward as follows for the final Protective Barrage:-

   <u>49th Inf. Bde. Group.</u> { 4 to UNNAMED WOOD SPUR and BLUE LINE.
   { 2 to NORTH HOUSE.

   <u>47th Inf. Bde. Group.</u> 6 to HILL 84.

   The remaining guns will await orders of D.M.G.O.

   (b) **48th Inf. Bde. Group.**

   The 48th Inf. Bde. Guns (less 4 at PARRET FARM) will search from the line separating squares N and O between the RED CHATEAU and NANCY DRIVE forward to a line 100 yards East of a north and south line through O.13.central and O.19.central. When the advance from the RED LINE begins at Zero plus 1 hour 5 minutes, they will creep forward to a N. and S. line through NORTH HOUSE from OBSTRUCTION DRIVE on the North to the WYTSCHAETE - TORREKEN FARM road on the south. On the advance from the BLUE LINE at Zero plus 3 hours 40 minutes they will creep forward until out of range. They will then come under the orders of G.O.C. 48th Inf. Bde.

   The rate of the Machine Gun creeping barrage is the same as that of the artillery.

   The 4 guns at PARRET FARM will at Zero begin searching from behind PETIT BOIS through BOIS DE WYTSCHAETE. They will eventually creep their barrage forward to the centre of WYTSCHAETE and cease when the advance from the BLUE LINE begins at Zero plus 3 hours 40 minutes. They will then come under the orders of G.O.C. 48th Inf. Bde.

(c) **33rd Inf. Bde. Group.**

At Zero hour a barrage will be opened on NANCY SUPPORT from NANCY DRIVE to NAP DRIVE. It will move forward until it reaches a line running due South from South-west corner of HOSPICE. When the advance from the RED LINE begins at Zero plus 1 hour 5 minutes it will continue forward to a line running from HILL 84 to the HOUSE 100 yards South of NORTH HOUSE. It will remain on this line until the advance begins from the BLUE LINE at Zero plus 3 hours 40 minutes and will then creep forward to the MESSINES - ST. ELOI Road, ceasing fire at Zero plus 4 hours. These guns will receive orders from the Corps on completion of task.

(d) D.M.G.O. will detail 4 guns from the above to pay particular attention to the targets mentioned in para. 5.

(e) Detailed instructions as to the above covering and barrage fire with charts will be issued by the D.M.G.O. direct to Group Commanders. No alteration is to be made in the barrage without reference to Divisional Headquarters.

8. **MACHINE GUN ACTION BEFORE ZERO.**

From now onwards until Zero hour D.M.G.O. will arrange for Machine Guns to co-operate for the purpose of :-

(a) Lowering the efficiency of the enemy working parties.

(b) Making the transport of material, and especially Trench Mortar ammunition, difficult.

(c) Causing deterioration in the enemy's moral.

This will be obtained by firing on -

(i) The wire and targets engaged during the day by the artillery.

(ii) Communication trenches and Avenues leading to the above.

(iii) The points of assembly of working parties, dumps, etc.

(iv) Trench Railways, Roads and Tracks; especially those leading to Trench Mortar Emplacements.

(v) Searching of Reverse Slopes.

49th I.B. No.S.C.60.
2nd June 1917.

SECRET.

Copy No 5.

49TH INFANTRY BRIGADE INSTRUCTIONS FOR THE OFFENSIVE.

Para. 36.   The wearing of captured German Head-dress, uniform or equipment is strictly forbidden.

Cancel Tables to appendix D and substitute the new Tables forwarded herewith; also cancel table attached to Appendix "A" and substitute the one forwarded herewith.

ACKNOWLEDGE.

F.W.M.William Captain,
Brigade Major, 49th Infantry Brigade.

Issued through Signals:

```
Copy No. 1 to G.O.C.
    "     2    Staff Captain.
    "     3    2nd R. Irish Regt.
    "     4    7th R. Innis Fus.
    "     5    8th R. Innis Fus.
    "     6    7/8th R. Irish Fus.
    "     7    49th M.G. Company.
    "     8    49th T.M. Battery.
    "     9    Bde. Signal Officer.
    "    10    Bde. Intelligence Officer.
    "    11    16th Division.
    "    12    16th Division.
    "    13    47th Inf. Bde.
    "    14    48th Inf. Bde.
    "    15    177th Bde., R.F.A.
    "    16    157th Field Coym R.E.
```

S E C R E T.

Copy No 5

G. O. C.
Staff Captain.
2nd R. Irish Regt.
7th R. Innis Fus.
✓ 8th R. Innis Fus.
7/8th R. Irish Fus.
49th M.G. Company.
49th T.M. Battery.
Bde. Signal Officer.
Bde. Intelligence Officer.
16th Division.
16th Division.
47th Inf. Bde.
48th Inf. Bde.
58th Inf. Bde.
177th Bde, R.F.A.
157th Field Coy, R.E.

49th Inf. Bde. No. S.O. 60 - 3-6-17.

     Herewith Copy No ...5... of Paras. 37 to 41 of 49TH INFANTRY BRIGADE INSTRUCTIONS FOR THE OFFENSIVE, also Appendix F.

     Kindly acknowledge receipt. ✓

H.W.H. Willcox, Captain,
Brigade Major, 49th Infantry Brigade.

SECRET.   Copy No ......

49TH INFANTRY BRIGADE INSTRUCTIONS FOR THE OFFENSIVE.

(CONTINUED).

37. After taking the BLACK LINE troops will be pushed forward to establish themselves on a more advanced line.

38. (a) The new objective will be known as the COSTAVERRE LINE. The portion allotted to IX Corps extends from O.28.b. 5.2 to O.16.c.4.2.
    (b) The 33rd Infantry Brigade and 68th Field Coy, R.E. from the 11th Division will be attached to the 16th Division for the purpose of this advance.

39. **ARTILLERY ACTION ON "Z" DAY UP TO THE TAKING OF THE BLACK LINE.**

   (a) <u>Action previous to Assault.</u>

   Previous to the assault there will be no intense bombardment - night firing and artillery work generally will be carried out as usual until Zero Hour. It is essential that there should be no alteration in the rate or volume of fire previous to Zero Hour, and that everything should appear normal.

   (b) <u>Action at Zero.</u>

   At Zero all guns will open at their maximum rate of fire, and the infantry will form up under the 18-pdr. Creeping Barrage.

   (c) <u>Barrage Arrangements.</u>

   The barrages will consist of :-
   (i) A Creeping Barrage of 18-pdr shrapnel moving in advance of the infantry at average lifts of 100 yards. The times of lifts and pauses in the Creeping Barrage up to the BLACK LINE are shown on Map G/16/8.
   (ii) Standing Barrages of 18-pdrs, 4.5" howitzers, medium and heavy howitzers, which will be established on successive trenches, strong points, etc. within the limits of safety of each gun or howitzer.

   These Barrages have been arranged in depth so as to ensure that all ground which commands the line of advance of our infantry is kept under fire from Zero onwards.

   (d) <u>Protective Barrages.</u>

   During the periods of consolidation of the RED, BLUE and GREEN LINES, the creeping barrage will form a protecting barrage 150 yards in front of our infantry. Fire will not be kept on the same points the whole time, but a system of searching and sweeping will be employed, so that all enemy movement in the area will be stopped.

   (e) <u>Protective Barrage in front of the BLACK LINE.</u>

   The Protective Barrage in front of the BLACK LINE will be placed 300 yards in front of our infantry. The infantry holding the BLACK line will push out their patrols as far as the barrage permits.

SECRET.   COPY NO........

CONTINUATION OF OPERATION ORDERS NO.1.ISSUED ON   /6/17.
SHEET 8.dated 4th./une.1917.

XXVII. OFFICERS.

The following Officers will accompany the Battalion:-
- Lieut.Colonel.K.C.Weldon D.S.O.   Commanding Officer
- Major.T.F.O'Donnell M.C.   2nd. in Command.

- Captain W.H.Stitt M.C.   Adjutant.
- Lieutenant D.M.H.W.Kinghan   Lewis Gun Officer
- 2/Lieut. G.J.Forbes   Signalling Officer.
- 2/Lieut.J.B.Drea   Intelligence Officer

"A" Company.
- Captain T.de C.Falle.
- 2/Lieut.H.B.Reynell.
- 2/Lieut.G.R.Attwood.
- 2/Lieut.J.V.L.McGarry.

"B" Company.
- Captain P.Jolliffe.
- 2/Lieut.V.J.Lynch.
- 2/Lieut.W.H.Waters.
- 2/Lieut.C.W.Pickett.

"C" Company
- 2/Lieut.W.H.Allen
- 2/Lieut.P.H.Wray.
- 2/Lieut.M.Jestin.
- 2/Lieut.G.Coombes.

"D" Company
- 2/Lieut.F.A.Moody.
- 2/Lieut.S.Turner.
- 2/Lieut.C.L.Henry.
- 2/Lieut.J.P.H.Bell.

XXVIII. SMOKING.
When the Battalion is forming up and is formed up in the Assembly Trenches,no smoking is to be allowed.

XXIX. WIRE.
Each Company Commander is directly responsible that the wire in front of his assembly position is cut and that sufficient gaps exist.

XXX. LEWIS GUN MAGAZINES.
The Lewis Gun Officer will deliver 50 filled Lewis Gun Drums in tins to No.4.Main Brigade Dump at N.17.a.15.25.when instructed.The remaining 174 Drums in tins are to be delivered at Battalion Dump at Junction BIRR and FERMOY TRENCHES on Y/Z Day.
They will be handed over to the Bomb Store Keepers.All Magazines will be filled with "K" or "K.N" Ammunition.

XXXI. STORES.
Reference para.4.The following stores will be dumped at BLACK COT:-
Picks,shovels,sandbags,rifle grenades,mills' No.5.Bombs,S.A.A.,
Lewis Gun Drums and S.O.S.Signals.

XXXII. BURIAL GROUNDS.
The following sites have been chosen as forward burial grounds, and will be used in case of severe losses in the line:-
- "A" Cemetery   N.17.d.5.7.   (Near S.P.13.)
- "B" Cemetery   N.23.d.½.7½. (Near IRISH HOUSE.

Marks are being placed at these points.Burial Parties are being detailed under Divisional arrangements.

XXXIII. SYNCHRONIZATION.
Watches will be synchronized daily at 9.0.a.m.,12 noon and 6.0.pm.

XXIV. FORWARD BRIGADE POST.
Brigade Forward Post will move to the corner of UNNAMED WOOD (O.13.c.15.45.)after our fourth wave.

XXV. FORWARD BATTALION HEADQUARTERS
Battalion Headquarters will move forward to BLACK COT when the BLUE objective has been taken.

XXVI. CONTACT PATROLS.
Aeroplanes for contact patrols will be R.E.8.Type.and will be specially marked by a black riap attached to the rear of each lower plane. One contact aeroplane will watch over WYTSCHAETE and the area N.of the village.

(Continued on Page 9.)

SHEET. 9.

XXXVI CONTACT PATROLS (Contd.)

Contact patrols will fly over the line and call for flares at the following hours and any hours subsequent to these hours at which special aeroplanes may be ordered. Troops will also be prepared to put out flares at any other time if the aeroplane calls for them:-

BY 7th. Royal Inniskilling Fusiliers and) at ZERO plus 45.minutes
  7/8th. Royal Irish Fusiliers.) at ZERO plus 2.Hours.

BY. 2nd. Battn. The Royal Irish Regiment) at ZERO plus 4.hrs.30 mins.
  ( ) at ZERO plus 5.hrs.30.mins.

Aeroplanes will call for flares and Watson fans by sounding a KLAXON HORN and firing a "VERY" White Light or by giving either of these two signals.

Green Flares will be used. They should be lit in bunches of three about 30.yards apart.

Watson fans will be used in conjunction with flares. The fans should be turned over every two seconds and not quicker. The White side will be exposed to the aeroplane for two seconds, and the dark side for two seconds, and so on.

XXXVII. TANKS.

It must be impressed on all ranks in the Infantry that the tanks are there to assist their advance if possible, but they must never for a moment suppose that success depends on their presence. The men must never wait for the tanks, but must push on to their objective irrespective of xxxxxx whether they come up or not. There is a great danger of the attack being held up if this is not thoroughly realized by all ranks

XXXVIII. EMPLOYMENT OF TUNNELLING COMPANIES ON DUGOUTS AND ROADS.

A party of the 250 Tunnelling Company will reconnoitre captured dugouts as soon as the objective is reached.

This party will mark habitable dugouts with the number of men which can be accommodated in them, and will carry out repairs where necessary

XXXIX. CORRECTION.

Sheet 3. para. VI. Stokes' Guns. Line 7. for S.W. read S.E.

W.H. Stitt.
Captain & Adjutant.

7/8th. (S) Battalion Royal Irish Fusiliers.

Issued through Signals at 7.30. p.m.

Copy No.		Copy No.	
1.	"A" Coy.	9.	Medical Officer.
2.	"B" Coy.	10.	49th. Infantry Brigade
3.	"C" Coy.	11.	8th. R. Innis. Fusrs.
4.	"D" Coy.	12.	7th. R. Innis. Fusrs.
5.	Signals.	13.	War Diary.
6.	Transport Officer.	14.	File.
7.	Intelligence Officer.	15.	2/Lieut. Taylor 49. T.M.B.
8.	Quartermaster.	16.	Lieut. C. May. 49. M.G. Co.

SECRET

The Officer Commanding - 8th R/Innis. Fus.

Reference Operation Order
No 30 of 29th May 1917
please note the following
amendments:-

Para 9 for "2.30" read "2 hours"
for "3.00" read "2.40"
for "3.15" read "3.10"

5/6/17

H. R. Pigott
Lieut Colonel,
Commanding 2/ the Royal Irish.

40

SECRET. Copy No...IX...

OPERATION ORDER No 37.
By,
Lieut Col H.N. Young, D.S.O. &

6. 6. 17.

Ref S.O/. d/31.5.17.
" " 1.6.17.
" " 2.6.17
" " 4.6.17.
" " 6.6.17.

and all Appendixes and Maps issued under S.O/I's of the dates quoted above.

1. The Instructions given in the reference quoted above will be now regarded in the same light as definite Orders.

2. Zero day will be the 7th of June 1917 on which date all troops are to be in position by 2 a.m.
   Zero hour will be notified later.

3. The Battalion will commence closing up to its assembly position at 10 p.m. 6.6.17.

4. WATLING STREET has been allotted to the Battalion for the purposes of para 3.

5. B Coy will commence the evacuation of that portion of the front line which is to be occupied by A Coy at 10.5 p.m. 6.6.17, and complete this evacuation as quickly as possible leaving a few sentry groups only, which will rejoin their own Company immediately that portion of the Trench they are evacuating is occupied by any man of A Coy.

6. A Coy will move at 10 p.m.

   D Coy " " " 10 p.m. followed by "C" Coy

   H.Q. Personnel, L/G's, Snipers etc will follow "C" Coy.

6. B Coy (8th R. Inn's Fus) attached to the Battalion as Moppers Up will enter WATLING STREET, at 11.25 p.m. 6.6.17.

7. "B" Carrying Party, No 3 platoon (A Coy 8th R. Inn's Fus) will enter WATLING STREET at 11.45 p.m. 6.6.17.

8. THE FOSSE is allotted to the T/M Battery and the 49th M.G. Coy from 10-30 p.m. - 11.5 p.m.

9. (a) The absolute necessity of strict silence being maintained throughout the move into the Assembly position and from then to Zero hour must be thoroughly impressed on all ranks.

   (b) No striking of matches, smoking or flashing of torches will on any account be permitted.

   (c) It is the duty of every Officer, N.C.O, or man to see that this order is enforced no matter whether the offender belongs to his Unit or no, and to see generally that they do nothing themselves or that nothing occurs in their vicinity that would possibly warn the enemy of the impending attack.

10. Coys and Units attached to the Battalion will report by Runner immediately they are in their assemble positions.

    Companies will also at the same time or in a later report, report whether the various units intermingled with them in the assemble positions in accordance with the instructions issued are in their proper positions.

11. All wire must be completely cut immediately companies reach their assembly positions.

12. A screen consisting of a chain of small outposts will be formed in front of our line so as to ensure that no enemy patrols come near our trenches.

OPERATION ORDER No 37 (continued).

12. The Brigade on our left and the Battalion on our right are forming similar screens.

13. Preparations will be completed by 2 a.m. for surmounting our own parapets.

14. Cpl McKenna and the 9 men of the Drums detailed as Auxiliary Stretcher bearers will be in MACAW TRENCH (N.16.d.3.4 - N.16.d.9.7) at 11-45 p.m. 6.6.17.

15. Verbal Orders will be issued to the Battalion Police re Battalion stragglers posts.

16. Battalion H.Q's will be in BYRON FARM H.Q's, USMAGH STREET at 10.30 p.m. 6.6.17.

17. ACKNOWLEDGE.

  ACTassant

  Captn & Adjutant.

Copy No
1. File
2. A Coy
3. B "
4. C "
5. D "
6. Bde for information
7. 2nd in Command.
8. B Coy 8th R.Innis Fus
9. 8th R.Innis Fus for information.
10. C Section, 49th M/G Coy.
11. No 2 section 49th T/M Btty

Dear Boardman.

In sending in my list of recommendations to the Brigadier, in my covering note I mentioned how extremely well Lieut W. a Browne had done his work for me. All your men did most excellent work whilst with me. and I trust that if ever any of mine are attached to you, they will give you as great satisfaction as yours did to me.

Yrs sincerely
H. R. Young

10/6/17

Dear Boardman

I should like to bring to your notice the very valuable services rendered by the patrol of the platoon which you attached to us as a carrying party. They gave us every possible assistance, & when the Reserve Line was reached we were able to get on at once with the work of consolidation as the carriers were on the spot with picks & shovels.

I am very grateful to you for lending me such a fine officer as Hartley, & will you please let him & his platoon know how very much their good work was appreciated by all of us

Yrs sincerely

H.G. Frigori

"A" Form — MESSAGES AND SIGNALS.

Army Form C. 2121 (in pads of 100).

Copy

TO: All Units

Day of Month: 8th

AAA

Situation now appears as follows aaa Cavalry patrols reports timed 11.20 am State aaa Enemy holding line O.11.6.8.0 - O.12.c.2.2. O.18 central O.24.c.2.8 and seen running about on ridge East of VAN HOTE FARM aaa Strong attachments at O.22.d.8.7 and GROENELINDE CABT. aaa Enemy counter attacked at 9.30 pm and 10.15 pm and was massing again aaa We hold JOYE FARM

SECRET.   S.O/1/2.

~~2nd in Command~~   ~~M.G. Officer~~
~~A Coy~~   Transport Officer
~~B "~~   ~~Q.M.~~
~~C "~~   ~~M.O.R.~~
~~D "~~

~~49th Infy Bde for information~~
~~B Coy 8th R.Innis Fus~~
8th R.Innis Fus; for information
7/8th R.I.F.   ; for information
~~No 2 Section M/G Coy~~
~~No 2 Section T/M Bty.~~

Herewith Instructions for the Offensive and Appendixes,
   S.O/I.d/30.5.17.
   S.O/I.d/ 1.6.17.
   App: A.
        ~~B/1.~~ C. ~~D.~~ ~~E.~~ ~~K.~~ ~~Y~~ and ~~Map A~~.
Those of the above not forwarded to you are struck out.
These instructions are on no account to be taken E of the
VIERSTRAAT SWITCH.
ACKNOWLEDGE. ✓

                                   a.c. Tassart.
                                      Captn & Adjt.
                                   Royal Inniskilling Fusrs.

1.6.17.

No S.O. 1.   SECRET: Copy No. 9

INSTRUCTIONS FOR THE OFFENSIVE.

30.5.17.

I. **GENERAL IDEA:**

The attack on the WYTSCHAETE RIDGE will be made by the 16th Division in conjunction with the 36th Division on its immediate Right. and 19th   "   "   "   Left:

(a) The 16th Division will attack with two Infantry Brigades in the line and one Infantry Brigade in Reserve.

Right Attack.	47th Infantry Brigade.
	156th Field Coy R.E.
	I Company 11th Hants (Pioneers)
Left Attack.	49th Infantry Brigade.
	157th Field Coy R.E.
	I Company 11th Hants (Pioneers).
Divisional Reserve.	48th Infantry Brigade.
	155th Field Coy R.E.
	11th Hants Pioneers (less 2 Coys).

(b) The Boundaries between the 49th Infantry Brigade and the Brigades on either flank are as follows:

Right boundary (with 47th Infy Bde).
German line at N.24.a.60.85. - North Corner of PETIT BOIS N.24.b.4.9.) - N.W.Corner of BOIS DE WYTSCHAETE (N.24.b.75.80) South corner of HOSPICE (O.19.a.70.70) - point where Tramway crosses ST ELOI - MESSINES ROAD at O.20.a.20.30 - O.20.a.40.28.

Left Boundary (with 19th Division).
German line at N.18.b.23.53. - VIERSTRAAT - WYTSCHAETE Road (inclusive) to NORTHERN BRICKSTACK (O.13.c.32.88) - South Corner of GRANDBOIS (O.13.c.92.70) - OBVIOUS AVENUE (exclusive) - ESTAMINET Cross Roads (O.20.a.30.87).

These boundaries are shown in YELLOW on Map A.

(c) The Objectives allotted to the 49th Infy Bde and to the Infantry on either flank are shown as follows on Map A :-

1st Objective	RED
2nd Objective	BLUE
3rd Objective	GREEN
4th Objective	BLACK.

(d) The following will be the times of arrival and departure from the various colored lines:

RED LINE	Arrive	0.35.
	Depart	1.05.
BLUE LINE	Arrive	1.40.
	Depart	3.40.
GREEN LINE	Arrive	4.10.
	Depart	4.20.
BLACK LINE	Arrive	4.40.

(e) The attack on the RED and BLUE lines will be made by the 7th R.Innis Fusrs.
Supported on its immediate Right by the 7/8th R.Irish Fus 49th I.Bde and   "   "   "   Left   "   " ....

The attack on the GREEN and BLACK lines will then be made by the 2nd R.Irish Regt which will advance through the frontage as laid down for this Battalion and the 7/8th R.Irish Fusrs on the BLUE line.

Sheet 2.

INSTRUCTIONS FOR THE OFFENSIVE (continued)

(f) The 8th R.Innis Fusrs are finding the necessary Moppers Up for the other three Battalions of the Brigade.

B Coy (Captn Green) 8th R.Innis Fusrs will be attached to this Battalion as Moppers Up.

2. **SPECIAL IDEA:**

(a) The Battalion will attack on a two Company frontage in four waves.

The first and second waves will be formed by A and B Coys attacking side by side, A Coy being on the Right of B Coy.

The third and fourth waves will be formed by C and D Coys attacking side by side, C Coy being on the right of D Coy.

The Moppers Up as detailed below will be attached to Companies and will move as stated.

(b) The approximate successive frontages occupied or passed through by the Battalion are as follows:-

1.	Our own Front line and Support line		460 yards.
2.	The German front line.		410 "
3.	NAIL SWITCH	"	360 "
4.	The RED CHATEAU	"	320 "
5.	The RED	" on Map A.	260 "
6.	The BLUE	" on Map A.	280 "

(c) The Boundaries of this Battalion are:-

On the Right with 7/8th R.Irish Fusrs:

N.17.b.80.00. to SHANNON TRENCH at N.18.a.32.00. our front line at N.18.a.55.00. - German Front line at N.18.d.20.75. along a line 30 yards south of NAIL DRIVE - Southern Corner of UNNAMED WOOD - 0.13.c.80.15. 20 yards north of the junction of OBVIOUS DRIVE and NANCY DRIVE.

This boundary is shown by a Purple line on Map A.

On the Left with ....

German line at N.18.b.23.33. VIERSTRAAT - WYTSCHAETE ROAD (inclusive) to NORTHERN BRICKSTACK, 0.13.c.32.88. - South Corner of GRAND BOIS (0.13.c.92.70) - OBVIOUS AVENUE (exclusive).

This boundary is shown by the Northern YELLOW LINE on Map A.1.

(d) The Dividing line between Companies will be:

SHANNON TRENCH	At N.18.a.53.40,	also see detailed instructions for assembly positions below.
British Front line	At 50 yds N. of MAYO STREET.	" " "
German " "	N.18.b.13,14,i.e. at point where the WYTSCHAETE BEEK crosses it.	" " "

N.18.b.36.08., i.e. Junction of HAG ROW and NAIL ROW, N.18.d.8.9., i.e. in the new or RED CHATEAU Trench 40 yards S of NAIL STREET.

Sheet 3.

INSTRUCTIONS FOR THE OFFENSIVE (continued)

    The N.W. Edge of UNNAMED WOOD 50 yards N.E. of its Western Corner.

    Thence through UNNAMED WOOD in a straight line running S.E. by E to where a tram line crosses the SUNKEN ROAD at O.13.c.50.55.

    Thence to 30 yards N of the Trench junction in the Salient of OBVIOUS ROW, i.e. the junction of OBVIOUS ROW and NANCY DRIVE.

    These boundaries are shown on Map A in black pencil.

    (e) <u>OBJECTIVES (Battalion)</u>

1st Objective	NAIL SWITCH.
2nd "	The RED CHATEAU Line including the RED CHATEAU itself.
3rd Objective	The RED line on Map A.
4th "	" BLUE " " "

    A and B Coys, with their Moppers Up, will be responsible for the capturing of the 1st and 2nd Objectives including all intervening ground, trenches, communication trenches etc etc up to and including the 2nd Objective.

    C and D Coys, with their Moppers Up, will be responsible for the capturing of the 3rd and 4th Objectives including all intervening ground, trenches, communication trenches etc etc from the 2nd Objective exclusive up to and including the 4th Objective.

3. <u>MOPPERS UP:</u>

    B Coy (Captn Green) 8th R.Innis Fusrs will be attached to the Battn as "Moppers Up".

        This Company will be divided for purposes of Mopping Up into three Platoons, each of an approximate strength of 34 O.R's. Each platoon will be divided into 4 sections.

4. <u>"B" CARRYING PARTY:</u>

    This party will be found by No 3 platoon, A Coy, 8th R.Inniskilling Fusrs and will be under the Command of 2nd Lieut Henderson of the 8th Battalion.

5.   The various lines will be composed and distributed as follows:-

Wave	Line	Objective	Unit
1st wave.	1st line.	2nd Objective.	A and B Coys.
" "	2nd "	" "	A and B "
	3rd "	See App: C.	Nos 1 and 2 Sections Moppers Up.
	4th "	" "	Nos 3, 4 & 5 Sections Moppers Up.
2nd Wave	5th "	1st Objective.	A and B Coys.
" "	6th "	" "	A and B Coys.
3rd Wave	7th "	3rd Objective	C and D Coys.
" "	8th "	" "	C and D Coys.
	9th "	See App: C.	Nos 6, 7 & 8 Sections Moppers Up.
	10th "	See App: E.	No 2 Section 49th T.M. Batty Lt Le Poton and Carriers.
4th wave	11th "	4th Objective	C and D Coys.
" "	12th "	" "	C and D Coys.

Sheet 4.

INSTRUCTIONS FOR THE OFFENSIVE (continued).

        13th line   See App: C.   Nos 9.10.11 & 12
                                                            Sections Moppers Up.

        14th "   See App: D.   Lt Bellamy & ½ section
                                                           (2 L/G's) of Bde
                                                           L/G Coy.

        15th "   See App: F.   1 platoon A Coy 8th
                                                           R.Inn's Fus for
                                                           carrying purposes.

6. ASSEMBLY POSITIONS:

    Front line. From N.18.a.55.00. to VIERSTRAAT ROAD (inclusive)

    Support line. SHANNON TRENCH from N.18.a.35.00. to the VIERSTRAAT
                      ROAD inclusive.

    The first six lines vide para 5 above will assemble in the Front line.

    The remaining 9 lines less the 10th line will assemble in the
        Support line.

    The 10th line (T.M's) will assemble in the T.M.Emplacements on the
        left (i.e.North) of MAYO STREET.

        Placards will be prepared thus:-

```
----------------------
|  No 1 Section.     |
|                    |
|   1 Platoon.       |
|                    |
|   Right Flank.     |
|                    |
|   1st line.        |
----------------------
```

    Assembly positions will be marked as follows:-

        1st Wave   White letters on Black.
        2nd Wave   "   "   " Blue.
        3rd wave   "   "   " Black
        4th wave   "   "   " Red.
    Moppers Up   Yellow letters on Black.

    These placards will be nailed on A Frames about ½ way up front leg
        on the right limit of each section and will be placed in position
        before the troops move into the assembly trenches.

        See also Appendix G.

7. HEADQUARTERS:

Bde H.Q's and left Art: Group.	The RIB N.16.d.35.50.
Bde Forward Station	About O.13.c.15.45.
Bn H.Q's will be in	USNAGH STREET. N.18.a.15.45.
Bn Forward Station	On left or N.Side of Brigade Forward station.
Bn H.Q's 7/8th R.I.F.	S.P. 13.
" " 2nd R.Irish Regt	S.P. 13 & then Bde Forward Station.
" " 8th R.Inn's Fusrs	KNOLL DUG OUTS. N.22.c.90.55.
A Coy H.Q's 7th R.Inn's Fus.	80 yards to right of MAYO STREET.
B " " " "	A few yards to left of TARA STREET.
C " " " "	100 yards to right of USNAGH STREET.
D " " " "	A few yards to left of TARA STREET.

Sheet 5.

INSTRUCTIONS FOR THE OFFENSIVE (continued)

HEADQUARTERS (continued)

B Coy 8th R.Innis Fusrs	In SHANNON TRENCH 50 yds to the left of its junction with USNAGH STREET.
Attached L.G. ½ Section.	Immediately on the right of the H.Q's of B Coy 8th R.Innis Fus.
1 platoon "A" Coy 8th R.Innis Fus. (Carrying party).	USNAGH STREET near its junction with SHANNON TRENCH.
Attached T.M.Personnel.	With their guns, vide para 6 above.

See also Appendix G.

8. Lewis Gun Sections.
   See Appendix H.

9. Signalling.
   See Appendix I.

10. Stokes Mortar.
    See Appendix J.

11. ½ Section M/G Company.
    See Appendix K.

12. COMMUNICATION TRENCHES:

   WATLING STREET.   IN Trench.
   THE FOSSE.   OUT   "

   USNAGH STREET.
   CLARE STREET.

   MAYO STREET.
   TARA STREET.

13. DATES AND HOURS:

   In making reference to times before or after which operations will commence, the following nomenclature will be adopted in future:-

   (a) Referring to days:

   "Z" is the day on which operations take place.

   One day before "Z"............."Y" day
   Two days before "Z"............"X" day
   Three days before "Z".........."W" day
   Four days before "Z"..........."V" day
   Five days before "Z"..........."U" day.

   Days before "U" day will be referred to as "Z" minus 6, "Z" minus 7, "Z" minus 8 etc.

   One day after "Z"............."A" day
   Two days after "Z"............"B" day
   Three days after "Z".........."C" days.

   Days after "C" day will be referred to as "Z" day plus 4, "Z" plus 5, "Z" plus 6, etc.

   (b) Referring to hours on "Z" day.

   Zero is the exact time at which operations will commence, and times will be designated in hours and minutes plus or minus from Zero, even if they encroach on "Y" day.

Sheet 6.

INSTRUCTIONS FOR THE OFFENSIVE (continued)

(c) In making references to times before and after which operations will take place the symbols + or - are not to be used. The word "PLUS" or "MINUS" is to be written in full.

In referring to times before or after Zero hour, the words "Zero plus...." or "Zero minus...." must be inserted, so as to prevent possible confusion with clock times.

14. **TIMES OF ARRIVAL AND DEPARTURE:**

The following will be the times of arrival and departure from the various coloured lines which directly concern the Battalion:

RED LINE.	Arrive	0.35.
	Depart	1.05.
BLUE LINE.	Arrive	1.40.
	Depart	3.40.

15. **CONSOLIDATION:**

Immediately an Objective is captured steps are at once to be taken to consolidate it.

NOTE:-
This does not by any means imply that the actual trench captured is the best line to consolidate probably the trench itself will be absolutely demolished and anyway a line of shell holes from 10 to 15 yards in front of the line captured might provide a better defensive position.

The 4th Objective (the BLUE line) is further to be strongly wired immediately.
See also Appendix F, re material.

The 3rd Objective (the RED line) is also to be wired and as soon as the 4th Objective has received all the wire it requires, wire will be sent to it (the 3rd Objective) for this purpose.

16. **STRONG POINTS:**

The 157th Field Coy R.E. will construct Strong Points to hold one platoon as follows on 4th Objective (BLUE line) being captured.

Strong Point A at ....
" " B at ....

Any Strong Point constructed within the Battalion area will on completion be immediately garrisoned by one Platoon. The Company Commander within whose area the Strong Point is, being responsible for supplying this garrison without further orders, reporting the fact to Bn H.Q's.

17. **MAPS, DOCUMENTS etc.**

Attention is directed to Bn R.Orders 219 & 728. 23.2.17 and 26.5.17 respectively.

Steps are at once to be taken to remind all ranks of their contents and they are to be informed that these orders will be strictly enforced and severe disciplinary steps taken for any breach of them, however trivial it may appear.

18. **GAINING OF OBJECTIVES:**

It is to be firmly impressed on every individual that his one and only thought is to be the reaching of his Objective no matter the casualties that may be taking place all round or the fact that units on either flank are held up.
The surest way to help them is to go straight on.

Sheet 7.
INSTRUCTIONS FOR THE OFFENSIVE (continued).

The protection of the front and flanks of a unit should be its first thought on reaching its Objective.

The handling of the wounded is NOT the duty of the fighting soldier; stretcher bearers and special parties are told off for this duty, and no combatant Officer or O.R. is on any account whatsoever to move to the rear either for the purpose of helping wounded back or conveying prisoners etc etc unless special definite orders to the contrary are issued.

Company and Platoon Commanders must keep in touch with the Commanders of similar formations or their flanks. They must further know the disposition and action being taken by their neighbours.

19. ACKNOWLEDGE.

                                                              A O Taggart   Captain & Adjutant.

Copy No 1 File.
         2 A Coy
         3 B "
         4 C "
         5 D "
         6 Brigade.
         7 ~~A Coy 8th R.Inn's Fus.~~
         8 B "   "   "   "
         9 8th R.Inn's Fusrs.
        10 M.G.
        11 T.M.
        12. 7/8th R.I.F. for information.

"A" Form.
MESSAGES AND SIGNALS.

Army Form C. 2121
(in pads of 100).

Secret

TO: 7th R Innis Fus, 8th R Innis Fus, H R Irish Fus, 49th M G Coy

Sender's Number: BM C 44
Day of Month: 3

Eleventh Artillery Barrage Maps on following scale

7th R Innis Fus — 6 copies
8th R Innis Fus — 3 "
1/8 R Irish Fus — 6 "
49th M G Coy — 1 "

Issued with reference to 49th Infantry Bde Instructions for the Offensive.
Acknowledge ✓

WB William Capt
Bde Maj 49 IB

Time: 12.30 AM

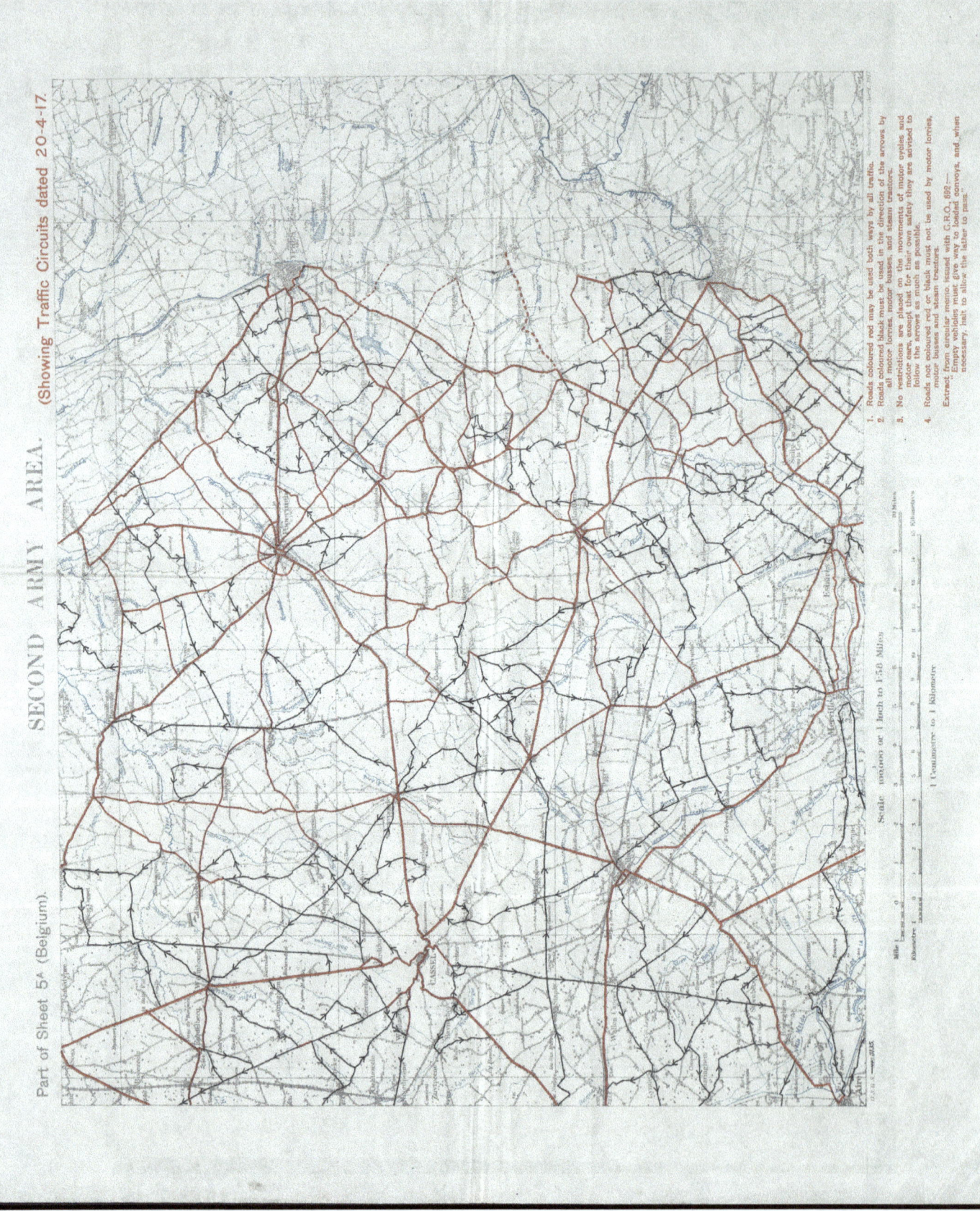

2nd/R. Irish Regt.
7th R. Innis Fus.
8th R. Innis Fus.
7/8th R. Irish Fus.
Staff Captain.
Bde. Bombing Officer.

S E C R E T.

49th Inf. Bde. No. S.O. 83 - 3-6-17.

The following will be the arrangements for Battalions to draw their complement of Bombs, Rifle Grenades, etc, to be carried on the man in the assault :-

2nd R. Irish Regt.

The 2 Coys. going to DONCASTER HUTS on the night of the 4th/5th will report by platoons at the YORK HOUSE Bomb Store on their way from the trenches and will draw their complement of Mills Bombs, Rifle Grenades (and "P" Bombs if they belong to Mopping Up Coy). Each Platoon Commander will have a list prepared showing the total number of each article he requires; this list will be handed to the Brigade Bomb Officer at the Bomb Store.

The 2 Coys remaining in the VIERSTRAAT SWITCH will draw their complement of Mills Bombs, Rifle Grenades and "P" Bombs (if they belong to Mopping Up Coy) from the YORK HOUSE Bomb Store during the morning of the 5th.

2. 7th R. Innis Fus. and 7/8th R. Irish Fus.

On the night of the 5th/6th the 2 Coys of each of the above Battalions that are going into the front line system, will report by Platoons to the following Brigade Dumps to draw their complement of Bombs and Rifle Grenades :-

7th R. Innis Fus. POLL TRENCH DUMP N.17.a.15.25.

7/8th R. Irish Fus. YORK HOUSE DUMP.

1 N.C.O per platoon should report at the Dump their Coy. is going to draw from at 2 p.m. on the afternoon of the 5th to take over his platoon's complement. He must be provided with a list showing the total number of Bombs and Rifle Grenades required by his platoon.

On the morning of the 6th the remaining Coys. of the above Battalions in the VIERSTRAAT SWITCH will arrange to draw from the same dumps their complement of Bombs and Rifle Grenades, and will issue them so as to be complete on the night of the 6th.

3. 8th R. Innis Fus.

"A", "B", "C" and "D" Carrying Parties will pick up their loads at the POLL TRENCH DUMP, N.17.a.15.25 on the night of the Y/Z as they proceed to the trenches.

The Mopping Up Coys will pick up their complement of Bombs and "P" Bombs at the YORK HOUSE Dump on their way up to the trenches on the night of Y/Z.

One N.C.O per Company Carrying Party and Platoon of Moppers Up will report to their respective dumps on the afternoon of the 6th to take over their loads and complement of Bombs.

2.

4. All Mills Bombs, Rifle Grenades and "P" Bombs issued from the Dumps will be detonated, all ranks should be warned accordingly.

5. On the night of the 4th June the 2nd R. Irish Regt, 7th R. Innis Fus and 7/8th R. Irish Fus. will each send half a limber to the YORK HOUSE Bomb Store to draw their Battalion Complement of Red Very Lights and Green Ground Flares. These will be distributed to Companies under Battalion Arrangements so that they will be complete by midday the 6th.

J.B.Wilken Captain,
Brigade Major, 49th Infantry Brigade.

40. **TANKS.**

One Section of TANKS (4 tanks) have been allotted to the 16th Division for the advance from the BLUE to the BLACK LINE.

Four Sections of Tanks and any others which can be rallied have been allotted to the 16th Division for the Advance from the BLACK LINE to the OOSTAVERNE LINE.

Details as to the employment of these tanks will be issued later to all concerned.

It must be impressed on all ranks in the Infantry that the Tanks are there to assist their advance if possible, but that they must never for a moment suppose that success depends on their presence. The men must never wait for the Tanks but must push onto their objective irrespective of whether they come up or not. There is a great danger of the attack being held up if this is not thoroughly realized by all ranks.

41. **EMPLOYMENT OF TUNNELLING COMPANIES ON DUGOUTS AND ROADS.**

(a) A party of 3 Officers and 30 Other Ranks from 250th Tunnelling Coy. provided with the necessary maps of the enemy trenches, will reconnoitre captured dugouts as soon as the objective is reached.

This party will mark habitable dugouts with the number of men which can be accommodated in them and will carry out repairs to other dugouts as required.

C.R.E. will issue any further instructions to this party through O.C. 250th Tunnelling Coy. and will arrange for lists of habitable dugouts to be prepared as rapidly as possible and passed to the Infantry Brigadiers in whose areas they lie.

SECRET.

Appendix F.

Copy No........

APPENDIX F.   CONTACT PATROLS.

1. Aeroplanes for contact patrols will be R.E. 8 type and will be specially marked by a black flap attached to the rear of each lower plane. Photographs are being issued.

2. Two contact aeroplanes will be in the air at the same time. One watching the area South of WYTSCHAETE and the other WYTSCHAETE and the area North of the Village.
   Contact patrols will fly over the line and call for flares at the following hours, and any hours subsequent to those hours at which special aeroplanes may be ordered. Troops will also be prepared to put out flares at any other time if the aeroplane calls for them :-

   BY 7ᵗʰ R INNIS FUS   (Zero plus 45 minutes.
   7/8 R IRISH FUS   (Zero plus 2 hours.
   BY 2ⁿᵈ R IRISH R.   (Zero plus 4 hours 20 minutes.
                         (Zero plus 5 hours 20 minutes.
   BY 48ᵗʰ & 33ᴿᴰ   (Zero plus 6 hours 30 minutes.
   INF BDES   (Zero plus 11 hours.

3. Aeroplanes will call for flares and WATSON Fans by sounding a Klaxon Horn and firing a "VERY" white light, or by giving either of those two signals.

4. Green Flares will be used. They should be lit in bunches of three each about 30 yards apart.
   WATSON Fans will be used in conjunction with flares. The fans should be turned over every two seconds and not quicker, that is, the white side will be exposed to the aeroplane for two seconds and the dark side for two seconds, and so on. An issue of fans will be made as they become available.

5. The Corps Dropping Ground will be in the field S.E. of the LA CLYTTE – LOCRE Road in M.17.b. and d, just West of the S in SCHERPENBERG, and will be in charge of 2nd Lieut. M.R. MONTGOMERY, 2nd Royal Dublin Fusiliers.
   The 7/8th R. Irish Fus. and 8th R. Innis Fus. will each detail one man from their reserve personnel to report to 2nd Lieut. MONTGOMERY at M.17.b.15.00 at 5 p.m. on "Y" day.

6. No aeroplanes will be in the air before Zero.

7. A Schedule of Code Calls for aeroplanes to be used by Brigades is attached.

8. X Corps contact aeroplanes will be distinguished by three broad white bands on the fuselage and also by a black board on the lower left plane.
   II Anzac contact aeroplanes will be distinguished by two black streamers on the lower right hand plane.

CODE LETTERS FOR LIAISON BETWEEN INFANTRY AND AIRCRAFT.

Corps.	Division.	Infantry Brigade.	Code Letters.
IX	16th.	47th 48th 49th	S T U

The addition of W, X, Y or Z to the Brigade Code Letter will give the particular Battalion of the Brigade, according to the "Order of Battle".

Secret

To O.C. 8th Inniskillings

I have seen the Right Group Commander & have arranged that the inside edge of Art Barrage should be moved outwards 50 yds either way.

So the Stokes gun had better take on the bit either side.

Rawson Tower Bny Gen
4 G.T.B
16/7/16

5/15. 36,000 Pads. L. S. & Co.

"B" Form   Army Form C. 2122.

MESSAGES AND SIGNALS.   No. of Message _____

Prefix _____ Code _____ m.	Received	Sent	Office Stamp.
Office of Origin and Service Instructions. Words.	At _____ m.	At _____ m.	
	From	To	
	By	By	

TO {				

*	Sender's Number	Day of Month	In reply to Number	**AAA**

MINEUR.

2 parties are in
8 of B etween Divisions
Opposite us

From			
Place			
Time			

* This line should be erased if not required.

"B" Form
MESSAGES AND SIGNALS.
Army Form C. 2122.

Prefix...... Code...... m.	Received	Sent	Office Stamp.
Office of Origin and Service Instructions. Words.	At......m.	At......m.	
	From	To	
	By	By	

TO {

Sender's Number	Day of Month	In reply to Number	AAA

12.15 M.N.
We hold the far lip
of the right crater
and the near lip
of the left crater
Driven off far lip of left crater.
12.30 Started shelling
Brig informed asked
retaliate. Art liaison
also sent through
12.30 am. The parties are in
12-34 - Sent party out
to retake far lip

From
Place
Time

"A" Form.
MESSAGES AND SIGNALS.
Army Form C. 2121.

TO: Senior L.M.G. Officer, PERCH
two O.C. Enterprise

Sender's Number: S747
Day of Month: 14th

AAA

Re "operation tomorrow night" you will take orders from O.C. Enterprise Captain Godslaud as to dispositions and action of all L.M. Guns. aaa Immediately after mines are blown 2 guns should be so placed as to enfilade to right and left behind SEAFORTH CRATERS but on no account whatever must they fire until orders are received from O.C. Enterprise or until it is certain that the raiding party has returned and is clear

From: C.O. PERCH
Place:
Time: 14.7.16 7 p.m.

H Mourgenwalton
Lt Col

"A" Form.   Army Form C. 2121.
MESSAGES AND SIGNALS.   No. of Message.......

Prefix...... Code...... m. | Words | Charge | This message is on a/c of: | Recd. at...... m.
Office of Origin and Service Instructions. | | | | Date......
SECRET | Sent At......m. | | ......Service. | From......
URGENT | To...... | | |
 | By...... | | (Signature of "Franking Officer.") | By......

TO: C.O. Stokes T M B Left Hut Sect &
through O.C. Enterprise

Sender's Number.	Day of Month	In reply to Number	A A A
* S.748	14th		

Re operation tomorrow night
you will take orders from
O.C. Enterprise Capt Goddard
as to dispositions and action
aaa Artillery V M G and L M G
will fire on enemy front
and support trenches outside
a zone of 200x from SEAFORTH
CRATER for 20 minutes
aaa if enemy continue
firing for long after we cease
we will reopen fire aaa
you will act accordingly
in cooperation aaa be very
careful not to fire within
200x zone of operations.

From: O.C. PERCH
Place:
Time: 7-5 p.m.

H Markwalter
t/Col

The above may be forwarded as now corrected. (Z)

Censor. | Signature of Addressor or person authorised to telegraph in his name.
* This line should be erased if not required.

(4198). Wt. W14042—M44. 300000 Pads. 12/15. Sir J. C. & S.

"A" Form.
MESSAGES AND SIGNALS.
Army Form C. 2121.

TO Salmon

* W 1   Day of Month 15   AAA

Perch agrees to DARN ~~DIAL~~ ~~DIAL~~

DALE

From Bde Major
Place
Time 12.15 PM

Wt. W. 1789-1402. 5/15. 36,000 Pads. L.S. & Co.			ARMY FORM C 2122
	"B" Form		Army Form C. 2122.
	MESSAGES AND SIGNALS.		No. of Message

Prefix_____ Code_____ m.	Received	Sent	Office Stamp.
Office of Origin and Service Instructions. Words.	At_____ m.	At_____ m.	
	From	To	
	By	By	

TO { | | | |

| * Sender's Number | Day of Month | In reply to Number | **AAA** |

12.50 AM. 16.7.16
15 Wounded

1.10 AM 16.7.16. One of our aeroplanes hog "conk" down on Bryan. 44.

1.18 Am. Quiet. Capt Godstank reports. Everything very quiet. and purports to go out and visit the craters permission given if situation permits. Capt Martin takes over charge

From			
Place			
Time			

* This line should be erased if not required.

"B" Form　　　Army Form C. 2122.
MESSAGES AND SIGNALS.　No. of Message ____

Prefix ____ Code ____ m.	Received	Sent	Office Stamp.
Office of Origin and Service Instructions. Words.	At ____ m.	At ____ m.	15/7/16
	From ____	To ____	Derek
	By ____	By	

TO {

| Sender's Number | Day of Month | In reply to Number | AAA |

Crater almost continuous to hold. enemy's post
cost ~~...~~ of? South
Side highest part

Green

From
Place
Time

This line should be erased if not required.

SECRET   S.138

To O.C. "B" Coy PRAWN.
O.C. "D" Coy

1. Two MINES will be blown together under SEAFORTH CRATER on our RIGHT FRONT (R.33.c) tonight at an hour not yet known to be communicated later.

2. The Explosion will be followed by a reconnaissance. Our own enemy trenches adjacent to Explosion and the CRATERS will be occupied, Bombing Post established and S.A.A. laid out to each. Our Artillery bombardment accompanied by M.G.'s and T.M. Guns will follow the Explosion for some 20 minutes — if the enemy opens in retaliation our bombardment will reopen.

3. Our front fire trench will be held by Vickers & Lewis M.G.'s and (approx) 50 rifles in the absence of raiding, crater and working parties.

4. Previous to Explosion trenches are to be cleared for a distance

of 140x from the Crater in order to avoid its effects.

(5) All troops in this subsection will act as to ours one hour before time of any action until stand-down is ordered from Bat. H.Q.

(6) "C" & "D" Coys will move up 2 platoons to SUPPORT line – one in support of Right front Coy and one in support of Centre front Coy – to take up positions by 2-30 p.m. These will be withdrawn to original positions on receipt of order to Stand down.

(7) Ration parties will carry on.

(8) Pass Word – CHIRPY.

(9) H.Q. of O.C. Picket in line (Capt. Godslaw) and forward dressing station will be in Right front Coy's H.Q. dug out in Support line of BLACK WATCH ALLEY.

(10) The platoons of D Coy DRAWN moved up to support will come under the orders of the front Coy Commanders & report accordingly.

H.S. Belgrave Watson
15.7.16.
C.O. PERCH Bat.

11-47 Art asked to open
again for 10'

11-50 pm Left crater - 30
yds, right crater
45 yds, ridge between
two craters,
Both craters. 40 fat deep

11-53 pm
Raiding party back
— officer's pack & Equipment
— prisoner may not
last

8th Divn
7th on Somme

Wt. W. 1789-1402. 5/15. 36,000 Pads. L.S. & Co.

"B" Form — Army Form C. 2122.

MESSAGES AND SIGNALS.

No. of Message _____

Prefix ___ Code ___ m.	Received	Sent	Office Stamp.
Office of Origin and Service Instructions. Words.	At ___ m. From ___ By St. Chr. G.	At ___ m. To ___ By ___	15/7/16 Devch

TO {

*	Sender's Number	Day of Month	In reply to Number	AAA
	11/25			

Crater almost contiguous to hold. enemy's post exist N of South side highest part

Runner Green

11.25 pm
Runner just come

11.20 pm / prisoner badly wounded

From			
Place			
Time			

* This line should be erased if not required.

[B]

[C]
95   54#
95
44/5 54/50 41 70 70 β!

2 Graders

1/60 Sundays   600 oft
6 6 bug out frames   "oad 4/3 12"
10 1/2 Sleepers   A per frame 10"
5   2 per 1/2 sl.
2/11 17 Shoes   tom 9 1
8   22 picks
                       6 Rs 226 #
4 Journeys   B

Mrs Reynolds Rg 155th 72 Coy Mazingarbe
Villa Ornand - 15 de Wire

"A" Form.
MESSAGES AND SIGNALS.

Army Form C. 2121.

Prefix......Code.......m.	Words	Charge	This message is on a/c of:	Recd. at.......m.
Office of Origin and Service Instructions.	Sent		...........Service.	Date...........
	At.......m.			From............
	To........			
	By........		(Signature of "Franking Officer.")	By........

TO { O.C. Enterprise.
     Capt Godsland

Sender's Number | Day of Month | In reply to Number

*   14th   A A A

Re operations to-morrow night the V.M.G. will place guns on our front parapet in order to sweep enemys front parapet up to a point 200 yds left of SEAFORTH CRATER. They will withdraw these when the situation becomes quiet aaa. Our L.M.G. must be disposed in front line ~~............~~ for same purpose until Raid is over and trenches are re-occupied by us. When they should return to their normal positions aaa STOKES and T.M.B must be carefully informed of Sphere of operation. They must not fire within 200 yd line left of SEAFORTH CRATER They will co-operate with Artillery and Machine guns on craters, front and support lines of enemy.

From
Place
Time

The above may be forwarded as now corrected.   (Z)

H.M. Greenwalton
Lt Col
Derek

Censor.   Signature of Addressor or person authorised to telegraph in his name.
* This line should be erased if not required.

5. I am having all MOUNDS & CRATERS on my front carefully examined & reported on as soon as possible.

H M E Mewalton
Lt Col
CO - PPCH.

12.7.16
8-50 pm

8" Inniskillings. Secret.

Herewith copy of scheme for the Artillery Barrage, and also sketch of what the new craters will be as far as it is possible to judge.

J B D Willem Capt
BRIGADE MAJOR 49' BRIGADE

14/7/16

HEAD-QUARTERS
No. SD 559
PLACE
DATE 14.7.16
49TH BRIGADE

APPENDIX.

SECRET.

49th Infantry Brigade Raid Scheme.

Left Sub-Section - LOOS Section.

(1). **Objects.** (1). To form Bombing Posts on near lips of 2 Craters to be blown under SEAFORTH CRATER (referred to as S1 and S2 South and North respectively).
    (2). To carry out a modified raid on enemy's trenches behind the exploded craters in order to take advantage of the occasion.
    (a) To obtain prisoners.
    (b) To obtain identifications.
    (c) To report on results of explosion on enemy garrison and trenches.

(2). **Personnel.**

		Offrs.	N.C.Os.	Men.	R.E.
Party No. 1	Raiding Party Left Front Line.	1	3	18	
" " 2	Covering Party S1. Right " "		2	12	
" " 3	" " S2 Left Front Line.		2	12	
" " 4	Bombing Post S1 Right " "		1	6	
" " 5	" " S2 Left " "		1	6	
" " 6	Consolidation S1 Right " " 1 R.E.(		1	4	1
" " 7	" S2 Left " " (		1	4	1
" " 8	Sap to crater S1 SEAFORTH ALLEY	1	2	25	5
" " 9	" " " S2 " "	1	2	25	5
	Total of all Parties.	4	15	112	12

(3). **Tasks.**

No. 1 Raiding Party: Starting Point "B", Left front line. Objective : to enter front line enemy trench, on enemy's side of craters in 3 parties, each consisting of 1 N.C.O. and 6 men.
One party to move up enemy's front trench to Right, another to Left, one party in centre. All parties to enter at same place.

No. 2 Covering Party for Crater S1. Starting Point "C" Right Front Line. Objective : to rush newly formed crater and occupy the far lip and South side in 2 Bomb parties to cover consolidation party and act as support to raiding party. On return of raiding party to retire on to Bombing Post and thence to return to trenches when ordered.

No. 3 Covering Party for Crater S2. Starting Point "B" Left Front Line. Objective : Same as No. 2 in respect of Northern Crater - occupying the NORTH side and the farlip.

No. 4 Party Bombing Post for Crater S1. Starting point "C" Right Front Line. Objective : To occupy and hold near lip of Crater S1.

No. 5 Party Bombing Post for Crater S2. Starting point "B" Left Front Line. Objective : To occupy and hold near lip of Crater S2.

No. 6 Party. Consolidation of Bombing Post on Crater S1. Starting Point "C" Right Front Line. Objective : Near lip of Crater S1, to assist R.E. in construction of bomb shelter, and to carry material out as required.

No. 7 Party. Consolidation of Bombing Post on Crater S2. Starting Point "B" Left Front Line.

Objective : Same as above in respect of Crater S2.
No. 8 Party. Sap to Crater S1. Starting Point "A" in SEAFORTH ALLEY, thence by SEAFORTH OLD SAP. Objective: To line out from Front Trench to Crater S1 and dig Sap to the Bombing Post on near Lip.
No. 9 Party. Sap to Crater S2. Same as above in respect of Crater S2.

(4). Tools and Material.
Sign Boards. - 3 lids of Hales Grenade Boxes, painted white with letters A,B,C, on each in black, - one letter on each board.
Bomb Shelters.- The R.E. will supply tools and material and arrange transport to starting point.
Sap digging Parties 8 & 9 - 70 picks and 70 shovels.
Raiding Party - 21 white cloth Armlets.

(5). Stretcher Bearers.
A dressing station will be established in the Right Coys H.Q. dug-out in Support Trench between NORTH STREET and BLACK WATCH ALLEY.

(6). Bombs for Parties Nos. 1, 2, 3, 4, & 5.

Each carrier of bomb parties to carry a bucket containing 20 Mills No. 5 Grenades and every N.C.O. and men to carry 6 bombs in his pockets.

(7). Officers.
O.C. Enterprise - Captain C.H. Godsland.
O.C. Raid Party - 2/Lieut. C.P.J. Wray.
In charge of Party No. 8 - 2/Lieut. H.A. Green.
In charge of Party No. 9 - 2/Lieut. G.W. Groombridge

(8). Strength.

	Officers	O.R.
Trench Strength of 3 Front Coys.) D.C.A. less Signallers, S.Bs. & Runners.	8	222
Total engaged in operations. (less above details).	3	127
Remaining in 3 Front Coys. (less above details).	5	95.

Probable date of Operations night of 15th/16th July.

(Sd). H.M. Dalzel Walton, Lieut.Colonel,
C.O. PERCH.

14/7/16.

49th Inf.Bde.Raid Scheme.

<u>Machine Guns.</u> O.C.49th M.G.Coy. will receive special instructions from O.C.Left Sub-Section to arrange for 2 Vickers Guns on either side of SEAFORTH CRATER to assist Lewis Guns to sweep enemy's parapets and check enemy's M.G. and rifle fire during raid and consolidation of Craters.

<u>Trench Mortars</u> will on mine being exploded form a barrage on enemy's front line on either side of Trenches to be raided. Instructions will be issued by O.C. Left Sub-Section. After to retaliate for any offensive action on part of enemy.

<u>Artillery barrage.</u> As per sketch for 20 minutes from time mine is fired.
Afterwards stand by in case retaliation is necessary.

Watches will be synchronised at 8 p.m.

Captain,
Brigade Major, 49th Infantry Brigade.

R.E. Scheme in conjunction with

49th Brigade Infantry Scheme.

----

1. **Object.** To construct two bombing posts at sapheads on lips of New Craters S1 and S2.

2. **Personnel.**

	Officers	N.C.Os.	Men.
No. 1 Party (S1 Right)	1	1	4
No. 2 " (S2 Left)	1	1	4

3. **Tasks.**

   These parties will move out from points C and P respectively at the same time as parties Nos. 6 & 7 in Infantry Scheme. They will carry their tools and part of the material with them, and move straight to lips of S1 Crater and S2 Crater. Work on the bombing posts will then be started at once.

4. **Guides.**

   The R.E. Officers in charge at S1 & S2 lips will take steps to help the parties which are carrying the remainder of the materials required - from points C & P - to find them ready to the sap heads. These two parties are being provided by the Infantry and will start from C & P directly after all the other parties have left these points.
   Guides should be sent half way from the sap heads to meet them.

5. **Bombs.**

   Every N.C.O. and man will carry 4 bombs in their pockets.

6. **Officers.**

   O.i/c No.1 party (S1 Right)   Lieut. HUGHES.
   "   No.2 party (S2 Left)   2/Lieut. HEGARTY.

   (signed) H.R.P. REYNOLDS Major,
   O.C. 155th Coy. R.E.

Copy.
Confidential.

H.Q. Inf. Bde.

Appendix III

Report on Operations 16th Aug 1917

UNIT. 8 Royal Inniskilling Fusiliers

Strength. Officers 19.
O.R. 462.

In Command. Lt. Col. A. J. Walkey M.C.

Attached Troops. C Coy. 9th R. Irish Fusiliers.
(Moppers up)

Strength Officers 5 or approx.
O.C. Coy. 2/Lt. C L HENRY

DISPOSITIONS
AT ZERO.   Frontage. D25a 75.05 — D25a 80.90.
           H.Q. LOW. F.M

The line was equally divided in two parts.
C & D Coys. in depth were on RIGHT; A & B Coys.
on LEFT.

Coy of Irish Fusiliers occupied whole front
forming 2nd WAVE of ATTACK, which consisted of 5 WAVES

At Zero, the troops advanced and were not affected by enemy Artillery Barrage, which was put down behind our FRONT LINE, — calibres mostly 4.2's and 5.9's

MACHINE GUN fire was encountered about 200ⁿ W of BORRY F^m causing very heavy casualties and at this stage Batt. on our RIGHT (the R.D.F.) swept across our front towards BORRY F^m but were held up by M.G. fire.

We advanced another 100ⁿ and were then completely held up. This was about 5.10 a.m.

RIGHT LEADING Coy made an attempt to take BORRY F^m from front by rushing under dim Cover of L/G fire.

This was unsuccessful and 2 FLANK ATTACKS were made by same Coy endeavouring to get in from N. side of the F^m which consists of 3 Concrete dugouts linked up by a Breastwork & was strongly garrisoned by about 100 men and at least 3 M.G.

The remnants of C Coy took Cover in shell holes about 100ⁿ W of BORRY F^m and held this position all day.

3.

T Coy here about 50x N.W. of C Coy.
As far as can be ascertained the LEFT
Coy advanced about 800x, in conjunction
with Batt on LEFT which fell back
after a time.

Germans advanced from dugouts and
made an encircling movement on
A & B Coys who stood their ground until
almost surrounded, & then fought their
way slowly back; only about 15 men
were left in each of these Coys.

No definite information was received
throughout the day as to action or
dispositions of Batt on R. & LT (R.D.F.)

About 8:30 a.m. I received a message
from 7 R. INNIS FUS to effect that
2" R. IR, SH REGT were sending forward
1 Coy to capture BORRY F.m.
This attack did not take place, but
a Coy certainly did take up a position
along general line D.25.c. 80.35 —
D.25.a. 70.80 (approx). This Coy was
on the right of the 7R. INNIS FUS
some 7/R R. Dusit FUS & LEFT

4.

At noon the LINE held by 49th I. Bde was
to best of my knowledge as follows:
D.19.c.5.5 — D.19.c.9.4 —
D.19.c.7.4 — D.25.a.9.5 —
D.25.a.9.3
Detached posts 100x W of BORRY F'M
(1 off + about 30 o.r.)

From about 10.0 am onwards enemy filtered
over RIDGE from direction DELVA F'M
+ HILL 35 and appeared to take some
of our men prisoners.

Troops near LOW F'M were able to fire
on enemy who made no organised
counter attack.

I attribute failure on my FRONT to
following factors.
(a) BORRY F'M was intact + strongly held
and no fresh troops were at hand to
press forward + take this place.
the ground being found was very much
cut up + wet. + rapid movement was
impossible. Many casualties were
suffered throughout day from Garrison
at BORRY F'M, from whence fire
was FRONTAL + ENFILADE

5.

(b) Lack of proper communication.
It was almost impossible to communicate with troops in front as orderlies were knocked out constantly, several being killed, and vicinity of LONE [?] was under shell fire nearly all day.
Communication backward had to be maintained solely by pack lines and much delay appears to have occurred in sending back messages from SQUARE F to Bgde HdQ.

(c) Heavy casualties among officers & NCO's during 1st hr. of attack, only one [?] officers survived and consequently any information is somewhat scanty.

A.J.W[...]

Lt. Col.
Comdg. 8 R. Innis. Fus.

18/8/17

O.C. 8. R. Innis Fus.

Herewith Copy No. 15 or Operation Orders No.4. They are not complete and will probably have to be amended as information is received on several points.

Please acknowledge.

August 14th.1917

Lieut & A/Adjutant.
7/8th(S) Battalion The Royal Irish Fusiliers

SECRET.   July 11. 15
   OPERATION ORDERS No 118
     R. INNIS FUS.   10.P.M.

1. On 12th R Innis Fus will relieve 9th R. Innis Fus in trenches at H/H Cny in support.

2. Guides will be at POTIJZE CHATEAU at 12.── noon. Trenches &c. will be own over as much as possible, and B.H.Qr will be in the cellar at POTIJZE CHATEAU but close at hand and considered for guides.

3. A Coy 9th R Innis Fus will be relieved by A Coy 7th R Innis Fus
   B   do   B   do
   C   do   C   do
   D   do   D   do

   O/C "C" Coy will detail 1 Lewis Gun and team to relieve like aircraft L.G. team of 2 R. Irish Rgt on CAMBRIDGE Rd at 11.P.M. 11th day. A guide will be at Byro 2.6, Menin Gate at 7.30 pm. to meet his team.

4. Order of march: A.B.C.D Coys. Hd. Platoon at 300". Leading platoon passes Gate THING POINT 1917 at O.C. at 10 p.m.

5. LG Limbers and trenches tools Carts will be collected as quickly as possible just before reaching POTIJZE Cross Rds. Machine Guns Cart will also be collected at this point.

6. Ammunition to be brought to POTIJZE CHATEAU in first line to be left there.

7. Servants hats. Officers valises etc will be sent down by Coys by 8.0 pm. L.G. Limbers & Machine Guns Carts parked by 9.0 pm.

Coys & Coy.

1. Bat HQ will close at this Camp at 6.00pm and open at 1.6a 2.7a arrival there.

2. Acknowledge

Issued through Sigs at 11.45p

Copy No 1   A Coy
       2   B
       3   C
       4   D
       5   Sig
       6   MD
       7   T.O
       8   G.M
       9   R.S.M.
      10   O.C R. Innis. Inn.
      11   Adj. R.I Rgn
      12   reserve

N. Hasan Rollins S/L
a/Adj O.R. Innis Inn.

SECRET.   COPY NO. 6

OPERATION ORDER. No 119
8 R INNIS FUS.   14-8-17

1. The 8 R. INNIS FUS. will relieve the 2 right Coys
b R. IRISH REGT in FRONT LINE and 2 right Coys
of 2 R. IRISH REGT in SUPPORT, on night
14/15 Aug.

2. Guides will be at BAVARIA HOUSE 12. midnight

3. A.C Coys will relieve 2 Coys b R. IRISH REGT front line Coy R.
B.D "   do   2 R IRISH REGT.

4. Order of march. A. C Coys H.Q. B. D Coys.
Platoons at 300⁰. Leading platoon to pass
STARTING PT. H.17.a.0.9 at 9.15 p.m.

5. 4/C LIMBERS will proceed with Coys. ½ LIMBER
to be filled with SHOVELS 1 for every 2 men.
They will be off loaded as quickly as
possible just before reaching POT IZE X Rds
MALTESE CART will also be unloaded at
this point.

6. Bn HQ will be at SQUARE F[m]

7. Acknowledge.
Issued through Sig 2.3 afor.

Copy No 1 A   11 D. R. Innis R.
        2 B   12 R City
        3 C   13 M J D.B
        4 D   14 W.
        5 S.
        6 M.o -
        7. 0
        8 Q m
        9 Sig D.B
        10 b.? Innis R

                          Mordaunt Robertson
                          a/Adj 8 R Innis Dns.

23

SECRET   Copy No.

8th R Innis Fus. Operation Order No 115   3-8-17

The following instructions are issued in continuation of
Provisional Orders issued under S/46.

1. (a) A . C Coys will pass starting point
   H.8. a 4.8. at 1.10 pm
   B . D Coys will move later and will relieve
   part of 1st R.M. Fus in CAMBRIDGE TRENCH

2. On completion of move dispositions of Battn will
   be as under :-
   Bn HQ :- LANCER F^m
   A.C Coy HQ - DRAGOON F^m
   B.D Coy HQ - CAMBRIDGE TRENCH.

3. Route - YPRES - POTITZE, interval of 200^x
   will be maintained between platoons. If the
   road is shelled troops will be moved across country.

4. Transport (a) A Cookers will move in rear of C Coy
   and take up position in POTIZE WOOD at
   present occupied by 1st R.M. Fus
   (b) Lewis Gun Limbers will accompany their Coys and
   will be off loaded opposite Coy Quarters, on completion of which they will return to Transport Lines
   H 16 d. 9. 4.
   (c) Water Carts will move in rear of C Coy and take up
   position in POTITZE WOOD Relieving to take place
   during night at first forward filling point near
   Swimming Baths N^E corner of YPRES

O.O. 115 Contd

(b) Mess Cart will move in rear of C Coy - halt on YPRES - POTITZE Rd opposite LANCER F⁵ offload and return to Transport Lines

(c) Machine Cart and medical personnel will move with B & D Coys to CAMBRIDGE Rd offload and return

5. Order of March A & C Coys Transport
6. Completion of moves to be reported by orderly to Bn HQ LANCER F⁵
7. Transport Lines will be at H.16.d.9.4 and not as notified in previous instructions
8. Rations will be dumped at 10.30 p.m. as under
   A & C Coys at I.4.a.8.2 (junction HAYMARKET - POTITZE Rd)
   B & D Coys   junction CAMBRIDGE T. - POTITZE Rd

9. Acknowledge

Issued by Sigs at 12.15 p.m.   Sn (W.E.F. MUIR)
Copy No 1 O C A Coy   Capt
     2   B   Adj 8/R INNIS FUS
     3   C
     4   D
     5   Signals
     6   MO
     7   QM
     8   T.O.
     9   Major A.J. Walkey MC
     10   File

SECRET.   Appendix I   Copy No. 16

PROVISIONAL ORDERS FOR THE ATTACK.   WM?m 14-5-17
      8th. R? INNIS. FUSILIERS.

1. GENERAL PLAN.
            The 16th. Division, in conjunction with Divisions on either flank, will attack the enemy's positions on a date to be notified later.
   The attack will be made in two bounds, each bound is shown by coloured lines on Map "A".
            First Bound   GREEN LINE
            Second Bound   DOTTED RED LINE.

2. OBJECTIVES OF BRIGADES.
            The 48th. Inf. Bde. (plus one Battn.) on the right and the 49th. Infantry Brigade (plus one Battn.) on the left will attack up to and including the RED DOTTED LINE. The 47th. Inf. Bde. less three Battns. and M.G. Coy. will be in Divnl. Reserve. The Left Battn. of the 48th. Inf. Bde. will be 2nd. R. Dublin Fus. The Right Battn. of the 108th. Inf. Bde. will be 9th. R. Irish Fus.

3. BOUNDARIES.
            The boundaries between the 49th. Inf. Bde., and the Bdes on either flank are as follows:-
Boundary with 48th. Inf. Bde.
   D.25.a.75.05 - where DOTTED RED LINE crosses the ZONNEBEKE stream.
Boundary with 108th. Inf. Bde.
   D.19.c.7.8. - D.19.b.70.50. - D.14.d.20.40.
These boundaries are shewn in BLUE on Map "A"

4. TASKS OF BATTALIONS.
            The attack on the GREEN and DOTTED RED LINES will be made by the 7th. R. Innis. Fus. on the Left and the 8th. R. Innis. Fus. on the Right. The dividing line between these two Battalions will be -
   D.25.a.60.90. - D.20.b.80.99.
This boundary is shewn in BLACK on Map "A".
The GREEN LINE is to be captured at Zero ZERO PLUS ....
There will be a pause of 20 minutes on the GREEN LINE.
The RED DOTTED LINE is to be captured at ZERO PLUS.......
As soon as the RED DOTTED LINE has been captured a line of posts will be pushed out as far as the Barrage permits.

5. DISPOSITIONS.
            "C" Coy. 7/8th. R. Irish Fus. (to be known for these operations as "E" Coy.) are attached and will assist in ATTACK and mop up, up to, and including ZEVENKOTE.
"C" Coy. and "A" Coy. will supply leading waves, "C" Coy. on RIGHT, "A" Coy. on the LEFT. "D" Coy. and "B" Coy. will be in rear, "D" Coy. on RIGHT, "B" Coy. on the LEFT. Dividing line between Coys. is shewn on Map "A".
The Battalion will attack in five waves of two lines each.
Distance between LINES 20 yards
   "   "   WAVES 100 Yards.
"E" Coy. will form the second WAVE of the ATTACK and are allotted tasks as follows.
RIGHT PLATOON (No. 10 2/Lt. YOUNG) will assist in capture of BORRY FARM
            Mop up and consolidate that position
RIGHT CENTRE PLATOON (No. 9 2/Lt. COOMBES) will assist in capture of
            COFFEE FARM and having mopped up will proceed to
            ZEVENKOTE.
            These two platoons will follow first WAVE of "C" Coy.
Nos. 11 and 12 Platoons (2/Lt. DICKSON) will follow 1st. WAVE of "A" Coy.
            will proceed direct to ZEVENKOTE.
The three Platoons of "E" Coy. at ZEVENKOTE having completed mopping up will choose and consolidate a suitable position about 250 yards in rear of GERMAN TRENCHES at ZEVENKOTE.
One Coy. 7/8th. R. Irish Fus. will provide Carrying parties.
Two Platoons will carry to 8th. R. Innis. Fus. at COFFEE FARM: after completing their task they will join the Coy. at ZEVENKOTE.

- 2 -

5 (contd.).

2 Platoons will carry to 7th R. Innis. Fus. at DELVA FARM, but will join the 2 Coys. at IBERIAN on completion of task.

The 2nd R. Irish Regt., will be in Brigade Reserve. At ZERO Hour 3 Coys. of the 2nd R. Irish Regt., will advance from their assembly positions and occupy the trenches vacated by the Assaulting Battalions, from D.25.a.80.65 to D.19.c.60.70. with a post at BECK HOUSE. 1 Coy. will remain in the assembly position on BLUE LINE.

The 6th R. Irish Regt., will be in Brigade Reserve in VLAMERTINGHE Area, and must be prepared to relieve the Assaulting Battalions on the RED DOTTED LINE if required.

6. MOPPING UP.

The 7th & 8th R. Innis. Fus. are responsible for Mopping Up all ground in their areas in front of DELVA FARM and ZEVENKOTE. The 7/8th R. Irish Fus., are responsible for Mopping Up in rear of DELVA FARM and ZEVENKOTE (inclusive).

7. CONSOLIDATION.

The RED DOTTED LINE, and all Supporting Points held by the 7/8th R. Irish Fus. will be consolidated as rapidly as possible after capture. "A" & "C" Coys. will consolidate FRONT LINE, pushing forward POSTS as ordered in para 4.

"B" & "D" Coys., will consolidate position in depth approximately along line of GERMAN TRENCHES at ZEVENKOTE.

8. ACTION OF MACHINE GUNS.

The Machine Guns will be under the direction of Divisional Machine Gun Officer.

12 Guns of the 49th M.G. Coy. will assist in the Machine Gun Barrage which will be 200 yards in advance of Arty. Creeping Barrage and will lift in conformity with that Barrage.

2 Guns will move in rear of the attacking Infantry to a position in vicinity of DELVA FARM and 2 Guns will move to a position near HILL 37 (D.20.c.).

9. ACTION OF STOKES MORTARS.

Two Stokes Mortars will be attached to each Assaulting Battalion. They will move in rear of the last wave, and will assist the Infantry to overcome opposition as required.

10. ACTION OF ARTILLERY.

The Divisional Artillery will form a Creeping Barrage covering the Advance of the Infantry.

At Zero Hour the Barrage will be put down 300 yards in advance of our present front line: BECK HOUSE will be specially dealt with. The first lift will take place at Zero plus 5 minutes, and it will then proceed forward at the rate of 100 yards in 5 minutes.

During the 20 minute pause on the GREEN LINE a protective barrage will be maintained 200 yards in advance of the Infantry.

After the capture of the DOTTED RED LINE a standing barrage will be established 300 yards in advance of it for a period of 1 hour, after which it will cease unless recalled by the "S.O.S." Signal.

11. ACTION OF TANKS.

One Section of Tanks, from "C" Battn., TANK CORPS, has been allotted to the 16th Division. These Tanks will not be available unless the weather conditions improve. In any case they are only likely to arrive behind the Infantry in time to act as "Moppers Up", In cases where isolated positions continue to hold out.

12. COMMUNICATIONS.

Brigade Headquarters, will remain at MILL COT.

The Bde. Forward Station will advance behind the last wave of the leading Assaulting Battalion, and will be established in the vicinity of IBERIAN.

Battn. Forward Posts will be established as follows:-

7th R. Innis. Fus.   DELVA FARM.
8th R. Innis. Fus.   COFFEE FARM. (D.20.c.2.2).
7/8th R. Irish Fus.   IBERIAN.

Battn. H.Qrs. will not move forward to these positions until communication has been established with them.

The attached Chart shows the various means of Communication except pigeons and runners.

- 3 -

12. (Contd.)

As many pairs of pigeons as available will be issued to Bde. Forward Station and Battalions. The latter will send half their issue with Battn. Forward Posts.

Runner Relay Posts will be established at -
- (a) IBERIAN
- (b) SQUARE FARM
- (c) BAVARIA HOUSE
- (d) BRIGADE HQRS.

Runners should not be used unless all other methods of communication fail.

The Bde. Forward Station of 48th. Inf. Bde. will be at VAMPIR
The Bde. Forward Station of 108th. Inf. Bde. will be at.........
The Bde. Visual Station and O.P. will be at C.29.d.8.7.

13. CONTACT AEROPLANES.

One Contact Aeroplane (Type......) and one Protective Aeroplane will be in the Air over the 16th. and 36th. Division Areas from Zero Hour onwards. Flares will be lit and WATSON FANS will be shown by the leading troops at the following hours

The leading troops will be prepared to light flares and show Watson Fans at other times if asked for by the aeroplane.

14. SYNCHRONISATION.

All Units will send a watch to Bde. H.Q. daily at 6 p.m.

15. S.O.S. SIGNAL.

The S.O.S. will be GREEN SIGNAL Cartridges.

16. PRISONERS.

All prisoners will be sent to BECK HOUSE, where they will be collected by the 2nd. R. Irish Regt., and sent down in batches to Bde. Prisoners' Cage at Brigade Headquarters.

17. MEDICAL ARRANGEMENTS.

Regtl. AID POSTS will be established at LOW FARM

18. ZERO HOUR.

Zero Hour will be notified later.

19. ACKNOWLEDGE.

Issued through Signals at

293 A. HODDER ROBBINS

2/Lieut.,

a/Adjutant, 8th. R. Inniskilling Fusiliers...

Copy No. 1 to O.C. "A" Coy.
" " 2 " " "B" "
" " 3 " " "C" "
" " 4 " " "D" "
" " 5 " Signalling Officer.
" " 6 " H.Q. 49th. Inf. Bde.
" " 7 " O.C. 7/8th. R. Irish Fus.
" " 8 " " 7th. R. Innis. Fus.
" " 9 " " 2nd. R. Irish Regt.
" " 10 " Medical Officer.
" " 11 " Quartermaster and Transport Officer.
" " 12 " O.C. 49th. T.M.B.
" " 13 " " 49th. M.G.C.
" " 14 " " 2nd. R. Dublin Fusrs.
" " 15/16 Retained.

NOTE.

MAP "A" issued to Coys. only.

17

COMMUNICATION CHART.

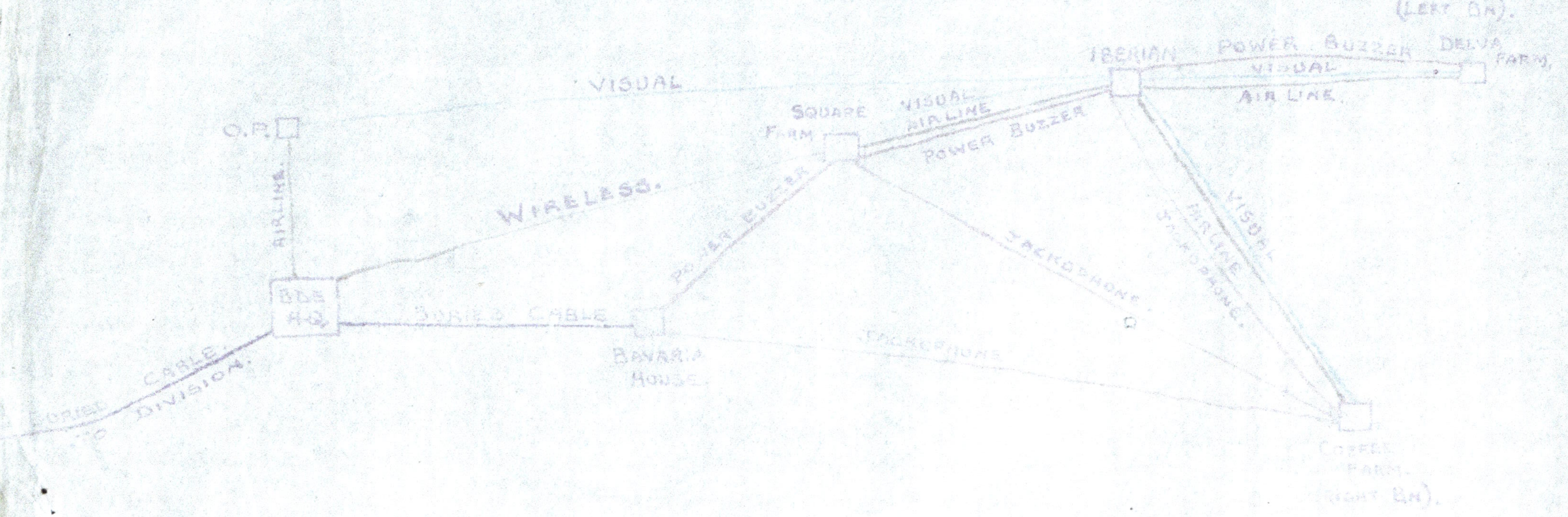

(LEFT BN).
DELVA FARM,
IBERIAN
POWER BUZZER
VISUAL
AIR LINE.
VISUAL
O.P.
SQUARE FARM
VISUAL
AIRLINE
POWER BUZZER
AIRLINE.
WIRELESS.
POWER BUZZER
VISUAL
AIRLINE
JACKOPHONE.
JACKOPHONE
BDE H.Q.
BURIED CABLE
BAVARIA HOUSE.
JACKOPHONE
BURIED CABLE.
DIVISION.
COFFEE FARM.
(RIGHT BN).

SECRET.   Appendix II Copy No 5
            OPERATION ORDER No 121
              8 R. INNIS. FUS.   16-8-17   Written

1. The PROVISIONAL ORDERS for ATTACK dated 14-8-17 hold good except in so far as altered or added to in these orders.

2. The ATTACK will take place 16-8-17.

3. LEFT BnBde will be 9th Royal Irish Rifles & right will be 9th R. DUBLIN FUS.

4. H.Q. 2 R. IRISH REGT. will move to SQUARE Fm when H.Q. 7th INNISKS. does for DELVA Fm.

5. M.G. GUNS will form M.G. Barrage behind the Centre of the FINAL OBJECTIVE. They will arrange an S.O.S. barrage & cover the pass.

6. 2. MESSAGE DOGS have been allotted to the Div. All ranks should be warned that DOGS carrying message pouches on their collars are not to be detained except for purpose of having message read by an officer. Messages sent by this means must be in CODE.

7. AEROPLANES.
   (a) 1 CONTACT AEROPLANE marked with BLACK PLAQUE projecting behind R. LOWER WING, and one PROTECTIVE AEROPLANE will be in the air over 16th & 36th DIV. areas from ZERO hour onwards.
   FLARES will be lit & WATSON FLARES FANS will be waved by leading troops.
      (b) When called upon to do so by CONTACT AEROPLANE by means of KLAXON horns & VERY LIGHTS. This call will, if attack proceeds as arranged, only be made at times when infantry are believed to have reached GREEN & DOTTED RED LINES.
      (c) When Infantry consider it advisable to make known position of their FRONT LINE.
   RED FLARES will be used & these should NOT be lit unless the sounding of KLAXON horns is accompanied by VERY LIGHTS.

8. ZERO hour will be notified later.

9. Acknowledge.
Issued through Sigs at 1.30pm.
Copy No 1 A
       2 B
       3 C
       4 D
       5 Sigs
       6 H.Q. 49th Inf. Bde.

                                          Jordan Roberts /.
                                          a/Adj. 8 R. Innis. Fus.

S E C R E T. AUGUST 14th. 1917   COPY NO. 15

OPERATION ORDERS No. 4.
BY.
Lieut.Colonel. K.C.WELDON D.S.O. Comdg Royal Irish Fusiliers

PROVISIONAL ORDERS FOR THE ATTACK.

1. GENERAL PLAN
The 16th.Division, in conjunction with Divisions on either flank, will attack the enemy's positions on a date to be notified later.
The attack will be made in two bounds, each bound is shewn by coloured lines on Map "A"

    First Bound   GREEN LINE.
    Second Bound   DOTTED RED LINE.

2. OBJECTIVES OF BRIGADES
The 16th.Division will attack with:-
48th.Infantry Brigade (plus 1 Battalion) on the Right.
49th.Infantry Brigade (plus 1 Battalion) on the Left.
47th.Infantry Brigade (less 3 Battalions) in reserve.
Left Battalion 48th.Infantry Brigade will be 2nd.R.DUBLIN FUSILIERS.
Right Battalion 108 Infantry Brigade will be 9th.R.IRISH FUSILIERS.

3. BOUNDARIES.
The Boundaries between the 49th.Infantry Brigade and the Bde. on either flank are as follows :-
Boundary with 48th.Infantry Brigade.
D.25.a.75.05\ -- where DOTTED RED LINE crosses the ZONNEBEKE STREAM.

Boundary with 108th.Infantry Brigade.
D.19.c.7.8. -- D.19.b.70.50. -- D.14.d.80.40.

These boundaries are shewn in BLUE on Map "A"

4. TASKS OF BATTALIONS.
The attack on the GREEN and DOTTED RED LINES will be made by the 7th. Royal Inniskilling Fusiliers on the Left and the 8th.Royal Inniskilling Fusiliers on the Right.
Boundary between Battalions is shewn in BLACK on Map "A"
The GREEN LINE is to be captured at ZERO PLUS..........
There will be a pause of 30 minutes on the GREEN LINE.
The DOTTED RED LINE is to be captured at ZERO PLUS.............
As soon as the DOTTED RED LINE has been captured a line of posts will be pushed out as far as the barrage permits.

The 7/8th.Battalion Royal Irish Fusiliers will support the attack and will find "MOPPERS UP" and Carrying Parties as under.

(a) "C" Company (2/Lieut.C.L.HENRY.)
No 10..Platoon (2/LIEUT.A.C.YOUNG.) to Mop Up BORRY FARM and hold it as a Supporting Point
No. 11...Platoon (2/LT. W.A.   ) These two platoons will Mop Up
No. 12...Platoon (DIXON.   ) ZEVENCOTE and hold it as a Supporting Point.
No. 9.. Platoon (2/LT.G.COOMBES.) to Mop Up COFFEE FARM, D.20.c.15.15.- and then join the two platoons at ZEVENCOTE.
These 4 Platoons will move into position on Y/Z Night and will advance in rear of the last wave of the 8.R.Inniskilling Fusiliers.

Continued on Page 2.

SHEET 2.   (Para 4. continued)

(b) "B" Company Captain V.J.LYNCH M.C.
No. 5. Platoon (2/Lt. C.W. PICKETT) to Mop Up DELVA FARM and will join the Platoon at IBERIAN when the H.Q.7th.R.Innis.Fusrs moves to DELVA FARM.
No. 6. Platoon (2/Lt. DICKSON) to form a Supporting Point about D.19.d.80.80.
The above two platoons will advance in rear of the first wave of the 7th. Royal Inniskilling Fusiliers (Right Half Battalion)

(c) No. 7. Platoon ( ) to Mop Up IBERIAN and the dugouts in the vicinity and form a Supporting Point there.
No. 8. Platoon ( ) One to Mop Up and hold as a Supporting Point the clump of trees at D.19.b.70.35.
The above two Platoons to advance in rear of the 1st wave of the 7th. R Innisk Fusrs. (Left Half Battalion)
"B" Company will move into position on Y/Z Night.

(d) "D" Company (Captain E.E.SARGINT M.C.)
This Company will assemble in the Front Line from D.25.a.80.90 to D.19.c.80.30.
At ZERO hour, this Company will advance and capture BECK HOUSE, and the ground as far East as the Stream, reform and on receipt of orders from Battalion H.Qrs.move to IBERIAN in support.

(e) "A" Company. (Captain E.H.FFORDE)
This Company will provide Carrying Parties as under :-
No. 1. Platoon (2/Lt. POWELL) and No. 2. Platoon (2/Lt.SHEPPARD) will carry to COFFEE FARM.
No. 3. Platoon (Capt OLIVER) and No 4. Platoon (Sgt TIMMINS) will carry to DELVA FARM.
Nos. 1 & 2. Platoons on completion of their tasks will join the Company at ZEVENCOTE.
Nos. 3 & 4. Platoons on completion of their tasks will join the two Coys at IBERIAN.
"A" Coy. will move into position on Y/Z Night

5. LOADS.

	COMPOSITION OF LOAD.	WHERE PICKED UP.
1st. LOAD		
2nd. LOAD		
3rd. LOAD		

The Officer or N.C.O i/c of any carrying party, when he has completed his journey will report the fact at the Battalion H'Qrs. of the Unit for which he is carrying and will on no account leave without obtaining the written authority of the O.C. to do so.
A detail of loads will be issued for the first three journeys, but if necessary more journeys will be made. The first load on YUKON PACKS will be picked up as they march past MILL COT. The number of YUKON PACKS available will be......

6. All Companies will remain under the orders of the O.C.7/8th.R.Irish Fusiliers

SHEET. 3.

7. ASSEMBLY POSITIONS.

On Y/Z Night the Battalion moves into Assembly Positions.
The order of march on leaving Camp at H.15.a.4.9. will be
Battalion H.Qrs.
"D" Company.
"A" Company.
"B" Company.
"C" Company

"D" Company 7/8th. Royal Irish Fusiliers will relieve "C" Coy. 7th. R. Innis. Fusrs. in the front line from D.25.a.80.90. to D.19.c.80.30. Four guides will be sent to BAVARIA HOUSE.

"A" Coy. 7/8th. R. Irish Fusiliers will move to an assembly position in rear of "D" Coy.
No. 1 & 2. Platoons on the Right
3. & 4. Platoons on the Left.
No guides will be sent for this Company.

"B" Company 7/8th. Royal Irish Fusiliers will move to assembly positions.
Nos. 5 & 7 Platoons to form up behind the 1st. wave of the 7. R. Innis. Fusrs. Left Half Battalion
Nos. 6 & 8. Platoons to form up behind the 1st wave of the 7. R. Innis. Fusrs Right Battalion.
4 Guides will be sent to BAVARIA HOUSE.

"C" Company 7/8th. Royal Irish Fusiliers will form up behind the 1st. wave of the 8th. Royal Inniskilling Fusiliers.
4 Guides will be sent to BAVARIA HOUSE.

8. RATIONS.

Rations for "Z" Day will be issued to each man on the afternoon of "Y" Day and will be carried up on the man

9. SHOVELS.

On moving into Assembly Positions "B", "C" and "D" Coys will take shovels from the Transport lines on a scale of one every other man. No picks will be taken

10. LEWIS GUNS.

The Four Lewis Guns of "A" Coy. will be attached :-
(a) Two to the 7. Royal Inniskilling Fusiliers
(b) Two to the 8th. Royal Inniskilling Fusiliers
Only two men with a bag of spare parts and 8 filled drums will accompany each Gun.
(a) These two guns will proceed to SQUARE FARM with Battalion H.Qrs.
(b) These two Guns will proceed with "D" Coy. O.C. "D" Coy will arrange to hand them over to O.C. 8. R. Innis. Fusrs. at LOW FARM.

11. MOPPING UP.

The 7th and 8th. Royal Inniskilling Fusiliers are responsible for Mopping Up all ground in their areas in front of DELVA FARM and ZEVENCOTE. The 7/8th. Royal Irish Fusiliers are responsible for Mopping Up in rear of DELVA FARM and ZEVENCOTE. (inclusive)

12 CONSOLIDATION.

The RED DOTTED LINE and all Supporting Points held by the 7/8th. Royal Irish Fusiliers will be consolidated as possible after capture. × Soon as
The R.E. will work under the direction of the C.R.E. 16th. Division, and will erect wire on the GHELUVELT --- LANGEMARCK LINE when captured. They will also prepare certain positions for defence in vicinity of DELVA FARM and IBERIAN.

SHEET 4.

13. MACHINE GUNS

The Machine Guns will be under the direction of the Divisional Machine Gun Officer.

12 Guns of the 49th.M.Gun Coy. will assist in the Machine Gun Barrage which will be 200 yards in advance of the Artillery Creeping Barrage and will lift in conformity with that Barrage.

Two Guns will move in rear of the attacking Infantry to a position in vicinity of DELVA FARM and 2 Guns will move to a position near Hill 37. (D.20.a.)

14. ACTION OF STOKES MORTARS.

Two Stokes' Mortars will be attached to each assaulting Battalion. They will move in rear of the last wave, and will assist the Infantry to overcome opposition as required. The remaining 4 Mortars will be left at Brigade Headquarters.

15 ACTION OF ARTILLERY

The Divisional Artillery will form a Creeping Barrage covering the advance of the Infantry. At ZERO HOUR the Barrage will be put down 300 yards in advance of our present front line; BECK HOUSE will be specially dealt with. The first lift will take place at ZERO plus 5. minutes, and it will then proceed forward at the rate of 100 yards in 5 minutes.

During the 20 minutes Pause on the GREEN LINE a protective barrage will be maintained 200 yards in advance of the Infantry.

After the capture of the DOTTED RED LINE a standing barrage will be established 300 yards in advance of it for a period of one hour, after which it will cease unless recalled by the "S.O.S." Signal.

16. COMMUNICATIONS.

BRIGADE H.QRS. will remain at MILL COT.

The Bde. Forward Station will advance behind the last wave of the leading Assaulting Battalions, and will be established in the vicinity of IBERIAN.

Battalion Forward Posts will be established as follows:-
7th. Royal Inniskilling Fusiliers   DELVA FARM
8th. Royal Inniskilling Fusiliers   COFFEE FARM (D.20.c.2.2.)
7/8th. Royal Irish Fusiliers   IBERIAN.

Battalion H.Qrs will not move forward to these positions until Communication has been established with them.

As many pairs of pigeons as available will be issued to the Battalion half of these will be sent to the Battalion Forward Post.

Runner Relay Posts will be established at :-
    (a) IBERIAN
    (b) SQUARE FARM
    (c) BAVARIA HOUSE.
    (d) BRIGADE H.Qrs.

Runners should not be used unless all other means of Communication fail.

The Brigade Forward Station of the 48th. Infantry Brigade will be at VAMPIR.

The Brigade Forward Station of the 108th. Infantry Brigade will be at ....

The Brigade Visual Station and O.P. will be at C.29.d.6.7.

17. CONTACT AEROPLANES.

One Contact Aeroplane (Type............) and One Protective Aeroplane will be in the air over the 16th. Division and 36th. Division Areas from ZERO HOUR onwards. Flares will be lit and WATSON FANS will be shown by the leading troops at the following hours.

The leading troops will be prepared to light flares and show WATSON Fans at other times if asked for by the aeroplane

SHEET...6.

No.18.S.O.S.SIGNAL.
The "S.O.S" will be GREEN SIGNAL CARTRIDGES.

19. PRISONERS
All prisoners will be sent to BECK HOUSE, where they will be
collected by the 2nd. The Royal Irish Regt. and sent down in batches
to the Brigade Prisoners Cage at Brigade H.Qrs.
Only one man to every ten prisoners will be sent down.

20. ZERO HOUR.
ZERO HOUR will be notified later.

21. TANKS. ACTION OF.
One Section of Tanks, from "C" Battalion, Tank Corps, has been allotted
to the 16th. Division. These tanks will not be available unless the
weather conditions improve. In any case they are only likely to
arrive behind the Infantry in time to act as "Moppers Up." In
cases where isolated positions continue to hold out.

22. SYNCHRONIZATION.
The Signal Officer will arrange to send a watch to Bde.H.Qrs. at
6.0.P.m. daily for synchronisation and will send same round to all
Officers daily.

23. HEADQUARTERS
The disposition of all Headquarters is as shown on attached plan.

24. ACKNOWLEDGE.

August 14th.1917.   Lieutenant & A/Adjutant,

7/8th.(S)Battalion The Royal Irish Fusiliers

ISSUED THROUGH SIGNALS AT 5.30 P.M.

COPY NO.1.	"A" Coy.	Copy.No.10.	Transport Officer.
2.	"B" Coy.	11.	War Diary
3.	"C" Coy.	12.	War Diary.
4.	"D" Coy.	13.	49th. Infantry Brigade.
5.	Lewis Gun Officer	14.	7.R.Innis.Fusrs
6.	Intelligence Officer	15.	8.R.Innis Fusrs.
7.	Signalling Officer.	16.	2.The R.Irish Regt.
8.	Medical Officer.	17.	Spare.
9.	Quartermaster	18.	O.C.Echelon "B"

Copy No.20.File.

SECRET   COPY N

OPERATION ORDER. No 120.
8 R INNIS FUS   15-8-17

1. The following moves will take place on night 15/16 Aug.

2. B & D Coys. will move up to their ASSEMBLY POSITIONS in rear of A & C Coys respectively.
   1st wave of B & D Coys will form up about 10 yds in rear of last wave of A & C Coys. 2nd wave of B & D Coys about 10 yds in rear of their 1st wave. Care should be taken that two waves are placed as near as possible on their proper portage and parallel to jumping off line which runs practically due NORTH & SOUTH.

3. 2 Guides from C Coy & 2 Guides from A Coy will be at BASIN CR HOUSE at 10 p.m. & will guide D & B Coys respectively to rear of present front line.

4. Batt. H.Q. will be at LEW F.C. from 11.0 p.m. 15 inst. onwards.

5. All companies will report to Batt. H.Q. as soon as they get into their ASSEMBLY positions which will be not later than _____ 16 inst.

6. Operation Orders, Maps, plans or _____ EXCEPT MAPS of our lines must not be taken into ASSEMBLY POSITIONS.

7. Absolute silence must be observed during the move and no lights must be shown.

8. Acknowledge.

Must reach Sigs at 4.30 a.m.
    Copy No. 1. B Coy
       "   2. D   "
                                        [signed] ....
                                        Major 8 R. Inn. Fus.

O.C. 7.R.F. Innis Fus.

SECRET
COPY NO. 15

Reference Operation Orders No.4. Copy.No. 15 issued to day please
note the following amendments:-

Para 10. LEWIS GUNS.

(a) For "D" Coy. in both places read "C" Company

Para 4. TASKS OF BATTALIONS.

(b) The 4 Platoons of "C" Coy will advance in rear of the first wave of
the 8th.R.Innis.Fus's, and not as previously stated.

Para 5. Add.
Unless further instructions are issued in the meantime, the loads for
the 2nd. and 3rd journeys and any subsequent journeys will be drawn
from the R.E. Dump at SIX TREES DUMP. It is possible that forward dumps
may be established at SQUARE FARM and LOW FARM for respective Battalions.

#8. WATER (Extra Paragraph.)
A forward WATER TANK will be established at C.30.d.5.5.

August 14th, 1917.   Lieutenant & A/Adjutant.
                7/8th.(S)Battalion The Royal Irish Fusiliers

Your copy has already been amended as regards paras 10 and 4.a.

SECRET.   Scheme for raid by 2nd. Battalion, The Royal
Irish Regiment.

Ref. WYTSCHAETE, 28 S.W. 2
Ed. 5.A. Map. Scale 1:10,000.

1. **Date.** A raid will take place on
   Zero hour will be notified later.

2. **Object.** To secure prisoners, ascertain strength and condition of trenches and obstacles, destroy M.G. and T.M. emplacements and dugouts, and to secure all information and documents possible.

3. **Strength.** Two platoons   Company.
   2 N.C.O's. 10 men, 16th. Div. Coy. R.E.
   O.C. Party.   Lieut.
   Total strength. 3 Officers. 82 O.R.

4. **Boundaries.** North. Enemy front line trench –
                            N.18.b.23.27. – NAIL SWITCH –
                            N.18.b.60.16. (Junction NAIL
                            SWITCH – NAG AV.)
                    South. Enemy front line trench –
                            N.18.d.20.96. – NAIL SWITCH –
                            N.18.d.61.88. (Junction NAIL
                            SWITCH – NAIL ST.)
   Final objective   NAIL SWITCH.

5. **Moppers up.** O.C. party will detail three small parties to mop up NAIL ROW, NAG ROW and front line.

6. **Time.** Zero – 15 minutes. Raiding party ready in our front line trench N.18.a.8.3. to N.18.c.60.95.
   Zero – 4 minutes. Raiding party leave trench and close up to barrage.
   Zero. Enter enemy's front line trench.

7. **Signal for withdrawal.** Signal for withdrawal will be golden rain rockets from our front line trench.
   Emergency. Two buglers in front line trench sounding "Cease fire".
   Under orders of O.C. Enterprise in each case.

8. **Action of Artillery.** 16th. Divnl. Artillery will cover raid.
   Wire cutting to be carried on for two days previous to raid along front and support lines to be raided, in conjunction with present artillery activity.
   Gaps created to be kept open by 49th. M.G.Coy. and Lewis Guns of Coy. in front line trench.
   Zero – 10 minutes. Intense bombardment on OBJECT SUPPORT N.7.c.9.9. to N.7.c.4.5.
   Zero – 5 minutes. Barrage enemy's front line trench between raid boundaries and on NAG and NAIL ROW and NAIL SWITCH.
   Bombardment NAGS NOSE and NAIL TRENCH.
   One battery to continue rapid on OBJECT SUPPORT.
   Zero. Barrage lifts to NAIL SWITCH.
   Zero plus 5 minutes. Box barrage to be continued till party re-enters our front line trench.
   Boundaries of Box Barrage. N.18.b.28.53. along SUNKEN ROAD to RED CHATEAU, thence along NANCY SUPPORT to N.18.d.71.29. (Junction with NAIL DRIVE) – to N.18.d.25.73. to N.18.d.00.03.

9. **Action of 49th. M.G.C.** 49th. M.G.C. will cover raid. O.C. will arrange his barrage to cover both

/flanks of raid.

flanks of raid, special attention being paid to sunken road.
Barrage to commence at Zero plus 5 minutes.
From Zero – 5 minutes to Zero plus 5 minutes he will engage NAGS NOSE, NAME TRENCH and their communications.

10. Action of 49th. T.M.B. O.C. 49th. T.M.B. will assist Artillery in wire cutting.
49th. T.M.B. will cover raid.
From Zero – 5 minutes to Zero – 2 minutes intense fire will be maintained on NAG ROW and NAIL ROW special attention being paid to any emplacements and dugouts suspected from aeroplane photographs.
Zero – 2 minutes to Zero plus 3 minutes. NAIL ROW from junction with NAG ROW (N.18.b.39.06.) to junction with NAIL SWITCH (N.18.b.60.16.).
From Zero plus 3 minutes to end of raid. Suspected emplacements, dugouts, etc., on immediate flanks of raid.

11. O.C. Enterprise. O.C. Enterprise will establish his Head Quarters at BYRON FARM whither all reports will be sent.

12. Prisoners, etc. All prisoners, documents, etc., will be at once sent back under orders of O.C. Raiding Party to H.Q. of O.C. Enterprise.
The R.S.M. will detail a party of 3 N.C.O's. and 12 men to stand by at H.Q. of O.C. Enterprise from Zero hour to immediately conduct prisoners to Brigade H.Q.

13. Dressing Station. M.O., 2nd. Bn., The Royal Irish Regt. will establish a dressing station besides H.Q. of O.C. Enterprise. He will arrange for evacuation of wounded.
S.B's. of   Coy's. will be stationed here under his orders from Zero hour.

14. Stretcher Bearers. Four stretcher bearers, with 2 stretchers to be included in personnel of raiding party.

15. Communications. Four signallers to be included in personnel of raiding party. They will lay two lines from H.Q., O.C. Enterprise to O.C. Raiding Party.
In the event of these being broken communication from enemy front line trench by lamp.
Signalling Officer will arrange for receiving station in our front line trenches, and immediate transmission to H.Q., O.C. Enterprise. He will also arrange a simple code for such an emergency.

16. Police arrangements. Provost Sergeant will post a policeman at tops of CROWBAR TRENCH and MAYO STREET also at junction of these trenches with WATLING STREET, one policeman at each place, from Zero – 15 minutes.
Before Zero MAYO STREET will only be used for "up" traffic, CROWBAR TRENCH for "down" traffic.
From Zero hour until end of raid both trenches will be available for "down" traffic, which will be limited

/to prisoners,

to prisoners, runners, and casualties. No "up" traffic except by special permit of O.C. Enterprise.

17. <u>Watches.</u> Watches will be synchronised at Zero - 4 hours and again at Zero - 1 hour at H.Q. of O.C. Enterprise.

18. <u>Guiding Tapes.</u> O.C. Raiding Party will arrange to have two guiding tapes firmly secured from our front line to NAIL SWITCH, one on either flank.

19. <u>Code word.</u> Code word for use in enemy's trenches "WEXFORD".

20. <u>Dress, Arms,</u> etc. Skeleton marching order, rifles, 30 rounds S.A.A. of which 5 to be in magazine and chamber, safety catch back, bayonets fixed. Each man 2 bombs in top pockets. Bombing sections 6 bombs per man extra, and 1 P bomb per man. N.C.O's. i/c sections. Revolver and 6 rounds ammunition.

O.O. No. 42, page 4, after line 12 insert :-

"(d) One Coy. will capture BECK HOUSE and the ground as far East as the Stream, reform and move to IBERIAN in support."

8th R. Innis Fus[rs]

SECRET. OPERATION ORDER No. 42   Copy No. 13
by
MAJOR J. D. SCOTT, COMMANDING,
2nd. BATTALION, THE ROYAL IRISH REGIMENT.
The Field.   15-8-1917.

1. GENERAL PLAN.   The 16th. DIVISION, in conjunction with Divisions on either flank, will attack the enemy's positions on 16th. August, 1917.
   The attack will be made in two bounds, each bound is shewn by Coloured Lines on map A.
   First bound   GREEN LINE.
   Second bound   DOTTED RED LINE.

2. OBJECTIVES OF BRIGADES.   The 48th. Inf. Bde. (plus 1 Battn.) on the Right, and the 49th. Inf. Bde. (plus 1 Battn.) on the Left will attack up to and including the RED DOTTED LINE. The 47th. Inf. Bde., less 3 Battns. and Machine Gun Company, will be in Divisional Reserve. The Left Battn. of the 48th. Inf. Bde. will be 9th. R. Dublin Fus. The Right Battn. of the 108th. Inf. Bde. will be the 9th. R. Irish Fus.

3. BOUNDARIES.   The Boundaries between the 49th. Inf. Bde. and the Brigade on either flank are as follows
   Boundary with 48th. Inf. Bde.
   D.25.a.75.05. - where DOTTED RED LINE crosses the ZONNEBEKE STEAM.
   Boundary with 108th. Inf. Bde.
   D.19.c.7.3. - D.19.b.70.50. - D.14.d.20.40.
   These Boundaries are shewn in BLUE on map A.

4. TASKS OF BATTALIONS.   The attack on the GREEN and DOTTED RED LINE will be made by the 7th. R. Innis Fus. on the Left and the 8th. R. Innis. Fus. on the Right. The dividing line between these two Battalions will be -
   D.25.a.80.90. - D.20.b.80.99.
   This boundary is shewn in BLACK on map A.
   There will be a pause of 20 minutes on the GREEN LINE.
   As soon as the RED DOTTED LINE has been captured a line of posts will be pushed out as far as the barrage permits.
   The 7/8th. R. Irish Fus. will support the attack and will find Moppers-Up and Carrying Parties as detailed below.
   (a) One Platoon to Mop-Up BORRY FARM and hold it as a supporting point.
   Two Platoons to Mop-Up ZEVENCOTE and hold it as a supporting point.
   One Platoon to Mop-Up COFFEY FARM, D.20.c.15.15. and then to join the two platoons at ZEVENCOTE.
   The above four Platoons will advance in rear of the first wave of the 8th. R. Innis. Fus.

2.

(b) One Platoon to Mop-Up DELVA FARM, and will join the Platoon at IBERIAN when the Hqrs. 7th. R. Innis. Fus. moves to DELVA FARM.

One Paltoon to form a supporting point about D.19.d.80.80.

The above two Platoons will advance in rear of the 1st. wave of 7th. R. Innis. Fus. (Right Half Battn.)

(c) One Platoon to Mop-Up IBERIAN and the dug-outs in the vicinity and form a supporting point there.

One Platoon to Mop-Up and hold as a supporting point the clump of trees at D.19.d.70.35.

The above two Platoons to advance in rear of the 1st. wave of the 7th. R. Innis. Fus. (Left Half Battn.)

(d) One Coy. will provide Carrying Parties.

Two Platoons will carry to the 8th. R. Innis. Fus. at COFFEE FARM; after completing their task they will join the Coy. at EEVINCOTT.

Two Platoons will carry to 7th. R. Innis. Fus. at DELVA FARM, and will join the two Coys. at IBERIAN on completion of task.

The Battalion will be in Brigade Reserve. At Zero Hour "A" Company, "C" Company (less two Platoons) and "D" Company will advance from their assembly positions and occupy the trenches vacated by the assaulting Battalions from D.25.a.80.05. to D.19.c.60.70.

"D" Company will be on the right from D.25.a.80.05. to D.25.a.80.80.

"C" Company (less two Platoons) in centre from D.25.a.80.80. to D.19.c.60.10.

"A" Company on left from D.19.c.60.10. to D.19.c.60.70.

O.C. "C" Company will detail two Platoons to form a post at BUCK HOUSE immediately it has been taken.

"B" Company will remain in its assembly position.

Battalion Headquarters will move to SQUARE FARM as soon as Hqrs. 7th. R. Innis. Fus. leaves for DELVA FARM.

The 6th. R. Irish Regt. will be in Brigade Reserve in the VLAMERTINGHE Area, and must be prepared to relieve the Assaulting Battalions on the RED DOTTED LINE if required.

5. MOPPING-UP. The 7th. R. Innis. Fus. and 8th. R. Innis. Fus. are responsible for mopping-up all ground in their areas in front of DELVA FARM and EEVINCOTT. The 7/8th. R. Irish Fus. are responsible for mopping-up in rear of DELVA FARM and EEVINCOTT (inclusive).

6. CONSOLIDATION. The RED DOTTED LINE, and all supporting points held by the 7/8th. R. Irish Fus. will be consolidated as rapidly as possible after capture.

The R.E. will work under the direction of C.R.E., 16th. Division and will erect wire on the GHELUVELT - LANGEMARCK LINE when captured. They will also prepare certain positions for defence in vicinity of DELVA FARM and IBERIAN.

7. ACTION OF MACHINE GUNS.   The Machine Guns will be under the direction of the Div. Machine Gun Officer.

40 guns will form the Machine Gun barrage. After the capture of the final objective they will arrange an S.O.S. barrage to cover the front.

2 guns will move in rear of the attacking Infantry to a position in vicinity of DELVA FARM and two guns will move to a position near HILL 37 (D.20.a.). In case of necessity Battalion Commanders can divert them to other positions for purposes of defence.

8. ACTION OF STOKES MORTARS. Two Stokes Mortars will be attached to each Assaulting Battalion. They will move in rear of the last wave, and will assist the infantry to overcome opposition as required. The remaining four Mortars will be left at Brigade Headquarters.

9. ACTION OF ARTILLERY.   The Divisional Artillery will form a creeping barrage covering the advance of the infantry. At zero hour the barrage will be put down as shown on barrage map: BECK HOUSE will be specially dealt with. The first lift will take place at zero plus 5 minutes and it will then proceed forward at the rate of 100 yards in five minutes.

During the 20 minutes pause on the GREEN LINE a protective barrage will be maintained 200 yards in advance of the infantry.

After the capture of the DOTTED RED LINE a standing barrage will be established 300 yards in advance of it for a period of 1 hour, after which it will cease unless recalled by the S.O.S. signal.

10. ACTION OF TANKS.   One section of Tanks from "C" Battalion, TANK CORPS, has been allotted to the 16th. Division. These Tanks will not be available unless the weather conditions improve. In any case they are only likely to arrive behind the Infantry in time to act as "Moppers-Up" in cases where isolated positions continue to hold out.

11. COMMUNICATIONS.   Brigade Headquarters will remain at
    MILL COT.

The Bde. Forward Station will advance behind the last wave of the leading Assaulting Battalions, and will be established in the vicinity of IBERIAN.

Battalion Forward Posts will be established as follows :-
7th. R. Innis Fus.   DELVA FARM.
8th. R. Innis Fus.   COFFEE FARM. (D.20.c.2.2.)
7/8th. R. Irish Fus.   IBERIAN.

Battalion Headquarters will not move forward to these positions until communication has been established with them. The attached chart shows the various means of communication except pigeons and runners. As many pairs of pigeons as available will be issued to Brigade Forward Station and Battalions.

Runner Relay Posts will be established at :-
(a) IBERIAN.
(b) SQUARE FARM.
(c) BAVARIA HOUSE.
(d) Brigade Headquarters.

Runners should not be used unless all other methods of communication fail.

The Brigade Forward Station of 48th. Inf. Bde. will be at VAMPIR.

The Brigade Forward Station of 108th. Inf. Bde. will be at SOMME. (D.13.c.4.4.) and later at GALLIPOLI (D.13.d.4.1.).

The Brigade VISUAL STATION and O.P. will be at C.29.d.8.7.

DOGS. Two Message Dogs have been allotted to the Division. All ranks should be warned that dogs carrying message pouches on their collars are not to be detained except for the purpose of having message read by an officer. Messages sent by this means should be in code.

12. CONTACT AEROPLANES. 1 Contact Aeroplane, marked with a BLACK plaque projecting behind the right lower wing and one protective aeroplane will be in the air over the 16th, and 36th. Division Areas from zero hour onwards. Flares will be lit and Watson fans will be waved by the leading troops -

(a) When called upon to do so by means of the contact aeroplane by means of Klaxton horns and very lights. This call will, if the attack proceeds as arranged, only be made at times when the infantry are believed to have reached the GREEN LINE and the DOTTED RED LINE.

(b) When the infantry consider it advisable to make known the position of their front line.

Red flares will be used.

Flares should not be lit unless the sounding of the Klaxton horn is accompanied by very lights.

13. SYNCHRONIZATION. The Battalion Signalling Officer will arrange to synchronise with Brigade Headquarters at 6 p.m. Y day. He will then send the correct time to all Companies.

14. S.O.S. SIGNAL. The S.O.S. will be GREEN SIGNAL CARTRIDGES.

15. PRISONERS. All prisoners will be sent to BECK HOUSE where they will be collected under the orders of the Officer Commanding the two Platoons of 'C' Company there. He will send them down to the prisoners cage at Brigade Headquarters in batches of thirty under an N.C.O. and 3 men. The Regimental Provost Sergeant and Regimental Police will move up to BECK HOUSE with the O.C.Post for escort duty.

16. **MEDICAL ARRANGEMENTS.** The Regimental Aid Post will be at BAVARIA HOUSE until Battalion Headquarters moves forward, when it will be established at SQUARE FARM.

All cases will be brought to BAVARIA HOUSE or SQUARE FARM whence they will be evacuated by R.A.M.C. stretcher bearers to POTIJZE CHATEAU.

17. **ZERO HOUR.** Zero Hour will be notified later.

18. **ACKNOWLEDGE.**

[signature]

Lieut. & Adjutant,
2nd. Battalion, The Royal Irish Regiment.

Hour of issue 3 p.m.

Copies No. 1. War Diary.
2. Senior Major.
3. O. C. "A" Company.
4. O. C. "B" Company.
5. O. C. "C" Company.
6. O. C. "D" Company.
7. Signalling Officer.
8. Intelligence Officer.
9. Medical Officer.
10. Regimental Sergeant Major.
11. H.Q., 49th. Inf. Bde.
12. 7th. R. Innis. Fus.
13. 8th. R. Innis. Fus.
14. 7/8th. R. Irish Fus.
15 and 16. File.

SECRET.

2/R. Irish Regt.
7/R. Innis. Fus.
8/R. Innis. Fus.
7/8th R. Irish Fus.
49th M.G. Coy.
49th T.M. Battery.

49th I.B. No. S.C.C. 9/306

The following 16th Division Medical Arrangements are notified for information:-

1. **Relay and Bearer Assembly Posts.**

BAVARIA HOUSE C.30.c.6.4.
POTIJZE CHATEAU I.4.a.6.5.

2. **Advanced Dressing Stations.**

PRISON YPRES.
MENIN Road Post.
BELGIAN BATTERY CORNER.

All above administered by 113th Fd. Ambulance.

3. **Reserve Stretcher Bearers.**

Headquarters at PRISON YPRES.

Detailed on a basis of 4 per Regimental Aid Post to assist Regimental Medical Officers and maintain touch with relay posts and Advanced Dressing Stations. Detachments of these Bearers will be located at BAVARIA HOUSE, POTIJZE and PRISON YPRES. Demands for Stretcher Bearers required at R.A.Ps, should be sent to the first two of above.

(To be read in conjunction with Bde. S.A.I. No. 7, "Medical Arrangements".)

Captain,
Staff Captain,
49th Infantry Brigade.

6-8-17.

SECRET.   S/629   Copy No. 5

49th INFANTRY BRIGADE.

SPECIAL ADMINISTRATIVE INSTRUCTION No. 15.

ISSUE OF AMMUNITION.

While in the line the system of the issue of ammunition will be as follows:-

1. There are two Divisional Grenade Dumps:-

    Main Divisional Dump   H.7.d.4.9.
    Advanced Divisional Dump I.3.d.4.4.

2. Issues will nominally be made from the Advanced Divisional Dump.

    A Brigade or Unit which wishes to draw ammunition will send a loading or carrying party and a requisition signed by a Brigade Staff Officer. This will be sufficient authority for the Officer in charge of Dump to issue, if the ammunition required is available.

3. There are a number of YUKON PACKS at the Advanced Divisional Dump which will be available if required but must be returned after use.

4. All ammunition issued will be issued detonated.

    Stokes ammunition has been detonated with 8 sec. and 13 sec. fuzes. The length of the fuze with which they have been detonated will be marked in green on the boxes, viz:- 8 sec.
    13 sec.

5. Lieut. L. BARNES, 16th D.A.C. is in charge of both dumps and is located at Divisional Headquarters.

3-8-17.

Captain,
Staff Captain,
49th Infantry Brigade.

Issued as laid down in para. 6 of S.A.I. No. 1
dated 3-7-17.

S E C R E T. S/628 Copy No. 5

49th INFANTRY BRIGADE.

AMENDMENT to
SPECIAL ADMINISTRATIVE INSTRUCTION No. 15.
re
ISSUE OF AMMUNITION.

1. Cancel para 3.

   No Yukon packs are now available.

   K P Bowen.

   Captain,
   Staff Captain,
   49th Infantry Brigade.

5-8-17.

SECRET.   Copy No............

8th. ROYAL INNISKILLING FUSILIERS OPERATION ORDER No. 122 - 20-3-17.

Ref. Map. Sheet 27 1/40.000.

1.   The 49th. Infantry Brigade Group will march to the BECK? AREA (Eastern Portion) on 20th. inst.

2.   Units will pass the Starting Points at the times shown :-
     Brigade Headquarters   4.10 p.m.
     4th. T.M. Battery   4.15 p.m.
     49th. M.G. Company   4.20 p.m.
     7th. R. Innis. Fus.   4.25 p.m.
     2nd. R. Irish Regt.   4.35 p.m.
     7/8th. R. Irish Fus.   4.45 p.m.
     8th. R. Innis. Fus.   4.50 p.m.
     157th. Fd. Coy. R.E.   5.5   p.m.
     144th. Coy. A.S.C.   5.10 p.m.
     113th. Field Ambulance   5.30 p.m.

3.   The Battalion will parade in Camp, and will be ready to move-off at 3.55 p.m. Head of column will pass Starting Point K.17.c.0.8. at 4.50 p.m. Dress - Marching Order less Packs. Steel Helmets will be worn.

4.   Order of March - H.Q., A, B, D, C, Transport.

5.   Route - K.17.c.0.8. - K.35.d.5.5. - O.11.d.8.1.

6.   Intervals of 500 yards will be maintained between Battalions. C.S.M. McDonnell will ride ahead of the Battalion at sufficient distance to warn traffic control.

7.   Advance Parties will meet the Battalion at Cross Roads K.35.d.5.5.

8.   Officers kits will be loaded by 3 p.m. Mess and Maltese Carts will be loaded by 3.30 p.m.

9.   O.C. Coys. will ensure that their lines are left in a clean and sanitary condition and will render certificate to that effect before moving off.

10. ACKNOWLEDGE.

                                                               W.S. *illegible* Capt
                                                               for 2/Lieut.,
                                                               a/Adjutant : 8th. R. Innis. Fusrs.

Issued through Signals at 11.30 a.m.

Copy No. 1 to O.C. "A" Coy.
  "   " 2 "   "   "B" & "D" Coy.
  "   " 3 "   "   "C" Coy.
  "   " 4 " Quartermaster.
  "   " 5 " Transport Officer.
  "   " 6 " Signals.
  "   " 7 " Medical Officer.
  "   " 8 " H.Q. 49th. Inf. Bde.
  "   " 9/10 Retained.

SECRET   Copy No. 13

8th R. Inniskilling Fusiliers Operation Orders No. 117.

1. The Batn. will be relieved in the front line on the night 7/8th Cent by the 7th R. Innis. Fus.

2. Coys of the 7th R. Innis Fus. will take over the exact frontages as now held by corresponding Coys of this Batn. in order I.C.B.A. Coys H.Q.

3. One guide per platoon + 2 for H.Q. will afford at Batn HQ SQUARE FM at dawn tomorrow 7th inst & will be at POTIJZE CHATEAU at 9.30 p.m. to conduct 7th R. Innis Fus into the Line. — route HAYMARKET & route best known to Guides avoiding POTIJZE – FREZENBERG Rd as far as possible.

4. On completion of relief the Batn will move back to Camp vacated by 7th R. Innis Fus at H17 a O.9. & will move by platoons at 300x distance — route — TRACK NORTH of POTIJZE–FREZENBERG Rd – HAYMARKET – then through YPRES to Camp.

5. All tools & defensive arrangements will be carefully handed over.

6. Completion of relief to be reported to Batn. H.Q.

7. Acknowledge.

Issued through Sigs 1.0 am. 7.8.17

Copy No 1. A Coy
     2 B .
     3 C .
     4 D .
     5 R. Echelon.
     6 M.O.
     7 T.O.
     8 Signals
     9 Q.M.
    10 R.S.M.
    11 7. R. Innis Fus.
    12 49th Inf Bde.
    13 retained.

                                J. Loggin
                                Lieut.
                                a/Adj. 8 R. Innis Fus.

SECRET   Copy No. 16

8th R.I. Innis. Ins. OO/11b/   5-8-17

In continuation of OO/11b of this date the following orders are issued.

1. Dispositions North to South.
    2 platoons D Coy will relieve 2 platoons D Coy 6th R.I. Regt
    'C' Coy   "   "   'C' Coy   "
    'B' "   "   "   'B' "   "
    'A' "   "   "   'A' "   "

   2 platoons D Coy will relieve 2 platoons D Coy 6th R.I. Regt in Support at LOW. F<u>m</u>

2. Order of march will now be
    H.Q.
    2 platoons D Coy
    C Coy
    B Coy
    A Coy
    2 platoons D Coy

3. Rations & Water will be dumped at Six Elms C.30.d.5.7 at 1.am.
   Coys & H.Q. will find their own ration parties

4. Acknowledge.

Issued through Sigs at 1.0 pm

Copy No 1   A Coy
       2   B "
       3   C "
       4   D "
       5   Signals
       6   Quartermaster
       7   Transport Off.
       8   Medical Off.
       9   H.Q. 49th Inf. Bgde
      10   6th R.I. Regt
     11/12 Retained

                                        N. Braden Robbins E/
                                        a/Adj 8 R. Innis. Ins.

SECRET.   Copy No. 11

8th R. Innis. Ins. Operation Orders No 116. 6·VIII·17

Ref. 1/20,000 Trench Map FREZENBERG.

1. The 48th & 49th Inf Bgdes will relieve the 47th Inf Bgde in the line on the 5th & night of 5/6th August.

2. The 48th Inf Bgde will relieve the Batt. of 47th Inf Bgde holding the Right Section. The 49th Inf Bgde will relieve the Batt. of the 47th I. Bgde holding the Left Section.

   The dividing line between Brigades will be notified later.

3. On Completion of reliefs the 49th Inf. Bgde will be disposed as follows:—

   Bgde H.Q.   JAMES Fm. (I.4.d. 65.15)
   Front Line.   8/R. Innis Ins, H.Q. SQUARE Fm
   Support Batt. 2 R/ Irish Regt. H.Q. (I. b an 20. 80.)
   Reserve Batt. 7 R/ Innis Ins . 7/8 R. Irish Rifles.
                        VLAMERTINGHE NO 3 AREA.

4. The 8th R. Innis Ins will take over the exact front held by 6 R. Irish Regt. left Bn. 47th Inf Bgde. This front extends from the road at D.25.c. 85.9a to the STEENBEEK at D 19 c 65.78, where the right of the 107th I Bgde 36th Div. rests.

   The front will be adjusted later to the proper Bgde Boundary.

5. Disposition of Coys in the line will be notified later.

6. The Batt. will move from present position in following order. H.Q. D.B. A. C. Coys. Leading unit will pass MILL COT at 9.15 pm. March will be by platoons at 200x distance.

7. Route. POTIJZE — FREZENBERG Rd to BAVARIA HOUSE where guides 1per platoon and 1 per Batt H.Q. will be met at 9.45 pm.

8. Field Cookers will be moved from their present positions to Transport Lines at 6.p.m. The Mess Cart will be at Batt. H.Q. at 7.30 pm to move surplus mess kit to Transport Lines Coy Mess Kits to be returned (if any) must be dumped at Batt H.Q. by that hour. Maltese Cart will be at AID POST CAMBRIDGE Rd. at 8pm for loading.

9. Ration arrangements will be notified later.

10. Completion of reliefs to be reported to Batt H.Q. SQUARE Fm.

OO. 116. Contd.

11 Acknowledge.

Issued through Sigs. at 10 AM

J. Hogan Robbins
p/c.
A/Adjt. 8 R/Innis Fus.

Copy No 1   O/C A Coy
     2   B
     3   C
     4   D
     5   Signals
     6   Quartermaster
     7   Transport Off.
     8   Medical Off.
     9   H.Q. 49' Inf Bde.
    10   6' R. I. Regt.
    11/12   Retained.

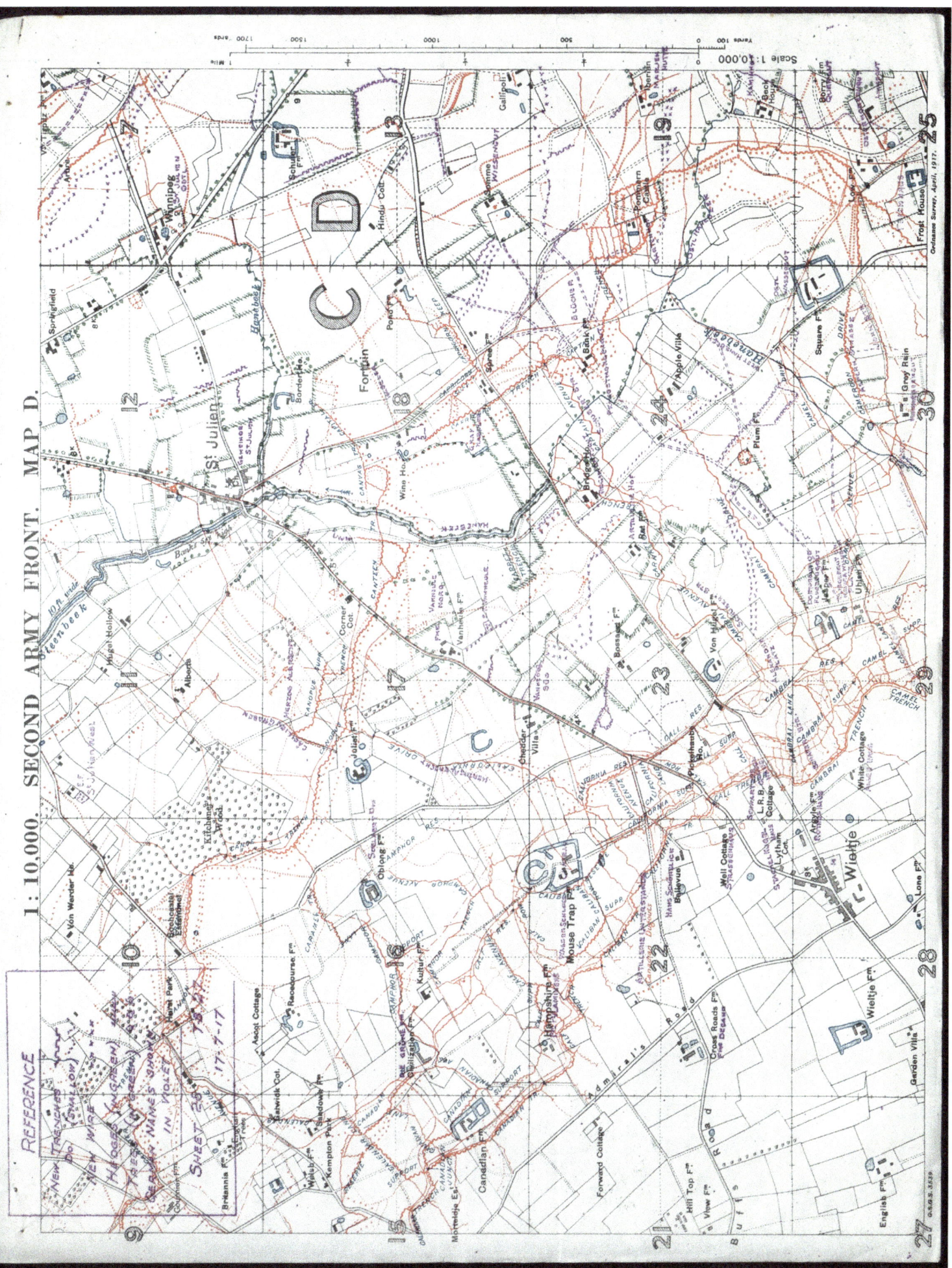

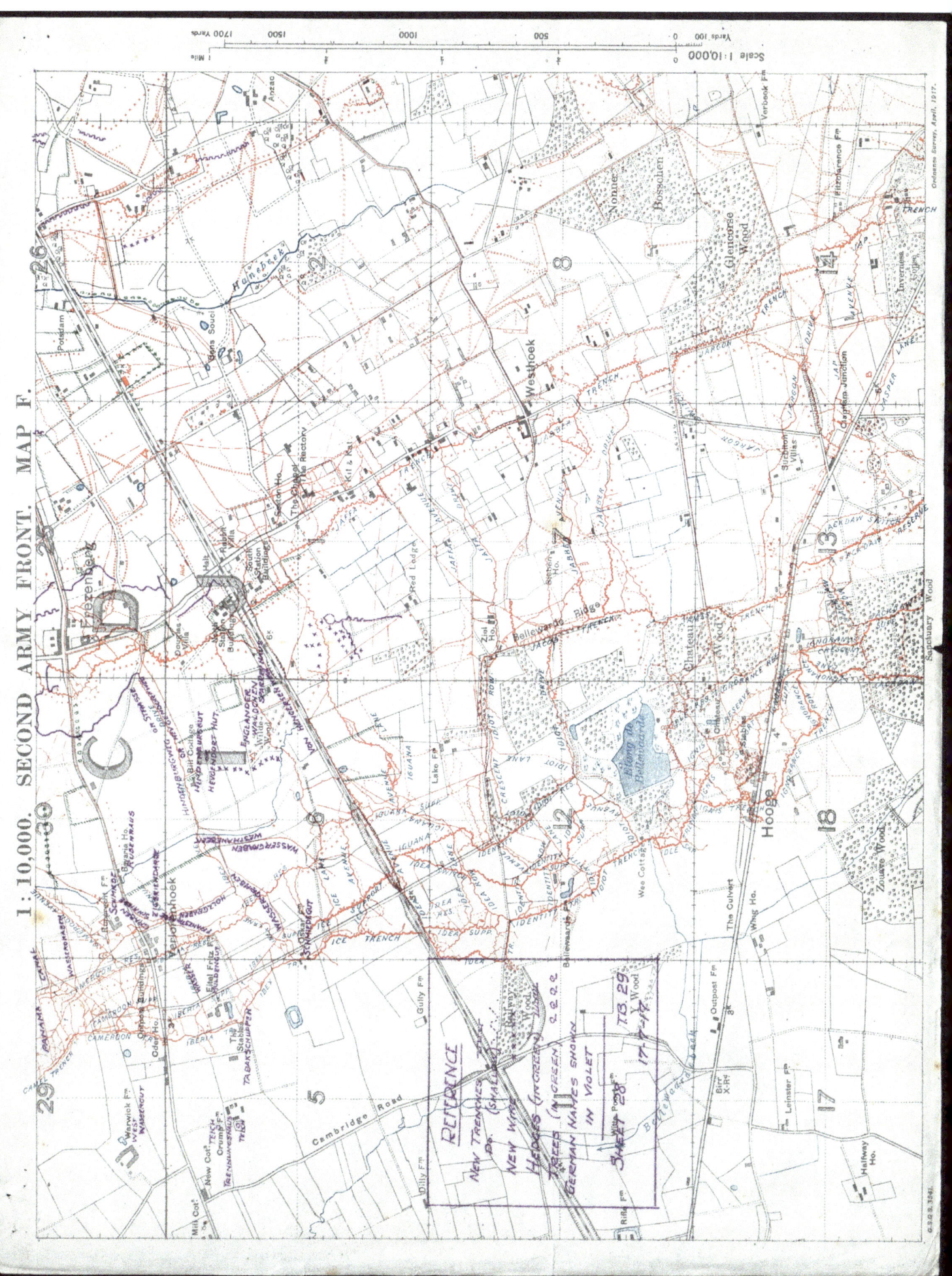

www.ingramcontent.com/pod-product-compliance
Lightning Source LLC
Chambersburg PA
CBHW081427300426
44108CB00016BA/2316